The Game Maker's Companion

Game Development: The Journey Continues

Jacob Habgood
Nana Nielsen
Martin Rijks
Kevin Crossley

Apress®

The Game Maker's Companion: Game Development: The Journey Continues

ISBN-13 (pbk): 978-1-4302-2826-4

ISBN-13 (electronic): 978-1-4302-2827-1

Printed and bound in the United States of America 9 8 7 6 5 4 3 2 1

President and Publisher: Paul Manning
Lead Editor: Steve Anglin
Development Editor: Matthew Moodie
Technical Reviewer: Sean Davies
Editorial Board: Clay Andres, Steve Anglin, Mark Beckner, Ewan Buckingham, Gary Cornell, Jonathan Gennick, Jonathan Hassell, Michelle Lowman, Matthew Moodie, Duncan Parkes, Jeffrey Pepper, Frank Pohlmann, Douglas Pundick, Ben Renow-Clarke, Dominic Shakeshaft, Matt Wade, Tom Welsh
Coordinating Editor: Kelly Moritz
Copy Editor: Ralph Moore
Compositor: MacPS, LLC
Indexer: Toma Mulligan
Artist: April Milne
Cover Designer: Anna Ishchenko

Distributed to the book trade worldwide by Springer Science+Business Media, LLC., 233 Spring Street, 6th Floor, New York, NY 10013. Phone 1-800-SPRINGER, fax (201) 348-4505, e-mail orders-ny@springer-sbm.com, or visit www.springeronline.com.

For information on translations, please e-mail rights@apress.com, or visit www.apress.com.

Apress and friends of ED books may be purchased in bulk for academic, corporate, or promotional use. eBook versions and licenses are also available for most titles. For more information, reference our Special Bulk Sales–eBook Licensing web page at www.apress.com/info/bulksales.

To the offspring of childish minds.

Contents at a Glance

Contents

Foreword

When I created the first version of Game Maker in 1999, I naturally had no idea that it would achieve its current status of the most-used game-creation package in the world. The program was still rather limited. You could only create very simple games with it and the package was downloaded only a few hundred times per month.

A lot has changed over the past ten years. New versions of Game Maker were released that made it possible to create sophisticated stand-alone games. The number of downloads rose to over 150,000 per month, and the company YoYo Games was formed that now develops and distributes the program. The site of YoYo Games (www.yoyogames.com) has already collected close to 100,000 games made with Game Maker and this number is rapidly increasing.

But one thing has not changed. Most of the games created with Game Maker are still very simple and do not use many of the advanced features that the program offers. They also often lack sophistication in their gameplay. One of the reasons for this is that there was no text book for the more advanced Game Maker users. That is, until this book came along. A book dedicated to those that have already created their first games and want to learn more.

Using the popular genre of platform games, the first part of the book introduces various advanced aspects of Game Maker. In an entertaining yet precise way, the authors show you how to create increasingly complicated versions of the game *Zool*, resulting in a game of commercial quality. Once you have worked your way through this part, you will be able to create many interesting platform games yourself.

To make great games, it is not enough to know the advanced aspects of the Game Maker program. It is equally important to understand the design principles on which good games are based. In the previous book, *The Game Maker's Apprentice*, that I wrote together with Jacob Habgood, we introduced some basic game design concepts such as challenges, level and feature design, and balance. In the second part of this new book, Jacob and his co-authors take this a step further.

In particular, they explain how to design fascinating storylines and characters and how to apply this in your games. As an example, you create a pirate game, *Shadows on Deck*, which also demonstrates the effect of using a very nice silhouetted graphical style. Good storylines will stimulate your players to continue playing your games. The players want to find out what is happening next. Good character design will create a bond between the player and the characters, making them care. They become attached to the characters, which further enhances the game play. Use it in your own games and players will appreciate your work a lot more.

The final part of the book consists of a large reference section with solutions to many features that you might want to put in your games. It handles such diverse topics as how to shoot to the mouse position, how to create fancy buttons, how to display a mini-map, how to make enemies patrol an area, and how to display scrolling text. It provides answers to many questions users might have, making this book a useful companion for every Game Maker user.

I am convinced that after reading this book, you will be an even better game maker than you are now and that you will be able to create games that many players will enjoy. Don't keep them to yourself, though. Share your creations with the rest of the world. You can publish them through the YoYo Games web site (www.yoyogames.com) so that everybody can play them for free. In 2010, YoYo games will also introduce the possibility to sell your games on the PC and PSP, preparing the way for other platforms in the future. So this book could actually be the start of your professional career as a console game designer. But, more importantly, it is a book that will help you enjoy creating exciting games.

Mark Overmars
Creator of Game Maker

About the Authors

Jacob Habgood

Jacob's career in the games industry spans 14 years, but he has been programming games as an amateur and professional now for a quarter of a century. During this time, he has worked on over a dozen published games for all the major console platforms, including as the lead programmer of the cult British game, *Hogs of War*. He has programmed, designed, and project-managed titles for such publishers as Gremlin, Infogrames, Atari, Disney, and Konami and he truly knows the meaning of the word "crunch."

Somehow he also found time to study a Ph.D. in the psychology of learning and has a passion for most things that connect video games and learning (including a whole lot of research involving zombies: `www.zombiedivision.co.uk`). This passion also extends to teaching game development, which he practices in his position as Senior Lecturer in Game Development at Sheffield Hallam University in the UK.

Jacob is the husband of a primary school teacher who is talented enough to inspire children without the need for a PlayStation controller, and the father of two beautiful daughters who are the product of their mother's inspiration.

Nana Nielsen

Nana Nielsen grew up in Denmark under the watchful eyes of two computer programmers: her parents. Being force-fed Tolkien books and text adventures on the Commodore 64, she developed a keen interest in both stories and games, and how the two intermingle. Since then, she has earned a degree in Interactive Media and worked in the games industry for more than a decade and published a dozen titles in different genres, including the platformer *Crash Bandicoot: Twinsanity*, the RPG *Sudeki*, the adventure series *Broken Sword*, and the sports title *Virtua Tennis*. She is currently working on the popular episodes of *Doctor Who—The Adventure Games*.

Martin Rijks

Martin Rijks wrote his first lines of code on paper, at the age of eight, using a book from the library that he probably returned too late. Not owning a computer himself until years later, little Martin had to wait for birthday parties at his uncle's to actually be able to test his programs on a TI99/4A. When he had finally bought his own, he wasted the best years of his youth dashing boulders, shooting mutant camels, raiding stars, or navigating several alternate realities carrying potions while swinging pointy weapons at critters.

Martin discovered Game Maker in 2001, and ever since has kept prodding it to see what it would do. Having played an important role in building and maintaining the lively Game Maker Community, you can still occasionally find him there telling people that They Are Doing It Wrong. For fear of not wanting to go home after working hours, Martin was fortunate enough to find a daytime job that has nothing to do with game development. These days hardly ever gaming, he still likes to challenge people for a multi-player match of *Duke Nukem 3D*, but he is unable to find anyone who is still willing to play it.

Having become a father while missing another deadline for the book, Martin is already planning to give his newborn son Dimar the same sermons he got from his own parents on the virtues of Playing Outside and Getting Some Fresh Air. This time, he hopes they will work.

About the Artists

Kevin Crossley

Kev Crossley began his long career as an artist at the tender age of three, when he discovered that rather than eating poster paint, it was actually useful for painting with. It was a while before he worked out that the teachers shouted less when you kept the brush on the paper, (rather than, for example, the trouser leg of Mr. Robinson!) Nevertheless, he displayed a precocious talent for one so young, and by the age of seven, he was composing vast battles between armies of Daleks and Hulked-up dinosaurs on his bedroom walls (as he still hadn't mastered the art of staying on the paper.)

Such a promising start augured well for the future, and after a distracting three years at University studying typography and how not to design stationary, he stumbled into a job as a video game artist. This was a role he enjoyed for 15 years before becoming a freelance illustrator, contributing to numerous RPG books and comics such as *2000AD* and *KISS4K*. His book *Fantasy Clip Art* was published in 2006, and he writes regularly for various art magazines, including *ImagineFX*.

His grueling work schedule is made bearable by the un-swaying support of his wonderful wife, Fiona, and thanks to the example set by his two-year-old son Aidan, Kev's brushes still stray from the paper....

Griffin Warner

Griffin is a technical artist specializing in animation and he was responsible for creating the character animations used for the *Shadows on Deck* example in this book. He is a former student of Jacob's, and graduated from Sheffield Hallam University in 2010 with a first-class degree in Games Software Development B.Sc. (Hons). At the time of writing, he is looking forward to a successful career in game development.

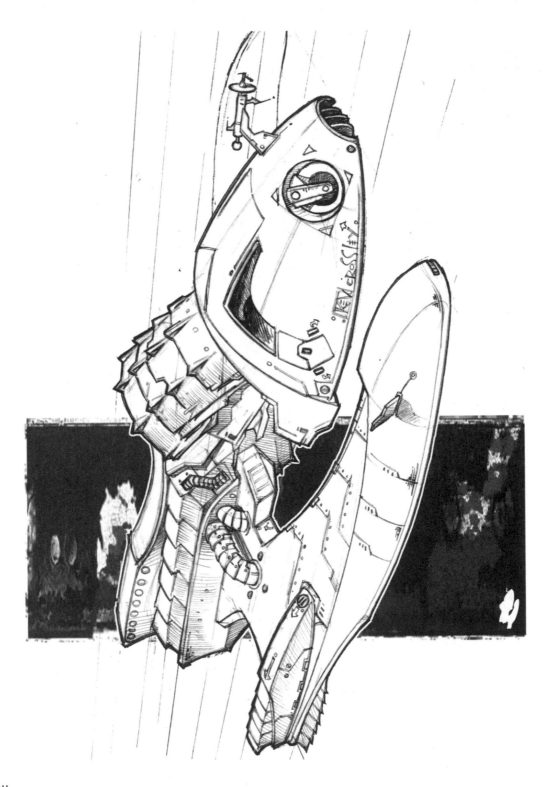

About the Technical Reviewer

Sean Davies

Sean was just 21 years old when his life was changed forever. Indoctrinated into a Top Secret government training program, Sean was transformed from a mild–mannered, floppy-haired guitarist into a cold-blooded coding machine. Rebuilt from the ground up (more than 70% of his blood replaced by machine code), he can now exist on diet of pure caffeine (with occasional pizza supplements) and has been forced to take on a treacherous double life. By day, he appears to be a perfectly normal early–30s male—chatty, outgoing, approachable. By night, he stalks the halls of Sheffield game development houses viciously optimising any code unfortunate enough to get in his way with the power of his bionic stare.

In the ten years since this change, he has worked on games for almost all of the major console platforms and for several major franchises including *Men in Black*, *Superman*, *Outrun*, *Virtua Tennis*, *Sega Superstars*, and *Doctor Who*.

Sean Davies does not sleep—he codes....

Acknowledgments

Writing a book like this one takes an enormous amount of time and commitment from all the people directly involved in its development, but these are not the only people who deserve recognition for their contribution to making this book a reality.

A huge debt of gratitude is owed to Ian Stewart for allowing us to reintroduce a lost icon of gaming history to a new generation of game developers. The original *Zool* resources and artwork have proved a fabulous addition to the offering of this book, while providing a fitting record of a retro classic. Further thanks go to Paul Hiley, Adrian Carless, George Allan, and Patrick Phelan for their assistance in reassembling the pieces after so much time.

Nonetheless, even intergalactic ninjas wouldn't get very far without the support of their nearest and dearest and we cannot express enough appreciation for the understanding and patience of our families while creating this book. Consequently, we extend our heartfelt thanks to Jenny, Elsie, and Jess Habgood, Pete Ellacott, Fiona and Aidan Crossley, Lucienne Klinkenberg, and Dimar Rijks. A particularly special welcome is extended to Jess and Dimar, who made their entrance into the world during the writing of this book.

Further thanks go to those who have tested and provided feedback on the book's content in some form, including Mark Overmars, Barry Lowndes, and Alex Aris. Our gratitude is also extended to Sandy Duncan of YoYo Games for providing permission to include Game Maker along with the CD.

Additional thanks goes to the members of the English Amiga Board forums for their support in obtaining *Zool* resources, and the Game Maker Community forums for their support and feedback on the plan for the book.

Finally, we would like to thank everyone at Apress for their unwavering support in our blind pursuit of another labor of love.

Introduction

Game Maker has become an extremely popular tool for beginners wanting to take their first steps into game development. This is hardly surprising, as its intuitive drag-and-drop programming system makes it very easy to start creating your own simple games. It's also possible to make very professional-looking games using Game Maker, and you've probably already come across some impressive offerings made with it on the YoYo Games web site. Nonetheless, it's not always easy for users to see how they can make that leap into creating more professional games for themselves—and that is exactly what this book is for.

We're focusing on creating platform games this time around, but the development principles you'll learn are applicable to other genres as well. We've organized this book into parts based around the example games. In **Part 1,** you'll be introduced to *Fishpod*: nature's first ever platform game character, which we'll use as a way of introducing some of the main issues involved in creating platform games.

In **Part 2,** we're going back in time to visit a ninja of the Nth dimension, as we revive the 90s classic that is *Zool*. You'll learn how to create a slick, commercial-quality platform game almost entirely using drag-and-drop programming, and without using any features from the Pro edition of Game Maker. Nonetheless, the principles you'll glean are just as applicable to GML and will form the foundation of the platform game "engine" used in the remainder of the book.

Zool: One of the games you'll learn how to make in this book

In **Part 3**, you'll follow the development of a new game called *Shadows on Deck* from its initial concept design through to the implementation of a vertical slice of game play. In the process, you'll learn how to create compelling storylines and interesting characters to inhabit your games and keep your players absorbed while they play. You'll discover how the role of a concept artist feeds into the design of a game and gain access to the original animations and graphics that we've used to create the resources for the game.

Shadows on Deck: The final game you'll learn how to make in this book

To implement the game play, you'll see how you can convert the *Zool* engine into GML and enhance it in the process. We'll gradually transform the colorful playground of *Zool* into a sinister world inhabited by skeletal pirates and filled with fatal traps. We'll conclude by adding the puzzles and dialogue that give this platform-adventure its character.

Part 4 is something a little different, providing a handy resource for all those essential Game Maker features that are needed time and time again in order to create all sorts of different games. If you want to know how to add cheat codes, a countdown clock, or smoke trails to your game, then it's all here for you to find. Numerous different game features are covered in this step-by-step "how-to" guide for Game Maker.

We really hope that you enjoy this book and that it will be as well-received as its predecessor. If you read *The Game Maker's Apprentice*, then we hope that it kindled a passion for game development that will be sustained in this sequel. If you're an old-hat to Game Maker, but new to our books, then we hope that *The Game Maker's Companion* will help you to realize your own gaming visions. Either way, we're confident this book will continue to convey our passion for creating games, and impart some of our combined years of experience along the way.

■ ■ ■

PART 1

Fishpod

"There's no point trying to run before you can walk," as the old saying goes. This must have been particularly true for the first creature to crawl out of the primeval oceans onto dry land. It's also true if you've never created a platform game before, so this prehistoric mudskipper will make the perfect companion as you take your first steps in platform game development.

■ ■ ■

CHAPTER 1

Greetings, Game Maker

So here we are, about to embark on another journey into the world of game development. You may have joined us last time in *The Game Maker's Apprentice: Game Development for Beginners* (Apress, 2006), or perhaps you taught yourself the basics of Game Maker under your own steam. Either way, we invite you to dust off your trusty keyboard and loosen up your mouse-arm as you join us in *The Game Maker's Companion*.

The path ahead is an exciting one and we have a host of new challenges in store to enhance your skills as a game developer. Nonetheless, it would be foolish to undertake such a journey without making suitable preparations first. Each of you will bring your own unique skills to the journey ahead, but you won't get very far without some level of background knowledge. This chapter will equip you with that knowledge, so please make sure you are familiar with it before continuing. The majority of this information was covered in our first book, so this chapter simply summarizes the important facts as a reminder. It won't take long to cover the essentials, so let's make a start. This chapter will also serve as a handy reference if you need to check back on something later on in the book.

Resources

Video games are made up of different kinds of digital resources such as animations, sounds, music, and backgrounds. Game Maker lists all of its resources down the left-hand side of the main window (see Figure 1–1). These are grouped together into folders according to the different kinds of resources that Game Maker supports. You don't need to know every detail of every kind of resource, but you should be generally aware of what each type of resource is for.

- *Sprites*: Sprite resources are the digital images that you use to represent foreground objects in your games. Game Maker supports loading sprite images from `.bmp`, `.jpg`, and `.gif` file formats and now in Game Maker 8, `.png` and `.gmspr` as well. You can load animated images using the `.gif` and `.gmspr` formats, or by treating `.png` files as sequential strips of images by using `_stripXX` at the end of the file name (where XX = the number of frames in the image).

- *Sounds:* Sound resources include both sound effects and music for your games. Game Maker supports `.wav`, `.mid` (MIDI), and `.mp3` formats, but `.mp3` music can take up a lot of space and often contributes to the large size of finished games.

- *Backgrounds:* Background resources are digital images that you use to represent the background scene of your game. Backgrounds can only contain single images and Game Maker can load these images from `.bmp`, `.jpg`, `.gif`, and `.png` formats.

- *Paths:* Path resources contain a series of points that define a route for *object* resources to follow in the game. These can be either closed looping paths or open paths with a start and finish point.

- *Scripts:* Script resources contain programming instructions written in Game Maker Language (GML). GML provides a more advanced way of programming in Game Maker.

- *Fonts:* Font resources provide a means of displaying text in your game using the fonts installed on your machine. Game Maker grabs images of each character in your chosen font so that the player doesn't need to have the same font installed on their machine.

- *Timelines:* Timeline resources provide a way of triggering many different *actions* at specific points of time in your game (see Objects for more on actions).

- *Objects:* Object resources are the most important of all the resource types in Game Maker as they are used to represent all of the active components of your game. Objects can respond to *events* in the game by following a series of *actions* that you add to the event. In this way, you can program the desired behavior for all the different components of your game.

- *Rooms:* Room resources provide spaces for staging all the visible aspects of your game (levels, menus, cut scenes, and so forth) and contain all sorts of settings relating to backgrounds, views, and the game window. It also provides an editor for placing *instances* of objects into your rooms to determine their starting positions.

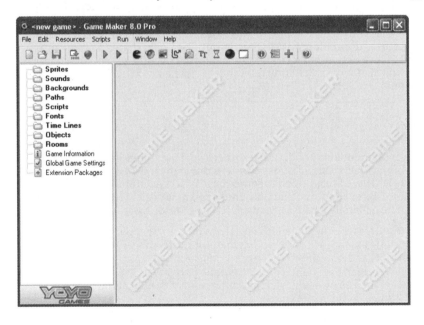

Figure 1–1. *The main Game Maker interface with the resource list on the left*

Instances and Objects

Objects are the programmable elements of your game and their behavior is directly determined by the *events* and *actions* that you choose to give them. However, there is an important distinction to be made between the *object resources*, which define the general behavior of objects, and the individual *object instances*, which occupy your game world. Once you have defined the behavior of an object resource, then you can place any number of instances of that object in your game. All these instances will behave in the same way (because they follow the same events and actions), but each has its own variables (position, speed, direction, and so forth) that are unique to that instance. If you like, you can think of object resources as being like jelly molds, and instances as the jellies you make with them. You only need one mold to make any number of jellies that have the same basic structure (see Figure 1–2).

Figure 1–2. Object resources are like jelly molds and you can use them to create any number of object instances

Variables

A variable is a general programming term for something that can store information. In Game Maker, variables can either store a number (for example, 3, -12, 151.33) or some text (for example, demons don't like dragons). You use variables in Game Maker to store all the unique information about individual instances, such as their position on the screen, or their speed. So if you create a new power variable in the **Create** event of a dragon object, then every dragon object will have this variable, but each instance can have its own different value for power. It's also worth noting that you must assign variables a value (using a **Set Variable** action, for example) before you can use them (with a **Test Variable** action); otherwise, Game Maker will produce an error.

Local Instance Variables

Game Maker uses a number of predefined variables for storing standard information about each instance in the game. All of the following variables either directly or indirectly affect the position of an instance in the room:

- x and y provide the current position of the instance in the room.

- xstart and ystart provide the starting position of the instance in the room.

- xprevious and yprevious provide the room position of the instance in the previous step.

- hspeed is the horizontal speed of the instance (in pixels per step).

- vspeed is the vertical speed of the instance (in pixels per step).

- direction is the instance's current direction of motion in degrees (360 degrees of rotation in an anticlockwise direction; 0 degrees is horizontally to the right).

- speed is the instance's current speed in the current direction.

- friction is the amount of friction reducing the speed of the instance (in pixels per step).

- gravity_direction is the current direction of influence for gravity (defaults to 270 = downwards).

- gravity is the amount of gravity that pulls the speed of the instance in gravity_direction every step (in pixels per step).

The following variables are also predefined for each instance and affect the appearance or collision of the instance in some way:

- sprite_index is the sprite displayed for the instance.

- image_index is the current index into the images of an animated sprite displayed for the instance.

- image_speed is the animation speed of an animated sprite (in subimages per step). This is typically set to a value between 1 (normal forward speed) and -1 (normal backwards speed).

- mask_index is the sprite used for collision detection (usually set to -1, which makes the mask_index the same as the sprite_index).

- depth is used to control the order in which instances are drawn on the screen. Highest depth values are drawn first and so appear behind those with lower values.

- image_xscale is a scaling value applied to the width of the sprite, where a value of 1.0 is 100% of the original width (normal size).

- image_yscale is a scaling value applied to the height of the sprite, where a value of 1.0 is 100% of the original height (normal size).

- image_angle is a rotation angle (0-360) applied to the sprite, where a value of 0 is no rotation. You can only change this variable in the registered, Pro version of Game Maker 8.

- image_alpha is the opacity of the sprite (how difficult it is to see through it), which can range from a value of 1.0 for fully opaque (unable to see through it at all) to a value of 0.0 for fully-transparent (invisible).

- image_blend is a color applied to the sprite when it is drawn. It is set to c_white by default, and using different values will change the color of the sprite when it is drawn. You can only change this variable in the registered, Pro version of Game Maker 8.

- visible determines whether the object is visible or invisible (true or false).

- solid determines whether the object is treated as solid in collisions (true or false).

- persistent determines whether the object will continue to exist in the next room, or whether it remains part of the room in which it was originally created (true or false).

■**Note** The constants true and false correspond to the values 1 and 0, respectively.

These two variables hold information about the identity of the instance:

- id is a unique identifying number that distinguishes the current instance from any other.

- object_index is the index of the object resource that the current instance is an instance of.

There are also a number of other variables that you cannot change, but are maintained internally by Game Maker for each instance depending on the current sprite. So you can check to see what values these variables hold (using a **Test Variable** action, for example), but you cannot change them (using a **Set Variable** action):

- sprite_width is the width of the current sprite displayed for the instance.

- sprite_height is the height of the current sprite displayed for the instance.

- sprite_xoffset is the x position of the origin within the sprite.

- sprite_yoffset is the y position of the origin within the sprite.

- image_number is the number of images in the current sprite.

- bbox_left is the x coordinate of the left edge of the sprite's bounding box in the room.

- bbox_right is the x coordinate of the right edge of the sprite's bounding box in the room.

- bbox_top is the y coordinate of the top edge of the sprite's bounding box in the room.

- bbox_bottom is the y coordinate of the bottom edge of the sprite's bounding box in the room.

Variables in Other Instances

You usually refer to an instance's variables within its own actions by entering their names in their basic form, as provided previously. Using actions to set or test an instance's variables in this way will only affect the instance concerned (hence, they are local to the instance). However, you can also refer to variables in other instances by using an object name followed by a dot (period/full-stop) and then the variable name (for example, obj_dragon.x). Used within a **Test Variable** action, this would retrieve the x position of the first instance of obj_dragon that was placed in the room (disregarding any other instances of obj_dragon). However, used within a **Set Variable** action, it would change the x position of *all* the instances of obj_dragon in the game—so be careful.

Game Maker also includes a number of special object names that you can use to refer to different objects in the game:

- `other` is an object that is used to refer to the other instance involved in a collision event. So `other.x` is the x position of the other object involved in a collision.

- `all` is an object that refers to all instances, so setting `all.visible` to 0 would make all instances of all objects invisible.

- `global` is an object used to refer to global variables that you create yourself.

Global Variables

You can also create *global variables*, which are common to all objects and instances in the game. These are useful for storing values that relate to the overall state of the game, such as the current player's name, or time playing the game. When you use a global variable of your own, you need to put the word `global` and a period (full-stop) in front of the variable name (for example, `global.player_name`). If you leave off the `global` part, then Game Maker will automatically assume you are referring to a local variable instead.

However, there are also a number of built-in global variables that do not require the use of the `global` object to access them. This can cause problems if you try and create local variables with the same name, so it's best to be aware of these so that you can choose different names:

- `score` is the global score value (as used by the actions on the **score** tab).

- `lives` is the global lives value (as used by the actions on the **score** tab).

- `health` is the global health value (as used by the actions on the **score** tab).

- `mouse_x` is the current x position of the mouse cursor in the room.

- `mouse_y` is the current y position of the mouse cursor in the room.

- `room_caption` is the caption shown in the window title bar.

- `room_width` is the width of the current room in pixels.

- `room_height` is the height of the current room in pixels.

Coordinates and Angles

If you want to position something in your room using actions (rather than the Room Editor), then you need to consider how Game Maker's coordinate system works. Traditionally, coordinates on computer screens are calculated slightly differently from how they are taught in school. As you might expect, the x-axis starts on the left-hand side of the screen with a value of zero and increases as you move horzontally to the right. However, the y-axis starts at the top of the screen with a value of zero and increases as you move vertically down (see Figure 1–3). This means that the origin of each room (x=0,y=0) is in the top left, rather than the bottom left and the y-axis is probably the other way from how you might have expected as well. Nonetheless, so long as you can remember that an increase in y moves something down the screen, then you won't go too far wrong.

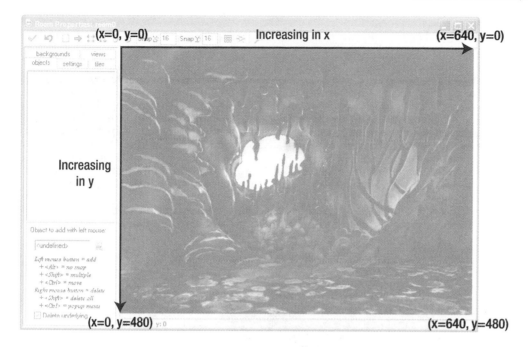

Figure 1–3. *The screen coordinate system used in Game Maker, illustrated for a standard 640x480 room*

Similarly, angles in Game Maker may not work in the way you expect, either. Angles can range from 0-360 degrees as normal, but an angle of 0 degrees represents a direction that points horizontally to the right. Game Maker angles also increase anti-clockwise, so 90 degrees points vertically upwards, 180 degrees points to the left, and 270 degrees points vertically downwards (see Figure 1–4). This can take a bit of getting used to, so it may be worth copying this diagram and sticking it to your monitor until you're completely comfortable with it.

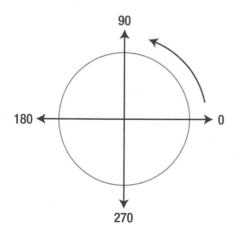

Figure 1–4. *The angle system used in Game Maker*

Transparency

One area that changed significantly in Game Maker 8 is the way that transparency works for sprites. Previous versions of Game Maker have only allowed one color to be transparent for each sprite, which meant that the pixels of sprites were either fully transparent or fully opaque (that is, nothing can be seen through it). This allowed simple *punch-through* transparency, where a single background color within the sprite is not drawn (see Figure 1–5). However, the edges of sprites could often seem quite harsh and jagged using this method—particularly when there was a large contrast in color between the sprites and the background behind them (see Figure 1–6, left).

Fortunately, Game Maker 8 supports a more advanced kind of transparency by which every pixel in a sprite can have its own level of opacity from 0 (fully transparent) to 255 (fully opaque). Opaque just means the opposite of transparent, so this value represents how hard it is to see through something. A low value means that it is easy to see through it (with a value of zero being invisible), and a high value means that it is hard to see through it (with a value of 255 being unable to see through it at all). A more general term for this measure in computer graphics is *alpha*, but you will come across both the terms opacity and alpha in Game Maker.

Figure 1–5. *A sprite displayed in front of a background with and without punch-through transparency*

Figure 1–6. *The jagged edges produced by punch-through transparency (left) compared to the smoother edges produced by alpha transparency (right)*

Figure 1–6 (right) shows how this new alpha transparency can improve the look of your sprites when they appear against contrasting backgrounds. Only two of the file types supported by Game Maker can include transparency in this way. PNG files (.png) support alpha transparency, and you can create them in many different graphics packages, but you need to use animation strips (using _stripXX at the end of the file name) to support multiple frames of animation. This is the most common format we use in this book, but Game Maker 8 includes a new sprite format (.gmspr) that supports both alpha transparency and animation frames, so we sometimes use that as well. There are plenty more cool effects that you can achieve with this new level of alpha control such as creating shadows and advanced particle effects.

■ **Note** Perhaps you're wondering why many things seem to be measured between such strange values as 0 and 255 in computing rather than 0 to 100 (red, blue, and green components of colors, are another example). The answer has to do with the way that numbers are stored on computers. The numbers 10, 100, 1,000, 10,000, and so forth have significance to us because we use a number system called *decimal*. Our number system is based on the number 10 (because we have 10 fingers) and each of the numbers above is 10 times the last. However, computers use a number system called *binary*, which is based on the number 2 (because in electronics, things can either be on or off), so the numbers that are significant to them are 2, 4, 8, 16, 32, 64, 128, 256, and so forth, where each number is 2 times the last.

Congratulations

Fantastic—the necessary preparations have been made, and we're ready to get started. We'll begin on easy ground, but there are trickier paths ahead, so make sure you take the opportunity to begin with a sure footing. Each chapter will build upon the challenges of the last, so you can't afford to take any shortcuts. Anyway, we hope you're not scared of heights, because that's the least of your worries when you're a character in a platform game....

CHAPTER 2

■■■

Platform Beginnings: An Idea with Legs

Not everyone agrees which game holds the honor of being the world's first platform game. Nonetheless, it was certainly the arrival of Donkey Kong back in 1981 that popularized this classic game genre and cemented many of its core mechanics. Mario (as he would later become known) ran, jumped, and climbed ladders between platforms in order to avoid a whole range of hazards and enemies. This seems to include all the key aspects we would expect to find in a platform game today, so it could well have been the first platform game—or at least the first *digital* platform game.

For *real-world* platform games have existed for thousands of years, and certainly long before Mario ever entered the scene. You only need to look as far as a children's playground to see the origins of this form of fun. You'll find plenty of platforms, ladders, slides, and swings—all of which have been incorporated into the platform game genre. Children have been making their own platform games for generations by jumping between tree stumps, walls, or anything else they can find to balance on.

So platform games may not be such a recent invention at all. In fact, although physical play of this kind is just something we do for fun, it has its origins in serious survival skills. Thousands of years ago, our ability to jump and climb could easily have made the difference between finding a meal and becoming one. That's why most animals develop their own survival skills through similar kinds of physical play. So perhaps the first *real-world* platform game was actually played by the very first animal to crawl out of the sea onto the land. Now there's an idea for a game....

A Fish Called Pod

Okay, so just for fun, let's base our first platform game example around one of these creatures. The fossil record suggests that the first backboned animals that "walked" out of the oceans were still very fish-like in appearance. Yet, they could breathe air and had articulated limb joints in their flippers that enabled them to walk on solid ground. The official name for this group of creatures is Tetrapodomorpha, which is not a very catchy name for a video game. Fortunately, they also have the nickname "Fishapods," so we will name our first character (and game) Fishpod (see Figure 2–1).

Figure 2–1. *A quick concept sketch of the Fishpod character, which resembles a modern-day Mudskipper*

This first example game is designed as both a refresher in drag-and-drop programming as well as an illustration of some of the problems involved in creating platform games. We assume that you're already familiar with the Game Maker interface and already have **Advanced Mode** enabled (under the **File** menu). If you're a bit rusty, then this example should bring you back up-to-speed, but all the examples in this book assume that you have had previous experience of drag-and-drop programming in Game Maker. If you haven't, then we strongly suggest you read our previous book (*The Game Maker's Apprentice*) first.

So we'll start this game with a short design description. This book covers game designs in a lot more detail in a later example, but for the time being, we'll stick to a very simple explanation of the idea:

> *You play the role of Fishpod: a sea creature whose life is threatened by the eruption of an underwater volcano. He is forced to flee the sulfurous, boiling waters that he once called home, for the relative safety of nearby caves. Unused to surviving on land, he must navigate his way through a series of perilous underground tunnels in order to find his way to a new home. To stay alive, he must learn how to make the most of his primitive limbs in order to avoid lava flows and poisonous pansies.*
>
> *The left and right arrow keys will move Fishpod horizontally to the left or right, and the space bar will make him leap diagonally upwards in the direction he is facing. Fishpod can stand, walk, and jump on horizontal rock platforms, but will automatically fall down the screen when he is not supported by one. If Fishpod comes into contact with any of the hazards or goes off the edge of the screen, then he dies and is sent back to the beginning of the level.*

From this simple description, we can get an idea of the resources we will need to create our game: a Fishpod character, rock platforms, lava flows, and poisonous pansies. However, we can be a bit more specific about the Fishpod character as the description says he will need to stand, walk, jump, and fall, which will require four different sprites. He will also need to do all of these things either facing left or right, so we'll actually need eight Fishpod sprites in total.

The platforms and lava flows will also require beginning, middle, and end sprites so that they can be made to any length we need. As a result, you will find a total of 16 different sprite images in the Chapter02/Resources directory on the CD, that are ready for you to use to make the game. Have a quick look through these and notice that they are all .png files and many of them contain multiple frames of animation (as indicated by _stripXX at the end of the file name). In the same folder, you will also find a .bmp file that holds the background image for the levels and a number of .wav and .mp3 files containing sound effects that we will use to add atmosphere to the game.

■**Note** We're going to begin by creating all the sprites for the game and a simple test room to work with. This is quite a simple and repetitive task, but we've included instructions on how to do it for the sake of completeness. Nonetheless, if you are a confident Game Maker user, then you might want to just read through the first couple of subsections without actually carrying out the step-by-step instructions. When you reach the section on State Machines, you will be provided with a version of the game that has the sprites and test room already set up for you. Make sure you do read the text, though; otherwise, you will miss out on important concepts that we will refer back to later!

Sprites

We will begin by preparing all of the sprites needed for our game. You should certainly already know how to load sprites into Game Maker, but here's a brief reminder in case you've forgotten.

■**Note** If you've been using an earlier version of Game Maker, then you'll notice that the sprite properties form is a little different in Game Maker 8. Don't worry, we'll explore its new features shortly. However, if you've still not upgraded, then now is the time to do it—you'll find the Game Maker 8 install program in the Program folder on the CD.

Creating and Loading a New Sprite

1. Select **Create Sprite** from the **Resources** menu (you can also create sprites by right-clicking on the **Sprites** folder in the resource tree, or using the little red Pac-Man button on the toolbar).

2. Click the **Load Sprite** button and open the first sprite from the Chapter02/Resources directory (that is, spr_gold_strip30.png).

3. Click on the **Name** field and enter the same name as the file name, but without the _stripXX.png part at the end (that is, spr_gold).

4. Click **Center** (under **Origin**) to move the reference point from which the sprite is positioned to the center of the image.

5. Click **OK** to close the Sprite Properties form.

6. Repeat this process, loading all the images until you have 16 sprites called: `spr_gold`, `spr_lava_begin`, `spr_lava_end`, `spr_lava_middle`, `spr_pansy`, `spr_pod_fall_left`, `spr_pod_fall_right`, `spr_pod_jump_left`, `spr_pod_jump_right`, `spr_pod_stand_left`, `spr_pod_stand_right`, `spr_pod_walk_left`, `spr_pod_walk_right`, `spr_rock_begin`, `spr_rock_end`, and `spr_rock_middle`.

This kind of thing should be second-nature to Game Maker users, so from now on, we will assume you can load and name resources appropriately without quite as much help. We will also assume that you will base your resource names on the original file names (removing the file extension from the end and `_stripXX` where necessary)—if you don't, then you may get confused when we refer to the names in this way later on in the instructions!

■**Tip** Don't forget to save your work regularly by clicking on the blue disk icon on the main toolbar.

Collision Masks

Before we can move on, there is something very important that we need to do to the sprites that may seem a bit counter-intuitive. One of the cool things about Game Maker's sprites is that they have a **Precise Collision Checking** option, which performs pixel-perfect collision detection between different instances in your games. Every new sprite you create has this option enabled by default, and it means that you'll only get collision events when there is a visible overlap between the sprites of two different instances in the game (see Figure 2–2). After all, why would you want anything else?

Figure 2–2. *The situation on the left wouldn't trigger a collision event with precise collision, as there are no overlapping pixels between the character and platform sprites. The situation on the right has overlapping pixels and so would trigger a collision*

Well, let's look at an example. In the Chapter02/Games directory, you will find two executables that show alternative approaches to collision detection in the game we're about to make. Begin by running `precise_collision.exe` and use the arrow keys and space bar to move and jump the green character around the level. This version illustrates precise collision detection in action where the shapes represent the exact *collision masks* that are used by Game Maker to determine collisions. These collision masks are simply the visible pixels of your sprites, allowing for perfect collision detection between instances in your games. Unfortunately, it's not difficult to spot that something is not quite right in this version, as the character frequently gets stuck while walking or jumping into platforms. This is because the collision masks are always changing to exactly match the pixels displayed in the animation frames of the character. So sometimes collisions can occur in one animation frame, but go away in the next when the sprite changes (see Figure 2–3). This can then result in the character getting stuck, flipping back and forth between sprites. There are also problems with the precise collision on the platforms themselves, where even tiny bumps stop the character from walking across them properly.

Now run `box_collision.exe` and compare the difference. This version illustrates a simpler box-based collision system for our platform game where the colored rectangles are now used for calculating collisions. Of course, you wouldn't see the bounding boxes in the finished game, but notice that it produces a much more solid and predictable playing experience. The result is better because all the character sprites use an identically sized bounding box and there are no dips or bumps in the shapes to give unpredictable results (see Figure 2–4).

Figure 2–3. *A precise collision has occurred between the falling pod sprite and the platform (left), which triggers a change to the standing pod sprite (right). However, as a result of the sprite change, there is no longer a collision with the platform, so it triggers a change back to the original falling sprite, and so begins an endless loop*

Figure 2–4. *Using box-based collision, the same collision is not triggered unless there is an overlap between the bounding boxes (left) and crucially when the sprite switches (right), the collision box remains the same*

It's also worth noting that box-based collision is faster than precise collision detection (because it is very quick to mathematically calculate whether two rectangles overlap, but slower to compare all the pixels between two images). Therefore, as far as collision in platform games is concerned, box-based collision is a safer, faster, and more reliable alternative to precise, pixel-based collision. That's why it's important that we make use of box-based collision detection in our game as well as ensuring that the dimensions of each box are the same for all the different sprites of the main character (otherwise, you could still get the kind of sprite-switching problem shown in Figure 2–3). So this is what we will do next.

Editing the Sprite Collision Masks

1. Reopen the Sprite Properties for `spr_pod_fall_left` by double-clicking on it in the resource list.

2. Click the **Modify Mask** button and the Mask Properties form will appear.

3. Under **Image**, ensure that the **Show Collision Mask** is enabled so that you can see the results of the changes you will make.

4. Under **Shape**, select **Rectangle** and under **Bounding Box**, select **Manual**.

5. Set the **Bounding Box** dimensions to **Left** 24, **Right** 40, **Top** 24, and **Bottom** 60, as shown in Figure 2–5. Notice how the shaded area on the collision mask alters to reflect the changes you make.

6. Repeat steps 1-5 with identical values for `spr_pod_fall_right`, `spr_pod_jump_left`, `spr_pod_jump_right`, `spr_pod_stand_left`, `spr_pod_stand_right`, `spr_pod_walk_left`, and `spr_pod_walk_right` (that is, all of the Fishpod sprites). All of these sprites must have the same bounding box dimensions for the game to work correctly.

7. Repeat steps 1-5 for `spr_rock_middle` using **Left** 0, **Right** 31, **Top** 5, and **Bottom** 20. This is the full-width platform sprite. Note that the bounding box doesn't include the top-most pixels of the rock, as this allows the character to have a small overlap when it is standing on the rock. It also doesn't include much of the spiky underside of the rock as it is cosmetic.

8. Repeat steps 1-5 for `spr_rock_begin` using **Left** 16, **Right** 31, **Top** 5, and **Bottom** 20. This is a half-width platform sprite, but it still needs to have the same **Top** and **Bottom** values as the full-width platform to ensure smooth movement across them.

9. Repeat steps 1-5 for `spr_rock_end` using **Left** 0, **Right** 15, **Top** 5, and **Bottom** 20.

The remaining five sprites (`spr_lava_begin`, `spr_lava_middle`, `spr_lava_end`, `spr_gold`, and `spr_pansy`) can actually keep their default **Precise Collision Checking** setting. Fishpod won't physically interact with them in the same way because they are either hazards that will kill him instantly or collectables that will disappear on contact. Because they don't have a physical effect on Fishpod, it isn't essential for them to use the same approach to bounding-box collision.

You may also be wondering why we set up a bounding box that is much smaller than the size of the character (after all, a *bounding* box suggests a boundary that is outside the sprite), but there are actually two good reasons to do this:

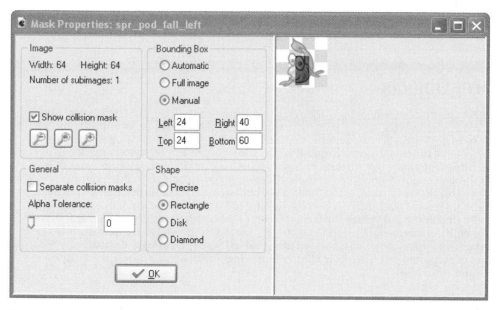

Figure 2–5. *Setting the Mask Properties for the main character*

- Firstly, it only takes a horizontal overlap of one pixel to support Fishpod standing on top of a platform (see Figure 2–4). If the bounding box extended right to the end of Fishpod's flippers, then he could support himself with the very tip of his flipper in a very unrealistic way. With the smaller bounding box, he needs at least a whole flipper in contact with a platform to stand on it.

- Secondly, there is nothing more annoying in a game than when an enemy or hazard kills you when there are clearly no overlapping pixels. If we used the larger, default bounding box, then collisions could potentially occur when there was actually no actual overlap between the sprites (see Figure 2–6). Using a smaller bounding box that remains within the center of the sprite helps to prevent this happening and makes for a less frustrating playing experience.

Figure 2–6. *With precise collision disabled and a full-size bounding box, the player would be killed by this pansy, even though they do not appear to have touched*

■**Tip** Don't forget to save your work regularly by clicking on the blue disk icon on the main toolbar.

Platform Objects

It's difficult to play a platform game without any platforms, so we'll get these made and out of the way first. We'll start by creating obj_platform, which is probably the most important object in the game—despite having no events, actions, or even a sprite. This is because it's going to be the *parent object* of all other platforms. Hopefully, you'll have come across *parent objects* before, but one of the things they allow you to do is group together similar kinds of objects so that they all behave in the same way. We only create three different platform objects in this example (obj_rock_begin, obj_rock_middle, obj_rock_end), but an average platform game would have many different kinds of platforms, so it's really useful to be able to treat them as a group. Most significantly, making obj_platform the *parent object* of these three platforms will mean that we can test for collisions between Fishpod and obj_platform and this will automatically include collisions with obj_rock_begin, obj_rock_middle, and obj_rock_end as well. Continue by following the next set of steps and you'll see how all this comes together when we create the Fishpod character later on.

Creating the Parent Platform Object

1. Click on the **Resources** menu and select **Create Object** (you can also create objects by right-clicking on the **Objects** folder in the resource tree, or using the blue ball button on the toolbar).

2. In the Object Properties form that appears, click on the **Name** field and enter obj_platform.

3. Click the **OK** button on the bottom left of the form to close it. Yes we're done with this object.

Now we will create the rock platform objects, which all use obj_platform as their parent:

Creating the Rock Platform Objects

1. Create a new object resource and enter the **Name** as obj_rock_middle.

2. Click on the icon at the end of the **Sprite** field and a list of all the available sprites will appear. Select the spr_rock_middle sprite.

3. Click on the icon at the end of the **Parent** field and a list of all the available objects will appear. Select the obj_platform object.

4. Click the **OK** button on the bottom left of the form to close it.

5. Repeat steps 1–4 for obj_rock_begin and obj_rock_end, using spr_rock_begin and spr_rock_end, respectively.

Next we'll do something to help make the process of creating levels a little less fiddly. We want it to be possible to create rock platforms of any length, but they always need to begin with an obj_rock_begin and end with an obj_rock_end. That will make positioning and repositioning platforms in the room editor a bit of a chore—particularly when trying to tweak level designs. Therefore, we'll automate the process by making every obj_rock_middle automatically create begin and end platforms either side of it where necessary. That way, we only have to worry about placing instances of the obj_rock_middle object in the room editor and the object events will handle the rest for us.

Adding a Create Event for the Rock Middle Object

1. Reopen the Object Properties for obj_rock_middle by double-clicking on it in the resource list.

2. Click on the **Add Event** button and select the **Create** event.

3. Click on the **control** action tab on the far right of the Object Properties form and drag the **Check Empty** action into the actions list.

4. In the **Check Empty** properties form, set **X** to 32 and leave **Y** set to 0. Set **Objects** to **all** and make sure that the **Relative** option is checked. This checks that there wouldn't be a collision if this instance was placed 32 pixels to the right of its current position. This is a conditional action (hexagonal in shape) and the action(s) immediately following it will only take place if this action evaluates to true. Click **OK** to close the **Check Empty** properties form.

5. Select the **main1** action tab and drag the **Change Instance** action into the actions list. Click on the menu icon at the end of the **Change Into** field and select obj_rock_end from the list. Also, set **Perform Events** to **yes**. This will turn the middle platform section into an end platform section if the previous check was true. In other words, a rock middle will be turned into a rock end when it is at the right-most end of a length of platform.

6. Repeat steps 3–5, this time checking 32 pixels to the left and creating obj_rock_begin (so you will need to use an X value of -32). Make sure that the left **Check Empty** is followed by the **Change Instance** for obj_rock_begin and the right **Check Empty** is followed by the **Change Instance** for obj_rock_end. You can rearrange the order of actions in the actions list by clicking and dragging them within the list.

7. Your list of actions should now look like the one shown in Figure 2–7. Click the **OK** button in the bottom left to close the Object Properties form.

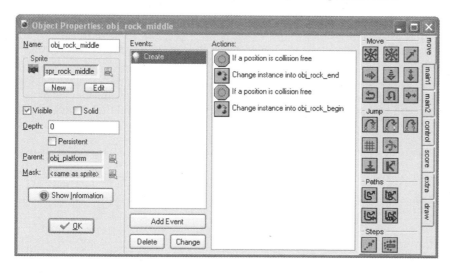

Figure 2–7. The actions for the create event of the middle rock object

Believe it or not, that's all the events and actions we will be creating for the platforms in this game. All the behaviors involving platforms will be controlled from within the Fishpod object.

Platform Waiting Room

It's not like there's much to see yet, but let's quickly make a level and test out our automatic platforms. Then we'll also have a level ready and waiting for Fishpod when we create him.

Creating a New Room with Platforms

1. From the **Resources** menu, select **Create Room** (you can also create rooms by right-clicking on the **Rooms** folder in the resource tree, or using the white window button on the toolbar).

2. Switch to the **settings** tab and set the **Width** of the room to 800 and the **Height** to 600. The default size of 640 by 480 is a little restrictive and 800 by 600 is the next logical size up that has the same ratio between the width and height.

3. On the Room Properties toolbar, set both **SnapX** and **SnapY** to 32, as this is the size of our platform segments.

4. Switch back to the **objects** tab and select obj_rock_middle from the menu below the **Object to add with left mouse** field (or by left-clicking anywhere in the object preview pane directly below the objects tab label).

5. Create a test level similar to the one shown in Figure 2–8 by clicking the left mouse button to add instances of obj_rock_middle to the level. This only needs to include instances of the obj_rock_middle object as its **Create** event will automatically create the obj_rock_begin and obj_rock_end instances where they are needed. However, you will need to put at least two platform instances next to each other in order for this to work properly. Remember that you can delete instances using the right mouse button or move them around by holding down the Control key and clicking the left mouse button at the same time.

6. Click on the little green tick in the top left of the toolbar to close the Room Properties form by.

Now run the game by pressing the green play button on the main Game Maker toolbar. Your room should appear with each platform neatly rounded off at either end. If this doesn't work correctly, then go back and check your steps up to this point. You will also find the current version of the game on the CD in the file Chapter02/Games/fishpod1.gmk.

■**Tip** Don't forget to save your work regularly by clicking on the blue disk icon on the main toolbar.

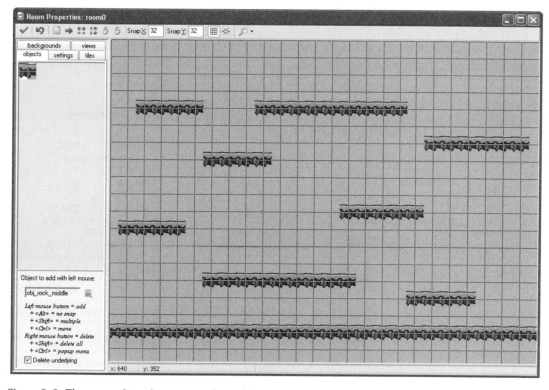

Figure 2–8. *The room editor showing just the middle sections of the platforms*

State Machines

Platform games are not trivial things to program and they usually require far too many different behaviors to be able to try and consider programming them all at once. *State machines* provide a way of breaking down large programming tasks into smaller chunks so that you can consider them more easily. They can help you to create programs that are more easily understood and contain fewer bugs as a result. In this example, we're going to use a state machine for our main character, as Fishpod has a number of different states that affect the way it behaves. Our game description at the start of the chapter listed five different states: standing, walking, jumping, falling, and dying. Apart from the obvious differences in appearance, the character's behavior in these five states should be quite different too. For example, you would expect him to automatically fall down the screen when he is in his falling state, but not in his standing state. We can briefly describe these different behaviors as follows:

- **Standing** motionless on a platform's surface.

- **Walking** horizontally across a platform's surface.

- **Jumping** diagonally under momentum and the influence of gravity.

- **Falling** under the influence of gravity.

- **Dying** under the influence of gravity and without collisions.

Obviously, it must be possible for Fishpod to change states as well, but the conditions for doing so also depend on the current state; so pressing the left arrow should change Fishpod into the walking state from the standing state, but not from the falling state. Figure 2–9 shows these five states and the relationships between them, with each arrow representing a different potential path for changing states.

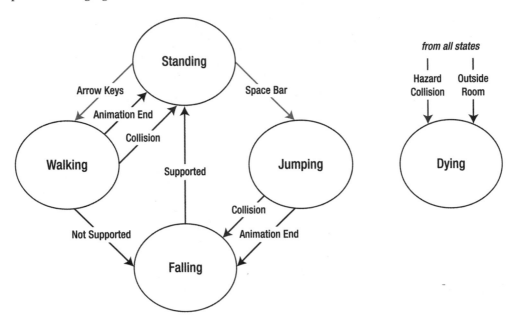

Figure 2–9. *A (finite) state machine diagram for the Fishpod character. "Collision" refers to a collision between Fishpod and a platform, unless otherwise specified. "Supported/not supported" refers to whether Fishpod has a platform directly below him or not. Note that the two blue arrows are the only state transitions directly controlled by the player by pressing keys*

If you read our previous book, then you'll know that it's possible to represent different states like this by creating separate objects for each state and using the **Change Instance** action to switch between them when required. **Change Instance** turns an instance of one type of object into another while keeping the same position, direction, and speed or any other individual properties of the instance. We'll see how this works in practice a bit later, but first we need to consider the additional complication created by the different directions the character can be facing.

Although we have shown five states in our state machine, there will actually be ten states in this game, as each of the five states can either be facing left or right. We could easily go ahead and create different left and right objects for each state, but this would seem to over-complicate the situation, and the whole point of a state machine is to make things easier. Instead, we will use a *variable* to keep track of which direction the character is facing, using a value of 1 for facing left and a value of 2 for facing right. This is great for Game Maker, as numbers are fast and easy for computers to process, but not so great for us because it is easy to forget what the values mean. Fortunately, Game Maker provides *constants* as a way of creating memorable names for important values you are using in your game.

■**Note** The following instructions show how to set up *constants* for use in our game. However, you won't be able to create these constants unless you have a registered **Pro** version of Game Maker 8. If you are using the **Lite** version of Game Maker, then you can achieve the same effect by creating a variable of the same name and value. You need to do this in the obj_pod object, which isn't created until a bit later, so we'll remind you to do it then. For the time being, if you are using the **Lite** version, then simply ignore the next four instructions and carry on as normal afterwards.

Adding Constants for Facing Left and Facing Right

1. From the **Resources** menu, select **Define Constants**. The User-Defined Constants form will then appear, as shown in Figure 2–10.

2. Click on **Add** and type FACE_LEFT (with an underscore between the words). We recommend using all capitals for constants so that you can easily identify them as constants when you use them in your actions. Press the Tab key and type 1. This assigns a value of 1 to the constant FACE_LEFT.

3. Click on **Add** again and type FACE_RIGHT. Press the Tab key and type 2. This assigns a value of 2 to the constant FACE_RIGHT.

4. Click **OK** to close the form.

Figure 2–10. *The User-Defined Constants form*

Now we can use the names FACE_LEFT and FACE_RIGHT in our actions to refer to the constant values of 1 and 2. You may wonder if this is worth the effort, but we can assure you that your programs will be more readable and you will create fewer bugs as a result. You will discover in this book that the ability to create neat, readable programs is essential to creating more complicated games.

State Objects

Okay, so most of the "meat" of our game is going to be in the state objects for the Fishpod character. Each state object will be simple in its own right, but as a whole, they will create a complex interactive object. Try to keep one eye on the bigger picture (Figure 2–9) as we go step-by-step through the implementation. We'll begin by tackling the simplest state object for the standing state.

Creating the Standing State Object and Its Create Event

1. Create a new object called obj_pod_standing. You can set its **Sprite** to be either spr_pod_stand_left or spr_pod_stand_right. This is just as a visual reminder for the resource list because we will be selecting the correct sprite manually in the **Create** event. Set its **Depth** value to -1 so that it appears in front of other objects, as the player's character is generally the most important thing for the player to see in the game.

2. Click on the **Add Event** button and select the **Create** event.

 3. Drag the **Move Fixed** action from the **move** tab into the actions list. Select the middle **Directions** button to indicate no direction of movement and leave the **Speed** set to 0. This ensures that the character stops moving when it enters the standing state. Click **OK** to close the action properties form (we won't remind you to do this from now on).

 4. Add the **Set Gravity** action (**move** tab) to the actions list and leave **Direction** and **Gravity** set to 0. This ensures that gravity is turned off for the character when it enters the standing state; otherwise, gravity would start it moving again.

 5. Include the **Test Variable** action (**control** tab) in the actions list. We're going to use a variable called facing to record whether the character is facing left or right, and use our constants instead of a numerical value. Type facing into **Variable**, FACE_RIGHT into **Value**, and leave **Operation** set to **equal to**. This checks to see whether the character is facing right and only performs the next action if this is true.

 6. Include a **Change Sprite** action (**main1** tab) in the actions list. Select the spr_pod_stand_right sprite and leave the other settings as they are.

 7. Include another **Test Variable** action (**control** tab) in the actions list. Type facing into **Variable**, FACE_LEFT into **Value**, and leave **Operation** set to **equal to**. This checks to see whether the character is facing left and only performs the next action if this is true.

 8. Include a **Change Sprite** action (**main1** tab) in the actions list. Select the spr_pod_stand_left sprite and leave the other settings as they are.

9. You should now have a list of six actions for your **Create** event, as shown in Figure 2–11. Notice how the names we have chosen for variables, sprites, and our constants all help to make it easier to understand what the actions are doing. The lazier alternative shown in Figure 2–12 is much harder to understand!

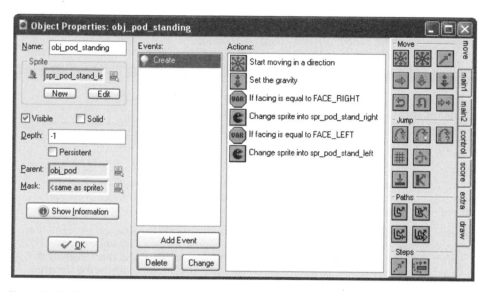

Figure 2–11. *The Create event actions for the standing state object*

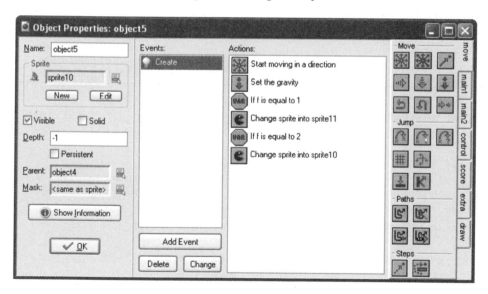

Figure 2–12. *How the Create event might have looked if we had taken less care with names and constants*

The **Create** event of `obj_pod_standing` now ensures that the character is not moving, which is basically all that is required for the behavior of this state. There are still a number of state transitions to handle, but we need to actually create the other state objects in Game Maker first, otherwise we can't include actions that would change into them (because they don't exist yet). We won't add any events or actions to the other state objects at this stage, but just create empty objects for us to continue to work with.

Creating the Remaining State Objects

1. Create a new object called obj_pod_walking. You can set its **Sprite** to be either spr_pod_walk_left or spr_pod_walk_right, as we will be selecting the correct sprite manually in the **Create** event. Set its **Depth** value to -1 so that it appears in front of other objects.

2. Create a new object called obj_pod_jumping. Set its **Sprite** to be either spr_pod_jump_left or spr_pod_jump_right and set its **Depth** to -1.

3. Create a new object called obj_pod_falling. Set its **Sprite** to be either spr_pod_fall_left or spr_pod_fall_right and set its **Depth** to -1.

4. Create a new object called obj_pod_dying. Set its **Sprite** to be either spr_pod_jump_left or spr_pod_jump_right and set its **Depth** to -1. The jump sprite shows Fishpod spinning, so we will also use this as a dying animation played as he falls from the screen.

There are now two state transitions that we need to handle for obj_pod_standing (see Figure 2–9). The first is to change into the walking state when the player presses the arrow keys and the second is to change into the jumping state when the player presses the space bar. This will require three separate events in total: two **Keyboard** events for the left and right arrow keys and one **Key Press** event for the space bar. These are implemented as follows.

Adding Key Events to the Standing State Object

1. Reopen the Object Properties for obj_pod_standing by double-clicking on it in the resource list.

2. Click on the **Add Event** button and select the **Keyboard <Left>** event. We are using a **Keyboard** event because we want Fishpod to keep walking when the player holds down the arrow keys.

3. Include a **Set Variable** action (**control** tab) in the actions list. Type facing into **Variable** and FACE_LEFT into **Value**. We will use this to make sure that Fishpod faces left when you press the left arrow key.

4. Include a **Change Instance** action (**main1** tab) in the actions list. Select obj_pod_walking from the **Change Into** menu and **yes** for **Perform Events**. This last setting means that the **Create** event of obj_pod_walking will be called as part of the change—the default is **not** to do so.

5. Repeat steps 2–4 using a **Keyboard <Right>** event and setting facing to FACE_RIGHT instead.

6. Click on the **Add Event** button and select a **Key Press <Space>** event. We are using a **Key Press** event here because we only want Fishpod to jump once for each press of the space bar.

7. Include a **Change Instance** action (**main1** tab) in the actions list. Select obj_pod_jumping from the **Change Into** menu and **yes** for **Perform Events** so that the **Create** event of obj_pod_jumping is called as part of the change.

That completes all the behaviors and transitions for the standing state object. We'll work on the walking state object next, as this will take us closer to something we can actually try out. As before, the **Create** event for the walking state object will set up the behavior of Fishpod in that state and a number of additional events that handle the transitions to other states.

Adding the Create Event for the Walking State Object

1. Reopen the Object Properties for obj_pod_walking.

2. Click on the **Add Event** button and select the **Create** event.

 3. Include a **Test Variable** action (**control** tab). Type facing into **Variable**, FACE_LEFT into **Value**, and leave **Operation** set to **equal to**. This checks to see whether the character is facing left and only performs the next actions if this is true.

 4. Include a **Start Block** action (**control** tab). This indicates the start of a block of actions grouped together so that all of them (not just the first) depend on the result of the previous test.

 5. Include a **Change Sprite** action (**main1** tab) and choose the spr_pod_walk_left sprite. Leave the other settings as they are.

 6. Include a **Speed Horizontal** action (**move** tab) and set the **Hor. Speed** to -2.

 7. Include an **End Block** action (**control** tab). This indicates the end of a block of actions that are grouped together.

8. Repeat steps 3-7 testing for FACE_RIGHT, changing the **Sprite** to spr_pod_walk_right, and setting the **Hor. Speed** to 2.

You should now have a set of ten actions for the **Create** event that looks like the one shown in Figure 2–13. The next step is to handle the transition from the walking state back to the standing state (refer back to Figure 2–9). The animations for Fishpod have been designed to depict a single hop, which would look odd if it was interrupted mid-flight, so there are going to be no **Keyboard** events for the walking state. Instead, Fishpod will return back to the standing state at the end of each walking animation loop, so that the player can control him again between hops. The **Animation End** event is triggered when the current sprite animation reaches its final frame, so this is the event we will use for the state transition.

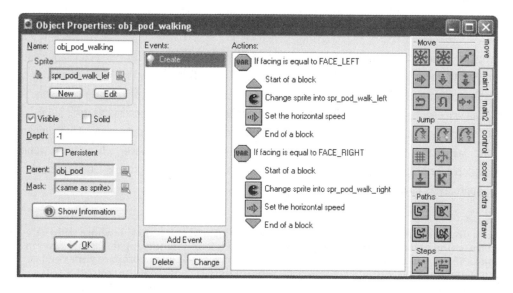

Figure 2–13. *The Create event actions for the walking state object*

Adding the Animation End Event to the Walking State Object

1. Click on the **Add Event** button and select the **Other, Animation End** event.

2. Include a **Change Instance** action (**main1** tab) that changes into obj_pod_standing and select **yes** for **Perform Events**.

We're now very close to being able to test our character events for the first time, but before we can do that, we're actually going to have to create another object for Fishpod. This isn't another state object but an object that sets up Fishpod's initial properties in the level. Normally, we would use the **Create** event of one of the state objects (probably obj_pod_standing) to provide any starting values (for things such as health and lives, for example). However, we are already using the **Create** events to set up the behavior of each state. If we put starting values in these **Create** events as well, then they would get reset between states (so you would go back to full health while walking, for instance). This is clearly not desirable, so instead we will create a new obj_pod object that sets up the initial properties for the character before changing itself into obj_pod_standing. In fact, we don't want to give our character health at this stage, but we do need to initialize the facing variable for the character. This will be done in the **Create** event of obj_pod, as it will only ever be created once at the very start of the level. It is essential that we initialize this value somewhere; otherwise, Game Maker will quite rightly give an error the first time we try and check what the value of facing is.

Creating a New Starting Object and Its Create Event

1. Create a new object called obj_pod. You can set its **Sprite** to any one of the Fishpod sprites.

2. Click on the **Add Event** button and select the **Create** event.

3. Include a **Set Variable** action (**control** tab). Type facing into **Variable** and FACE_LEFT into **Value**. This sets the initial facing direction of Fishpod to the left.

4. Include a **Change Instance** action (**main1** tab). Select obj_pod_standing from the **Change Into** menu and **yes** for **Perform Events**. This will put the object into the standing state and it will never return to the starting object again.

■**Note** If you are using the **Lite** version of Game Maker, then now is the time to "fake" the constant values by including **Set Variable** actions (**control** tab) at the very start of the **Create** event for obj_pod that to create variables called FACE_LEFT with a value of 1 and FACE_RIGHT with a value of 2. Unlike constants, these variables will only be accessible in Fishpod objects, rather than globally (as constants are), but it makes no difference to this example. You might wonder if we could have achieved the same thing simply by setting the facing variable to the *strings* "FACE_LEFT" or "FACE_RIGHT". However, while strings would be just as readable for people, they are much harder and slower for machines to process, so the variable or constant approach is much more advisable.

You can now reopen your test room and place an instance of obj_pod somewhere within the level. Run the game and check that you can move Fishpod left and right using the arrow keys on the keyboard. If you can't, then go back and check your steps carefully or compare your version against our version in Chapter02/Games/fishpod2.gmk on the CD. Note that the character will currently walk on thin air and through platforms as we've not handled those things yet. Pressing the space bar will also cause Fishpod to spin endlessly and you'll have to quit the game (this is because he is stuck in the jumping state and there is no way out of that state yet).

Collision

Before we can make any more progress on the game, we need to look at the way collision works in video games and the problems it can create for game programmers. Try and make sure you understand the explanations that follow, because these issues are encountered again and again in game programming and are common to both 2D and 3D games.

Problem 1: Just Passing Through

Games create the illusion of motion by drawing images at slightly different positions on the screen over the course of time (much like a cartoon). In Game Maker, each of these positions is called a *step*, where there are usually 30 steps in 1 second. This means that if Fishpod moves from the top to the bottom of your screen in 1 second, then Game Maker will have redrawn its sprite in 30 different positions during its journey. This is called *discrete time sampling*, and it has a big impact on collision detection. For when we add a collision event to Fishpod, Game Maker will also perform a collision test in each of these positions to see if it has collided with anything during that step. When an object moves slowly (as on the left of Figure 2–14), the position of the bounding boxes overlap from one step to the next and so collisions are detected continuously. However, when the sprite is moving much faster (Figure 2–14, right) it creates gaps between the positions of bounding boxes in each step. A collision event is only called when two instances overlap during a step, so it is now possible to create situations where Fishpod is above a platform in one step but below it in the very next step. As a result, the collision event would never be called and Fishpod would appear to pass straight through the platform. Worse still, if two instances are travelling toward each other at speed (for example, a character and an enemy missile), then the chances of them missing each other in this way is even higher. So one problem we must solve for our platform game is to make sure that moving instances don't move so fast that they can pass through each other.

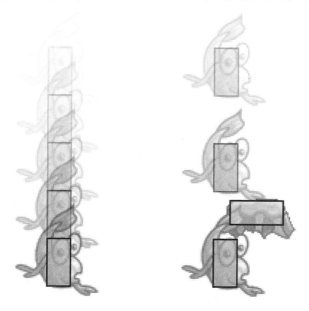

Figure 2–14. *Discrete time sampling produces gaps in collision detection when instances are moving very fast*

Problem 2: Get Your Inside Out

We also face another problem as a result of *discrete time sampling* in collision detection (see Figure 2–15). Even if two instances are not colliding at all in one step (a), they can still have a large overlap by the time the collision event is triggered in the next step (b). The collision event may stop Fishpod moving, but if the instances remain overlapping in this way, then the collision event will continue to get triggered in every step. Therefore, we need to make sure that after instances collide, they finish up touching—but not overlapping. Unfortunately, we only know about the collision after it happens, so putting it right means going back in time to the previous step to work out the exact point at which the collision should have occurred (c). You can then move the sprites toward each other one pixel at a time until they reach the precise point of collision (d). Don't worry—there is an action in Game Maker to do this for you, but it will help a lot if you can understand the approach.

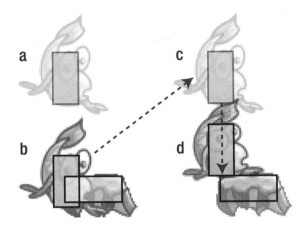

Figure 2–15. *Discrete time sampling means that instances may be inside each other when they collide (left), so we need to move them back to their position in the previous step and lower them to the contact point (right)*

Walk On

Now that we know a bit more about what we need to achieve with the collision events, we can start to handle the remaining state transitions for our walking state object. This needs to include an event for handling (sideways) collisions with platforms, as well as a way of detecting whether the character is supported by a platform or not (see Figure 2–9). We'll add the collision event first, which—as discussed previously—needs to go back in time to the previous step and then position Fishpod at the point of collision with the platform.

Going back in time is not actually as impossible as it sounds. You may recall that every object has x and y variables that store the position of an instance in the room. Well, every object also has xprevious and yprevious variables that store the previous position of the instance in the room (in the previous step). By setting x to xprevious and y to yprevious, we can effectively move the instance back in time to the step before the collision happened. You can then find the exact collision point using the **Move to Contact** action. This action moves the instance in a given direction, one pixel at a time, until it collides with something. All objects also have a direction variable, which indicates an instance's current movement direction, so we can use this in the **Move to Contact** action to make sure we get the contact point with a colliding platform. Putting all these things together we can create our collision event.

Adding a Collision Event to the Walking State Object

1. Reopen obj_pod_walking and add a **Collision** event with obj_platform. Recall that all the platform objects have obj_platform as their parent, so this collision event will be triggered for collisions between obj_pod_walking and any kind of platform.

2. Include a **Set Variable** action (**control** tab). Type x into **Variable** and xprevious into **Value**. This sets the x position back to the value it had in the last step.

3. Include another **Set Variable** action. Type y into **Variable** and yprevious into **Value**. This then does the same for the y position.

4. Include a **Move to Contact** action (**move** tab). Type direction into **Direction,** leave **Maximum** as -1, and select **all objects** for **Against**. This will find the contact point in the direction Fishpod is moving. The **Maximum** value indicates the distance (in pixels) that the action will check for a collision before giving up. A value of -1 means it will check for collisions an arbitrary distance away, but sometimes it is useful to be able to limit this.

5. Include a **Change Instance** action (**main1** tab). Select obj_pod_standing from the **Change Into** menu and **yes** for **Perform Events**. This will put the object into the standing state after a horizontal collision.

Keep the walking state object open, as we now need to handle the transition from the walking state to the falling state when there is no longer a platform supporting the character's feet. We can achieve this using the **Check Object** action.

Adding a Step Event to the Walking State Object

1. Add a **Step, Step** event to obj_pod_walking. We're going to use a **Step** event because the walking object is constantly moving and the ground could stop supporting it at any point (a **Begin Step** or **End Step** would have an almost identical effect in this case).

2. Include a **Check Object** action (**control** tab). Select obj_platform for **Object**, leave **X** as 0, and set **Y** to 1. Check both the **Relative** and **NOT** options. This checks to see if there would be a collision with an instance of obj_platform if Fishpod was moved down one pixel and only performs the next action if this is *not* true (that is, if Fishpod is standing in thin air).

3. Include a **Change Instance** action (**main1** tab). Select obj_pod_falling from the **Change Into** menu and **yes** for **Perform Events**. This will now put the object into the falling state when it is no longer supported by a platform.

That completes the walking state object, which now has all the state transitions originally shown in Figure 2–9. Now we've just got the jumping and falling state objects to complete.

Jump Up

Finishing off the remaining state objects should be pretty easy now, as there is nothing particularly new to consider. Starting with obj_pod_jumping, we'll set the default behavior in the **Create** event as usual, then handle the state transitions in **Collision** and **Animation End** events.

Adding a Create Event for the Jumping State Object

1. Reopen obj_pod_jumping and add a **Create** event.

 2. Include a **Speed Vertical** action (**move** tab) and type -24 into **Vert. Speed**. A negative vertical speed moves the character up the screen, so this will launch Fishpod up into the air.

 3. Include a **Set Gravity** action (**move** tab). Type 270 into **Direction** (downward) and 2 into **Gravity**. This tells Game Maker to increase the vertical speed by 2 in every step, as if it was being pulled downward by the force of gravity.

 4. Include a **Test Variable** action (**control** tab). Type facing into **Variable**, FACE_LEFT into **Value**, and leave **Operation** set to **equal to**. This checks to see whether the character is facing right and only performs the next action(s) if this is true.

 5. Include a **Start Block** action (**control** tab). This indicates the start of a block of actions grouped together so that all of them (not just the first) depend on the result of the previous test.

 6. Include a **Change Sprite** action (**main1** tab) and choose the spr_pod_jump_left sprite. Leave the other settings as they are.

 7. Include a **Speed Horizontal** action (**move** tab) and set the **Hor. Speed** to -6.

 8. Include an **End Block** action (**control** tab). This indicates the end of a block of actions that are grouped together.

9. Repeat steps 4–8, testing for FACE_RIGHT, changing the **Sprite** to spr_pod_jump_right, and setting the **Hor. Speed** to 6.

Our collision event for the jumping state object is actually going to be very similar to the collision event for the walking object, so we'll copy it to save some time. Remember that we used the direction variable as a parameter to the **Move to Contact** action, so the actions we're copying automatically handle collisions in whatever direction Fishpod is travelling. However, we'll need to change the **Change Instance** action from obj_pod_standing to obj_pod_falling and we'll require an additional action in there that brings the jumping Fishpod to a halt.

Copying a Collision Event for the Jumping State Object

1. Reopen obj_pod_walking and select the **Collision** event with obj_platform (left-click on it) so that the actions for this event are visible in the actions list.

2. Right-click anywhere in the actions list and choose **Select All** from the menu. Right-click again and choose **Copy**.

3. Reopen obj_pod_jumping and add a **Collision** event with obj_platform.

4. Right-click anywhere in the actions list and choose **Paste** from the menu. All four actions from `obj_pod_walking` should be copied over.

5. Drag the **Move Fixed** action (**move** tab) into the actions list before the **Change Instance** action. Select the middle **Directions** button to indicate no direction of moment and leave the **Speed** set to 0.

6. Double-click the **Change Instance** action in the actions list to reopen it. Change the **Change Into** option to `obj_pod_falling`.

■**Note** Although we told you to put the **Move Fixed** action before the **Change Instance** in the previous instructions, it doesn't actually make any difference if you put it at the end of the actions list in this case. This is because after the **Change Instance** action is called (along with the appropriate **Create** event of the object it is changing into), Game Maker will come back and finish off any remaining actions in this event. Nonetheless, in principle, we want the **Create** event called by the **Change Instance** action to override any previous settings, so we make sure that it is last in the list.

Actually, you may think it's a bit strange that we always change into the falling state when an instance of the jumping object collides with a platform. There are actually two different situations in which this collision might occur. The first is when Fishpod neatly jumps onto a platform's surface, and the second is when it collides with the underside of a platform. Both cases are neatly handled by the **Move to Contact** action with the `direction` variable. However, you might expect the first to result in a change to `obj_pod_standing` and the second in a change to `obj_pod_falling`. Indeed, we could test the `direction` variable and make the appropriate choice, but this is unnecessary. Once in the falling state, it will get back to the standing state within a couple of steps anyway through its own state transitions.

Finally we will handle the **Animation End** event, which just needs to switch from the rotating jumping animation into the static falling animation at the end of one full rotation.

Adding an Animation End Event for the Jumping State Object

1. Add an **Other, Animation End** event to `obj_pod_jumping`.

2. Include a **Change Instance** action (**main1** tab) that changes into `obj_pod_falling` and set **Perform Events** to **yes**.

Fall Down

Now the only missing state behavior is for the falling state object. It's not particularly complicated, as it just needs to be affected by gravity. However, the **Set Gravity** action in Game Maker continues to increase the speed of an object indefinitely, so we must be careful not to break our collision detection by making the object move too fast (refer back to Figure 2–14). Anyway, we'll begin with the **Create** event, which sets up the default object behavior:

Adding a Create Event to the Falling State Object

1. Reopen the `obj_pod_falling` object and add a **Create** event.

2. Include a **Set Gravity** action (**move** tab) in the actions list. Set **Direction** to 270 (downwards) and **Gravity** to 2.

3. Include a **Test Variable** action (**control** tab) and check that `facing` is **equal to** `FACE_RIGHT`.

4. Include a **Change Sprite** action (**main1** tab) and select `spr_pod_fall_right` (leave the other settings as they are).

5. Include another **Test Variable** action (**control** tab) and check that `facing` is **equal to** `FACE_LEFT`.

6. Include a **Change Sprite** action (**main1** tab) and select `spr_pod_fall_left` (leave the other settings).

Next, we will copy the collision event from the jumping state object, and implement the transition back into the standing state when Fishpod is supported by a platform (see Figure 2–9). This collision needs to check whether there is actually a platform beneath Fishpod's feet, as he may have fallen diagonally into the side of a platform after making a jump.

Copying a Collision Event for the Falling State Object

1. Reopen `obj_pod_jumping` and select the **Collision** event with `obj_platform` (left-click on it) so that the actions for this event are visible in the actions list.

2. Right-click anywhere in the actions list and choose **Select All** from the menu. Right-click again and choose **Copy**.

3. Reopen `obj_pod_falling` and add a **Collision** event with `obj_platform`.

4. Right-click anywhere in the actions list and choose **Paste** from the menu. All five actions from `obj_pod_jumping` should be copied over.

5. Double-click the **Change Instance** action in the actions list to reopen it. Change the **Change Into** option to `obj_pod_standing` and set **Perform Events** to **yes**.

6. Include a **Check Object** action (**control** tab) directly *above* the **Change Instance** action. Set **Object** to `obj_platform`, set **Y** to 1, and check the **Relative** option. This will now only switch to the standing state if Fishpod is supported after colliding with the platform. This is important in the situation where Fishpod falls sideways into a platform as it doesn't make sense for him to change state when that happens.

Finally, we need to handle the problem of gravity making Fishpod fall too fast for the collision detection. We'll do this in a **Step** event, as this will constantly keep the speed in check.

Adding a Step Event to the Falling State Object

1. Add a **Step, Step** event to the `obj_pod_falling` object.

2. Include a **Test Variable** action (**control** tab) and use it to check that `vspeed` (the object's vertical speed) is **larger than** 12.

3. Include a **Set Variable** action (**control** tab) and use it to set `vspeed` to 12. This is equivalent to using a **Speed Vertical** action, which sets the **Vert. Speed** to 12. This will ensure that the vertical speed of Fishpod never exceeds 12 pixels in each step. Its bounding box is 36 pixels high, so there should never be any gaps in the collision detection when it is falling.

That's just about it for Fishpod's state objects. There is one more change we should make to `obj_pod` before running the game. We originally set the initial state of Fishpod to be `obj_pod_standing`, as this was the only state we had implemented at that stage. It makes more sense now to start Fishpod in the falling state, as this handles the situation where he is not supported by a platform at the start of the level.

Editing the Create Event of the Fishpod Object

1. Reopen the `obj_pod` object and select the **Create** event.

2. Edit the **Change Instance** action and set it to `obj_pod_falling`.

Now, run the game and it should start to feel like a platform game for the first time. You should be able to walk along platforms and jump between them. Try not to jump off the screen at the moment, as we've not implemented a way to restart the level without stopping the game yet. Make sure that you have saved your work and then compare your version against the version in `Chapter02/Games/fishpod3.gmk` to check that everything is working as it should.

Challenges

Now that we have the basic platform game mechanics in place, we should be able to turn this into a simple game by adding a few challenges. We'll do this by adding poisonous pansies and lava flows that send the player straight back to the start as soon as Fishpod collides with them. All of these objects need to have the same behavior, so we will use a parent object (`obj_hazard`) to make it possible to handle them all in the same collision event.

It would also be nice if our lava flows finished themselves off automatically in the same way as the rock platforms. So instances of the middle lava object will turn themselves into instances of the begin and end lava objects if there are no more hazards to either side of them. We will also make the begin and end lava objects add instances of platform objects to finish them off if there is nothing there already.

Creating Hazard Objects and Their Create Events

1. Create a new object called `obj_hazard` and close the properties form.

2. Create a new object called `obj_pansy`. Select the `spr_pansy` sprite and set `obj_hazard` as the parent of this object. Set its **Depth** to -2 (in front of Fishpod, as this will ensure that the player can clearly see a hazard like this one when they collide with it).

3. Create a new object called `obj_lava_begin`. Select the `spr_lava_begin` sprite and set `obj_hazard` as the parent of this object. Unlike the pansy hazard, we will leave the **Depth** set to 0 for all the lava hazards because they are part of the platforms.

4. Add a **Create** event to `obj_lava_begin`.

5. Include a **Change Sprite** action (**main1** tab) with **Sprite** set to spr_lava_begin, **Subimage** to 0, and **Speed** to 0.5. This will slow the lava sprite's animation down by half.

6. Include a **Check Empty** action (**control** tab) that checks that there wouldn't be a collision if this instance was placed 32 pixels to the left of its current position (set **X** to -32, **Objects** to **all**, and check the **Relative** option).

7. Include a **Create Instance** action (**main1** tab) that creates an instance of obj_rock_begin 32 pixels to the left of the current object (Set **X** to -32 and check the **Relative** option).

8. Create a new object called obj_lava_end. Select the spr_lava_end sprite and set obj_hazard as the parent of this object.

9. Add a **Create** event to obj_lava_end.

10. Include a **Change Sprite** action (**main1** tab) with **Sprite** set to spr_lava_end, **Subimage** to 0, and **Speed** to 0.5.

11. Include a **Check Empty** action (**control** tab) that checks that there wouldn't be a collision if this instance was placed 32 pixels to the right of its current position (set **X** to 32, **Objects** to **all**, and check the **Relative** option).

12. Include a **Create Instance** action (**main1** tab) that creates an instance of obj_rock_end 32 pixels to the right of the current object (set **X** to 32 and check the **Relative** option).

Creating the Middle Lava Object and Its Create Event

1. Create a new object called obj_lava_middle. Select the spr_lava_middle sprite and set obj_hazard as the parent of this object.

2. Add a **Create** event to obj_lava_middle.

3. Include a **Change Sprite** action (**main1** tab) with **Sprite** set to spr_lava_middle, **Subimage** to 0, and **Speed** to 0.5.

4. Include a **Check Object** action (**control** tab) that checks if there would *not* be a collision with an instance of obj_hazard if the lava instance was placed 32 pixels to the right of its current position (Set **X** to 32 and check both the **Relative** and **NOT** options).

5. Include a **Start Block** action (**control** tab) to group together the following actions.

6. Include a **Change Instance** action (**main1** tab) that changes into obj_lava_end with **Perform Events** set to **yes**.

7. Include an **Exit Event** action (**control** tab). This stops the remaining actions in the event from being executed.

8. Include an **End Block** action (**control** tab) to mark the end of the grouped actions.

9. Include a **Check Object** action (**control** tab) that checks that there would *not* be a collision with an instance of obj_hazard if the lava instance was placed 32 pixels to the left of its current position (set **X** to -32 and check both the **Relative** and **NOT** options).

10. Include a **Start Block** action (**control** tab) to group together the following actions.

11. Include a **Change Instance** action (**main1** tab) that changes into obj_lava_begin with **Perform Events** set to **yes**.

12. Include an **Exit Event** action (**control** tab).

13. Include an **End Block** action (**control** tab) to mark the end of the grouped actions.

■**Note** Poisonous pansies may seem like an odd choice for a hazard, but they have an established gaming heritage. They appeared in the underground caverns of Manic Miner in 1983—one of the first games to popularize the platform game genre in the United Kingdom.

That should handle the automatic creation of lava platforms. Next, we need to make sure that Fishpod restarts the level when he comes into contact with a hazard or goes off the edge of the screen. We already have a parent object for all hazards, which should make this easier, but things are a little more complicated for Fishpod. There are four different state objects that would require their own collision event with the hazard object (all of the states apart from the dying state object). So, rather than repeat ourselves four times, we will make obj_pod (the starting Fishpod object) a parent of these four states and then just handle the one collision event between obj_pod and obj_hazard.

Adding Inherited Events to the Fishpod Object

1. Open each of these state objects in turn: obj_pod_standing, obj_pod_walking, obj_pod_jumping, and obj_pod_falling (but not obj_pod_dying) and set the parent of each one to be obj_pod.

2. Reopen obj_pod and add a **Collision** event with obj_hazard.

3. Include a **Change Instance** action (**main1** tab) that changes into obj_pod_dying with **Perform Events** set to **yes.**

4. Add an **Other, Outside Room** event.

5. Include a **Test Variable** action (**control** tab) and check that the y **Variable** is **larger than** 0. This means that the next action will only occur if Fishpod is lower than the top of the screen (remember that y values start at 0 and increase down the screen). Gravity will bring Fishpod back down again if he jumps off the top of the screen, so there is no need to restart the level in this case.

6. Include a **Change Instance** action (**main1** tab) that changes into obj_pod_dying with **Perform Events** set to **yes.**

■**Note** If you accidently try and make obj_pod a parent of obj_pod as well, then you will get an error saying that this will create a loop in parents. It cannot be the parent of itself and we don't need it to be.

So although we have only added these **Collision** and **Outside Room** events to obj_pod, they will also work for the four Fishpod state objects that have obj_pod as a parent. This is because objects inherit events from their parents. The Fishpod state objects have no **Collision** event defined with obj_hazard themselves, but their parent object (obj_pod) does, so they inherit this event and all its actions. Likewise for the **Outside Room** event. However, when both parent and child objects have the *same* event (like the Fishpod objects do for the **Create** event), the child's event overrides (replaces) the event of its parent. Try and make sure this makes sense as we will continue to make full use of parenting in the remainder of this book. You'll find that parenting is a really powerful and useful concept once you understand it.

Now we need to create the correct behavior for the dying state object, as we haven't handled that yet. We'll make Fishpod fall off the screen and then restart the game when he's outside the room.

Adding Behaviors for the Dying State Object

1. Reopen `obj_pod_dying` and add a **Create** event.

2. Include a **Speed Vertical** action (**move** tab) and type -15 into **Vert. Speed**. This will push Fishpod up into the air slightly before he gets pulled down by gravity.

3. Include a **Set Gravity** action (**move** tab). Type 270 into **Direction** (downward) and 2 into **Gravity**.

4. Include a **Test Variable** action (**control** tab). Type `facing` into **Variable**, `FACE_LEFT` into **Value**, and leave **Operation** set to **equal to**. This checks to see whether the character is facing left and only performs the next action(s) if this is true.

5. Include a **Change Sprite** action (**main1** tab) and choose the `spr_pod_jump_left` sprite. Leave the other settings as they are.

6. Repeat steps 4 and 5 testing for `FACE_RIGHT` and changing the **Sprite** to `spr_pod_jump_right`.

7. Add an **Other, Outside Room** event and include a **Restart Room** action (**main1** tab) without setting any **Transition**.

You might want to test out your dying state before continuing by placing a few hazards in your test room and checking that they kill off Fishpod correctly. Remember that for lava you only need to place instances of `obj_lava_middle`, but that they need to be in lengths of at least two sections to work.

Goals

Our game won't provide much of a challenge without a goal, so the final addition we will make to the game play will be to include some gold nuggets that Fishpod must collect in order to complete each level. Exactly what a prehistoric fish-creature would do with gold is unclear, but perhaps if he evolves into a hedgehog, then he could make them into rings. Once there are no gold nuggets left on the current level, the game will automatically progress onto the next room.

Creating the Gold Object

1. Create a new object called `obj_gold` and give it the `spr_gold` sprite.

2. Add a **Create** event and include a **Change Sprite** action (**main1** tab). Set **Sprite** to `spr_gold`, **Subimage** to `random(30)`, and **Speed** to 0.5. This will set the gold sprite's start frame to a random subimage between 0 and 29 (as there are 30 frames in the sprite) and slow its animation down by half.

3. Reopen `obj_pod` and add a **Collision** event with `obj_gold`.

4. Include a **Destroy Instance** action (**main1** tab) and select **Other**. This will destroy the gold as it is the other instance in the collision.

5. Include a **Test Instance Count** action (**control** tab) to test when the number of instances of obj_gold is **equal to** 0. This means that the next action will only happen when the last instance of obj_gold has been collected.

6. Include a **Next Room** action (**main1** tab) and select your preferred **Transition**.

You could now begin to create some interesting levels for your game, but many of the objects in the resource list shouldn't actually be placed on the level, so let's tidy that up a bit first.

Creating a Resource Group for Private Objects

1. Right-click on the **Objects** folder in the resources menu and select **Create Group**. Call the group Private, or something similar. This will contain all the objects that should not be placed in a room using the Room Editor.

2. Drag the following objects into the new group folder: obj_pod_standing, obj_pod_walking, obj_pod_jumping, obj_pod_falling, obj_pod_dying, obj_rock_end, obj_rock_begin, obj_platform, obj_hazard, obj_lava_begin, and obj_lava_end.

3. You should now just be left with five objects outside of the new group folder: obj_rock_middle, obj_pod, obj_pansy, obj_lava_middle, and obj_gold.

Now it's much easier to focus on the five relevant objects when creating your rooms. Have a go at creating a few levels now. You can place obj_rock_middle and obj_lava_middle in lengths of two or more and the ends will be added automatically. Consider the placement of lava carefully as it will kill Fishpod when he collides with it from both above and below. Each level you create should have one instance of obj_pod and at least one instance of obj_gold. Also include a final room that has a congratulatory message spelled out using gold instances as a final reward.

Finishing Touches

Our final task will be to improve the presentation of the game by adding a few finishing touches in the form of backgrounds and sound effects.

Adding the Finishing Touches

1. From the **Resources** menu, use the **Create Sound** option to create new sound resources for the five sound effects in the Chapter02/Resources directory on the CD (you can also create sounds by right-clicking on the **Sounds** folder in the resource tree, or using the little speaker button on the toolbar). Give them the same names as their filenames without the .wav or .mp3 extensions and leave other settings as they are.

2. Reopen obj_pod and add an **Other, Game Start** event. Include a **Play Sound** action (**main1** tab) for snd_thunder and set **Loop** to **true**.

3. Now select the **Collision** event with obj_gold. At the start of the actions list, include a **Play Sound** action (**main1** tab) for snd_gold and leave **Loop** as **false**.

4. Reopen obj_pod_walking (now in your new group folder) and select its **Create** event. At the start or end of the actions list, include a **Play Sound** action for snd_walk and leave **Loop** as **false**.

5. Reopen obj_pod_jumping and select its **Collision** event with obj_platform. At the start of the actions list, include a **Play Sound** action for snd_splash and leave **Loop** as **false**.

6. Reopen obj_pod_falling and select its **Collision** event with obj_platform. At the start of the actions list, include a **Play Sound** action for snd_splash and leave **Loop** as **false**.

7. Reopen obj_pod_dying and select its **Create** event. At the start or end of the actions list, include a **Play Sound** action for snd_die and leave **Loop** as **false**.

8. From the **Resources** menu, use the **Create Background** option to create a new background resource using bgd_cave.bmp from Chapter02/Resources directory on the CD (you can also create backgrounds by right-clicking on the **Backgrounds** folder in the resource tree, or using the little landscape picture button on the toolbar).

9. Reopen each room in turn and select the **backgrounds** tab. Look halfway down where it currently says **<No Background>** and select the new background from the menu next to this.

Make sure that you have saved all your work and then run your game to see the finished result. Now compare your version against the final version of the game in Chapter02/Games/fishpod4.gmk (see Figure 2–16). Check that everything is working as it should and try out our three levels to see if you can actually complete them yourself.

Figure 2–16. *The finished Fishpod game*

Congratulations

Congratulations! You have now completed your first platform game using Game Maker. Even a simple platform game like Fishpod brings together a huge range of knowledge and programming skills, so you can rightly be proud of yourself. You have already learned about the importance of using box-based collision, seen the orderly power of state machines, and overcome the perils of discrete time-sampling. Imagine saying all that at the start of the chapter! All this should also have brought you back up-to-speed with drag-and-drop programming in Game Maker. Try to make sure you are comfortable with everything we've done in this chapter before continuing, as we will have to take much of it for granted as we look at more advanced platform games.

Now that you can play the finished game, its worth reflecting on the game play for a moment. Fishpod is a simple, enjoyable game that provides a decent challenge, but it can sometimes be quite frustrating as the player doesn't have full control when maneuvering around the hazards. This is something that arises as a result of the kind of animations we have chosen for Fishpod. We deliberately gave him a floppy hopping animation that would emphasize the clumsy movement of a "fish out of water." However, you can't easily stop a hop in mid-air without strange-looking results, so Fishpod moves around a kind of artificial grid where he hops from one grid square to the next. This control system is part of the game's challenge, but it can also leave the player feeling unfairly punished and unmotivated. This is certainly something that we would need to address if we were to take the Fishpod idea further. Unfortunately, only the fittest survive in the competitive world of platform game characters, so we shall be leaving Fishpod behind in his own prehistoric niche. Don't worry, though; there are plenty of other interesting characters out there, including ninjas from at least N different dimensions....

■ ■ ■

PART 2

Zool

The pioneering developers of the platform game genre learned their art by breathing life into incredible characters from fantastic worlds.[1] It was the trials and challenges of developing these early games that turned these young people from bedroom coders into professional game developers. Now is your chance to emulate their journey by recreating a genuine classic in Game Maker.

---

[1] *Zool* illustrations by Alan Batson , reproduced with kind permission of Urbanscan Ltd.

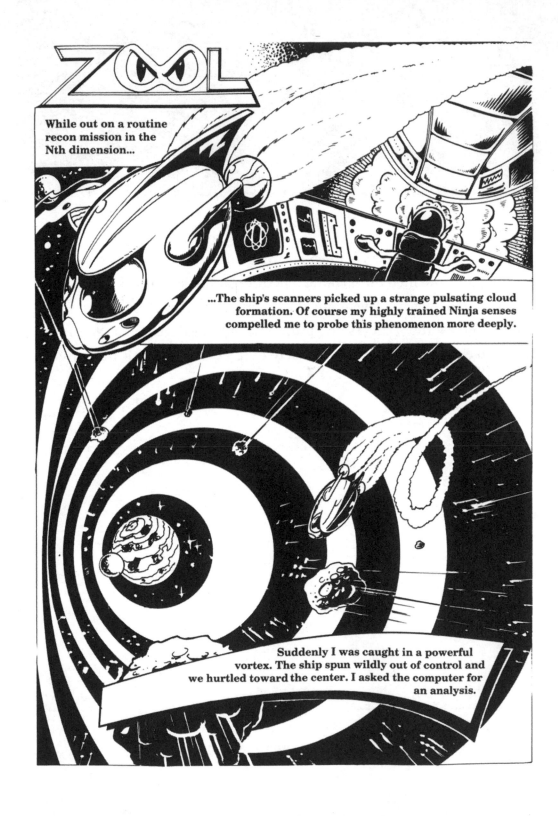

CHAPTER 3

■ ■ ■

Zool: Taking It to the Nth Dimension

Gremlin Graphics was responsible for bringing a menagerie of video-game franchises to the gaming world, including the likes of Monty Mole and Jack the Nipper in the 1980s, Premier Manager and Zool in the early 90s, and Actua Soccer and Loaded before the turn of the millennium. If you're young enough not to have heard of Zool, then you may be surprised to know that he was once seen as the gaming mascot for Amiga computers in the same way that Sonic was for SEGA and Mario is for Nintendo. Zool was a best-selling title that was bundled with every new Amiga 1200, as well as being ported to all the major game consoles of the day. There was even a sequel that featured Zooz (Zool's girlfriend) and Zoon (Zool's alien dog).[1]

However, Zool's popularity declined with that of the Amiga platform he was associated with and, unlike his contemporaries, he's not been seen or heard of since. Until now, that is, for in the next few chapters, we will continue our journey by reviving this lost icon of platform gaming history for one last candy-fuelled excursion....

Designing a Ninjalien

Back in 1991, a fresh young artist at Gremlin was asked to come up with an idea for a video-game character to rival Sonic the Hedgehog. That artist's name was Adrian Carless. He went on to become Gremlin's lead game designer and spent the following decade as the prolific studio's game design front-man. So who better then to explain the origins of Zool than the man himself:

---

[1] ZOOL and the ZOOL logo are registered trademarks of Urbanscan Ltd. All rights reserved. The Zool game resources are provided solely for use with *The Game Maker's Companion* and should not be distributed without written permission from the copyright holder.

We originally set out to make a platform game that took influences from early 16-bit Japanese games, with a character that could become a mascot for the Amiga (which we saw as a vacant position). The Studio boss, Ian Stewart, gave us a simple brief: he wanted an alien character, and he wanted him to do things that no other character could. This was a pretty wide open theme, so after a bit of brainstorming I came up with the 'Ninja of the Nᵗʰ Dimension' line: the theory being if we knew where he came from, we could start to visualize him. His name came last of all. I think he was originally called ZOON, but I changed it to ZOOL (and never thought about Zuul in Ghostbusters until it was mentioned later).

Visually, the first goal was to make him easy to read in the confined sprite constraints imposed by the Amiga: 48 x 48 pixels and just 16 different colors. The second goal, which fell out of the first, was that he'd be easy to animate. When you look at Zool, he's made of two basic geometric spheroids, with a few sticks. I wanted him to have a stripped down look, similar to that seen in Bomberman, with just a little more highlighting to help define his shape.

First came the eyes. As Zool was such a minimal character with few adornments, his mouth (if he had one) hidden behind his mask, I wanted his eyes to be as large and expressive as possible. Cats are agile and inscrutable, so he got a pair of feline eyes (three, the first time I drew him, but we decided the traditional two were better). His eyes were also his brightest feature. I wanted them to 'pop' at all times, so the player could see the determined look in his eye, or the look of panic when he was precariously balanced. As his eyes were so large and prominent in proportion to the rest of him, they pretty much became his stand-out feature by default, and I even designed the logo based around them.

Zool would be a combination of black (ninjas wear black, right?) and green (default alien color—though I tried a couple of alternatives), with a highlight color to help sell his movement. Black stripes around both his head and body helped with rotation animations, and the red at his wrists and ankles helped with tracking limbs. The limbs were made green to prevent him turning into a black mass when he did some fancy rotation. I think the end result fitted well into the fast-paced game we were attempting to create. The final character was dynamic, versatile and a tad enigmatic—everything you want from a Ninja from the Nᵗʰ dimension.

Figure 3–1. *A screenshot from the Mega Drive version of Zool to show what we're aiming for*

The success of the original Zool game on the Amiga meant that it was ported to numerous other gaming platforms as well. Each new version had a slightly different interpretation of the game's controls and core mechanics. We will actually take the SNES/Mega Drive versions as our main reference point, as they were the later versions of the game. Yet we're not aiming to be completely true to the original, so we will mix and match to suit Game Maker's strengths as well. So in our version of the game, Zool will have the following behaviors:

- **Standing**, **Walking**, **Skidding**, **Slipping**, and **Kicking** while supported by a platform.

- **Jumping**, **Falling**, and **Spinning** under the influence of gravity.

- **Shooting** at the same time as any of the above.

- **Clinging** to and **Climbing** vertical surfaces.

- **Dying**, **Invulnerability**, and **Object Collection** at the same time as any of the above.

We will concentrate on Zool's movement-related behaviors to begin with, as they are central to creating a core mechanic that is fun to play. But before we get down to work, let's get an overview of the job ahead.

Long-Term Challenge

Making a complex game like Zool is not an easy task—even in Game Maker. It took a team of professional programmers, artists, and designers many months to create the original game. Of course, they didn't have Game Maker, but it would still be impossible to try and explain the development of the whole game in just a single chapter. That's why we have split the game into four chapters that divide it into more manageable chunks. Unless you have super-human powers of concentration, then you shouldn't expect to create the whole game in a single sitting, either. Example games like those found in *The Game Maker's Apprentice* were designed so that they could be made in just a few hours, but this is very unusual in game development. This time we are recreating a professional game that was sold in high-street stores all around the world, so it's undoubtedly going to be more of a challenge. It's going to require your full concentration to succeed and we recommend that you reward yourself with a treat (and a break) at the end of each chapter. We've even included our own little reward for you, in the shape of a new page from the Zool comic strip at the beginning of each new chapter.

Nonetheless, we think you'll agree that the finished product is well worth the time and effort and you might even want to play it first to see what the pay-off is. You'll find it in the `Finished` directory on the CD.

Short-Term Challenges

The four chapters detailing the development of Zool will be broken down into the following areas, gradually progressing toward the finished game:

- **Chapter 3: Zool: Taking It to the Nth Dimension**
  Getting to know the resources and making Zool walk and jump around the test level.

- **Chapter 4: Empowerment: Sliding Ninjas**
  Adding Zool's full range of movement abilities and making them as slick as a whistle.

- **Chapter 5: Kroole's Forces: Sweetening the Challenge**
  Bolstering the challenge of the game by adding a range of Krool's evil minions.

- **Chapter 6: Fighting Talk: The Empower Strikes Back**
  Giving those minions what's coming to them—ninja style!

Now that you know a bit more about what's in store, we'll return to the first task of looking at all the resources we're going to need in order to realize the vision for this game.

Ready-Baked Resources

By now, you should be very familiar with the more routine tasks involved in making a game, such as loading and creating resources. There are going to be a lot of resources involved in making Zool, so you'll be relieved to hear that we provide an initial version of the game that has all the sprites, backgrounds, some objects, and even a test room already created for you. None of the objects have any behaviors, so the game doesn't actually do anything yet, but we've saved you some of the simpler, monotonous tasks. All the same, we'll begin by looking at what has already been created so that you don't miss out on any important details.

Exploring the Sprite Resources

1. Use Game Maker to open `zool0.gmk` from the `Chapter03/Games` directory on the CD and take a look at the sprite resources. The `Zool` group contains all the sprites required for Zool's movement (combat moves will come later), including standing, walking, falling, jumping, climbing, slipping, and skidding[2] (see Figure 3–2).

2. Notice that most of Zool's sprites have a **Width** and a **Height** of 48 pixels (the climbing sprite is a little bit taller), but they all have their **Origins** set to X=24, Y=24 (the center of a 48x48 sprite). It is important that the origin of each Zool sprite corresponds to the same reference point on the character's body so that they match up correctly when switching between sprite animations.

3. Observe that **Precise collision checking** is turned off for all of the Zool sprites. Click on **Modify Mask** and see that each sprite has a **Manual, Rectangle** bounding box with identical dimensions (**Left**=14, **Right**=34, **Top**=6, **Bottom**=42). As we saw in Chapter 2, both of these are crucial to smooth movement and collision.

4. The `Platforms` group contains all the collision mask sprites that define the physical boundaries of solid parts of the landscape. Different colored sprites are used for the masks of platforms, walls, ledges, ramps, and slopes to distinguish them from each other in the room editor. They all have a **Width** and **Height** of 16 pixels with **Precise collision detection** turned off and **Automatic** bounding boxes that adapt to the visible area of the sprite. Note that these are only used for collision and the visual appearance of the landscape comes from a tile set, described in the next section.

5. There are even more collision mask sprites in the `Ramps` and `Slopes` groups but these have **Precise collision detection** turned *on* for the simple reason that you cannot represent sloped collision areas using a bounding box.

---

[2] These sprites came from the original Deluxe Paint image files created for the SEGA Mega Drive console version of the game (known as the SEGA Genesis in North America).

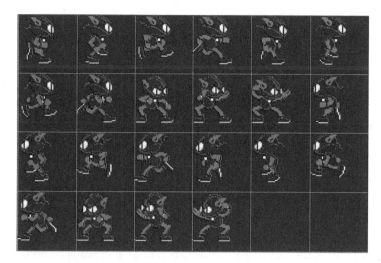

Figure 3–2. One of the original sprite sheets from the Mega Drive version of the game. It is interesting to see how they were laid out in a 48x48 grid against a single color background (lines added)

Kitchen Tiles

You are probably quite used to thinking about your levels being divided into a grid of equal-sized squares, as this is the way that Game Maker usually works. The original Zool game also divided the landscape into squares. These were only 16x16 pixels so that a relatively small number of tiles could be rearranged in different combinations to produce a wide variety of levels. In Zool's era, it was extremely common to construct levels out of very small tiles in this way because of the limited memory available on the hardware platforms. Figure 3–3 shows tiles from the Sweet World, which was the first enemy world encountered in the game and the one we'll be using in this book.

Game Maker supports *tile sets*, as a way of representing a level in a similar way. You may have used them before, perhaps even in the Koalabr8 game in *The Game Maker's Apprentice*. A *tile set* is used to create the visible parts of the landscape, but tiles are non-interactive (they can't have events and actions), so invisible objects are placed on top to handle any interactive behaviors. It also means that any number of tiles can make use of an identical object behavior: providing visual variety without adding hundreds of objects to your game.

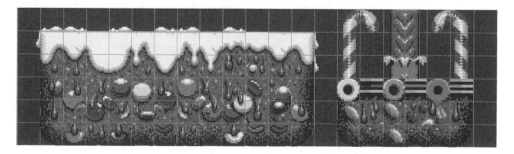

Figure 3–3. Some of the 16x16 tiles originally taken from the SNES version of the game

Exploring Tiles and Rooms

1. Open `tile_sweet` from the Background resources. It has **Use as tile set** selected so Game Maker automatically subdivides it into around 500 different 16x16 pixel tiles that you can rearrange to create the visual composition of a level. It's worth noting that, unlike individual sprites, tiles do not have a movable origin. Their origin is effectively always **X=0, Y=0**, so all the corresponding sprite collision masks (in the `Platforms` group) also have their origins set to **X=0, Y=0**, to match up precisely with the tiles.

2. Open up `room_test` from the Room resources to see the example level we've created for you using this tile set. If you select the **settings** tab, you'll see that the size of the entire room is `2048x640` pixels. Have a look around using the scrollbars. It's not nearly as big as an original Zool level, but it'll work fine for our testing purposes.

3. Now switch to the **tiles** tab (see Figure 3–4). From here, you can see our `tile_sweet` tile set displayed in the tab on the left hand side, and the room itself on the right. You'll need to expand the right edge of the tab by some way in order to see all of the tiles from the tile set. You can change the currently selected tile by left clicking on the tile set, and then place copies of that tile by left clicking in the room. As with objects, you can also delete tiles again using the right mouse button. Have a go at creating an area of landscape using the tile set, but be careful to undo your changes again afterward (either by using the Undo button or by closing the room and selecting **No** when asked to save the changes). You can see how much time and effort went into putting just this small level together!

4. There are two separate tile layers in this room: a background layer (at a depth of `1000`), which will appear behind Zool, and a foreground layer (at a depth of `-1000`), which will appear in front of Zool. This helps to give the game a more 3D effect by making Zool appear behind some items of scenery and in front of others. You can select between editing these different layers by clicking on the drop-down menu where it says **Current tile layer**. You can only add or delete tiles from the currently selected layer.

■**Tip** To view only the tile layer you are currently editing, uncheck the **Show Tiles** option from the drop-down menu next to the magnifying glass on the Room Properties toolbar (see Figure 3–4). When the **tiles** tab is selected, this only shows the current tile layer. When the **tiles** tab is not selected, it hides all tiles.

---

5. Now, switch to the **objects** tab in the Room Properties with the **Show Tiles** option still unchecked. All the pretty graphics should disappear and you should now be able to see through to the green collision objects that define the physically solid parts of the level. All these collision objects have a **Depth** of `0`, so they appear in-between the two tile layers (although they also have their **Visible** setting unchecked so they aren't visible at all when you run the game—just in the editor).

6. It's difficult to tell, but worth noting that we have placed additional collision objects so that the floor extends some way beyond the left and right boundaries of the room. We want the room to work as an infinitely looping level, so this helps Zool to smoothly wrap around the boundaries of the room without accidently falling down outside of the room. This also means you might occasionally get a message from Game Maker telling you that there are objects outside of the room and asking you if you want to delete them. Obviously, you need to select **No** when you get this message.

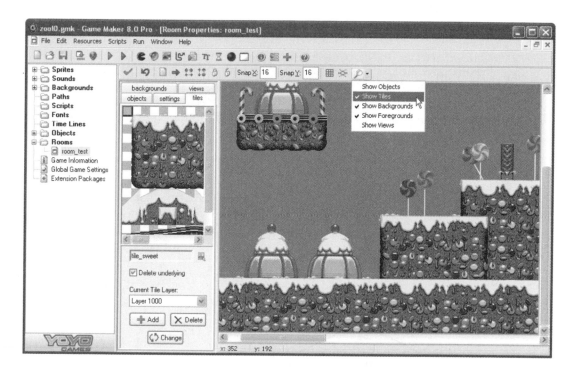

Figure 3–4. *Disabling Show Tiles in the Room Properties allows you to view the foreground and background tile layers separately as well as reveal the collision objects*

7. Finally, go to the **Objects** resources folder and open the Platforms group to examine the objects themselves. You'll see that a whole range of collision objects have been created for you and assigned the appropriate sprites. The first three are "standard" objects and you should have already seen plenty of instances of these in the test room:

obj_platform (green) —This object is used to represent all the horizontal platform sections that make up the ground that Zool walks on. They are also used to create the underside of solid areas of ground that Zool can't jump up through.

obj_wall (blue) —This object is used to represent all the vertical wall sections that make up the cliffs that Zool will climb and cling to.

obj_ledge (almost invisibly thin magenta line) —This object is used for horizontal platforms that Zool can jump up through but still walk on top of.

The next three are only used as parent objects, so you'll never actually see instances of these objects placed on the landscape. They just exist to group similar kinds of objects together in useful ways:

obj_ramp (black) —Ramps are just platforms that have a slope up or down. You'll find the actual ramps that get placed on the level (and so have the sloped collision masks) in the Ramps group.

obj_slope (grey) —Slopes are just steeper ramps that are made of ice, and therefore slippery. Again, you'll find the actual slopes that are placed on the level (and have the sloped collision masks) in the Slopes group.

obj_solid (no sprite) —This is a parent object that is used for all objects that are considered to be solid parts of the landscape.

8. Notice that all the objects in the Ramps group have obj_ramp set as their parent and all the objects in the Slopes group have obj_slope set as their parent. You can think of this kind of parent relationship as meaning "a kind of." So all the ramps are "a kind of" obj_ramp and all the slopes are "a kind of" obj_slope.

9. There are more "a kind of" relationships set up for the other types of collision objects. The obj_slope object (which represents icy slopes) has obj_ramp set as its parent because slopes are "a kind of" slippery ramp. Both obj_ramp and obj_ledge have obj_platform as their parent because they are "a kind of" platform. Finally, both obj_platform and obj_wall have obj_solid as their parent because they are "a kind of" solid object. Figure 3–5 shows the complete hierarchy of parent relationships used for the landscape objects. Take a good look at this and make sure that the parent relationships make sense to you before continuing.

10. Crucially, this makes it possible to consider collisions with objects that are "a kind of" something. For example, a collision with obj_solid now includes every kind of landscape object, and a collision with obj_platform would include everything apart from walls.

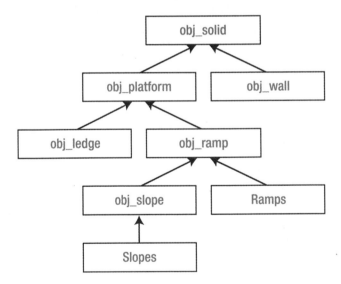

Figure 3–5. *The hierarchy of "is a kind of" relationships as defined by the parent settings of each object*

PARENTING

If all this use of parenting still seems confusing, then try to remember that there are two different effects of giving an object a parent in Game Maker:

1. The child object inherits all the events and actions of its parent (unless it has identical events, in which case the child's events override those of its parent).

2. All collisions events with the parent object (for example, `obj_solid`) are now also triggered by collisions with the child object (for example, `obj_platform`).

An Alien State

You probably won't be surprised to learn that we're going to make use of state objects again in this game. When we made Fishpod, we had a very clear rule: every different behavior and/or appearance had its own state object to handle it. Now this may work fine with simple games like the Fishpod example, but it is not always practical when things get more complex. For a start, we already know Zool will have seven different appearances for movement alone, and we'll need to add several more later for attack moves. If we apply the same rule about appearances, then that could mean ten or more different state objects for Zool. There would be many common behaviors between these different appearances, producing a lot of duplicated or subtly different versions of the same actions (for example, look back at the platform collision events for `obj_pod_jumping` and `obj_pod_falling` in the Fishpod game). Our events will contain a lot more actions than the ones in Fishpod and duplicated actions can be dangerous if they need to be modified: it's easy to introduce errors by forgetting to change all of them.

Now we could use *Parents* as a way of reducing duplicated code and sharing common behaviors between state objects. Making one object a parent of another allows it to inherit all of its events and actions or override those events with its own when differences are required. However, complex inheritance hierarchies can quickly become difficult to follow, so too many parents and use of inheritance could be just as problematic as too many state objects.

The bad news is that there are no hard and fast rules about how much you should use such mechanisms as state machines or inheritance in programming, and you have to develop a gut instinct for it. However, you should always bear in mind that they are designed to make your life easier—not as some kind of programming philosophy. It is never right to use parents, state objects, or any other programming mechanism just "because you can." You should always consider whether it actually makes your life easier or harder as a result!

To this end, we have tried to group our states together into a smaller number of state objects that include common behaviors. There will be eight moving-related states in all (one for each appearance and two for climbing) grouped into four different state objects. We will simply store the current state in a variable, and manage this *state variable* from within the events and actions of the four *state objects*. Combined with a small amount of parenting to cope with behaviors common to all states, we believe this will provide an effective and manageable result:

- `obj_zool`—The parent object for all Zool state objects. This will handle any behaviors that are common to Zool in all states.

- `obj_zool_land`—This state object will handle all states and behaviors relating to moving on land: **standing**, **walking**, and **skidding**.

- `obj_zool_air`—This state object will handle all states and behaviors relating to moving in the air: **jumping** and **falling**.

- `obj_zool_wall`—This state object will handle the states and behaviors relating to moving on walls: **clinging** and **climbing**.

- `obj_zool_ice`—This state object will handle the **slipping** state behavior relating to moving on icy slopes in all different directions.

We can also attempt to draw these state objects and the relationships between them as a guide to implementing the object behaviors (see Figure 3–6). It looks pretty frightening, doesn't it? Don't worry—you don't need to memorize it, and the whole point of drawing a complicated diagram like this is to help us focus on one state at a time, without worrying about how complicated the overall structure is. It is impossible to capture the finer details of a system like this in one diagram, but it should help us plan our general approach.

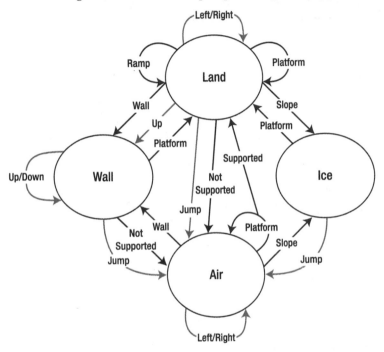

Figure 3–6. *A (Finite) State Machine diagram for our implementation of Zool. Red arrows indicate collisions and blue arrows indicate player interactions. "Supported/Not Supported" refers to whether Zool has a platform directly below him or not*

■**Note** We are going to begin by defining a set of *constants* for use in our game. Just as with the Fishpod example, you won't be able to create these constants unless you have a registered **Pro** version of Game Maker 8. If you are using the **Lite** version of Game Maker, then you can achieve the same effect by including **Set Variable** actions (**control** tab) at the very start of the **Create** event for the parent Zool object. Each one should have the same name and value as the constant. Unlike constants, these variables will only be accessible in Zool objects, rather than globally (as constants are), but it makes no difference to the rest of this example.

An Alien's First Steps

So with a plan in place, we can now set about implementing some functionality for our game. While it's all still fresh in our head, we'll begin by setting up constants for the eight different movement states we're going to need, as well as creating empty objects for the four different state objects.

Setting up State Constants and State Objects

1. Make sure you have an unaltered version of zool0.gmk opened and go to **Define Constants** on the **Resources** menu.

2. Create the following state constants with their respective values: ZSTATE_STAND = 0, ZSTATE_WALK = 1, ZSTATE_JUMP = 2, ZSTATE_FALL = 3, ZSTATE_CLIMB = 4, ZSTATE_CLING = 5, ZSTATE_SLIP = 6, ZSTATE_SKID = 7. Note that we have prefixed all of these with the letter Z (for Zool) in case we need to define states for other characters in the game later.

3. While it's open, create two more constants for facing left and right: FACE_LEFT = -1, FACE_RIGHT = 1. Note that we are using a negative value for left and a positive value for right this time. These will be particularly useful as we can make regular use of the relationship between these values and movement on the x-axis (as x-1 is one pixel to the left, and x+1 is one pixel to the right). More of that later.

4. Create a new object called obj_zool, give it the spr_zool_stand_right sprite, and set its depth to -1 (just in front of 0).

5. Create four more object resources called obj_zool_land, obj_zool_air, obj_zool_wall, and obj_zool_ice. Give each object the corresponding sprite: walk for land, jump for air, climb for wall, and slip for ice. The facing direction of the sprite is not important, but if you use the wrong sprite, then you may end up with a Zool that doesn't animate properly. Set their depth to -1 and make obj_zool their parent.

6. Open up the test room and place a single instance of obj_zool on the bottom left of the room so that he is standing in mid-air just above the floor.

Now let's create some simple walking functionality for Zool. We'll begin by setting up the parent object, which can contain any functionality that is common to all Zool state objects. All the child objects will inherit the events and actions of this object. One of the key functions we'll make the parent object perform for *all* state objects will be to draw the appropriate sprite for Zool's current state. The parent object will also be the first Zool object that gets created on each level, so we'll use its **Create** event to set default values for variables as well.

The Zool Parent Object

1. Add a **Create** event to obj_zool and include a **Set Variable** action (**control** tab) that sets a **Variable** facing to FACE_LEFT. We will use this variable to keep track of which way Zool is facing just like before. Setting it to left in here makes Zool default to facing left whenever he starts a level.

2. Now include a **Change Instance** action (**main1** tab) that changes into obj_zool_land and sets **Perform Events** to yes. This last option makes sure that the **Destroy** event of the current object (obj_zool) and the **Create** event of the object we're changing into (obj_zool_land) are both called as part of this action (in that order). We've only mentioned the **Create** event in the past, as we don't use **Destroy** events very often.

3. Add an **Other, Outside Room** event and include the **Wrap Screen** action (**move** tab) with **Direction** set to horizontal. We have a relatively small room, so this will help us to maximize the available space. Remember that we have added platform objects beyond the edges of the room so that Zool can wrap smoothly.

4. Add a **Draw** event. Adding this **Draw** event to the parent will not just disable drawing for this object, but all its children as well. So next we will include actions to draw the appropriate sprite for all the different states—otherwise Zool will not appear!

5. Include a **Test Variable** action (**control** tab) that tests if the **Variable** facing is **equal to** the **Value** FACE_RIGHT.

6. Immediately follow this with a **Start Block** action to group the following actions together under this test.

7. Include a **Test Variable** action that tests if the **Variable** state is **equal to** the **Value** ZSTATE_STAND.

8. Immediately follow this with a **Draw Sprite** action (**draw** tab) that draws spr_zool_stand_right at a **Relative** position of **X=0, Y=0**.

9. Include a **Test Variable** action (**control** tab) that tests if the **Variable** state is **equal to** the **Value** ZSTATE_WALK.

10. Immediately follow this with a **Draw Sprite** action (**draw** tab) that draws spr_zool_walk_right at a **Relative** position of **X=0, Y=0**.

11. Add an **End Block** action (**control** tab) to end the group of actions.

12. Now repeat steps 5-11, replacing FACE_RIGHT with FACE_LEFT and right-facing sprites with left-facing ones, appropriately. Once completed, this event should contain the actions shown in Figure 3–7.

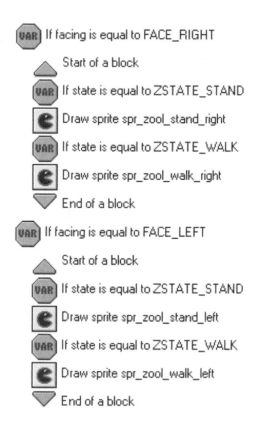

VAR If facing is equal to FACE_RIGHT

Start of a block

VAR If state is equal to ZSTATE_STAND

Draw sprite spr_zool_stand_right

VAR If state is equal to ZSTATE_WALK

Draw sprite spr_zool_walk_right

End of a block

VAR If facing is equal to FACE_LEFT

Start of a block

VAR If state is equal to ZSTATE_STAND

Draw sprite spr_zool_stand_left

VAR If state is equal to ZSTATE_WALK

Draw sprite spr_zool_walk_left

End of a block

Figure 3–7. The current state of the Draw event for the parent Zool object

■**Note** If you run the game at the moment, it will exit immediately. Why is this? Well, if you think about it, the **Create** event of `obj_zool` changes the instance into `obj_zool_land`, performing the **Destroy** and **Create** events of `obj_zool` and `obj_zool_land`, respectively. Yet, `obj_zool_land` inherits its **Create** event from `obj_zool`, so its **Create** event will also change the instance into `obj_zool_land`. This sets an infinite loop in motion, and Game Maker aborts the program.

The Zool Land State Object

1. Reopen `obj_zool_land` and add a **Create** event. Include a **Set Variable** action (**control** tab) that sets a variable `state` to `ZSTATE_STAND`.

2. Include a **Set Gravity** action (**move** tab) that sets **Direction** to 270 (downward) and **Gravity** to 0 (off). All the land-based movement will work with gravity turned off, as it makes things simpler that way.

3. Include a **Set Friction** action that sets **Friction** to 1. This adds a force to Zool that will gradually slow him down by reducing his speed by 1 pixel every step.

4. Include a **Speed Vertical** action that sets **Vert. Speed** to 0. This makes sure that Zool stops any vertical movement if he had any in a previous state.

5. Add a **Keyboard, Left** event and include a **Speed Horizontal** action (**move** tab) that sets **Hor. Speed** to a **Relative** value of -2.5. This applies a force on Zool toward the left when the left key is held. The size of this movement force is one greater than the friction force, so he will gradually build up speed by 1.5 pixels per step (the difference).

6. Include a **Set Variable** action (**control** tab) that sets the **Variable** state to ZSTATE_WALK.

7. Include another **Set Variable** action that sets the **Variable** facing to FACE_LEFT.

8. Repeat steps 5-7 for a **Keyboard, Right** event containing the same three actions. These should set **Hor. Speed**, **Relative** to 2.5, the **Variable** state to ZSTATE_WALK and the **Variable** facing to FACE_RIGHT.

9. Now add a **Step, Begin Step** event and include a **Set Variable** action that sets the **Variable** state to ZSTATE_STAND. You might think that putting this in a **Begin Step** event would mean that Zool always ends up being drawn in the standing state, but we will explain why that's not the case in the next section.

10. Add a **Collision** event with obj_solid. The parent hierarchy we have set up between collision objects means that obj_solid will include collisions with every other kind of solid object (platforms, walls, ledges, ramps, and slopes).

11. Include a **Set Variable** action (**control** tab) that sets the **Variable** x to xprevious.

12. Include another **Set Variable** action that sets the **Variable** y to yprevious. These two actions set Zool back to the position he was in before the collision happened.

13. Include a **Move to Contact** action (**move** tab) with **Direction** set to direction, **Maximum** set to -1 (no maximum), and **Against** set to **all objects**.

14. Finally, include a **Speed Horizontal** action with **Hor. Speed** set to 0. This now provides us with the same kind of collision event as used in the Fishpod game. The obj_zool_land object should now look like Figure 3–8.

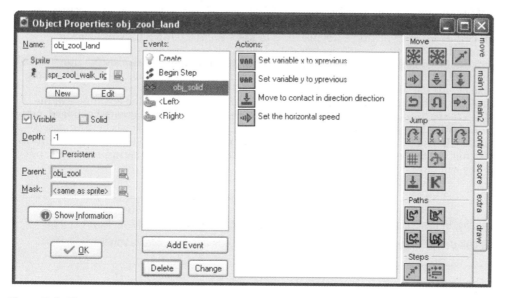

Figure 3–8. *The current state of the land Zool state object*

■**Note** If you run the game now, then the previous problem has fixed itself. The `obj_zool_land` object now has its own **Create** event that overrides that of its parent and so prevents the infinite loop occurring.

Marching Order

So before moving on, it's worth looking at the order of events in Game Maker, as it is critical to why this particular combination of events works. If you've ever wondered why there are three different kinds of **Step** events in Game Maker, then this should help to explain things. In every game step, Game Maker executes all the different events for all the different objects in the game. However, it does this by performing each kind of event for every object before moving on to the next kind of event. The order in which it does this is as follows:

- Any **Begin Step** events for all objects

- Any **Alarm** events for all objects

- Any **Keyboard**, **Key Press**, and **Key Release** events for all objects (in that order)

- Any **Mouse Button**, **Mouse Press**, and **Mouse Release** events for all objects (in order)

- Any normal **Step** events for all objects

- [At this point all instances are set to their new positions based on their current speed and direction.]

- Any **Collision** events for all objects with all other objects

- Any **End Step** events for all objects

- And finally, any **Draw** events for all objects

One of the things that seems to be missing from Game Maker when you first start to create games is an event for when a specific key is *not* being pressed. You start something moving in a **Keyboard, Left** event and you add a **Keyboard, <No Key>** event to stop it moving again. Unfortunately the **<No Key>** event only gets called when no keys are being pressed on the keyboard *at all*. So once you have started an object moving left, then you can keep it moving left by holding *any* key down on the keyboard —even the right arrow key! Similarly, solutions using **Key Release** events can also be tricky to make work in all situations.

So for Zool, we have created a solution to this kind of problem by taking advantage of the event order. We set the state to ZSTATE_STAND in the **Begin Step** event, and create **Keyboard, Left** and **Keyboard, Right** events that reset the state to ZSTATE_WALK. If neither key is being pressed, then the state will still be ZSTATE_STAND in any of the **Step**, **Collision**, **End Step**, or **Draw** events as they occur after the keyboard events. The left and right keys will set the state appropriately, but any other key will have no effect on the outcome.

■**Note** Actually, in the registered, Pro version of Game Maker 8, you can now add your own **Trigger** events that can detect the user pressing (or not pressing) any combination of keys you like.

Room with a View

If you try running the game at the moment, then you will discover that your entire room is displayed in one very large window. Fortunately, Game Maker provides *views* as a means of changing how much of the room you can see at once, and even settings to make that view automatically follow a particular object around the room. We know that the entire test room is 2048 pixels wide by 640 pixels high (see Figure 3–9), but how much of it do we want to see at once? The screen resolution on the original (Amiga) version of Zool was only 320x256 pixels, which didn't give a wide view of Zool's surroundings. We're going to be a bit more generous and adapt our aspect ratio to fit a widescreen monitor by giving players a 512x300 pixel view window into the room. However, modern monitor resolutions are much higher than this, so this would create a pretty small window on your desktop. Therefore, we will also scale up the output of this view by doubling it up to 1024x600 pixels—you can always hit F4 to go full-screen if you have a really high desktop resolution and you want the full effect.

Setting Up the Room View

1. Open room_test from the **Rooms** resources folder and select the **views** tab. Check the **Enable the use of views** option and select **View 0** from the pane below it. The settings below this pane now refer to **View 0**.

2. **Check** the **Visible when room starts** option and set **View in room** to X=0, Y=0, W=512, H=300. You should see a rectangular outline appear in the room panel marking the boundary of the view we will be *copying*. The X and Y positions of the view are actually irrelevant, as we will make the view follow the position of the Zool object below.

3. Set **Port on screen** to X=0, Y=0, W=1024, H=600. So if you think of the previous step as a *copy* operation, then this is the *paste*. It will paste the view to an X,Y position of (0,0) on the player's window, but scale up the width and height to double its original size as part of the pasting process.

Figure 3–9. *The entire Zool test room, with the size of the player's view area shown in the top left corner*

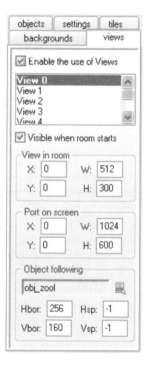

Figure 3–10. *The view panel settings for this view*

4.   Select obj_zool from the drop-down menu next to **Object following** and set the **Hbor** (horizontal border) to 256, **Vbor** (vertical border) to 160, and both **Hsp** and **Vsp** (horizontal and vertical speed) to -1. Because obj_zool is the parent of all the other Zool objects, the view will know to follow any kind of Zool object. The border values determine the distance Zool needs to be from the edge of the view before the view starts to move. Setting these to half the width and height of the view means that the view will always try and keep Zool in its center. The speed values allow you to set a limit on the speed at which the view can move and a value of -1 means no limit.

5.   Your **View** tab settings should now look like Figure 3–10.

Now when you run your game, you should have a much better view of Zool as he moves around the level (albeit in mid-air and at incredible speeds). He should also stop when he collides with walls (but pass through ramps). If you have problems, then you will find a version of the game at this point in the file `zool1.gmk` in the `Chapter03/Games` directory on the CD.

Crash Landing a Ninja

Clearly, walking on thin air is not right, so we'll start by putting some limits on Zool's speed and then we'll get his feet on the ground. We know from the previous chapter that it is necessary to limit the speed of moving objects to prevent them from moving so fast that they pass through other objects (one of the problems of discrete time sampling). We'll do this in the **Step** event because this takes place immediately after the keyboard events that change Zool's speed. We'll put this **Step** event in `obj_zool` (the parent Zool object) because then the event will be inherited by all Zool objects and that will save us repeating the same actions in each object.

Limiting Zool's Speed

1. Define two new constants using the **Define Constants** option on the **Resources** menu (or two new variables in the **Create** event of `obj_zool`, if you are using Game Maker Lite). Set both MAX_HSPEED and MAX_FALL_SPEED to 14.

2. Add a **Step, Step** event to `obj_zool` and include a **Set Variable** action. Set the **Variable** vspeed and type min(MAX_FALL_SPEED, vspeed) into **Value**. Here, min is a Game Maker function that returns the minimum value of its arguments (the values separated by commas). So while vspeed is smaller than MAX_FALL_SPEED, the min function will return the value of vspeed and the action will set vspeed to the value of vspeed (which changes nothing). Yet, when vspeed is greater than MAX_FALL_SPEED, the min function will return MAX_FALL_SPEED and the action will set vspeed to MAX_FALL_SPEED. In this way, the min function limits Zool's falling speed to a maximum of 14 pixels per step.

3. Include another **Set Variable** action. This time, set the **Variable** hspeed and type median(-MAX_HSPEED, hspeed, MAX_HSPEED) into **Value**. Here, median is a different function that computes the middle value of its arguments when they are arranged in order of size. So while hspeed is less than MAX_SPEED and more than -MAX_HSPEED, the middle value will be hspeed. However, if hspeed is greater than MAX_HSPEED, then the middle value becomes MAX_HSPEED and if hspeed is smaller than -MAX_HSPEED, then the middle value becomes -MAX_HSPEED. In this way, we can keep hspeed between -14 and +14 pixels per step just using a single action.

■**Caution** We'll need to remember that if we create a **Step** event for any of the other Zool objects (which have `obj_zool` as a parent), then the new **Step** event will replace this inherited **Step** event. That means our speed clamping actions won't be called for that object and Zool will potentially move too fast again.

If you play the game now, Zool is limited to a sensible running speed—also notice how he slides to a halt when you release a key when he is moving fast. This is a result of the friction gradually bringing him to a halt when you are no longer applying a force to move him. Next, we'll start to implement behaviors for `obj_zool_air` and add a bit of gravity into the equation.

For our purposes, we will consider a "normal" gravity setting to be a downwards force of 2 pixels per step. Logically, `obj_zool_air` should always be subject to this same gravitational pull, so this shouldn't need to change. However, many platform games of this type include a feature whereby the character can jump higher if you continue to hold down the jump key rather than releasing it immediately. So we will make gravity a little weaker (1.5 pixels per step) when the player initially presses the spacebar so that Zool can jump a little higher, but revert back to normal gravity as soon as the player releases it again. So to get the maximum height out of a jump, the player will need to hold the spacebar down for the duration of the jump.

The Zool Air State Object

 1. Reopen `obj_zool_air` and add a **Create** event. Include a **Set Variable** action (**control** tab) with **Variable** set to `state` and **Value** set to `ZSTATE_JUMP`.

 2. Include a **Set Gravity** action (**move** tab) with **Direction** set to 270 and **Gravity** set to 1.5. This sets an initial downwards force of 1.5 pixels per step on Zool when he is jumping.

 3. Include a **Set Friction** action with **Friction** set to 0. We don't want any friction in the air.

 4. Add a **Step, End Step** event and include a **Test Variable** action (**control** tab) with **Variable** set to vspeed, **Value** set to 0 and **Operation** set to **larger than**.

 5. Immediately follow this with a **Start Block** action to group together the following actions.

 6. Include a **Set Variable** action with **Variable** set to `state` and **Value** set to `ZSTATE_FALL`.

 7. Include a **Set Gravity** action (**move** tab) with **Direction** set to 270 and **Gravity** set to 2. This sets a downward force of 2 pixels per step to Zool when he is falling.

 8. Immediately follow this with an **End Block** action to end the grouped events.

9. Add a **Collision** event with `obj_solid`. The first four actions in this event will be very similar to the `obj_solid` collision event for `obj_zool_land`. You'll need to set Zool back to his previous position, move him to the contact position in his current direction (against **all objects**), and then stop his movement. Try doing this for yourself and look back at `obj_zool_land` (or Figure 3–8) to make sure you've got it right. Your last action will need to be a **Move Fixed** action rather than a **Speed Horizontal**, to stop movement in both directions.

 10. After these four actions, include a **Check Object** action (**control** tab) to check for the **Object**, `obj_platform` at a **Relative** position of **X**=0, **Y**=1 (underneath Zool).

 11. Immediately follow this with a **Change Instance** action (**main1** tab) that changes into `obj_zool_land` and performs (**Destroy** and **Create**) events as it does so. This will now revert Zool back to the land state after a collision if he is supported by a platform.

 12. Add a **Key Release, Space** event and include a **Set Gravity** action (**move** tab) with **Direction** set to 270 and **Gravity** set to 2.

This last **Key Release** event may seem a bit odd without the corresponding **Key Press** event, but the player will already have pressed the spacebar in another state object if they are jumping. This **Key Release** event sets the gravity back to normal when the player releases the spacebar to create the variable height jumping effect we're after. There are now a few changes we need to make to `obj_zool` to accommodate the new object.

Modifying the Parent Zool Object

1. Reopen `obj_zool` and select the **Draw** event again. Within the grouped actions for FACE_RIGHT, include a new **Test Variable** action (**control** tab) to check if the **Variable** state is **equal to** the **Value** ZSTATE_JUMP.

2. Immediately follow this with a **Draw Sprite** action (**draw** tab) to draw `spr_zool_jump_right` at a **Relative** position of **X**=0, **Y**=0.

3. Follow this with another **Test Variable** action (**control** tab) to check if the **Variable** state is **equal to** the **Value** ZSTATE_FALL.

4. Immediately follow this with a **Draw Sprite** action (**draw** tab) to draw `spr_zool_fall_right` at a **Relative** position of **X**=0, **Y**=0.

5. Now use `spr_zool_jump_left` and `spr_zool_fall_left` to create left-facing equivalents of these four new actions within the grouped actions for FACE_LEFT. The actions of the **Draw** event should now look like Figure 3–11.

6. Select the **Create** event of `obj_zool` and edit the **Change Instance** action to **Change Into** `obj_zool_air` rather than `obj_zool_land`.

If you try running the game now, then Zool should fall to the ground and run across it as you would expect, but we really need to jump up to see the real effect of our new behaviors. This will require some changes to the land state object.

VAR If facing is equal to FACE_RIGHT

△ Start of a block

VAR If state is equal to ZSTATE_STAND

e Draw sprite spr_zool_stand_right

VAR If state is equal to ZSTATE_WALK

e Draw sprite spr_zool_walk_right

VAR If state is equal to ZSTATE_JUMP

e Draw sprite spr_zool_jump_right

VAR If state is equal to ZSTATE_FALL

e Draw sprite spr_zool_fall_right

▽ End of a block

VAR If facing is equal to FACE_LEFT

△ Start of a block

VAR If state is equal to ZSTATE_STAND

e Draw sprite spr_zool_stand_left

VAR If state is equal to ZSTATE_WALK

e Draw sprite spr_zool_walk_left

VAR If state is equal to ZSTATE_JUMP

e Draw sprite spr_zool_jump_left

VAR If state is equal to ZSTATE_FALL

e Draw sprite spr_zool_fall_left

▽ End of a block

Figure 3–11. The new state of the Draw event for the parent Zool object

Modifying the Zool Land State Object

1. Reopen `obj_zool_land` and add a new **Key Press, Space** event. Include a **Speed Vertical** action (**move** tab) with **Vert. Speed** set to `-22`.

2. Include a **Change Instance** action (**main1** tab) to **Change into** `obj_zool_air` and **Perform events** (**Destroy** and **Create**) as it does so.

3. Add a new **Step, End Step** event. Remember this event happens after all the movement and collision of the object has been resolved but before the object is drawn, so it is a good place to change the state of an object if its new position requires it.

4. Include a **Check Object** action (**control** tab) to check for the **Object,** `obj_platform` **NOT** being at a **Relative** position of **X=**0, **Y=**1 (underneath Zool).

5. Immediately follow this with a **Change Instance** action (**main1** tab) that changes into `obj_zool_air` and performs (**Destroy** and **Create**) events as it does so. This will now revert Zool back to the air state if he is no longer supported by a platform.

Run the game now and you should have your first reasonably mobile version of Zool. You can only interact with the solid, sweet-encrusted parts of the landscape (and still not ramps), but if you're careful, you can make the jump up to the nearest platform and fall back down again. You will find a version of the game at this point in the file `zool2.gmk` in the `Chapter03/Games` directory on the CD.

Congratulations—Phase 1 Complete!

You're now 25% of the way toward creating the finished Zool game! Already you've covered a lot of key concepts and done important groundwork for the remaining chapters. You've surveyed the alien landscape and boldly taken on the grand plan for the Zool state objects without losing your nerve. You've assimilated a fearsome set of parent hierarchies and helped our inter-dimensional ninja to take his first steps (and jumps) around the hostile sweet planet—closely tracked by your camera view.

Clearly there is still a long way to go, so we'd understand if you'd prefer to save your progress and resume your journey at some later date. Although, before you go, you may as well turn over to see what happens on the next page of the Zool comic first, and then you might as well quickly skim through the next chapter to see what's coming up next. Actually, there's an intriguing-looking picture of an athlete and another of a knight fighting a giant skeletal hand, but... they can wait. There are also several diagrams of Zool head-butting a cake, which is quite strange. Nonetheless, there's bound to be a perfectly good reason why and there's no need to read on at all. No, it can all wait for another time....

■ ■ ■

CHAPTER 4

Empowerment: Sliding Ninjas

Games like Zool and Sonic are at their most enjoyable when they empower the player with a feeling of control over a fluid gameplay experience. In other words, the player is able to execute very cool moves without too much effort. The player feels in control, but somehow their normal abilities seem to be enhanced beyond what they should realistically be able to achieve. Sonic routinely flies about the landscape at incredible speeds, grabbing rings mid-flight and narrowly avoiding perilous-looking hazards—and that makes the player feel powerful. Naturally, some of this is just good level design, but the levels wouldn't work if Sonic didn't have a beautifully fluid movement mechanic in the first place.

In contrast, our own movement mechanic is currently very unresponsive and actually makes Zool awkward and frustrating to control. In this chapter, we add Zool's full range of movement abilities and develop a control system that actively assists the player to move fluidly around the landscape in order to boost their feeling of empowerment.

Balance of Power

In practice, there is a balance to be struck between making the player feel *powerful* on the one hand, while remaining in *control* on the other. We can illustrate this by looking at extreme examples. Foddy Athletics (see Figure 4–1) is a popular online Flash demo that gives the player separate control over a sprinter's calves and thighs in order to try and make him run along a track. Basically, you are asked to learn how to walk all over again in a new medium! There is an enormous amount of *control* in this concept, but it doesn't make you feel *powerful*. Running is not typically considered to be something that is hard to do, but this game makes it feel that way. It is more of a "running simulation" than a game.

Dragon's Lair was released in 1983 with visuals to rival any modern video game (see Figure 4–2). The stunning graphics were possible because the game was basically an interactive movie running on a forerunner to the DVD. The hero, Dirk, could do seemingly anything that a cartoon knight might do in a Disney animation, and so the feeling of *power* was potentially huge—especially compared to the pixel-based games of the day. As a result it became an enormously popular and financially successful format. However, the *control* the player had over Dirk's powerful actions were generally limited to a single button press in each scene, which often stopped the player from feeling empowered by the experience.

These games illustrate that players only feel *empowered* by a game when there is both *power* and *control*. However, sometimes one comes at the expense of the other; at their best, modern Prince of Persia titles are enormously empowering, allowing the player to achieve incredible acrobatic moves with no effort at all. The game provides a lot of help to make sure your moves work out for you, and the results are often breathtaking. Yet, sometimes this can also make the player feel as if they are not actually in control at all, again dispelling the feeling of empowerment and reducing the challenge offered by the game.

Figure 4–1. *Foddy Athletics is an extremely difficult game to master (reproduced with kind permission of Dr. Bennett Foddy: www.foddy.net)*

Figure 4–2. *Dragon's Lair was originally an arcade game, but these days you can buy the game for your iPhone or DSi ("Dragon's Lair" is a registered trademark of Dragon's Lair LLC ©1983-2010)*

Empowering Up

So we need to provide Zool with an empowering movement mechanic that makes it easy to fluidly navigate the landscape of the level. We'll aim to make movement as unchallenging as possible, as the game's real challenge will come from the mobile enemies and platforms that we will add in the next chapter. That way, the player should feel appropriately empowered, but still get an enjoyable challenge from playing the game.

The main problem with Zool's movement at the moment is that every time he bumps into anything mid-jump, he comes to a dead stop and falls to the ground (see Figure 4–3, left).

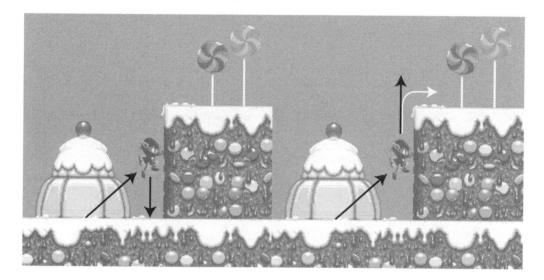

Figure 4–3. *Zool's jumping mechanic as it is (left) and as we would like it to be (right)*

Even landing back on the ground after a running jump awkwardly breaks Zool's stride by bringing him to a stop for an instant. This is pretty unusual for platform game characters and it's easy to see why. The more common approach is to get the character to slide against solid objects, continuing to move in whatever direction of movement is not blocked. The red arrow in the right panel of Figure 4–3 shows a basic sliding effect, but we'd like to go one stage further for our game, as indicated by the yellow arrow. More about how to achieve that later, but we'll start by implementing the basic (red arrow) form of wall sliding.

Making the Zool Air State Object Slide Against Solid Objects

1. We're continuing from where we left off in the last chapter, so either reopen your saved file, or start from zool2.gmk in the Chapter04/Games directory on the CD.

2. Reopen obj_zool_air and select the **Collision** event with obj_solid. Select the **Move Fixed** action that stops Zool moving and delete it.

3. Include a **Check Object** action (**control** tab) at the end of the list to check for **Object** obj_solid at a position of **X**=x, **Y**=yprevious+vspeed.

Now take a look at Figure 4–4. At the start of this event, Zool is set back to his position before the collision (xprevious and yprevious—the blue cross), but then the **Move to Contact** action moves Zool's x and y position to the collision point with obj_solid (red cross). The variable vspeed provides Zool's vertical speed in pixels per step (orange arrow), so yprevious+vspeed gives us the vertical position of Zool if he had never collided with obj_solid (black cross). Therefore, by checking for instances of obj_solid at the position X=x, Y=yprevious+vspeed, we are seeing if there is anything in the way if Zool continues to slide vertically (but not horizontally) after the collision.

4. Immediately follow this with a **Speed Vertical** action (**move** tab) that sets **Vert. Speed** to 0. This makes sure that Zool stops moving vertically if there *is* something in the way, and leaves Zool's position at the collision point (red cross in Figure 4–4).

5. Follow that with an **Else** action (**control** tab).

6. Then include a **Set Variable** action that sets **Variable** y to yprevious+vspeed. This will move Zool's position to the sliding point (black cross in Figure 4–4) if there isn't anything in the way and maintain Zool's vertical speed after the collision.

7. Now we repeat the process for horizontal movement. Include a **Check Object** action to check for **Object** obj_solid at a position of X=xprevious+hspeed, Y=y. In a similar way, we are checking if there is anything in the way if Zool continues to slide horizontally (but not vertically) after the collision.

8. Immediately follow this with a **Speed Horizontal** action (**move** tab) that sets the **Horiz. Speed** to 0.

9. Follow that with an **Else** action (**control** tab).

10. And then follow that with a **Set Variable** action that sets **Variable** x to xprevious+hspeed. This will now maintain Zool's horizontal movement if there isn't anything in the way after the collision.

11. All of the new actions we've added actually need to take place before the check to see if Zool is standing on solid ground, so we'll need to move those two actions to the end of the list again. Click and drag the first **Check Object** action to the end of the actions list. Now do the same for the (only) **Change Instance** action. You should now have 13 actions in the **Collision** event with obj_solid and it should look like Figure 4–5.

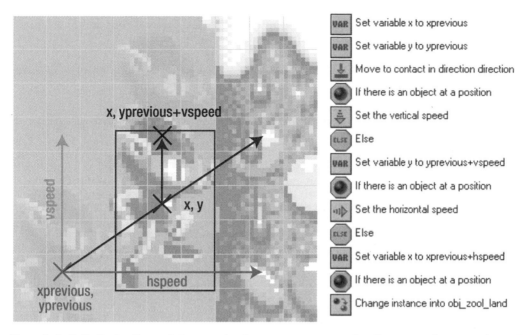

Figure 4–4. *(left). Zool will now slide upward as he jumps into a vertical wall, retaining his x coordinate from the collision position (red) but continuing his vertical movement by setting his y position to his y position in the previous step (blue) plus his vertical speed (orange)*

Figure 4–5. *(right). The new sequence of actions for the collision event of the Zool air state object*

You Cannae Break the Laws of Physics

If you play the game now, then it is certainly an improvement. Zool no longer stutters when he lands from a running jump and he slides upward against vertical walls when you jump into them. However, it would be even nicer if he could drift across onto the top of the platform surface when he slides above the top (see Figure 4–3, right). In many platform games, this is achieved by adding a drifting mechanic to allow the character to have a small amount of control over horizontal movement even when they are in mid-air. We will actually add just such a drifting mechanic later, but in fact we can achieve the desired outcome without needing the player to actively hold a key to drift Zool over the edge. We can do this simply by maintaining Zool's horizontal speed when he collides horizontally with objects in mid-air. Clearly, this goes against the laws of physics, but it produces a nice result and, after all, this is the Nth dimension.

Tweaking the Air State Object's Sliding Collision Mechanic

1. Reopen the `obj_zool_air` object and select the **Collision** event with `obj_solid`. Edit the **Speed Horizontal** action that stops Zool moving horizontally when there is a horizontal obstruction. Change the **Hor. Speed** setting from 0 to `hspeed` (that is, not changing the horizontal speed at all—don't remove it completely as this is only temporary).

Try running the game again and see the result when you jump against the same wall as shown in Figure 4–3. It works, but it looks quite unnatural, so we're going to impose some limits on how much of the horizontal speed can be retained after a collision.

2. Use the **Define Constants** option on the **Resources** menu (or a new variable in the **Create** event of `obj_zool` if you are using Game Maker Lite) to define a new constant called `MAX_DRIFT_SPEED`, which is set to `8`.

3. Now go back to the **Speed Horizontal** action in the **Collision** event of `obj_zool_air` and change the **Hor. Speed** setting from `hspeed` to `median(-MAX_DRIFT_SPEED, hspeed, MAX_DRIFT_SPEED)`. Just like when we used this function in the **Step** event of `obj_zool`, this will limit the size of `hspeed` to within plus or minus `MAX_DRIFT_SPEED` (+8 to -8).

Now try playing the game again. If you jump at the same wall again, it should be a little more believable now. Also try standing right next to the wall at the bottom and making a horizontal jump to the right. You'll find you land neatly on the top edge of the platform, which is very helpful! If you play around with it for long enough, you will also find a small bug. If you fall against one of the walls, you will slide down to the bottom and get stuck! This is because Zool's horizontal speed keeps him colliding with the wall so he never reaches the bottom. This is a side effect of our little tweak, which never resets the horizontal speed. This bug will actually solve itself as we add more of Zool's movement mechanics, but if you're applying this technique to your own games, then it might be easier to stick with the "basic" form of sliding (setting **Hor. Speed** to `0`) and relying on the drifting mechanic described in the next section to get the player over the edge of the platform.

A Floating Garage Worker

So we're going to add the drifting mechanic next, which gives the player a limited amount of control over Zool's horizontal movement in the air. We will only allow Zool to slowly change his speed in the air (by 1 pixel per step), and we won't allow drifting to increase his air speed beyond `MAX_DRIFT_SPEED`.

Adding a Drifting Mechanic to the Zool Air State Object

1. Add a new **Keyboard, Left** event to the `obj_zool_air` object and include a **Set Variable** action (**control** tab) that sets the **Variable** `facing` to the **Value** `FACE_LEFT`.

2. Include a **Test Variable** action that checks if the **Variable** `hspeed` is **larger than** `-MAX_DRIFT_SPEED`. So, in other words, it checks that Zool is not already moving left at a speed that is greater than the maximum drifting speed (negative means left).

3. Follow this with a **Speed Horizontal** action (**move** tab) with **Hor. Speed** set **Relative** to `-1` to increase his speed to the left by 1 pixel per step.

4. Add a new **Keyboard, Right** event to the `obj_zool_air` object and include a **Set Variable** action (**control** tab) that sets the **Variable** `facing` to the **Value** `FACE_RIGHT`.

5. Include a **Test Variable** action that checks if the **Variable** `hspeed` is **smaller than** `MAX_DRIFT_SPEED`. Similarly, this checks that Zool is not already moving right at a speed that is greater than the maximum drifting speed.

6. Follow this with a **Speed Horizontal** action (**move** tab) with **Hor. Speed** set **Relative** to `1` to increase his speed to the right by 1 pixel per step.

Play the game again and see what you think. It works, but it doesn't provide that much control in the air—particularly when changing direction. Being able to change direction mid-flight in order avoid an inevitable collision is actually one of the most important reasons to have drifting. We could increase all the speeds, but this provides a bit too much control (try it if you like). So, instead we will reset the horizontal speed to zero whenever Zool changes direction in the air. This will give him the ability to do an instant about-turn to avoid a moving enemy, but not fly around the level like Superman.

Tweaking the Drifting Mechanic for the Zool Air State Object

1. Select the **Keyboard, Left** event for the obj_zool_air object and include a **Test Variable** action (**control** tab) at the start of the actions that checks if the **Variable** hspeed is **larger than** the **Value** 0.

2. Follow this with a **Speed Horizontal** action (**move** tab) with **Hor. Speed** set to 0. You should now have five actions in the **Keyboard, Left** event that look like Figure 4–6.

3. Select the **Keyboard, Right** event and include a **Test Variable** action (**control** tab) at the start of the actions that checks if the **Variable** hspeed is **smaller than** the **Value** 0.

4. Follow this with a **Speed Horizontal** action (**move** tab) with **Hor. Speed** set to 0.

Play the game one more time and hopefully you'll agree that we now have reasonably polished walking and jumping mechanics. We've also already gone half way to solving our bug, as the drifting controls now allow you to get out of the situation where Zool was stuck. You will find this version of the game in the file Zool3.gmk in the Chapter04/Games directory on the CD.

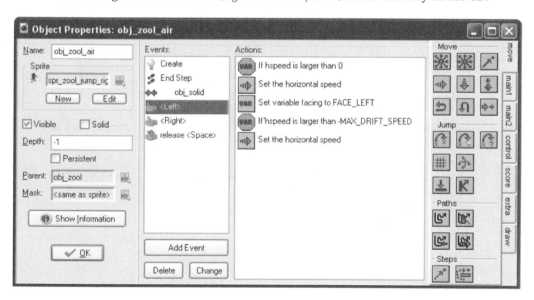

Figure 4–6. *The sequence of events for the Keyboard, Left event of the Zool air state object*

Underground, Overground

Now that we have our standard platforms working, we can quite easily create behaviors for the ledge platforms too. Ledges support Zool in the same way as normal, but he can jump up through from underneath them and land on top. In the Sweet World, these ledge platforms are represented by colorful square-shaped jellies, and there are a few of these around our test level. However, they don't yet have the collision objects in place to collide with, so you'll need to do this before we can start. Reopen room_test from the resources list and add instances of obj_ledge along the top surface of each block of jelly. The ledge collision objects are made up of a thin, horizontal line, so be careful not to leave any stray ledge objects around. It's easier to see what you are doing if you temporarily turn off the room grid by clicking on the grid icon on the toolbar. There are two separate areas of jelly blocks that need ledges: one in the middle of the level and the other on the far right-hand side. Once these are in place, there are not too many changes to make to the actions.

Adding Support for Ledges to the Land and Air Zool State Objects

1. Reopen obj_zool_land. Add a new **Collision** event with obj_ledge and include an **Exit Event** action (**control** tab). We want Zool to ignore collisions with ledges when he is walking on the landscape. However, because obj_ledge is "a kind of" obj_solid, the obj_solid collision event would have been called for collisions with obj_ledge as well. Adding a collision event specifically for obj_ledge excludes ledges from the obj_solid collision event and makes nothing happen instead using the **Exit Event** action.

2. Reopen obj_zool_air. Right-click on the **Collision** event with obj_solid to **Duplicate Event** for a **Collision** with obj_ledge. Again, this creates a specific collision event for obj_ledge, which was previously handled by the collision event with obj_solid. Both events are currently identical, but we will change that next.

3. At the start of the list of actions, include a **Test Variable** action that checks if the **Variable** yprevious+18 is **larger than** other.y. This compares the position directly below Zool's feet in the previous step to see if it was below the y position of the ledge platform (see Figure 4–7). If it is, then Zool must be approaching the platform from below (rather than above) and the collision should be ignored.

4. Immediately follow this with an **Exit Event** action to ignore the collision. This should now be the second action in the list.

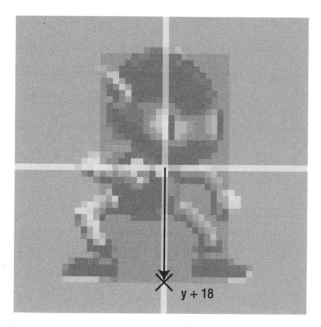

Figure 4–7. *Zool's origin is at X=24, Y=24 and his bounding box extends 18 pixels above and below this. That means that the pixel on the bottom row of his bounding box is 18 pixels below his y position*

Give it a try. It's not such a pretty-looking sequence of actions any more, but it works and that's what counts! Next, we will begin to open up the test level a bit more by adding the climbing movement mechanic.

Driven up the Walls

One of Zool's unique abilities as a platform game character was to be able to cling to vertical walls. We're going to implement this behavior using the (as yet untouched) obj_zool_wall state object. We're not going to make Zool's climbing speed increase and decrease gradually like it does on the ground, but just set his speed to a constant value when the player presses a key. When Zool is moving, he will be in the climbing state, and when he isn't, he'll be in the clinging state; there is no separate sprite for this and clinging will just use the first frame of the climbing sprite. As in previous state objects, we will use the **Begin Step** event to set his default state (clinging) and use the **End Step** to update his state when there is no longer a wall to cling to:

The Zool Wall State Object

1. Begin by reopening obj_zool_wall and setting the depth to -1001. Unlike the other state objects, we want Zool to appear in front of both tile layers when he is climbing up a wall.

2. Add a **Create** event and include a **Set Variable** action (**control** tab) with **Variable** set to state and **Value** set to ZSTATE_CLIMB.

3. Include a **Set Gravity** action (**move** tab) that sets **Direction** to 270 and **Gravity** to 0. Gravity is not helpful while Zool is climbing.

4. Include a **Set Friction** action that sets **Friction** to 0. Friction is not good either.

5. Include a **Move Fixed** action with the middle **Directions** button selected and a **Speed** of 0. This time we actually do want Zool to stop as soon as he grabs a wall.

6. Add a **Step, Begin Step** event and include a **Set Variable** action (**control** tab) with **Variable** set to state and **Value** set to ZSTATE_CLING. The default state will be clinging, but this will get overridden in the keyboard events if the player is moving up or down.

7. Include a **Speed Vertical** action (**move** tab) with **Vert. Speed** set to 0. In doing so, we will default the speed to zero as well.

8. Add a **Keyboard, Up** event and include a **Check Object** action (**control** tab) that checks for the obj_wall **Object** at the **Relative** position X=facing, Y=-4. This is where the facing variable comes in particularly useful, as facing will be -1 if Zool is facing left and +1 if Zool is facing right. So this makes it easy to detect if Zool is facing a wall. We are checking 4 pixels above because the climbing speed will be 4 pixels per step, so we need to check that there will still be a wall facing Zool at the position we want to move him to.

9. Include a **Start Block** action.

10. Include a **Speed Vertical** action (**move** tab) with **Vert. Speed** set to -4.

11. Include a **Set Variable** action (**control** tab) with **Variable** set to state and **Value** set to ZSTATE_CLIMB.

12. Include an **End Block** action. The **Keyboard, Up** event should now have the five actions shown in Figure 4–8.

13. Repeat steps 8-12 in order to create a **Keyboard, Down** event that checks that there will be a wall facing Zool 4 pixels below him, before setting his **Vertical Speed** to 4 and his state to ZSTATE_CLIMB.

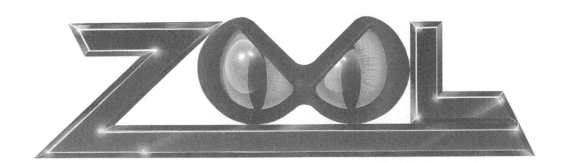

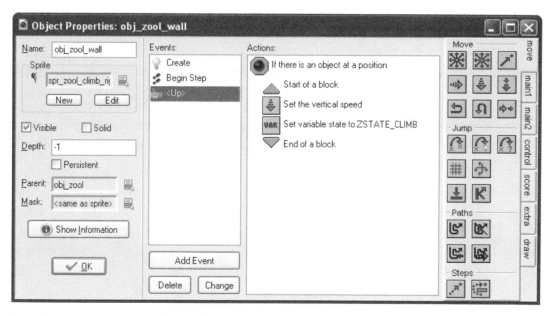

Figure 4–8. *The actions for the Keyboard, Down event of the Zool wall state object*

 14. Next, add a **Key Press, Space** event to obj_zool_wall to allow Zool to release himself from walls by jumping. Include a **Speed Horizontal** action (**move** tab) with **Horiz. Speed** set to -facing*2. This applies a horizontal speed of 2 pixels per step in the opposite direction to which Zool is facing.

15. Include a **Speed Vertical** action with **Vert. Speed** set to -15. This will make Zool jump upward as he leaps back from the wall.

16. Include a **Change Instance** action (**main1** tab) that will change into obj_zool_air and **Perform Events** (**Destroy** and **Create**) as it does so.

17. Now add a **Collision** event with obj_solid and include a **Set Variable** action (**control** tab) that sets the **Variable** x to xprevious. This collision event will be similar to ones we have used before, but not as complicated as the one for obj_zool_land.

18. Include a second **Set Variable** action that sets the **Variable** y to yprevious.

19. Include a **Move to Contact** action (**move** tab) with **Direction** set to direction, **Maximum** set to -1, and **Against** set to **all objects**.

20. Include a **Move Fixed** action with the middle **Directions** button selected and **Speed** set to 0. This creates the simpler kind of collision event, which is fine for climbing.

21. Include another **Set Variable** action (**control** tab) with **Variable** set to state and **Value** set to ZSTATE_CLING. This makes sure the climbing animation stops after a collision. You should now have five actions for the **Collision** event, as shown in Figure 4–9.

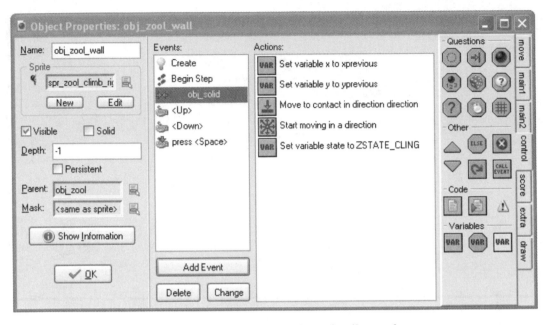

Figure 4–9. The actions for the obj_solid Collision event of the Zool wall state object

22. Finally, add a **Step, End Step** event and include a **Check Object** action that checks if there is **NOT** an obj_wall **Object** at the **Relative** position **X**=facing, **Y**=0.

23. Immediately follow this with a **Change Instance** action (**main1** tab) that will change into obj_zool_air and **Perform Events** (**Destroy** and **Create**) as it does so. This makes sure that Zool falls off the wall if it should disappear for any reason later on.

There are now a few changes we need to make to the other Zool objects to incorporate obj_zool_wall. First, we'll add appropriate transitions to the wall state from both the air and land state objects. Then we need to include the sprite drawing for ZSTATE_CLING and ZSTATE_CLIMB in the parent Zool object.

Adding State Transitions and Sprite Drawing to the Wall State Object

1. Reopen obj_zool_land and select the **End Step** event. Include a new **Check Object** action (**control** tab) that checks for the **Object** obj_wall at the **Relative** position **X**=facing, **Y**=0.

2. Immediately follow this with a **Change Instance** action (**main1** tab) that will change into obj_zool_wall and **Perform Events** (**Destroy** and **Create**) as it does so. This will now make Zool automatically grab onto walls if there is a wall directly in front of him at the end of a step.

3. Reopen obj_zool_air and select the **End Step** event. Directly below the **Set Gravity** action (as part of the events grouped in the block), include a new **Check Object** action (**control** tab). This should check for the **Object** obj_wall at the **Relative** position **X**=facing, **Y**=0.

4. Immediately follow this with a **Change Instance** action (**main1** tab) that will change into obj_zool_wall and **Perform Events** (**Destroy** and **Create**) as it does so. This will now make Zool automatically grab onto walls if there is a wall directly in front of him at the end of a step—but only he is traveling downward. This is actually a good feature, as it allows him to quickly scale walls in a number of successive jumps. You should now have seven actions in the **End Step** event for obj_zool_air, as shown in Figure 4–10.

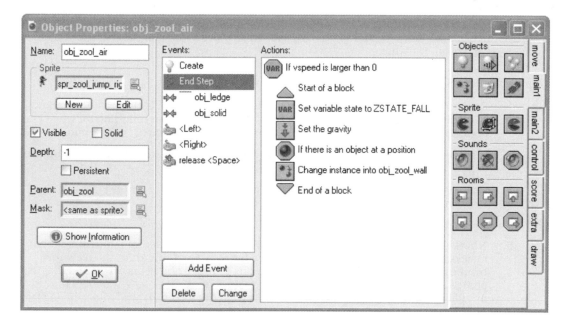

Figure 4–10. *The actions for the End Step event of the Zool air state object*

5. Now reopen obj_zool and select the **Draw** event. Within the grouped actions for FACE_RIGHT, include a new **Test Variable** action (**control** tab) to check if the **Variable** state is **equal to** the **Value** ZSTATE_CLIMB.

6. Immediately follow this with a **Draw Sprite** action (**draw** tab) to draw spr_zool_climb_right at a **Relative** position of X=0, Y=0.

7. Include another **Test Variable** action to check if the **Variable** state is **equal to** the **Value** ZSTATE_CLING.

8. Immediately follow this with a **Draw Sprite** action to draw spr_zool_climb_right at a **Relative** position of X=0, Y=0 and a **Subimage** of 0. This overrides the animating frame of the sprite and stops it at the first frame when Zool is in the clinging state.

9. Now use spr_zool_climb_left to create left-facing equivalents of these four new actions within the grouped actions for FACE_LEFT.

Finally, you can now run the game and you should have a crude form of wall-climbing working. Like our first walking mechanic, it's a little rough around the edges, but don't worry, as we're going to sort that out next.

Wall Polish

We're going to need to make some serious improvements to the climbing mechanic before it's as slick as Zool's movement on land and in the air. For a start, it's really easy to grab onto a wall, but a bit of a pain getting detached again. He appears to cling on to thin air at the top or bottom of walls and you're forced to jump off awkwardly in order to get free. It's also annoying when he accidently slides into a wall while walking in one direction, but then is forced to jump off again before he can walk back in the other. These are all fairly minor issues to fix, but will drastically improve the responsiveness of Zool's controls. They will involve a few changes to the keyboard events, so we'll begin with those.

Improving Detachment for the Zool Wall State Object

1. Reopen obj_zool_wall and select the **Keyboard, Down** event. Include an **Else** action (**control** tab) at the end of the actions list. This adds a separate condition for when Zool is climbing down and there is no longer an obj_wall below and in front of him.

2. Include a **Start Block** action. It's not strictly necessary, as we will only be including one action, but it looks neatest as we used a block further above.

3. Include a **Change Instance** action (**main1** tab) that will change into obj_zool_air and **Perform Events** (**Destroy** and **Create**) as it does so.

4. Include an **End Block** action (**control** tab).

5. Now select the **Keyboard, Up** event. Edit the **Check Object** action (**control** tab) that checks for the **Object** obj_wall and change the **Y** setting from -4 to -22. We know from earlier that Zool's bounding box extends 18 pixels above his origin and that he climbs at 4 pixels per step. Therefore, this test will make sure that Zool only moves up if his bounding box would not extend beyond the top of the wall after moving (see Figure 4–11).

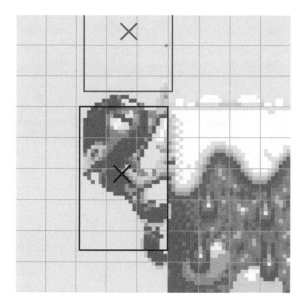

Figure 4–11. *We check to make sure that there would still be a wall object above and to the right of Zool after climbing up another 4 pixels*

6. Include an **Else** action at the end of the actions list. This adds a separate condition for when Zool is climbing up but there is no longer an obj_wall above and in front.

7. Include a **Start Block** action to group the following actions.

8. Include a **Speed Vertical** action (**move** tab) with **Vert. Speed** set to -16. This will make Zool automatically jump up when he reaches the top of the wall.

9. Include a **Speed Horizontal** action with **Hor. Speed** set to facing. This will give Zool a very small push toward the wall he is facing as he jumps up. You might think this is pointless, as he will immediately collide with the wall and stop moving horizontally again. But remember that we maintain the horizontal speed in collisions, provided it is less than MAX_DRIFT_SPEED, so he will keep this speed until he is clear of the top of the wall and it will bring him neatly onto the top edge of the platform.

10. Include a **Change Instance** action (**main1** tab) that will change into obj_zool_air and **Perform Events** (**Destroy** and **Create**) as it does so.

11. Include an **End Block** action (**control** tab). There should now be a sequence of 11 actions in the **Keyboard, Up** event for obj_zool_wall, as shown in Figure 4–12.

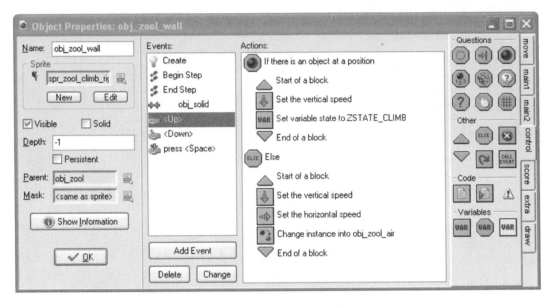

Figure 4–12. The actions for the Keyboard, Up event of the Zool wall state object

12. Now select the **End Step** event and include a **Check Object** action that checks if there is **NOT** an obj_wall at the **Relative** position X=facing, Y=-20. If there isn't a wall at this position, then Zool's upper body is above the top of the wall. Although the **Keyboard, Up** event in the previous step will stop Zool from moving up into this position, he could still jump into a wall and cling on in this unrealistic position without this check.

13. Include a **Jump to Position** (**Move** tab) that moves Zool to a **Relative** position of X=0, Y=5. This will make him slide back down again until his hands appear to grab onto the top of the wall. Note that we are only checking 20 pixels above Zool to trigger the slide down, which is not quite as far as the 22 pixels that triggers the automatic jump in the **Keyboard, Up** event. This is because we don't want the slide down to happen before the jump up when Zool is climbing up a wall.

14. Next, we're going to allow Zool to walk away from walls without needing to jump. Add a **Keyboard, Left** event and include a **Test Variable** action (**control** tab) that tests if the **Variable** facing is **equal to** FACE_RIGHT.

15. Immediately follow this with a **Check Object** action that checks to see if there is an obj_platform at a **Relative** position of X=0, Y=1. He should only be able to walk off a wall when there is a platform directly below his feet.

16. Include a **Start Block** action.

17. Include a **Set Variable** action that sets the **Variable** facing to the **Value** FACE_LEFT.

18. Include a **Change Instance** action (**main1** tab) that will change into obj_zool_land and **Perform Events** (**Destroy** and **Create**) as it does so.

19. Include an **End Block** action (**control** tab). The **Keyboard, Left** event should now contain six actions, as shown in Figure 4–13.

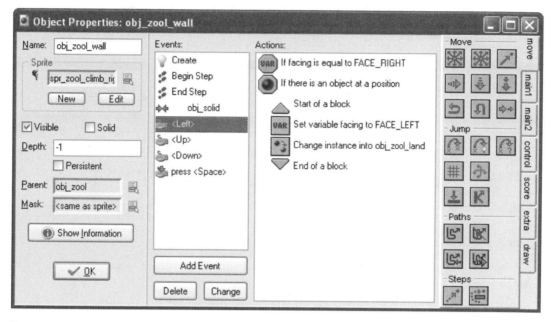

Figure 4–13. *The actions for the Keyboard, Left event of the Zool wall state object*

20. Repeat steps 14–19 to create a similar **Keyboard, Right** event that checks that `facing` is equal to `FACE_LEFT` and sets it to `FACE_RIGHT`.

Try out this latest version and see what a difference it makes. Zool should now spring neatly off the top and bottom of walls, as well as being able to walk into them and walk away again without needing to jump. This works pretty well now and you will find this version of the game in the file `Zool4.gmk` in the `Chapter04/Games` directory on the CD.

Ramping Up

All is well and good for horizontal and vertical surfaces in the game, so it's about time we tackled those slopes and ramps. Ramps are actually not too difficult to add, so we'll do those first. There are currently no ramp collision objects placed on the level (that's why you can walk straight through the ramp tiles), so you're going to need to add these first.

Placing Ramp Collision Objects in the Room

1. Reopen `room_test`, make sure that the **objects** tab is selected, and scroll to the position of the first ramp that slopes gently up and down again. Now turn off **Show Tiles** (next to the magnifying glass) and all the tiles should disappear to reveal that there is just a flat row of `obj_platform` collision objects beneath where the ramp tiles are.

2. Turn **Show Tiles** back on and carefully right-click on the two squares marked with blue crosses in the top left panel of Figure 4–14. This will delete the collision objects that are currently hidden behind the tiles and mark the boundaries of the ramp for you, as shown in the middle left panel.

3. Turn **Show Tiles** back off and place one instance of each of the 16 different Ramps group objects (obj_ramp_u1 to obj_ramp_d8), as shown in the bottom left panel of Figure 4–14. Also, delete the unneeded platform instances underneath the ramp as shown.

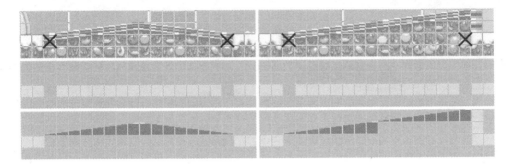

Figure 4–14. *Adding ramp collision objects to the room*

4. Turn **Show Tiles** back on and scroll to the second ramp over on the far right of the room.

5. Carefully right-click on the two squares marked with blue crosses in the top right panel of Figure 4–14 to delete the collision objects. Again, this will mark the boundaries of the ramp for you when you turn the tiles off.

6. Turn **Show Tiles** back off again and place instances of the first eight different Ramps group objects (obj_ramp_u1 to obj_ramp_u8), as shown in the bottom right panel of Figure 4–14. Also, delete the unneeded platform instances and add two extra to fill the gap on the right-hand side of the ramp as shown.

Believe it or not, probably the hardest part of ramps is finished! If you play the game now, you will see that you can already collide with ramps, as the hierarchy of parents means that all these different ramp objects are eventually a kind of obj_solid. However, the general-purpose obj_solid collision events are not always suitable for ramps. The one in obj_zool_land simply brings Zool to a halt on rising ramps, preventing him from walking up them. The sliding mechanism in the collision event of obj_zool_air can cause Zool to slide uncontrollably down falling ramps as well. Fortunately, we can simply add collision events between these state objects and obj_ramp in order to handle this specific case differently from other solid objects.

Adding Specific Collision Events for Ramp Objects

1. Reopen obj_zool_land and create a **Collision** event with obj_ramp. Include a **Set Variable** action (**control** tab) that sets the **Variable** y **Relative** to -speed. This moves Zool up by a distance equal to the speed he is traveling. The faster Zool is moving, the further he may have moved inside the ramp during the collision, so the further he needs to move up in order to be above the surface again (see Figure 4–15). This method should work for angles up to and including 45 degrees.

Figure 4-15. *The faster Zool is traveling, the further up or down he needs to be moved in order to place him back on the ramp's surface*

 2. Include a **Move to Contact** action (**move** tab) with **Direction** set to 270, **Maximum** set to -1, and **Against** set to **all objects**. This will bring Zool back down in contact with the ramp.

3. Select the **End Step** event and delete the **Change Instance** action that changes into the obj_zool_air when there is no platform one pixel beneath Zool's feet. Every time Zool walks forward on a descending ramp, he will find himself with no platform beneath his feet, so we need to be more careful about this test.

 4. Include a **Start Block** action in its place (**control** tab) to group together the following actions that will now depend on there being no platform directly beneath Zool's feet.

 5. Follow this with a **Check Object** action that checks for the **Object** obj_platform, at a **Relative** position of X=0, Y=speed. This checks to see if there is actually a platform (which includes ramps) a little bit further below Zool's feet. The distance depends on his speed, as the faster he is moving, the further above the ramp he could be (see Figure 4-15).

 6. Follow this with a **Move to Contact** action (**move** tab) with **Direction** set to 270, **Maximum** set to -1, and **Against** set to **all objects**. This will bring Zool back down on top of the ramp.

 7. Follow this with an **Else** action (**control** tab).

 8. Follow this with a **Change Instance** action (**main1** tab) that will change into obj_zool_air and **Perform Events** (**Destroy** and **Create**) as it does so. This will start Zool falling if he isn't traveling down a ramp.

 9. Follow this with an **End Block** action (**control** tab). The End Step event should now have nine actions, as shown in Figure 4-16.

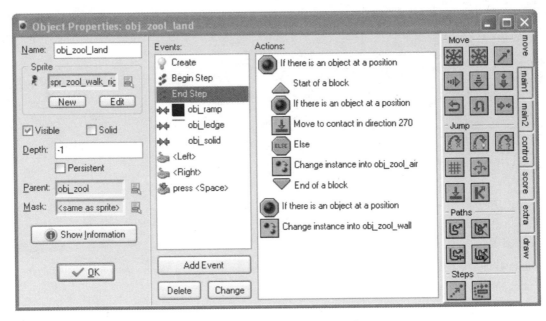

Figure 4–16. *The actions for the End Step event of the land Zool state object*

10. **Reopen** obj_zool_air and add a **Collision** event with obj_ramp. Again, this creates a specific collision event for obj_ramp to override the general obj_solid collision event that was making Zool slip down ramps. Include a **Set Variable** action that sets the **Variable** y **Relative** to -speed.

11. Include a **Move to Contact** action (**move** tab) with **Direction** set to 270, **Maximum** set to -1, and **Against** set to **all objects**. This places Zool on the ramp as before.

12. Include a **Change Instance** action (**main1** tab) that will change into obj_zool_land and **Perform Events** (**Destroy** and **Create**) as it does so. We have just placed Zool on top of a ramp, so obviously he will need to be in the land state.

Play the game now and ramps should be working in the way you would expect them to, so let's continue to think about slopes....

Sliding Down

The original Zool game included slippery slopes as a feature in many levels. These would make the player automatically (and uncontrollably) slide down towards the bottom. The only way of getting up these slopes was to repeatedly jump like you were trying to climb a descending escalator. The icing-covered slopes toward the top right of the test room are supposed to behave in this way and that's what we will implement next. This is going to require behaviors for our final state object, obj_zool_ice, but before we start implementing these, let's break down the problem a bit more.

If you consider all of the slope collision objects in the Platforms and Slopes groups, you will see that there are only five different gradients of slopes:

- Ascending at 22.5 degrees (spr_slope_u1 and spr_slope_u2)

- Ascending at 45 degrees (spr_slope_u3)

- Horizontal (spr_slope)

- Descending at 45 degrees (spr_slope_d1)

- Descending at 22.5 degrees (spr_slope_d2 and spr_slope_d3)

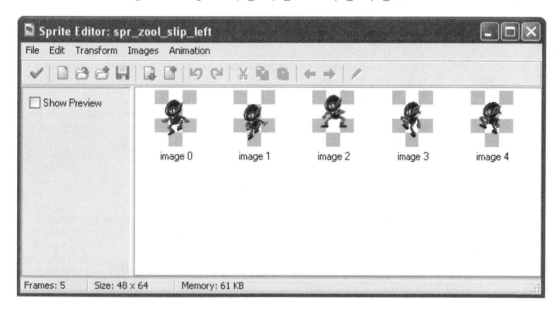

Figure 4–17. *The five different sprite sub-images for spr_zool_slip_left*

Note that there are two different objects for each of the 22.5-degree slopes, as it needs two objects to create a slope that is as high as one grid square. Now go to the Zool group in the sprite resources, open spr_zool_slip_right, and click on **Edit Sprite** to look at the sub-images. You'll see that there are also five sub-images corresponding to these same angles in the same order. Likewise for spr_zool_slip_left, but all facing to the left (see Figure 4–17). Part of the behavior that we need to implement is therefore to display the correct sprite sub-image according to the angle of slope Zool is standing on. We're also going to make him slide by simply changing his gravity direction to match that of the slope he's standing on. Therefore, we want Zool's gravity direction to depend on the angle of this slope as well.

Let's start to get some of this working by adding basic support for the new state object to the other Zool objects, and then begin work on the ice state object itself.

Editing the Zool State Objects to Support the Ice State Object

 1. Reopen obj_zool and select the **Draw** event. Within the grouped actions for FACE_RIGHT, include a new **Test Variable** action (**control** tab) to check if the **Variable** state is **equal to** the **Value** ZSTATE_SLIP.

 2. Immediately follow this with a **Draw Sprite** action (**draw** tab) to draw spr_zool_slip_right at a **Relative** position of X=0, Y=0.

3. Now use `spr_zool_slip_left` to create left-facing equivalents of these two new actions within the block for `FACE_LEFT`. This is now a very long event containing 34 actions, but all following the same simple structure that you should be familiar with by now.

4. Reopen `obj_zool_land` and select the **End Step** event. Include a new **Check Object** action (**control** tab) to check for the **Object** `obj_slope`, at a **Relative** position of X=0, Y=1.

5. Immediately follow this with a **Change Instance** action (**main1** tab) that will change into `obj_zool_ice` and **Perform Events** (**Destroy** and **Create**) as it does so.

6. Reopen `obj_zool_air` and add a **Collision** event with `obj_slope`. Include a **Set Variable** action (**control** tab) to set the **Variable** y **Relative** to –speed*2. Just as for the ramp object, this moves Zool upward to compensate for the overlap with the slope object. We multiply speed by 2 this time because Zool is not just moving horizontally and so can be even further below the surface of the slope.

7. Include a **Move to Contact** action (**move** tab) that sets **Direction** to 270, **Maximum** to -1, and **Against** to **all objects**. This will bring Zool back down in contact with the slope.

8. Include a **Change Instance** action (**main1** tab) that will change into `obj_zool_ice` and **Perform Events** (**Destroy** and **Create**) as it does so.

Implementing Behaviors for the New Ice State Object

1. Open `obj_zool_ice` and add a **Create** event. Include a **Set Friction** action (**move** tab) that sets **Friction** to 0.25 (we want our slopes to be quite slippery). Unlike the other state objects we're not going to set the state variable in the **Create** event as this will immediately affect the sprite that is drawn. We need to do some tests on the steepness of the slope before we can decide which subimage of the slipping sprite to use, so it's best not to switch to the slipping sprite until then. We'll do all this in a **Begin Step** event instead.

2. Add a **Step**, **Begin Step** event and include a **Set Variable** action (**control** tab) that sets the **Variable** state to the **Value** ZSTATE_SLIP.

3. Include a **Set Gravity** action (**move** tab) with a **Direction** of -1 and a **Gravity** of 1. This is the default gravity setting for when the slope is horizontal and Zool should keep moving forward at a tiny downward angle (as that seems the most logical default).

4. Include a **Set Variable** action (**control** tab) that sets the **Variable** image_index to the **Value** 2. This makes sure the horizontal sprite sub-image is shown by default too.

5. Include a **Check Object** action that checks for the **Object** `obj_slope_u1` at the **Relative** position of X=0, Y=1.

6. Immediately follow this with a **Start Block** action.

7. Include a **Set Gravity** action (**move** tab) with a **Direction** of 202.5 and a **Gravity** of 1. We have to add 180 to 22.5 degrees to get an angle slopping downwards and to the left.

8. Include a **Set Variable** action (**control** tab) that sets **Variable** image_index to **Value** 0.

9. Include an **End Block** action. This set of actions now sets the appropriate gravity setting and sub-image for `obj_slope_u1`.

10. Repeat steps 5-9 to check for `obj_slope_u2` using the same settings for the **Set Gravity** and **Set Variable** actions. If you want to cut and paste the five actions, then try including a **Comment** action (**control** tab) at the very end of the list of actions first. Highlight the five actions (hold control and left-click each one) and then right-click and select **Copy**. Next, right-click on the **Comment** action and select **Paste**. The actions should appear in front of the comment, allowing you to repeat the procedure.

11. Repeat steps 5–9 to check for `obj_slope_u3` using a **Direction** of 225 for the **Set Gravity** action and an `image_index` of 1 for the **Set Variable** action. Again we have to add 180 to 45 to get an angle sloping dowards to the left.

12. Repeat steps 5–9 for `obj_slope_d1` using a **Direction** of -45 and `image_index` of 3.

13. Repeat steps 5–9 for `obj_slope_d2` using a **Direction** of -22.5 and `image_index` of 4.

14. Repeat steps 5–9 for `obj_slope_d3` also using a **Direction** of -22.5 and `image_index` of 4. There should now be 33 actions in the **Begin Step** event for `obj_zool_ice`, as shown in Figure 4–18.

15. Add a **Step, End Step** event and include a **Check Object** action (**control** tab) that checks for the **Object** `obj_slope`, **NOT** at a **Relative** position of X=0, Y=1. This next series of actions will be similar to the ones that help Zool to walk down ramps smoothly, but a bit more complicated, as it needs to check for both slopes and platforms.

16. Follow this with a **Start Block** action.

17. Include a **Check Object** action that checks for the **Object** `obj_slope`, at a **Relative** position of X=0, Y=speed. This checks if there is actually a slope a bit further below Zool's feet that he could move down onto.

18. Follow this with another **Start Block** action.

19. Include a **Move to Contact** action (**move** tab) with **Direction** set to 270, **Maximum** set to -1, and **Against** set to **all objects**. This brings Zool back down on top of the slope if there is one to move down onto.

20. Follow this with an **End Block** action (**control** tab).

21. Include an **Else** action.

22. Follow this with another **Start Block** action.

23. Include a **Check Object** action (**control** tab) that checks for the **Object** `obj_platform`, at a **Relative** position of X=0, Y=1. This checks if Zool is actually standing on a normal platform if he's not standing on a slope.

24. Include a **Change Instance** action (**main1** tab) that will change into `obj_zool_land` and **Perform Events** (**Destroy** and **Create**) as it does so. If he is on a normal platform, then he needs to switch state.

25. Include an **Else** action (check Figure 4–19 if you're losing track).

26. Include a **Change Instance** action (**main1** tab) that will change into `obj_zool_air` and **Perform Events** (**Destroy** and **Create**) as it does so. This will start Zool falling if he isn't sliding down a slope or supported by a normal platform.

27. Include an **End Block** action (**control** tab).

28. Include a second **End Block** action. There should now be 14 actions in the **End Step** event for `obj_zool_ice`, as shown in Figure 4–19.

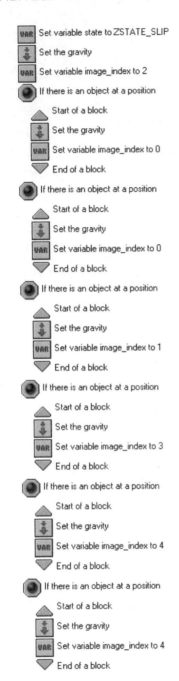

Figure 4–18. *The actions for the Begin Step event of the ice Zool state object*

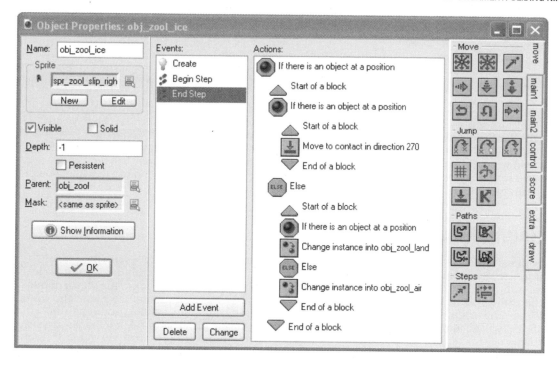

Figure 4–19. *The actions for the End Step event of the ice Zool state object*

29. Add a **Collision** event with obj_slope and include a **Set Variable** action to set the **Variable** y **Relative** to -speed*2.

30. Include a **Move to Contact** action (**move** tab) that sets **Direction** to 270, **Maximum** to -1, and **Against** to **all objects**. This will bring Zool back down in contact with the slope.

31. Add a **Key Press, Space** event and include a **Speed Vertical** action that sets **Vert. Speed** to -22. Jumping is the player's only way of controlling the slide.

32. Include a **Change Instance** action (**main1** tab) that will change into obj_zool_air and **Perform Events** (**Destroy** and **Create**) as it does so.

If you spend a little time on the slopes now, you should see that we've already nearly got this cracked. There is just one bug: if you jump back up the slope and manage to slide up to the top and back onto a non-slippery platform, then you will get stuck. This is because we have not handled collisions with other kinds of solid objects. We would really like this to have the same sliding behavior as the obj_zool_air object because it would look quite strange to suddenly come to a halt at the bottom of a slope. Therefore, we will copy the actions of that event and use it for this one.

Adding a General Solid Collision Event to the Ice State Object

1. Open obj_zool_air and select the **Collision** event with obj_solid. Right-click on the list of actions and choose **Select All** from the menu. Right-click again and choose **Copy**.

2. Now reopen obj_zool_ice and add a **Collision** event with obj_solid. Right-click on the empty list of actions and choose **Paste**.

You should now have a fairly solid slope mechanic, so give it a whirl, and if you have any problems then you will also find this version of the game in the file zool5.gmk in the Chapter04/Games directory on the CD. There are still some situations that you should probably avoid when designing your own levels: placing a wall directly next to a slope will not produce great results, for example. However, as long as you apply a bit of common sense to where you put them, then slopes should be a great additional feature to the game.

Sound Movement

Well we're nearly there with our movement mechanics, but actually there is something really important missing from Zool's movement—and that's sound. You might think that sound is just an optional extra, but sounds can play a massive role in providing feedback to the player about the game. Instant feedback is critical to creating an empowering movement mechanic and sound is one way to supply it. Sound effects for walking, skidding, jumping, landing, grabbing, and sliding will all add to the feeling that Zool is occupying a real, physical world that the player has the power to control. We will begin by adding a range of sound effects that are easy to implement and then add in a new skidding state with its own sound effect.

Adding Basic Sound Effects

1. You'll need to begin by creating sound resources for all the sound effects, which you'll find in the Chapter04/Resources directory on the CD. At the end of it you should have snd_footstep, snd_skid, snd_jump, snd_ice, snd_land, snd_grab, and snd_hiya.

2. Reopen obj_zool and select the **Create** event. At the start of the actions list, include a **Set Variable** action (**control** tab) that sets the **Variable** step_count to the **Value** 0. We're going to use this variable to decide how often to play some sound effects.

3. Select the **Step** event and include a **Set Variable** action that sets the **Variable** step_count **Relative** to the **Value** 1. In this way, step_count will keep track of how many steps there have been since Zool was first created.

4. Reopen obj_zool_ice and select the **Create** event. At the start of the actions list, include a **Play Sound** action (**main1** tab) to play the **Sound** snd_ice with **Loop** set to **true**. This will play an icy-sounding slipping sound continually while Zool is in the ice state.

5. Add a **Destroy** event and include a **Stop Sound** action to stop the **Sound** snd_ice. We don't use **Destroy** events very often, but this will get called whenever obj_zool_ice gets changed into another state object and stop the ice sound effect from looping (because we have the **Perform Events** option checked).

6. Select the **Key Press, Space** event and include a **Play Sound** action to play the **Sound** snd_jump with **Loop** set to **false**.

7. Reopen obj_zool_land and select the **Create** event. At the start of the actions list, include a **Test Variable** action (**control** tab) that tests if the **Variable** state is **NOT equal to** ZSTATE_SLIP. We're going to include a sound effect for landing on the ground here, but we don't want it to be played if Zool has slid into the land state rather than fallen into it.

8. Immediately follow this with a **Play Sound** action (**main1** tab) to play the **Sound** snd_land with **Loop** set to **false**.

9. Select the **Key Press, Space** event and include a **Play Sound** action to play the **Sound** snd_jump with **Loop** set to **false**.

10. Select the **End Step** event. At the start of the list of actions, include a **Test Variable** action (**control** tab) that checks if the **Variable** state is **equal to** ZSTATE_WALK.

11. Follow this with a **Start Block** action and place the following actions within that block.

12. Include a **Test Variable** action that checks if the **Variable** step_count mod 8 is **equal to** 0. The mod operator takes the value on its left, divides it by the number on the right, and returns the remainder. So 10 mod 8 equals 2 because 10 divided by 8 is 1 with 2 left over. Likewise 18 mod 8, 26 mod 8, and 2 mod 8 are all equal to 2 because their remainders are all 2 as well. So using step_count mod 8 means that the remainder will increase by one each frame, until it reaches 8 and then it will go back down to 0. It will only be equal to 0 once every 8 frames, so the following action to play a footstep sound effect will only be executed once every 8 frames—that's all we're trying to do here.

13. Immediately follow this with a **Play Sound** action (**main1** tab) to play the **Sound** snd_footstep with **Loop** set to **false**.

14. Include an **End Block** action (**control** tab). There should now be 16 actions in the **End Step** event of obj_zool_land, as shown in Figure 4–20.

15. Reopen obj_zool_wall and select the **Create** event. Include a **Play Sound** action (**main1** tab) to play the **Sound** snd_grab with **Loop** set to **false**.

16. Now select the **Keyboard, Up** event. We're going to add a sound effect for when Zool automatically leaps up from the top of a wall. This needs to be included within the second block of actions: directly before the **Change Instance** action will do. Include a **Play Sound** action here to play the **Sound** snd_hiya with **Loop** set to **false**.

Now that the easy ones are out of the way, run the game and see what difference it already makes to the way the game feels to play. Next, we're going to add a skidding state and sound effect to go with it. It will make no difference to the actual movement handling, but will add a significant amount of "cool" factor to running about the level.

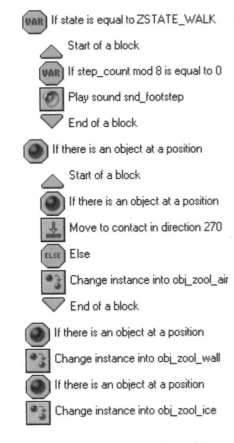

Figure 4–20. *The actions for the End Step event of the land Zool state object (part 1)*

Adding Skidding

1. Define a new constant called SKID_SPEED and set it to 10 (either through the **Define Constants** option on the **Resources** menu or a new variable in the **Create** event of obj_zool if you are using Game Maker Lite).

 2. Reopen obj_zool and select the **Draw** event. Within the grouped actions for FACE_RIGHT, include a new **Test Variable** action (**control** tab) to check if the **Variable** state is **equal to** the **Value** ZSTATE_SKID.

 3. Immediately follow this with a **Draw Sprite** action (**draw** tab) to draw spr_zool_skid_right at a **Relative** position of X=0, Y=0.

4. Now use spr_zool_skid_left to create left-facing equivalents of these two new actions within the grouped actions for FACE_LEFT.

 5. Reopen obj_zool_land and select the **Begin Step** event. Include a **Test Variable** action (**control** tab) immediately before the existing **Set Variable** action. Make this check whether the **Variable** state is **equal to** the **Value** ZSTATE_WALK. This will now only set the default state to standing if the previous state was walking, as otherwise this would interfere with skidding.

6. Select the **End Step** event and include all the following actions above the existing ones.

7. Include a **Test Variable** action that tests if the **Variable** state is **equal to** ZSTATE_STAND.

8. Immediately follow this with another **Test Variable** action that tests if the **Variable** speed is **larger than** SKID_SPEED. This will ensure that the following actions will only be executed if Zool is standing but still moving quite fast—that is, he has just stopped running and friction hasn't brought him to a standstill yet.

9. Include a **Start Block** action.

10. Include a **Set Variable** action that sets the **Variable** state to the **Value** ZSTATE_SKID.

11. Include a **Play Sound** action (**main1** tab) to play snd_skid with **Loop** set to **false**.

12. Include an **End Block** action (**control** tab). This covers switching into the skid state, so now we need to make sure that it goes back to standing again afterwards.

13. Include a **Test Variable** action that tests if the **Variable** state is **equal to** ZSTATE_SKID.

14. Immediately follow this with another **Test Variable** action that tests if the **Variable** speed is **smaller than** 1.

15. Follow this with a **Set Variable** action that sets the **Variable** state to the **Value** ZSTATE_STAND. The **End Step** event of obj_zool_land should now contain the 25 actions shown in Figure 4–21. Give yourself a round of applause!

And that's it—you can now skid Zool around the test level to your heart's content. Give the game a really good play-test to iron out any mistakes, or alternatively you can use the file zool6.gmk in the Chapter04/Games directory on the CD.

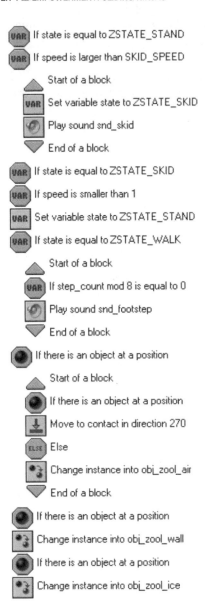

If state is equal to ZSTATE_STAND

If speed is larger than SKID_SPEED

  Start of a block

  Set variable state to ZSTATE_SKID

  Play sound snd_skid

  End of a block

If state is equal to ZSTATE_SKID

If speed is smaller than 1

Set variable state to ZSTATE_STAND

If state is equal to ZSTATE_WALK

  Start of a block

  If step_count mod 8 is equal to 0

  Play sound snd_footstep

  End of a block

If there is an object at a position

  Start of a block

  If there is an object at a position

  Move to contact in direction 270

  Else

  Change instance into obj_zool_air

  End of a block

If there is an object at a position

Change instance into obj_zool_wall

If there is an object at a position

Change instance into obj_zool_ice

Figure 4-21. *The actions for the End Step event of the land Zool state object (part 2)*

Congratulations—Phase 2 Complete!

Half-way is a significant milestone in any journey—it's the point of no return, the point at which it is as far to go back as it would be to carry on to the end. We've made a lot of progress in this chapter, and hopefully learned some practical lessons about empowerment (and bending the laws of physics) along the way. But you've probably got action icons spinning in front of your eyes by now, and the last thing you want to hear about is the next chapter. Actually, that's just as well, because you're almost certainly not ready to know about the horrors that await you there. Giant insects are undoubtedly not for everyone, and dead factory owners are a topic probably best left for another day as well. Perhaps you're not even interested in whether Zool escapes from his crashed ship in the cartoon on the next page, let alone how he will overcome an army of walking liquorices that spit deadly aniseed balls. Anyway, what fun can there possibly be in squaring off against the forces of Krool with nothing more than a ninja ant from the 2345th dimension? Maybe you should go and read a cookery book instead....

CHAPTER 5

■ ■ ■

Krool's Forces: Sweetening the Challenge

One-hundred and fifty years before Gremlin came up with the idea for Zool, his home city of Sheffield (in the UK) witnessed the birth of a quite different sort of company. This was George Bassett and Co. Limited, the confectioner who would go on to produce Licorice Allsorts, Jelly Babies, and Wine Gums. So, although it may be somewhat surreal, it's actually quite fitting that the first world in Zool was inspired by the colorful and tempting wares of a candy store.

It's difficult to know exactly what kind of nightmares a 19th century confectioner might have had, but being attacked by his own candy would almost certainly qualify as a particularly bad one. Of course, Zool's resemblance to an ant hasn't gone unnoticed over the years either, and ants in the sweet factory would probably be up there on George's list of nightmares, too. Our next task then, is to turn this confectioner's nightmare into a game-player's dream by beefing up the challenges of our game with a range of strange, but deadly enemies.

Figure 5–1. *The enigmatic Krool: he's probably quite nice once you get to know him*

Challenging Ingredients

We already have a movement mechanic that turns our level into an interactive playground, but we don't have something we could call a game yet, because we haven't provided the player with any challenges. The original game provided a range of challenges relating to the various short- and long-term goals of the game (including the role of Krool—see Figure 5-1). You will have already started to discover the back story behind the game through the Zool comic strip, and the overall goal of the game is described in the original Amiga manual as follows:

> *In Zool you play the interstellar cosmos dweller from the Nth dimension. You must guide Zool through thousands of screens of surreal and bizarre action in a bid to bring the intergalactic Ninja back home to the Nth dimension. You must take Zool to the outer limits of the known universe, through quite a bit of the unknown universe, and beyond the "fairly well-known, but I wouldn't want to walk through it at night on my own" universe.*
>
> *Before reaching home, Zool has to successfully work through all manner of bizarre situations, worlds and enemies. The only way to do this is by exploring each world until the exit is found, and progressing onto the next one.*

So, the long-term goal is to get Zool back home, and each level has a medium-term goal of finding the exit. Simply adding an exit to our existing level would technically provide the missing challenge required to call it a game. Nonetheless, reaching this exit could actually be pretty unchallenging unless there were some additional constraints. We can describe the constraints from the original version of the game as follows:

- **Movement**—The exit is placed in a position that is difficult for Zool to reach, requiring him to employ a full range of movement mechanics in order to get to it.

- **Bonus Collection**—The exit is unavailable until Zool has collected a certain percentage of the bonus pickups on each level (25% on easy, 50% on normal, and 75% on hard).

- **Enemies and Hazards**—If an enemy, enemy missile, or hazard touches Zool, then he will lose one bar of health. However, Zool can destroy enemies by shooting them with missiles, sliding or spinning into them, or jumping on top of them.

- **Lives**—Once he has lost three bars of health, Zool loses a life. He starts with only three lives with which to complete the game (the original game had continues too, but we will ignore these in our version).

- **Time Limit**—Zool has a limited amount of time to reach the exit before he loses a life (the time limit depends on the difficulty setting and the level).

The goal of reaching the exit under these constraints characterizes the challenge of Zool as a game. Including them in our version will not only make the game more fun, but will make it recognizable to players as belonging to the Zool series. Many of these features will be relatively easy to implement, but there are some challenges ahead for *you*, too. In this chapter, we will concentrate on bonuses, enemies, and hazards, and in the next (and final) chapter on Zool, we'll deal with lives and time limits.

Reheated Resources

In order to save time (and paper), we have provided you with a new version of the game, which contains all the new sprite and sound resources you'll need for this chapter. Although setting these up is trivial, there are still a few things you should take note of, so we'll give you another quick tour so that you don't miss anything crucial.

Exploring the Sprite Resources

- Use Game Maker to open zool7.gmk from the Chapter05/Games directory on the CD and take a look at the sprite resources. The Zool group now contains left- and right-facing sprites for three new actions (kick, spin, and die), as well as a missile sprite for shooting. Open up some of the new sprites and click on the **Modify Mask** button. Notice that the new action sprites have **Precise Collision Checking** turned off and share the same bounding box and origin settings as the previous Zool sprites (in order to ensure that the collision area doesn't change when switching sprites).

- Zool's missile sprite also has **Precise Collision Checking** turned off and has an appropriately smaller bounding box set up. From now on, you can assume that we have turned the **Precise Collision Checking** off and used **Rectangular** collision, unless we specify otherwise. However, precise collision would actually work just as well in this case, as Zool's missiles will get destroyed on contact with anything.

- The Platforms group now contains a new group called Lifts, which itself contains all the sprites needed for moving platforms later on. It is not practical to use tiles for moving objects, so these sprites are used for both the collision mask and the visual image of lifts. Most of these have their **Origins** at X=0, Y=0, and use the **Full image** option for the bounding box (which just means that the bounding box is the full size of the sprite).

- The new Hazards group contains all the hazards we will be adding in this chapter. First comes a range of spikes in varying orientations. All of these use the **Full image** option for the bounding box, which just means that the bounding box is the full size of the sprite.

- Next comes six different sprites for the Sweet Beastie enemy. These all have **Manual** bounding boxes set up with identical boundaries (**Left**=8, **Right**=24, **Top**=4, **Bottom**=43). They also share the same **Origin** settings (X=16, Y=28), which are not at the center of the sprite. This origin is offset in the y direction so that the base of the bounding box rests on top of the platform's surface when the Beastie object is placed in the room editor.

- The collision settings for the die sprites and the splat sprite (further down) are irrelevant, as they are only included for visual effect and we will not handle their collisions.

- The Beastie missile uses a **Rectangular**, **Full image** bounding box. It will be expected to react to collisions and bounce across the landscape. In practice, you probably wouldn't notice any difference using **Precise Collision Checking** in this case (as the missile is such a simple, solid shape and is unlikely to get stuck), but we'll keep to the principle that precise collision is the not the best choice for reactive collisions.

- The collision and origin settings for the Jelly enemy sprites are different from the Sweet Beastie, but follow identical logic.

- The Bee enemy sprites are slightly different insofar as they do not need to rest neatly on the surface of platforms, so their origins are in the center of the sprites.

- Finally (in the Hazards group), the enemy limit sprite has a **Full image** bounding box, as it is just used as an invisible barrier to enemy objects when they move about the level.

- The Icons group contains all the sprites relevant to the game's user interface (score, lives, time, and so forth). As they are purely visual, their collision settings are irrelevant, but they all have their **Origin** placed at the center for ease of reference.

- The Misc (miscellaneous) group contains all of the remaining sprites in the game that don't justify a group of their own. The first three (spr_pickups, spr_100pts, and spr_twinkle) all relate to the basic collectible items on the level. These need to align precisely with the landscape, which is determined by the tiles. You will recall that all tiles behave as if they have **Origin** settings of **X=0, Y=0**, so these are the same origin settings used for these sprites. Only the pickups will be collidable and they use a **Full image** setting to make them as easy as possible to collect.

- The exit sprite uses the **Disk** collision shape to create a circular collision area in the very center of the exit.

- The cloud sprites are not used for collision.

Gotta Get 'Em All

Collection is a common game mechanic in many games and Zool had collectibles by the bucket load. Each level contained items which were appropriate to the theme of the world, so it won't surprise you to learn that the Sweet World contained enough candy to rack up a sizable dentist bill. Nonetheless, collectibles of this kind can serve all sorts of useful roles in level design by providing a way to guide the player through the level and even encourage them to explore levels to the full. Now let's set about creating the items themselves. These sweets will disappear when Zool collides with them and be replaced by a 100pts graphic that drifts upward and then disappears in a twinkle effect. Achieving this will require three new objects.

Creating Objects for the Level Collectibles

1. We're going to add a lot more objects to the game in the remaining chapters, so we'll try to keep our object resources organized by mirroring the group structure from the sprite resources. We've already created all the empty groups for you, so it's up to you to create each new object in the appropriate place.

2. Right-click on the Misc group within the **Objects** resource folder and select **Create Object** from the menu. In this way, create three new objects within the group called obj_collect, obj_100pts, and obj_twinkle. Give each one the sprite of the same name.

3. Reopen obj_collect and add a **Create** event. Include a **Change Sprite** action (**main1** tab) that changes into spr_collect, but sets the **Subimage** to random(7) and the **Speed** to 0. If you look again at spr_collect, you will see that the sprite contains seven separate images that are not part of an animation, as each image represents a different kind of sweet. So this action randomly selects one of these subimages (from 0-6) and stops the sprite from animating.

4. Reopen obj_zool (now in the Zool group) and add a **Collision** event with obj_collect. As usual, we try and handle all collisions with Zool in the Zool objects. Adding this event to obj_zool (the parent of all the Zool states) also means that all of Zool's different object states will inherit it.

5. Include a **Play Sound** action (**main1** tab) to play snd_collect.

6. Include a **Change Instance** action that changes the **Other** instance (the obj_collect instance) into obj_100pts, with **Perform events**.

7. Reopen obj_100pts and add a **Create** event.

8. Include a **Set Score** action (**score** tab) that increases the score by 100 (that is, sets the score **Relative** to 100).

9. Include a **Speed Vertical** action (**move** tab) that sets **Vert. Speed** to -0.5 (remember, up is negative).

10. Include a **Set Alarm** action (**main2** tab) that sets **Alarm 0** to 30 steps (one second). This is how long the instance will drift upward before it turns into a twinkle object.

11. Add an **Alarm, Alarm 0** event and include a **Change Instance** action (**main1** tab) that changes the instance into an obj_twinkle with **Perform events**.

12. Reopen obj_twinkle and add a **Create** event.

13. Include a **Change Sprite** action that changes into spr_twinkle, and sets the **Subimage** to 0 and the **Speed** to 1. This may seem unnecessary, but remember that the **Create** event of obj_collect sets the **Speed** of the sprite to 0 (that is, not animating) and the **Change Instance** action does not start it animating again automatically.

14. Add an **Other, Animation End** event that includes a **Destroy Instance** action to destroy itself at the end of the twinkle animation.

Spoil Your Dinner

Now reopen the test room and disable the **Show Tiles** option (from the drop-down menu beside the magnifying glass toolbar icon). Place numerous instances of obj_collect all around the level, being careful not to destroy the existing platform objects as you go. Holding the Shift key down at the same time as pressing the left mouse button will allow you to place multiple objects more easily (provided you have a steady hand). You should be aiming to place between 50-75 instances of obj_collect all around the level for the player to find, but many of these should be in long lines for the player to slide into and collect in one smooth movement.

Run the game and see the result. This already adds a bit more of a purpose to the game, even if it's somewhat artificial at the moment. However, it also reveals a real problem with the way collisions work in our game! Try jumping on top of a long row of collectibles and see what happens. You should find that rather than landing on his feet as you might expect, Zool slides across the row of collectibles while hovering slightly above the ground. This isn't right!

Figure 5–2. *Zool cannot collide properly with the platform because the 100pts instances are in the way*

A Solid Problem

So what is happening here? Reopen `obj_zool_air` and select the **Collision** event with `obj_solid`. This event is triggered by collisions with solid objects, such as when Zool lands on top of a platform. There's nothing wrong with that, but now open the **Move to Contact** action within this event. This moves the Zool instance downward until it comes into contact with **all objects**—and *all objects* includes instances of `obj_100pts`.

The problem occurs when Zool lands on a collectible immediately before colliding with the platform beneath it. The collision event with `obj_solid` will move him back to his position before the collision, and then he *should* get moved down to the contact position with the platform. However, he can't because there will be an instance of `obj_100pts` in the way that was created by the collectible (see Figure 5–2). So he doesn't get moved down by the **Move to Contact** action and there won't be a platform directly beneath his feet at the end of the **Collision** event. That means he won't change into `obj_zool_land` and will float across the line of collectibles, until either he reaches the end, or they eventually turn into twinkles and disappear. This may not seem like a disaster, but think about it. Every new object we add to the game will start to interfere with collisions even when they are not supposed to be solid. This is going to cause a huge number of bugs and problems with our game!

The Solid Wheel

So at this stage you may be thinking the solution is simple: everybody knows that Game Maker has a built-in option to distinguish between objects that should be treated as solid and those that should not. All we need to do is enable this **Solid** option for all the different kinds of platforms and then select the **solid objects** option in all our **Move to Contact** actions. Then the likes of collectibles will be ignored and the problem will be solved. In fact, why have we been bothering with this strange `obj_solid` object anyway—surely it's just reinventing the wheel? Why spend time coding something that Game Maker already does for us?

Well yes, Game Maker *does* contain a check box for every object to enable you to flag it as being **Solid**, and yes many of the actions, such as **Move to Contact,** allow you to distinguish between objects that do or don't have this flag set. It's also true that we've deliberately been creating a similar mechanism for ourselves using obj_solid. We *are* reinventing the wheel, but with very good reason. Although Game Maker's **Solid** option may just seem like a simple way of tagging objects, that's not the case. Game Maker treats collisions with objects tagged as **Solid** in a completely different way from normal collisions. It is not a simple wheel, but a wheel with a mind of its own....

Reinventing the Solid Wheel

Recall from Chapter 3 that collision events take place directly after all instances are moved to their new positions based on their current speed and direction settings. When a collision occurs, you might expect Game Maker to execute the actions you have put into that collision event and nothing else. However, when a collision takes place between two instances and *either* of them has its **Solid** flag set, it automatically triggers a number of extra steps as part of the collision event:

1. Both instances are set back to their previous position before the collision (including setting them back to their previous path positions if they are following a path).

2. The collision events for both instances are then executed in the usual way, performing all the actions you've included in the action list for those events.

3. Both instances are then set to their new position based on their (potentially changed) speed and direction (and path where relevant).

4. An additional collision check is made to make sure that the instances are no longer colliding with each other. If they are still colliding, then they are set right back to their previous position before the collision again.

So in step one, Game Maker effectively performs the same task as the two **Set Variable** actions we have been including at the start of our collision events to set x to xprevious and y to yprevious. That means if we were to enable the **Solid** flag, then we could remove these two actions and save some effort—okay, that's not so bad. Next, the collision events are performed as usual: the assumption being that the actions of your collision event should attempt to change the speed and direction of the instances so that they no longer collide. In step three, the objects are moved again based on their current settings, but if they still collide afterward, then step four undoes all the movement of *both* instances and puts them back where they were before the collision occurred (back to xprevious, yprevious).

Game Maker's **Solid** option is designed to make it easy for beginners to create impenetrable objects like walls. However, the behind-the-scenes "magic" described here can cause problems and confusion when you try to take a more advanced approach. In fact, steps three and four would completely break the collision system of our game. Remember that we don't actually reset the horizontal speed of Zool to zero when he jumps into a wall because we want him to slide up and over the top edge of platforms (refer back to Figure 4-3). Normally, we have the ability to move Zool's position so he is no longer colliding, but maintain his horizontal speed "for future use" in this way. However, if the **Solid** option was enabled for the wall, then Zool's horizontal speed would cause him to collide with the wall again in step three, and then move right back to his original position in step four. Basically, we have to choose between either using the **Solid** option *or* keeping our sliding movement mechanic that we've worked so hard on.

Nonetheless, the big picture here has nothing to do with the details of Zool's movement mechanic. It is quite simply not a good idea to use the **Solid** option unless you are a beginner, as it ties your hands unnecessarily. If you think about it, then all of the automatic steps performed during a **Solid** collision can be created in drag-and-drop actions anyway, so you don't need Game Maker to do any of this for you. Furthermore, you don't actually need all of these steps in most situations, and it is better to maintain full control (and a full understanding) of what is really going on in your game. This is why we have been reinventing the wheel by creating an obj_solid object to act as our replacement for the **Solid** option, as well as including our own **Set Variable** actions that set x to xprevious and y to yprevious at the start of each collision event. For advanced games, it is an approach that will prove far less problematic in the long run than using Game Maker's built-in method.

A Scripted Rescue

This is all very well, but we haven't actually solved our original problem of collectible objects getting in the way of collisions. Unfortunately, the truth is that this can't be solved just using Game Maker's built-in drag-and-drop actions. What we need is the equivalent of a **Move to Contact** action, which allows us to specify contact with obj_solid, rather than just **all objects**. We can achieve this fairly easily by creating our own script and using the **Execute Script** action to execute it. We'll call the script move_to_contact_with and it will provide all the same options as the **Move to Contact** action (a direction, a maximum distance to move, and the type of thing to move against). However, the final option will not just be a choice between solid or all objects, but you will be able to provide the name of an object or even a specific instance. We're not going to explain how the script works just now, but we will come back to it in Chapter 11. For now, simply follow these instructions to set up the script.

Loading the Alternative Move to Contact Script

1. From the **Scripts** menu, select **Import Scripts**.

2. Select move_to_contact_with.gml from the Chapter05/Resources directory on the CD. This will add this script to the **Scripts** folder in the resource tree. Double-click on it if you're curious to take a look, but be careful not to change anything.

3. Reopen obj_zool_air and select the **Collision** event with obj_solid. Locate the **Move to Contact** action and reopen it. Notice the settings (direction, -1, **all objects**) and then close it again. Now delete this action from the action list (click on it and press Delete).

 4. In its place (directly after the second **Set Variable** action), include an **Execute Script** action (**control** tab). Set **Script** to move_to_contact_with, **Argument0** to direction, **Argument1** to -1, and **Argument2** to obj_solid. Notice how these settings are in the same order as **Move to Contact**, but have generic names (**Argument0**, and so forth). As you can use the **Execute Script** action to call any script, you have to remember the order (or refer back to the script). The new script also allows us to use obj_solid instead of **all objects**, making our action only move into contact with solid objects and not with collectibles.

If you run the game now, you will find that our problem seems to be fixed. Nonetheless, there are many more places where we use the **Move to Contact** action with **all objects** and any of these could cause similar problems with our game at some point. So, we now need to go through and systematically change all of the rest over too. You can either follow the steps here or skip to the end and load the file zool8.gmk from the Chapter05/Games directory on the CD.

Replacing the Remaining Move to Contact Actions

1. Select and **Copy** the **Execute Script** action that you just created in the obj_solid **Collision** event of obj_zool_air.

 2. Select the obj_ledge **Collision** event. Highlight the **Move to Contact** action and **Paste** the **Execute Script** action in its place. Delete the old **Move to Contact** action afterward.

3. Select the obj_slope **Collision** event. Highlight the **Move to Contact** action and **Paste** the **Execute Script** action in its place. Edit the **Execute Script** action and change **Argument0** to 270. Delete the **Move to Contact** action .

4. Select the obj_ramp **Collision** event. Highlight the **Move to Contact** action and **Paste** the **Execute Script** action in its place. Edit the **Execute Script** action and change **Argument0** to 270. Delete the **Move to Contact** action.

5. Reopen obj_zool_land and select the **End Step** event.

6. Highlight the **Move to Contact** action (some way down) and **Paste** the **Execute Script** action in its place. Edit the **Execute Script** action and change **Argument0** to 270 and **Argument2** to obj_platform. Delete the **Move to Contact** action.

7. Select the obj_ramp **Collision** event. Highlight the **Move to Contact** action and **Paste** the **Execute Script** action in its place. Edit the **Execute Script** action and change **Argument0** to 270. Delete the **Move to Contact** action .

8. Select the obj_solid **Collision** event. Highlight the **Move to Contact** action and **Paste** the **Execute Script** action in its place. No need to edit the **Execute Script** action this time. Delete the **Move to Contact** action afterward.

9. Reopen obj_zool_ice and select the **End Step** event.

10. Highlight the **Move to Contact** action and **Paste** the **Execute Script** action in its place. Edit the **Execute Script** action and change **Argument0** to 270 and **Argument2** to obj_slope. Delete the **Move to Contact** action afterward.

11. Select the obj_slope **Collision** event. Highlight the **Move to Contact** action and **Paste** the **Execute Script** action in its place. Edit the **Execute Script** action and change **Argument0** to 270. Delete the **Move to Contact** action .

12. Select the obj_solid **Collision** event. Highlight the **Move to Contact** action and **Paste** the **Execute Script** action in its place. No need to edit the **Execute Script** action this time. Delete the **Move to Contact** action afterward.

13. Reopen obj_zool_wall and select the obj_solid **Collision** event.

14. Highlight the **Move to Contact** action and **Paste** the **Execute Script** action in its place. No need to edit the **Execute Script** action this time. Delete the **Move to Contact** action.

Note that all the **Collision** events should use obj_solid for **Argument2**. This is because Zool may collide with more than one type of object in a single step (at the join between a ramp and a platform, for example). In this situation, both collision events would be called, and either could produce incorrect results if they didn't take into account all solid objects when moving to contact position. Now give your game a thorough retest to make sure that nothing has been broken by this switch over. If you have any problems, then revert to the file zool8.gmk in the Chapter05/Games directory on the CD.

Health Hazards

There can't be many ninjas that regularly go up against licorice-based opponents, but that's exactly what Zool will do in our Sweet World. Spikes, Jellies, Beasties, and Bees are just some of the hazards Zool will have to overcome if he's to make it to the minty freshness of the exit. In this section, we'll take these hazards in turn and make them get in Zool's way.

Spiky Fright

Spikes are by far the simplest of the hazards, so we will begin by creating these and making Zool react appropriately when he collides with them.

Creating Spike Hazards

1. Begin by creating a new object in the `Misc` group called `obj_controller`. You might recognize this kind of object from *The Game Maker's Apprentice*. It is used to carry out behaviors that affect the whole game.

2. Include a **Create** event with a **Set Variable** action (**control** tab) that sets the **Variable** `global.step_count` to 0.

3. Include a **Step, Step** event with a **Set Variable** action that sets the **Variable** `global.step_count` **Relative** to 1. This creates a global counter that records the number of steps performed in the game so far. This will prove useful later on.

4. Reopen `obj_zool` and select the **Create** event. Delete the first **Set Variable** action that sets `step_count` to 0. The Zool object had its own step count, but we would rather use the global one from now on.

5. Likewise, select the **Step** event of `obj_zool` and delete the corresponding **Set Variable** action that sets `step_count` **Relative** to 1.

6. Reopen `obj_zool_land` and select the **End Step** event. Edit the **Test Variable** action that checks if `step_count` mod 8 is **equal to** 0. Change **Variable** to `global.step_count` mod 8. This now ties in the Zool object to our global step count instead.

7. Right-click on the `Hazards` group within the object resources and select **Create Object** from the menu. You should create all the enemies and hazards within this group to keep them organized. Call this one `obj_hazard` and close it again. This will be the parent object for all hazards in the game.

8. Create a new object called `obj_spike_left` and give it the `spr_spike_left` sprite. Set its parent to be `obj_hazard` and then close it. It does not need any actions.

9. Repeat the previous step to create two more spike objects called `obj_spike_right` and `obj_spike_up` using the appropriate sprites.

10. Reopen `obj_zool` and select the **Create** event.

11. Directly above the final **Change Instance** action, include a **Set Variable** action (**control** tab) that sets the **Variable** `hurt` to `false`. We will use this to keep track of when Zool gets hurt by a hazard and make him invulnerable to being hurt again for a short period of time.

12. Add a **Collision** event with `obj_hazard` and include a **Test Variable** action that checks if the **Variable** `hurt` is **equal to** `false`. In other words, the following events will only take place if Zool is not already hurt.

13. Immediately follow this with a **Start Block** action. This following block of actions will make Zool jump up and back from a hazard when he collides with it.

14. Include a **Test Variable** action that sets **Variable** to abs(hspeed), **Value** to 1, and **Operation** to **larger than**. Colliding with a hazard should make Zool jump back diagonally, unless he falls straight down onto it (when a vertical jump would make more sense). The abs() function returns the "absolute" value (or magnitude) of the variable, turning any negative numbers into positive ones. That means that the next action will trigger if Zool is moving horizontally (left or right) faster than 1 pixel per step.

15. Include a **Speed Horizontal** action (**move** tab) that sets **Hor. Speed** to -facing*4. This will make Zool's horizontal speed four times as large, but in the opposite direction.

16. Next, include a **Speed Vertical** action that sets **Vert. Speed** to -18 (upward). This is not part of the previous condition, so the vertical jump will take place regardless of Zool's horizontal speed.

17. Include a **Play Sound** action (**main1** tab) that plays snd_hurt. From now on, we'll include sound effects as we go along.

18. Include a **Set Variable** action (**control** tab) that sets the **Variable** hurt to true.

19. Include a **Set Alarm** action (**main2** tab) that sets **Alarm 0** to 90 steps (3 seconds).

20. Include a **Set Health** action (**score** tab) that takes 1 off the health **Value** (**Relative** to -1).

21. Include a **Change Instance** (**main1** tab) action that changes to obj_zool_air with **Perform events**.

22. Follow this with an **End Block** action (**control** tab). There should now be 11 actions for the **Collision** event with obj_hazard that look like Figure 5–3.

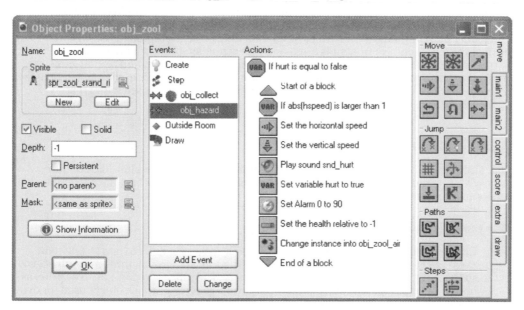

Figure 5–3. *The obj_zool Collision event with obj_hazard*

23. Add an **Alarm, Alarm 0** event and include a **Set Variable** action that sets the **Variable** hurt to false. This alarm event will end Zool's period of invulnerability after three seconds, as that's what it was set to previously.

24. Reopen the **Draw** event and include a **Test Variable** action at the start of the list of actions. Use it to check whether the hurt **Variable** is **equal to** true.

25. Follow this with another **Test Variable** action with **Variable** set to global.step_count mod 6, **Value** set to 0, and **Operation** set to **equal to**. Recall that the mod operator divides the left value by the right value, and then provides the remainder. In other words, this will provide a number from zero to five based on the global step counter that increases by one every step. That means this condition will fire once every six steps.

26. Immediately follow this with an **Exit Event** action. So Zool's sprite will periodically not be drawn if he is hurt—making his sprite flash on and off in a way that is often used to represent invulnerability in games.

Now return to the room editor and add a range of spikes in interesting places around the level (it's usually best to hide the tiles again while you're doing this). You'll also need to add an instance of obj_controller to the room. Play the game and check that it all works as intended because we're going to tackle some more animated hazards next.

Bitter Sweets

Computer-controlled opponents often play a big part in the challenge of a video game, and we'll be tackling these next. So what makes a good computer opponent? This might be the kind of question that fires your imagination with thoughts of advanced artificial intelligence (AI) and team-based tactics. Okay, let's imagine for a moment that all the computer opponents in Zool had AI that allowed them to work together in order to stop the player from reaching the objective (the exit). Would that create a fun game to play? It might be entertaining to find yourself suddenly ambushed in all directions by 50 opponents the first time around, but it would quickly lose its charm!

The reality of AI in games is that, more often than not, artificial stupidity is a more appropriate term. A "good" opponent is often one that is predictable and has a clear vulnerability for the player to exploit. Remember that the player is not your opponent, and a good game balances a theatrical threat of failure with a true desire to assist the player in their mastery of the game. So the minions of Krool we're about to implement may not be blessed with great intelligence, but that's exactly the way we like them.

Jelly and I Scream

The first, and simplest, of Krool's dimwitted automatons is the Jelly. This blob-like creature roams slowly back and forth regardless of Zool's approach, and can only hurt the player if he is clumsy enough to bump into him.

Creating the Jelly Enemy

1. Create three new objects called obj_enemy, obj_enemy_die and obj_splat (all in the Hazards group). Give obj_splat the spr_splat sprite and give all three a **Depth** of -1001 so that they appear in front of all of the scenery. The other two don't need a sprite, as one will just be a parent object and the second a general-purpose object used for dying enemies (and its sprite will change).

2. Reopen obj_enemy and add a **Destroy** event. Include a **Play Sound** action (**main1** tab) to play snd_enemy_die.

3. Include a **Repeat** action (**control tab**) to repeat the following action 4 **Times**. When an enemy dies, it splits into four pieces, so we need to create four objects from one.

4. Immediately follow this with a **Create Moving** action (**main1** tab) that creates an instance of obj_enemy_die at a **Relative** position of X=0 Y=0, with a **Speed** of 4 and a **Direction** of random(180). Note that a random angle between 0 and 180 will range from horizontally right through vertically up and to horizontally left.

5. Include a (normal) **Create Instance** action that creates an instance of obj_splat at a **Relative** position of X=0 Y=0.

6. Now add a **Key Press, Letters, K** event and include a **Destroy Instance** action to destroy **Self**. We'll use this to test dying enemies before we've implemented Zool's attacks.

7. Add a **Create** event for obj_enemy_die and include a **Set Variable** action (**control** tab) that sets the **Variable** sprite_index to global.die_sprite_index. Setting sprite_index is equivalent to the first part of a **Change Sprite** action where you would normally select the desired sprite from a drop-down menu. However, the drop-down menu doesn't include variables and we want to set the sprite from a global variable (die_sprite_index), so this allows us to do that. You'll see where this variable comes from a little later.

8. Take a quick peek at one of the enemy die sprites in the sprite resources (Hazards group). You can see that these sprites are not animations of an enemy dying, but separate pieces of the enemy as if they had just exploded into pieces of a puzzle.

9. Include another **Set Variable** action that sets the **Variable** image_index to random(image_number). Setting image_index is equivalent to the second part of a **Change Sprite** action where you set the subimage. The variable image_number holds the total number of subimages in the current sprite, so we're just setting the subimage to be a random image between 0 and image_number. The random function only returns numbers small than the value in brackets.

10. Include another **Set Variable** action that sets the **Variable** image_speed to 0. Setting the variable image_speed is equivalent to the third part of a **Change Sprite** action where you set the animation speed of the sprite. So this stops the sprite from animating.

11. Include a **Set Gravity** action (**move** tab) that sets **Gravity** to 1 in **Direction** 270 (down). At this point, you should have four actions for the **Create** event of obj_enemy_die, as shown in Figure 5–4.

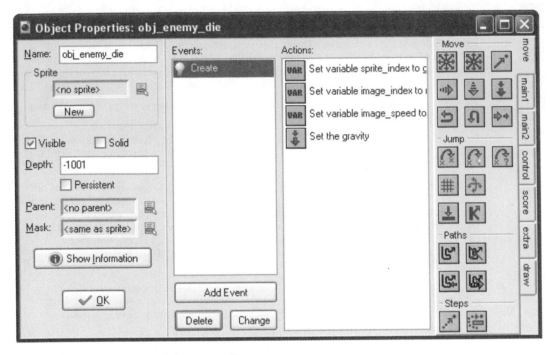

Figure 5–4. *The Create event of obj_enemy_die*

12. Finally (for obj_enemy_die), add an **Other, Outside Room** event and include a **Destroy Instance** action (**main1** tab) to destroy **Self**. This makes sure the enemy pieces get destroyed when they fall off screen.

13. Reopen obj_splat and add a **Create** event. Include a **Set Variable** action (**control** tab) that sets the **Variable** image_speed to 0.5 to slow down the animation speed.

14. Add an **Other, Animation End** event and include a **Destroy Instance** action (**main1** tab) to destroy the splat at the end of the animation.

15. Now we can actually create the Jelly enemy. Create a new object called obj_jelly (Hazards group), give it the spr_jelly sprite, and make obj_enemy its parent.

16. Add a **Create** event and include a **Set Variable** action (**control** tab) that sets the **Variable** facing to FACE_LEFT. If you are using Game Maker Pro, then FACE_LEFT is a constant that is available to use in all objects. If you are using the Lite version, then FACE_LEFT is currently just a local variable to obj_zool, so you can't use it here. Don't worry—just set the variable to -1 instead as it's the only time it is used for this object.

17. Add a **Step, Step** event and include a **Speed Horizontal** action (**move** tab) that sets **Hor. Speed** to facing*1.5. In other words, give it a speed of +1.5 or -1.5, depending on the direction the jelly is facing. Next, we must consider the situations in which it should change direction.

18. Include a **Check Object** action (**control** tab) that checks for there **NOT** being a collision with an instance of obj_platform at a **Relative** position of **X**=facing*16 and **Y**=8. This means we're checking that there will be a platform to continue to support the Jelly if it keeps moving in the direction it is traveling.

19. Follow this with a **Set Variable** action that sets the **Variable** facing to –facing and thus reverses the Jelly's direction of travel.

20. Include a **Check Object** action that checks for there being a collision with an instance of obj_hazard at a **Relative** position of **X**=facing*16 and **Y**=0. This checks whether the Jelly has collided with a hazard (spike), as we want it to reverse direction in this case too.

21. Follow this with another **Set Variable** action that sets the **Variable** facing to –facing.

22. Add a **Destroy** event and include a **Set Variable** action that sets the **Variable** global.die_sprite_index to spr_jelly_die. This is the global variable that gets passed on to the obj_enemy_die object so that it knows which sprite to use.

23. Include a **Call Parent Event** action. The Jelly's parent object (obj_enemy) already has a **Destroy** event, so the current event overrides that event with the Jelly's own version. However, that's not what we want, as it is the **Destroy** event of obj_enemy that creates the exploding instances of obj_enemy_die. Fortunately, Game Maker provides a way of allowing us to explicitly call inherited events from the parent object *as well* using the **Call Parent Event** action.

24. Finally, reopen obj_zool. Right-click on the **Collision** event with obj_hazard and select **Duplicate Event** to create a **Collision** event with obj_enemy. This now provides the same behavior for a collision with enemies as we already had for hazards.

Now return to the room editor and place a few instances of the new Jelly object around the level. Test them out to make sure they roam back and forth as they should and try killing them all by pressing the K key. The only problem now is that the Jelly doesn't move up and down ramps properly (it's not designed to go on the steep icy slopes, so avoid putting it there). So it needs to change orientation and height when it moves up and down shallow ramps. This could involve a lot of different checks for all the different ramp objects, so we'll group all the up ramps together, and all down ramps together, using parent objects. This will then allow us to detect collisions with all the up or down ramps at once, and while we're dealing with collisions, we'll also add a limiter object that will force enemies to turn around if they collide with it.

Creating Enemy Limits and Coping with Ramps

1. Create a new object called obj_enemy_limit (Hazards group). Give it the spr_enemy_limit sprite, but uncheck the **Visible** option. This will be our invisible marker that turns enemies around. It will eventually affect all enemies, but we'll start with the Jelly.

2. Create two new objects (outside of any groups at the top level) called obj_ramp_up and obj_ramp_down. Set both of their parents to obj_ramp.

3. Now go through all of the inclining ramp objects (with names ending u1 to u8) and change their parents to be obj_ramp_up. This was made a lot easier because obj_ramp_up was not in a group, but it should really live in the Platform, Ramps group, so drag it there afterward.

4. Repeat for all the declining ramp objects (with names ending d1 to d8) and change their parents to be obj_ramp_down. Now, drag obj_ramp_down to the Platform, Ramps group as well. All this has no effect on the rest of the game, but now allows us to easily distinguish between up and down ramps in collisions.

5. Reopen obj_jelly and select the **Step** event. Include a **Check Object** action (**control** tab) that checks if there would be a collision with an instance of obj_enemy_limit at a **Relative** position of **X**=facing*16, **Y**=0.

6. Follow this with a **Set Variable** action that sets the **Variable** facing to -facing.

7. Include a **Check Object** action that checks if there would **NOT** be a collision with an instance of obj_platform at a **Relative** position of **X**=0, **Y**=1.

8. Follow this with an **Execute Script** action that sets **Script** to move_to_contact_with, **Argument0** to 270, **Argument1** to -1, and **Argument2** to obj_platform. This will move the Jelly down when descending slopes.

9. Include a **Change Sprite** action (**main1** tab) that sets the **Sprite** to spr_jelly, **Subimage** to -1 (unchanged), and **Speed** to 0.2. This provides a default state for the sprite and reduces the animation speed to a fifth because the wobble animation only has two frames and was running much too fast.

10. Include a **Check Object** action (**control** tab) that checks if there would be a collision with an instance of obj_ramp_up at a **Relative** position of **X**=0, **Y**=1 (that is, directly underneath the Jelly).

11. Follow this with a **Change Sprite** action (**main1** tab) that sets the **Sprite** to spr_jelly_up, the **Subimage** to -1, and the **Speed** to 0.2 again.

12. Include another **Check Object** action (**control** tab) that checks if there would be a collision with an instance of obj_ramp_down at a **Relative** position of **X**=0, **Y**=1.

13. Follow this with a **Change Sprite** action (**main1** tab) that sets the **Sprite** to spr_jelly_down, the **Subimage** to -1, and the **Speed** to 0.2. The **Step** event for obj_jelly should now contain 14 actions, as shown in Figure 5–5.

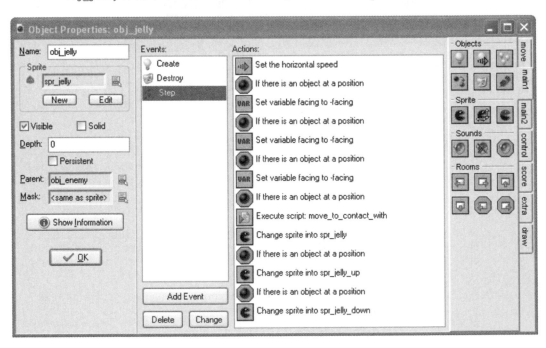

Figure 5–5. *The Step event of obj_jelly*

14. Add a **Collision** event with `obj_ramp` and include a **Set Variable** action (**control** tab) that sets the **Variable** y **Relative** to -2 (that is, moves it up a little).

15. Include an **Execute Script** action that sets **Script** to `move_to_contact_with`, **Argument0** to 270, **Argument1** to -1, and **Argument2** to `obj_solid`. Together with the previous action, this will move the Jelly up when climbing slopes.

So you now have your first enemy to obstruct Zool from completing his objective. Place a few more around the level and make sure that they cope with ramps correctly and that you can control their movement using the limiters. If in doubt, you can check your version against the file `zool9.gmk` from the `Chapter05/Games` directory on the CD.

> **Note** We're going to take you through the implementation of two more enemies in this chapter: the Sweet Beastie and the Bee. However, there is nothing particularly new to learn here, so if you find yourself suffering from drag-and-drop fatigue, then it probably won't hurt to just read through the steps and then load `zool10.gmk` for the completed Beastie and `zool11.gmk` for the completed Bee.

Beastly Licorice

Next on our list of enemies is the Sweet Beastie. According to the Zool manual, these are "*the meanest critters you will come across in the Sweet World. They not only get in your way, but launch a whole load of projectiles at you at any given opportunity.*" This will be a more complicated enemy that can face both left and right, so we will take a different approach from the Jelly and use a state machine to control its different behaviors (see Figure 5–6). Nonetheless, it is a fairly basic state machine, so we will only use a single object and handle all the states using a state variable. This enemy simply wanders back and forth along platforms like the Jelly, but occasionally stops in his tracks and shoots projectiles at Zool. In order to make him seem a little more "intelligent," we will only make him shoot when Zool is close by:

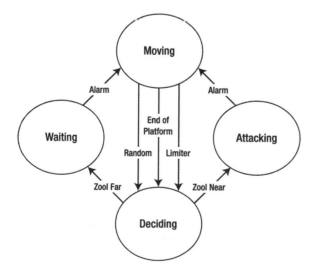

Figure 5–6. *The Beastie state machine diagram*

Creating the Sweet Beastie Object

1. Go to the **Resources** menu and select **Define Constants**. Add four new constants called ESTATE_WAIT, ESTATE_MOVE, ESTATE_DECIDE, and ESTATE_ATTACK and assign them the values 0 to 3, consecutively. If you don't have the Pro version of Game Maker, then you will need to define these as variables at the start of the **Create** event instead (in step three).

2. Create a new object called obj_beastie (Hazards group), give it spr_beastie_walk_right, and set its parent to obj_enemy.

3. Add a **Create** event and include a **Set Variable** action (**control** tab) that sets the **Variable** state to ESTATE_MOVE. This will be the starting state for the Beastie.

4. Include a second **Set Variable** action that sets the **Variable** facing to FACE_LEFT.

5. Include a third **Set Variable** action that sets the **Variable** image_speed to 0.2. This slows down the animation speed of the sprite without needing a **Change Sprite** action.

6. Add a **Destroy** event and include a **Set Variable** action that sets the **Variable** global.die_sprite_index to spr_beastie_die.

7. Include a **Call Parent Event** action that will thereby handle the rest of the process of creating dying enemy instances and the splat.

8. Add a **Draw** event. This will handle the drawing of the correct left- and right-facing sprites in different states in a similar way to the Zool object.

9. Include a **Test Variable** action that checks if the **Variable** facing is **equal to** FACE_LEFT.

10. Follow this with a **Start Block** action.

11. Include a **Test Variable** action that checks if the **Variable** state is **equal to** ESTATE_WAIT.

12. Follow this with a **Draw Sprite** action (**draw** tab) that draws spr_beastie_stand_left at a **Relative** position of **X**=0, **Y**=0.

13. Include a **Test Variable** action (**control** tab) that checks if the **Variable** state is **equal to** ESTATE_MOVE.

14. Follow this with a **Draw Sprite** action (**draw** tab) that draws spr_beastie_walk_left at a **Relative** position of **X**=0, **Y**=0.

15. Include another **Test Variable** action (**control** tab) that checks if the **Variable** state is **equal to** ESTATE_ATTACK.

16. Follow this with a **Draw Sprite** action that draws spr_beastie_attack_left at a **Relative** position of **X**=0, **Y**=0.

17. Follow this with an **End Block** action. Note that there is no case for ESTATE_DECIDE, as this state will automatically switch to ESTATE_MOVE or ESTATE_ATTACK before it is drawn.

18. Repeat steps 9-17 and create the right-facing equivalents. You should be able to handle this on your own by now. If you want to **Copy** and **Paste**, then try adding a **Comment** action (**control** tab) to the end of the list of actions first and pasting over that.

19. Add a **Step, Step** event and include a **Test Variable** action that checks if the **Variable** state is **equal to** ESTATE_WAIT. We're going to use the **Step** event to control the Beastie's state machine using the state variable, so there will be a check for each state in turn and a different set of behaviors for each one.

20. Follow this with a **Speed Horizontal** action (**move** tab) that sets **Hor. Speed** to 0. The wait state is the simplest state—the Beastie just stands still. There is no transition out of this state in the **Step** event, as we will handle this with an **Alarm** event in a moment.

21. Include a **Test Variable** action (**control** tab) that checks if the **Variable** state is **equal to** ESTATE_MOVE.

22. Follow this with a **Start Block** action. The move state is going to be more complicated.

23. Include a **Speed Horizontal** action (**move** tab) that sets **Hor. Speed** to facing. The basic behavior of the move state is simply that—moving. However, we also need to cope with transitions into other states when required.

24. Include a **Check Object** action (**control** tab) to check if there would **NOT** be a collision with an instance of obj_platform at a **Relative** position of **X**=facing*16, **Y**=1. This checks for when the Beastie has reached the end of the platform he is walking along.

25. Follow this with a **Set Variable** action that sets the **Variable** state to ESTATE_DECIDE. This is the default state for deciding what to do next.

26. Include a **Check Object** action to check if there would be a collision with an instance of obj_enemy_limit at a **Relative** position of **X**=facing*16, **Y**=0. The enemy limiter objects will turn Beastie enemies around too.

27. Follow this with a **Set Variable** action that sets the **Variable** state to ESTATE_DECIDE.

28. Include a **Test Chance** action with 150 **Sides**. We want the Beastie to randomly change state sometimes and at a room speed of 30 steps per second, we would expect this event to fire once every 5 seconds (on average).

29. Follow this with a **Set Variable** action that sets the **Variable** state to ESTATE_DECIDE.

30. Include an **End Block** action.

31. Include a **Test Variable** action that checks if the **Variable** state is **equal to** ESTATE_DECIDE. This is the state that will decide what to do next.

32. Follow this with a **Start Block** action.

33. Include a **Test Variable** action with point_distance(x,y,obj_zool.x, obj_zool.y) for **Variable, smaller than** for **Operation,** and 150 for **Value.** Make sure you type that first part of this very carefully with all the commas, dots, and parenthesis in the correct places, otherwise you'll get problems. Actually, this is not a variable at all, but Game Maker allows us to treat the result of a function like point_distance as a value. This function calculates the distance between two points, which in our case are x,y (the position of the Beastie) and obj_zool.x, obj_zool.y (the position of Zool).

34. Follow this with a **Set Variable** action that sets the **Variable** state to ESTATE_WAIT. Of course, this should really be ESTATE_ATTACK because we want the Beastie to shoot when Zool is closer than 150 pixels away. However, we're not going to add the attack state until a little later on, so we'll always just switch to the wait state for now and come back and change this later.

35. Follow this with an **Else** action.

36. Follow this with a **Set Variable** action that sets the **Variable** state to ESTATE_WAIT.

37. Include a **Set Alarm** action (**main2** tab) that sets **Alarm 0** to 30 **Steps.**

38. Include an **End Block** action (**control** tab). There should now be 20 actions in the **Step** event of obj_beastie, as shown in Figure 5–7. Notice how the actions for ESTATE_DECIDE occur after the actions for ESTATE_MOVE, which is the only way of getting into the ESTATE_DECIDE state. Also note that by the end of these ESTATE_DECIDE actions, it is impossible for the state to still be in ESTATE_DECIDE. This is important, as we have no sprite to draw for ESTATE_DECIDE, so it shouldn't ever finish in that state.

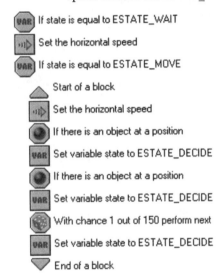

Figure 5–7. *The Step event of the Beastie object. Note that both of the state transitions from ESTATE_DECIDE go to ESTATE_WAIT at this stage*

39. Add an **Alarm, Alarm 0** event and include a **Check Object** action to check if there would **NOT** be a collision with an instance of obj_platform at a **Relative** position of **X**=facing*16, **Y**=1.

40. Follow this with a **Set Variable** action that sets the **Variable** facing to -facing. This turns the Beastie around at the end of the wait or attack states if he has reached the end of a platform.

41. Include a **Check Object** action to check if there would be a collision with an instance of obj_enemy_limit at a **Relative** position of **X**=facing*16, **Y**=0.

42. Follow this with a **Set Variable** action that sets the **Variable** facing to -facing.

43. Include a **Set Variable** action that sets the **Variable** state to ESTATE_MOVE.

Now place an instance of the Beastie in the room; the top of the second hill in front of the start point seems like a good place (see Figure 5–8). When you run the game, you should observe him walking back and forth along the top of his platform, pausing briefly to turn at each end and sometimes just randomly pausing as well. This gives the impression that he is a little bit on edge or is responding to something that the player might have done. We know it is just random behavior, but players will often project human-like characteristics onto computer enemies in this way. Next, we need to give this Beastie some teeth....

Figure 5–8. *The Beastie enemy guarding the top of the hill*

Spitting Mad

Life is about to get a lot more dangerous for our ninja friend, and there is a smell of aniseed in the air as his enemies start to spit missiles in his direction. These projectiles will bounce around the landscape for a while too, making them an even more lethal hazard.

Creating the Sweet Beastie Missiles

1. Create a new object called obj_beastie_missile (Hazards group), give it the spr_beastie_missiles sprite, and set its **Parent** to obj_hazard.

 2. Add a **Create** event and include a **Play Sound** action (**main1** tab) to play snd_enemy_missile.

 3. Include a **Change Sprite** action for spr_beastie_missiles that sets **Subimage** to random(image_number) and **Speed** to 0. This randomly selects one of the multicolored missile images and stops the sprite from animating.

 4. Include a **Set Gravity** action (**move** tab) that sets the **Gravity** to 1 in **direction** 270.

 5. Include a **Set Alarm** action (**main2** tab) that sets **Alarm 0** to 90 steps. This will be the lifespan of the missile (three seconds).

 6. Add an **Alarm, Alarm 0** event and include a **Destroy Instance** action (**main1** tab) to destroy **Self**.

 7. Add a **Step, Step** event and include a **Test Variable** action (**control** tab) that checks if the **Variable** speed is **larger than** 8. This is to make sure that the missile doesn't accelerate too fast under gravity and break the collision (discrete time sampling again).

 8. Include a **Set Variable** action that sets the **Variable** speed to 8.

 9. Add a **Collision** event with obj_platform and include a **Set Variable** action that sets x to xprevious. We're handling the collision with the platforms in the usual way, but we'll make the missiles bounce as well.

 10. Include a second **Set Variable** action that sets y to yprevious.

 11. Include an **Execute Script** action that sets **Script** to move_to_contact_with, **Argument0** to direction, **Argument1** to -1, and **Argument2 to** obj_solid.

 12. Include a **Reverse Vertical** action (**move** tab).

 13. Repeat steps 9-12 for collisions with obj_wall, but use the **Reverse Horizontal** action instead. Alternatively, you could duplicate and edit the platform collision event.

 14. Add a **Collision** event with obj_zool and include a **Destroy Instance** action (**main1** tab) for **Self**. The fact that the missile has obj_hazard as a parent already means that Zool will be hurt by missiles in the same way as the spikes, but unlike the spikes, we want the missiles to disappear on contact.

15. Now reopen obj_beastie and select the **Step** event.

16. Find the **Test Variable** action that uses the point_distance function. Edit the **Set Variable** action that comes directly after it to set state to ESTATE_ATTACK instead of ESTATE_WAIT.

17. At the end of the actions list, include a **Test Variable** action (**control** tab) that checks if the **Variable** state is **equal to** ESTATE_ATTACK.

 18. Follow this with a **Start Block** action.

 19. Include a **Speed Horizontal** action (**move** tab) that sets **Hor. Speed** to 0.

 20. Include a **Test Variable** action (**control** tab) with global.step_count mod 4 for **Variable**, **equal to** for **Operation,** and 0 for **Value**. This will now perform the next action every fourth step as we have done in a similar way before. This makes sure that there will be gaps in the stream of missiles coming from the Beastie.

 21. Include a **Create Moving** action (**main1** tab) that creates an instance of obj_beastie_missile at a **Relative** position of **X**=0, **Y**=-12 with a **Speed** of 6 and a **Direction** set to point_direction(0,0,facing,0). This last part is another function that provides the angle between two points. By using 0,0 and facing,0 as the two points, we are simply obtaining an angle for the facing direction (that is, 0 degrees for FACE_RIGHT and 180 degrees for FACE_LEFT).

22. Include an **End Block** action (**control** tab). There should now be 26 actions in the **Step** event for obj_beastie, as shown in Figure 5–9.

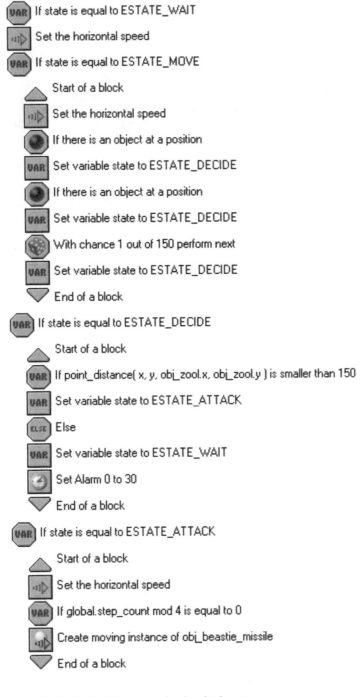

If state is equal to ESTATE_WAIT

Set the horizontal speed

If state is equal to ESTATE_MOVE

Start of a block

Set the horizontal speed

If there is an object at a position

Set variable state to ESTATE_DECIDE

If there is an object at a position

Set variable state to ESTATE_DECIDE

With chance 1 out of 150 perform next

Set variable state to ESTATE_DECIDE

End of a block

If state is equal to ESTATE_DECIDE

Start of a block

If point_distance(x, y, obj_zool.x, obj_zool.y) is smaller than 150

Set variable state to ESTATE_ATTACK

Else

Set variable state to ESTATE_WAIT

Set Alarm 0 to 30

End of a block

If state is equal to ESTATE_ATTACK

Start of a block

Set the horizontal speed

If global.step_count mod 4 is equal to 0

Create moving instance of obj_beastie_missile

End of a block

Figure 5–9. *The final Step event for the obj_beastie*

That's it for the Sweet Beastie, and you'll be pleased to know that that was the most complicated of the enemies we'll be adding to the game. See if you can get past him now that he is armed with this new weapon. If there are any problems with your version, then check it against the file zool10.gmk in Chapter05/Games on the CD.

Let it Bee

The final enemy we'll be tackling for the Sweet World are the Bees. These differ from the other enemies in that they can fly and will actively follow Zool around the level. This is actually much easier than it sounds, as Game Maker has built-in path-finding actions to help us do this. We will use states for the Bee, but it only has two alternating states—move and wait—so it isn't worth drawing a diagram. The bee will move very quickly for just a few steps and then hover for a while before it moves again. Unlike the original game, Bees won't actually try to touch Zool and will hover around him in order to give it the impression of a buzzing insect that is trying to size up Zool instead. Of course, that still makes it very easy to touch one accidently:

Creating the Bee Enemy Object

1. Create a new object called obj_bee (Hazards group), give it spr_bee_fly_right, and set its **Parent** to obj_enemy.

2. Add a **Create** event and include a **Set Variable** action (**control** tab) that sets the **Variable** state to ESTATE_MOVE.

3. Include a second **Set Variable** action that sets the **Variable** facing to FACE_LEFT.

4. Include a third **Set Variable** action that sets the **Variable** targetx to 0. We'll use this later to work out the position for which the Bee is heading.

5. Include a **Set Alarm** action (**main2** tab) that sets **Alarm 0** to 5 steps. The Bee will move quite fast, so five steps of movement will be plenty.

6. Add a **Destroy** event and include a **Set Variable** action (**control** tab) that sets the **Variable** global.die_sprite_index to spr_bee_die.

7. Include a **Call Parent Event** action that will thereby handle the rest of the process of creating dying enemy instances and the splat.

8. Add a **Draw** event. This will handle the drawing of the correct left- and right-facing sprites, although the Bee's appearance is the same in all states.

9. Include a **Test Variable** action that checks if the **Variable** facing is **equal to** FACE_LEFT.

10. Follow this with a **Draw Sprite** action (**draw** tab) that draws spr_bee_fly_left at a **Relative** position of X=0, Y=0.

11. Include a **Test Variable** action (**control** tab) that checks if the **Variable** facing is **equal to** FACE_RIGHT.

12. Follow this with a **Draw Sprite** action (**draw** tab) that draws spr_bee_fly_right at a **Relative** position of X=0, Y=0.

13. Add a **Step, Step** event and include a **Test Variable** action (**control** tab) that tests if state is **equal to** ESTATE_MOVE. Again, we will use the **Step** event to control the behaviors and transitions for each state.

14. Include a **Start Block** action.

15. Include a **Test Variable** action that tests if x is larger than obj_zool.x. In other words, this is testing whether the Bee is to the right of Zool. If it is, then we want it to aim for a target position just to the right of Zool.

16. Include a **Set Variable** action that sets targetx to obj_zool.x+32.

17. Include an **Else** action.

18. Include a **Set Variable** action that sets targetx to obj_zool.x-32.

19. Include a **Test Variable** action with point_distance(x,y,obj_zool.x,obj_zool.y) for **Variable**, **smaller than** for **Operation,** and 256 for **Value**. Flying Bees have no physical restrictions on their movement, but we don't want them to swarm in on Zool from all over the map, so this makes sure they only react to him as he gets close.

20. Include a **Step Avoiding** action (**move** tab) that steps toward the point X=targetx, Y=obj_zool.y, at a **Speed** of 10 and avoids **all instances**.

21. Include an **End Block** action (**control** tab).

22. Include a **Test Variable** action that tests if x is **larger than** obj_zool.x (again).

23. Follow this with a **Set Variable** action that sets facing to FACE_LEFT.

24. Include an **Else** action.

25. Follow this with a **Set Variable** action that sets facing to FACE_RIGHT. This last set of actions ensures that the Bee always faces Zool, even when hovering—adding to that buzzing insect feel. There should now be 13 actions in the **Step** event for obj_bee, as shown in Figure 5–10.

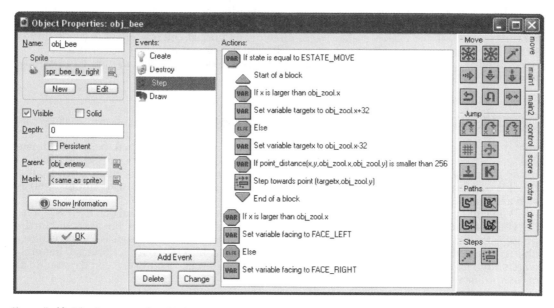

Figure 5–10. *The Step event for obj_bee*

 26. Add an **Alarm, Alarm 0** event and include a **Test Variable** action that tests if state is **equal to** ESTATE_WAIT.

 27. Include a **Start Block** action.

 28. Include a **Set Variable** action (**control** tab) that sets state to ESTATE_MOVE.

 29. Include a **Set Alarm** action (**main2** tab) that sets **Alarm 0** to 5 steps. This makes sure that the bee only moves for five steps again (1/6 of a second).

 30. Include an **End Block** action (**control** tab).

 31. Include an **Else** action.

 32. Include a **Start Block** action.

 33. Include a **Set Variable** action that sets state to ESTATE_WAIT.

 34. Include a **Set Alarm** action (**main2** tab) that sets **Alarm 0** to 30 steps. This makes sure that the bee waits for one second before moving again.

 35. Include an **End Block** action (**control** tab).

Space a few of the Bees around the level and check that they are working correctly. One of the nice side effects of Game Maker's path finding (around **all objects**) is that the Bees also avoid each other and sometimes end up buzzing round and round each other as they seem to fight to face off against Zool. Give your game a thorough play test to make sure everything works just as it should, and if you find any problems, then compare your version to zool11.gmk in the Chapter05/Games directory on the CD.

This is the last of the enemies we will be implementing, but the original game contained another kind of enemy that turned up just as frequently in the Sweet World. You will find sprites for the Wall Slob in the `Chapter06/Resources` directory on the CD, but it is left up to you to bring it to life. This creature is basically the same as a Jelly, but it goes vertically up walls instead of horizontally along platforms. It shouldn't be too difficult to duplicate the Jelly object and modify it for the Wall Slob.

Congratulations—Phase 3 Complete!

So that's it for another chapter. You've survived the forces of Krool and helped them to dominate the far reaches of the Sweet World. There are ninja-repelling spikes on every corner and ankle-biting Jellies sliding down every ramp. An army of walking licorice is spitting lethal candy from the skies, and swarms of Bees are poised to lock in on Zool's position. Hold on a minute—whose side are you on anyway?

You can't possibly leave now! It would be a crime to leave Zool alone and defenseless against the vile evil that *you've* just unleashed on the peaceful Sweet World. Besides, the next (and final) phase is the best yet by a long way. Ninja aliens are renowned for their combat skills and you're about to have the pleasure of teaching Zool the art of kicking butt ninja-style. Krool had better watch out because the Sweet world is about to get a lot less sweet. Of course, if you'd rather do a crossword or something, then I'm sure he'd understand....

■ ■ ■

CHAPTER 6

Fighting Talk:
The Empower Strikes Back

Clearly, it's high time our inter-dimensional friend went ninja on the asses of this particular line of confectionary. There's only so much disrespect one alien can take—particularly after consuming his own bodyweight in sugar and artificial colorings. There was only ever going to be one outcome from this confrontation, and it's going to produce the kind of wholesale massacre of candy that children will dream about for generations to come.

Okay, so we might be exaggerating a little. Nonetheless, our main goal will be to maintain the flow of Zool's movement around the level as he smashes his enemies into a shower of sugar-glazed fragments. If we do our job right, then this is when the game should suddenly become both more challenging and far more enjoyable at the same time.

Figure 6–1. *Zool: those swords are not for decoration, you know*

Ant Attack

In the original game, the precise mechanics of Zool's attack moves actually varied quite a bit between different platforms. As usual, we're not trying to be completely faithful to a particular version, but pick and choose features that work well with the Game Maker platform. There will be a number of new states to support jumping, kicking, spinning, and shooting attacks, but most of these will be incorporated into the existing state object structure. In fact, only one new state object needs to be created, and that's for the dying state.

Adding the New States to the Zool Object

1. Go to the **Resources** menu and select **Define Constants**. Insert three new constants for the new Zool states: ZSTATE_KICK, ZSTATE_SPIN, and ZSTATE_DEAD and assign them the values 8 to 10, consecutively. If you don't have the Pro version of Game Maker, then you will need to define these as variables in the **Create** event of obj_zool instead.

2. Reopen obj_zool and select the **Draw Event**.

3. Immediately before the **End Block** of the block of actions for facing right, include a **Test Variable** action (**control** tab) that tests if state is **equal to** ZSTATE_KICK.

4. Follow this with a **Draw Sprite** action (**draw** tab) that draws spr_zool_kick_right at a **Relative** position of X=0, Y=0.

5. Repeat steps 3-4 for ZSTATE_SPIN and ZSTATE_DEAD, using the appropriate sprites but the same other settings.

6. Repeat steps 3-5 within the block of actions for facing left using the corresponding left-facing sprites. You now have more actions in the **Draw** event than anyone cares to count and you'll be pleased to hear that that's the last of them!

Splitting Headache

Since the early beginnings of platform games, it has become accepted that even the most terrifying enemies that inhabit them are liable to roll over and die after the gentlest downward contact between their head and the player's feet. Strange as it is, it's a great game mechanic that worked for many games, and Zool was no exception. So we'll begin by changing the way we handle collisions between Zool and the enemies.

Adding Jump Attack Behavior to Zool

1. Reopen obj_zool and select the **Collision** event with obj_enemy. This event currently provides the same "jumping back and losing health" behavior for a collision with enemies that we already had for hazards. However, we actually only want this behavior to apply if Zool *isn't* jumping on the enemy's head.

2. Include a **Test Variable** action (**control** tab) at the very start of the list of actions that tests whether vspeed is **larger than** 0.

3. Immediately follow this with a **Start Block** action.

4. Follow this with a **Speed Vertical** action (**move** tab) that sets **Vert. Speed** to -14.

5. Follow this with a **Destroy Instance** action (**main1** tab) with **Applies to** set to **Other** (the enemy instance).

6. Follow this with a **Change Instance** action to `obj_zool_air` and **Perform events**.

7. Follow this with an **Exit Event** action (**control** tab).

8. Follow this with an **End Block** action.

Go on—give it a try and teach those stupid sweets a lesson. One of the nice side effects of the damage mechanic is that when you are hurt by an enemy, you get launched into the air and provided with the chance to get back at your enemy by landing on its head. Very satisfying! Don't play the game for too long though—there are more ways to bother a sweet coming up.

Slide Kick

Being of ninja persuasion, Zool was not just limited to using his feet on the heads of his enemies and it could often be more effective and satisfying to take out an entire row of enemies with a sliding kick. This will be activated by holding down the down arrow key while running or skidding on the ground. We've already paved the way for these with the new constants and **Draw** event actions completed earlier. We will make use of a new variable to indicate that Zool is attacking (either with a kick or a spin), as it will reduce the number of checks in different states.

Adding Kick Attack Behavior to Zool

1. Reopen `obj_zool`, `obj_zool_air`, `obj_zool_land`, `obj_zool_ice`, and `obj_zool_wall` in turn (that is, all of the Zool objects) and include a **Set Variable** action within each of their **Create** events that sets the **Variable** attacking to false. This makes sure that Zool is reset into a non-attacking mode whenever he changes state.

2. Reopen `obj_zool` and select the **Collision** event with `obj_enemy` again and include a **Test Variable** action immediately after the first **End Block** action. Use it to test if attacking is **equal to** true.

3. Immediately follow this with a **Start Block** action.

4. Follow this with a **Destroy Instance** action (**main1** tab) with **Applies to** set to **Other**.

5. Follow this with an **Exit Event** action (**control** tab).

6. Follow this with an **End Block** action. The **Collision** event with `obj_enemy` should now contain 23 actions, as shown in Figure 6–2.

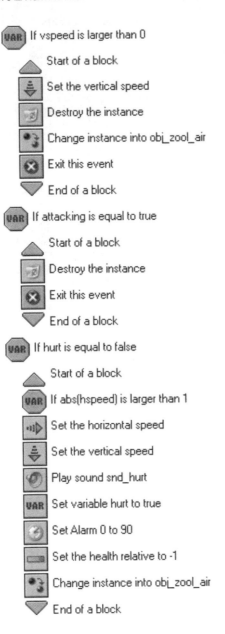

If vspeed is larger than 0

  Start of a block

  Set the vertical speed

  Destroy the instance

  Change instance into obj_zool_air

  Exit this event

  End of a block

If attacking is equal to true

  Start of a block

  Destroy the instance

  Exit this event

  End of a block

If hurt is equal to false

  Start of a block

  If abs(hspeed) is larger than 1

  Set the horizontal speed

  Set the vertical speed

  Play sound snd_hurt

  Set variable hurt to true

  Set Alarm 0 to 90

  Set the health relative to -1

  Change instance into obj_zool_air

  End of a block

Figure 6-2. The complete list of actions for the obj_zool Collision event with obj_enemy

7. Reopen `obj_zool_land` and add a **Keyboard, Down** event.

8. Include a **Test Variable** action (**control** tab) that tests if `state` is **NOT equal to** `ZSTATE_KICK`.

9. Include a **Start Block** action.

10. Include a **Set Variable** action that sets state to ZSTATE_KICK.

11. Include a **Set Variable** action that sets attacking to true.

12. Include a **Set Friction** action (**move** tab) that sets **Friction** to 0.67.

13. Include a **Test Variable** action (**control** tab) that checks if speed is **larger than** 2.

14. Follow this with a **Play Sound** action (**main1** tab) that plays snd_skid.

15. Include an **End Block** action (**control** tab).

16. Include a **Test Variable** action that tests if speed is **equal to** 0.

17. Follow this with a **Set Variable** action that sets image_index to 1. The kicking sprite has two images, one with the leg raised during the skid and one lowered for when Zool has come to a halt, so these actions will set the correct subimage.

18. Include an **Else** action.

19. Follow this with a **Set Variable** action that sets image_index to 0. The **Keyboard, Down** event should now have 12 actions in it, as shown in Figure 6–3.

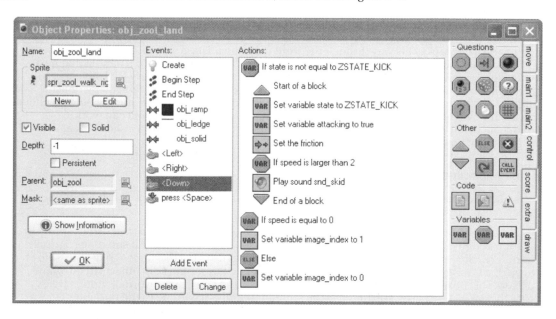

Figure 6–3. *The Keyboard, Down event for obj_zool_land*

20. Add a **Key Release, Down** event and include a **Set Friction** action (**move** tab) to set Friction to 1. This event restores the standard settings when the player releases the skid.

21. Include a **Set Variable** action (**control** tab) that sets state to ZSTATE_STAND.

22. Include a **Set Variable** action that sets hspeed to 0.

23. Include a **Set Variable** action that sets attacking to false.

24. Select the **Keyboard, Left** event and include a **Test Variable** action at the start of the actions list that tests if state is **NOT equal to** ZSTATE_KICK. We don't want the player to be able to walk and kick at the same time.

25. Immediately follow this with a **Start Block** action.

26. Include an **End Block** action at the end of the actions list for this event.

27. Repeat steps 24-26 for the **Keyboard, Right** event.

And now you can slide your way through multiple enemies at once. You can actually kill enemies both in front of and behind the skidding Zool (if they walk into you from behind, for example). You could fix this by making some additional tests, but we're choosing to put that down to the remarkable abilities of an inter-dimensional ninja.

Top Spinning

The cover artwork for Zool typically depicted him wielding some kind of glowing ninja swords in each hand as he kicked his way through the front of the box. These swords actually only seem to make an appearance in the spinning attack move, but it's pretty cool so we'll handle that next. While he's spinning, Zool will demolish any enemy in his path, so it is a very advisable way to travel. In fact, some versions of the game seemed to make Zool spin by default every time he jumped. We're not going to do that, but we will make it possible for him to spin by holding either the up or down arrow keys during a jump. This is actually quite intuitive and can work particularly well with the down arrow key if you want to move straight into a slide kick at the end of a spinning jump.

Adding Spinning Attack Behavior to Zool

1. Reopen obj_zool_air and change the **Sprite** to spr_zool_spin_right. It is not immediately obvious why this is necessary, so we'll explain.

Game Maker automatically handles the animation of sprites based on the current sprite. It cycles through all the frames of animation and then returns back to the first subimage again when it reaches the end. You can easily set the current sprite using the sprite_index variable or through a **Change Sprite** action, but actually we never do this for the Zool objects in our game. Instead, we chose to use the **Draw** event of obj_zool to draw the correct sprite for ourselves. Nonetheless, Game Maker still updates the animation frame according to the number of subimages in the default sprite (spr_zool_jump_right), but this only had one subimage—so it never actually changes. In order to make sure that the spinning sprite (which has four subimages) can animate properly, we need to use this as the default sprite instead. Try setting the sprite back to spr_zool_jump_right at the end of this sequence of steps if you need to prove it to yourself.

2. Add a **Keyboard, Down** event and include a **Set Variable** action (**control** tab) that sets state to ZSTATE_SPIN.

 3. Include a **Set Variable** action that sets attacking to true.

4. Right-click on the **Keyboard, Down** event and **Duplicate Event** as a **Keyboard, Up** event.

 5. Select the **End Step** event and include a **Test Variable** immediately after the **Start Block** action to test if state is **NOT equal to** ZSTATE_SPIN. We want the player to be able to spin while falling and jumping, so we don't want to override the state here. The actions for the **End Step** event should now look like those shown in Figure 6–4.

Now give your new ninja skills a whirl. One nice side effect of the way this works is that you tend to end up putting Zool into a spin when he automatically jumps at the top of a wall. This makes it easy to elegantly demolish any enemies waiting at the top in the process.

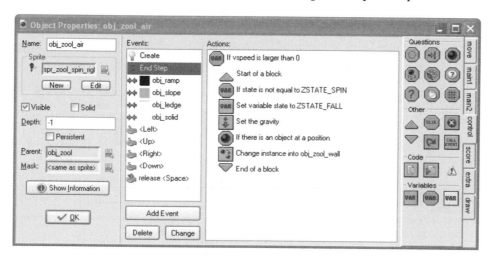

Figure 6–4. *The End Step event for obj_zool_air*

Shooting Stars

The ability to shoot is something fairly unusual for platform games, as it can potentially make them a bit too easy. Shooting was a core skill for Zool, so we felt it had to be included, but we wanted to do it without making it the dominant strategy. We tried out a range of controls, including using the up arrow key to jump and the space bar to shoot. Putting the shooting mechanic on the primary key (space bar) made it much easier to shoot, but turned the game into more of a platform-based shoot-'em-up. This wasn't what we wanted, so we decided that the primary key should be the jump key and there should be a secondary fire key. This makes the player use the shooting mechanic more sparingly and restores the prevalence of jumping as the core-mechanic of our platform game:

Adding Shooting Behavior to Zool

1. Create a new object called `obj_zool_missile` (Zool group) and give it the `spr_zool_missile` sprite.

2. Add a **Create** event and include a **Play Sound** action (**main1** tab) for `snd_shoot`.

3. Add a **Collision** event with `obj_enemy` and include a **Destroy Instance** action for **Other**.

4. Include a second **Destroy Instance** action for **Self**. We want missiles to destroy enemies, but the missile should be destroyed as part of the collision too.

5. Add a **Collision** event with `obj_solid` and include a **Destroy Instance** action for **Self**.

6. Add an **Other, Outside Room** event and include a **Destroy Instance** action for **Self**. We don't want missiles flying along forever when they will never come back into play.

7. Reopen `obj_zool` and add a **Key Press, Ctrl** event. Include a **Create Moving** action (**main1** tab) that creates an instance of `obj_zool_missile` at a **Relative** position of **X**=`facing*8`, **Y**=`0` with a **Speed** of `(facing*8)+hspeed` and a direction of `0`. We use this **X** position so that the missile appears just in front of Zool (rather than the center of Zool's body). Similarly, we use this **Speed** because we want the missile to move in the direction Zool is facing, but we need to add on Zool's moving speed, otherwise he could shoot bullets that are actually travelling slower than he is. We can always use a **Direction** of `0` because the speed of the bullet will be negative if it is moving left.

8. Reopen `obj_zool_wall` and add a **Key Press, Ctrl** event that includes an **Exit Event** action (**control** tab). As we have put the previous event in the parent object, it would be possible to shoot in all the different Zool states. However it doesn't really make sense for Zool to be able to shoot while climbing so this simply overrides the **Key Press** event with one that does nothing when Zool is in the wall state.

At this point, you should have a fighting-fit ninja to take on the enemies we created earlier. If you've not done so already, then now might be a good time to populate the level with a range of enemies and test out your ninja skills. As usual, you can save time by loading our version from the file `zool12.gmk` in the `Chapter06/Games` directory on the CD.

Uplifting Platforms

Up until now, we've avoided the concept of moving platforms as they are potentially quite tricky to implement. After all, they have to move the character as well as themselves and the character still needs to be able walk and jump across them as if his movement was relative to theirs. The easiest way to implement moving platforms is to have a platform of a fixed size, so that you are just working with a single platform object, but this isn't the way they worked in Zool. They were made up of individual segments, so that platforms could be constructed of any length. However, as you'll discover, this makes things trickier....

Up and Down

The good news is that making separate platform segments move vertically is not so hard. As the platforms themselves are horizontal, each segment can move vertically without having to worry about the segments on either side of them getting in the way. We're going to call our moving platforms "lifts" and make them children of obj_ledge, as we want to be able to jump up through the lifts and land on top of them. We're going to create separate objects for moving in different directions, as this makes the horizontal platforms possible later. We'll also create some limiter object for the lifts, like we did for the enemy objects.

Creating Vertical Lifts

1. Begin by defining a new constant called LIFT_SPEED that is set to 2. It's a good idea to declare constants in this way if you are going to use them in several different objects, as it saves you from having to find and edit all the different actions if you want to change the value. However, if you are using the Lite version, then just replace this constant with a "hard–coded" value of 2 when you see it in this list of steps.

2. Create a new object called obj_lift (create all of these lift-related objects in the Platforms, Lifts group) and set its **Parent** to obj_ledge.

3. Create a new object called obj_lift_vlimit, give it the spr_lift_vlimit sprite, and disable the **Visible** option.

4. Create two new objects called obj_lift_up and obj_lift_down. Give them the appropriate lift sprites, set their **Depth** to -1001, and their **Parent** to obj_lift.

5. Add a **Create** event to obj_lift_up and include a **Speed Vertical** action (**move** tab) that sets **Vert. Speed** to 0. The platforms will stand still for a while as they change direction.

6. Include a **Set Alarm** action (**main2** tab) that sets **Alarm 0** to 90 **Steps** (3 seconds). This alarm will start the platform moving again.

7. Add an **Alarm, Alarm 0** event and include a **Speed Vertical** action (**move** tab) that sets **Vert. Speed** to -LIFT_SPEED.

8. Add a **Collision** event with obj_solid and include a **Set Variable** action (**control** tab) that sets y to yprevious. We don't need to bother with x, as this platform doesn't move horizontally.

9. Include a **Change Instance** action (**main1** tab) that changes into obj_lift_down with **Perform events** set to yes.

10. Right-click on the **Collision** event with obj_solid and **Duplicate Event** to create an identical **Collision** event with obj_lift_vlimit. The same actions are required when colliding with the limiter, but limiters are not solid (otherwise Zool would start colliding with them too).

11. Repeat steps 5-10 for obj_lift_down, setting the **Vert. Speed** in the **Alarm 0** event to LIFT_SPEED and using obj_lift_up for the **Change Instance** action instead.

You can now add instances of either obj_lift_up or obj_lift_down to the test level in order to see their effects. Obviously, you will eventually want to avoid situations that would squash the player against the underside of a platform, so that's what obj_lift_vlimit is for. However, this is arbitrary at the moment, as Zool can't yet stand properly on the platforms. But before we do that we will tackle the trickier horizontal platform segments.

Left and Right

The basic problem with horizontal lift segments is that we expect them to move together in a long line, but the segment at the back of the line has no idea when the segment at the front of the line has collided with obj_solid. Our lift segments are children of obj_solid themselves, so you might think that when the segment at the front stops, the next segment would collide into it, and so on, until all the segments come to a halt. This is kind of true, but these collisions would actually happen in subsequent steps, producing a messy "train crash" effect. As a result, the **Alarm** event would get set in different steps and the line of segments would start breaking apart as they began moving again (try it if you like).

So what we need is the ability to instantly let all the segments in the line know that there has been a collision, so that they all can stop moving in the same step. One potential way to do this would be to apply a **Set Alarm** action to all lift objects at the same time (just by using the **Applies to** option on the top of the action form). Unfortunately, this would mean that all the lifts in the same room would receive the alarm and come to a halt, so unless we only have one horizontal lift on each level, then that won't work either.

A better solution is to use a *loop* to let all the adjacent segments know about the collision. We've used a **Repeat** action before to create multiple obj_enemy_die objects when an enemy dies, but it has all sorts of uses. We will use it here to repeatedly check along a line looking for other instances of the same lift object that are linked to the one that has collided. We then just need to change each one into an instance of the lift object that moves in the opposite direction.

Unfortunately, although Game Maker provides a **Check Object** action that we could use to check for adjacent instances, there is no way of calling **Change Instance** on that adjacent instance. What we need is an equivalent of the **Check Object** action that also provides us with the actual instance found. We then need an equivalent of the **Change Instance** action that can be called for another instance. Fortunately, both of these are easy to create using scripts that we can then apply in the horizontal lift objects to achieve the desired effect.

Creating Horizontal Lifts

1. Use the **Import Scripts** option (**Scripts** menu) to load check_object_returned.gml and change_instance_for.gml from the Chapter06/Resources directory on the CD. This will add these scripts to the **Scripts** folder in the resource tree.

2. Create a new object called obj_lift_hlimit (in the Platforms, Lifts group), give it the spr_lift_hlimit sprite, and disable the **Visible** option.

3. Create two new objects called obj_lift_left and obj_lift_right. Give them the appropriate lift sprites, set their **Depth** to -1001, and their **Parent** to obj_lift.

4. Add a **Create** event to obj_lift_left and include a **Speed Horizontal** action (**move** tab) that sets **Hor. Speed** to 0. The horizontal platforms will also stand still for a while as they change direction.

5. Include a **Set Alarm** action (**main2** tab) that sets **Alarm 0** to 90 **Steps**.

6. Add an **Alarm, Alarm 0** event and include a **Speed Horizontal** action (**move** tab) that sets **Hor. Speed** to –LIFT_SPEED.

7. Add a **Collision** event with obj_solid and include a **Set Variable** action (**control** tab) that sets horizontal_offset to 16. This is a new variable that we will use to keep track of how far to the left or right we are looking for platform segments.

8. Include a **Repeat** action with **Times** set to 10. Setting this number to 10 means that we will stop looking for adjacent platform segments after we have found 10—so platforms can't be longer than 10 segments. If you want longer platforms, then increase this.

9. Include a **Start Block** action.

10. Include an **Execute Script** action for the **Script** check_object_returned with **Argument0** set to obj_lift_left, **Argument1** set to horizontal_offset, **Argument2** set to 0, and **Argument3** set to true. The arguments for this script take the same form as the original **Check Object** action with the **Object** to check for first, followed by **X** and **Y** coordinates, and then an option to treat the co-ordinates as **Relative**. Therefore, initially this action checks for instances of obj_lift_left 16 pixels to the right of the current object. Significantly, though, this script creates a variable called returned that either contains the instance found or a negative value if no instance is found.

11. Include a **Test Variable** action that tests if returned is **larger than** 0. If the value is negative, then there are no more instances and we have reached the end of the line.

12. Include a **Start Block** action.

13. Follow this with another **Execute Script** action for the **Script** change_instance_for with **Argument0** set to returned, **Argument1** set to obj_lift_right, and **Argument2** set to true. The first argument is the instance to be changed. In the original **Change Instance** action, this could only be the current object, but our new script can be called on any instance. The remaining arguments take the same form as the original action with the object to **Change into** coming next, followed by an option for **Perform Events**. Therefore, this action changes the instance returned previously into an instance of obj_lift_right and performs **Destroy** and **Create** events.

14. Include a **Set Variable** action (**control** tab) that sets horizontal_offset **Relative** to 16. This moves the position we are checking 16 pixels along the line.

15. Include an **End Block** action.

16. Include a second **End Block** action.

17. Include a **Change Instance** action (**main1** tab) that changes into obj_lift_right with **Perform events**. There should now be 11 actions in the **Collision** event for obj_solid, as shown in Figure 6–5.

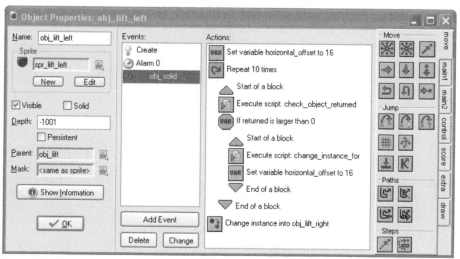

Figure 6–5. *The Collision event with obj_solid for obj_lift_left*

18. Right-click on the **Collision** event with `obj_solid` and **Duplicate Event** to create an identical **Collision** event with `obj_lift_hlimit`.

19. Add a **Destroy** event and include a **Set Variable** action (**control** tab) that sets x to xprevious. This was done in the **Collision** event for the up and down lifts, but *all* of the lift sections need to move back—not just the one that collided. Therefore, this action has been moved to the **Destroy** event that is then called by each lift segment as part of changing instance.

20. Repeat steps 4–19 for `obj_lift_right` or copy all the actions from each event in `obj_lift_left`. This time, set the **Hor. Speed** in the **Alarm 0** event to `LIFT_SPEED` and use `-16` for both of the `horizontal_offset` **Set Variable** actions. You'll also need to use `obj_lift_right` for **Argument0** of the `check_object_returned` script and `obj_lift_left` for **Argument1** of the `change_instance_for` script. Don't forget to **Change into** the `obj_lift_left` object in the last **Change Instance** action as well.

Now add a few horizontal lifts around the level and make sure that they work too. Bear in mind that there is nothing stopping moving enemies from walking onto moving platforms, so it's best to use some enemy limiters around the end points if that might be a possibility.

Relativity

Zool can already walk on top of the lift objects because they use `obj_ledge` as their **Parent**. However, he generally falls off as soon as they move because he is not physically carried along with them as if he was standing on their surface. To achieve this, we need to make Zool's movement relative to the movement of any lift he is standing on. Actually changing Zool's horizontal and vertical speed can be problematic, so it is easier to modify Zool's position directly by the movement speed of the lift in each step.

Making Lifts Lift

1. Reopen `obj_zool_land` and select the **Begin Step** event.

2. Include an **Execute Script** action (**control** tab) for the **Script** `check_object_returned` with **Argument0** set to `obj_lift`, **Argument1** set to `0`, **Argument2** set to `1`, and **Argument3** set to `true`. Therefore, this action checks for instances of `obj_lift` 1 pixel below Zool and puts the result into the `returned` variable.

3. Include a **Test Variable** action that tests if `returned` is **larger than** `0`.

4. Include a **Start Block** action.

5. Include a **Set Variable** action that sets x **Relative** to `returned.hspeed`. In other words, this is adding the platform's horizontal speed to Zool's position.

6. Include a **Set Variable** action that sets y **Relative** to `returned.vspeed`. In other words, this is adding the platform's vertical speed to Zool's position.

7. Include an **End Block** action. The **Begin Step** event of `obj_zool_land` should now contain eight actions, as shown in Figure 6–6.

8. Select the **End Step** event and reopen the **Check Object** action that appears directly before the **Execute Script** action that calls `move_to_contact_with`. Recall that this action is checking a little bit further beneath Zool's feet to see if there is a platform close enough to move down onto automatically without falling. We need this to be a bit more generous for use with our lifts, so change **Y** to `max(speed,LIFT_SPEED+1)`. In other words, this action will look at least 3 pixels below Zool's feet and further if he is moving faster.

Now run the game and try standing on the lifts again.

■**Note** If you're observant, then you'll have noticed that there is a tiny lag in the movement of Zool compared to the platforms. This is because Zool checks the movement speed of the lift he is standing on in his **Begin Step** event, but the lifts start moving in the **Alarm** event and stop moving in the **Collision** event—both of which occur after the **Begin Step** in the order of events. That means Zool's speed is always one step behind, and this creates the lag. You could solve this by moving the preceding actions into the **End Step** event, but be wary of doing so. This would mean we were moving Zool after his collisions have been resolved and so it would potentially allow lifts to push him into the landscape and get him stuck.

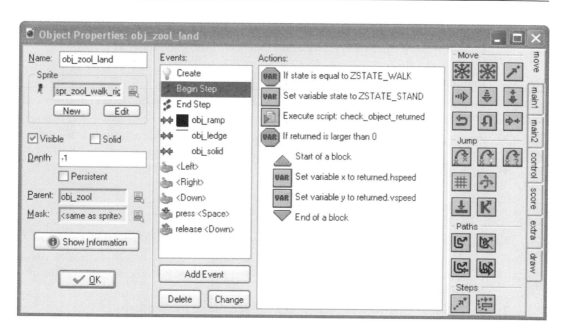

Figure 6–6. *The Begin Step event of obj_zool_land*

Not So Solid Ground

Falling platforms are another common feature in platform games. In Zool, these resemble static lifts, but fall away beneath the player's feet a moment or two after the player stands on them. This keeps the player on their toes and makes sure they keep moving. We'll also make them respawn after a certain amount of time to give the player another chance at getting through a tricky set of falling platforms.

Creating Falling Platforms

1. Create a new object (Platforms, Lifts group) called obj_ledge_fall, give it the spr_ledge_fall sprite, the obj_ledge **Parent**, and set **Depth** to -1001.

 2. Add a **Create** event and include a **Set Variable** action (**control** tab) that sets falling to false.

 3. Add a **Step, Step** event and include a **Check Object** action to check if there would be a collision with an instance of obj_zool at a **Relative** position of X=0, Y=-16.

 4. Follow this with a **Test Variable** action that tests if falling is **equal to** false.

 5. Follow this with a **Start Block** action.

 6. Include a **Set Variable** action that sets falling to true.

 7. Include a **Set Alarm** action (**main2** tab) that sets **Alarm 0** to 30 **Steps**.

 8. Include an **End Block** action (**control** tab).

 9. Add an **Alarm, Alarm 0** event and include a **Set Gravity** action (**move** tab) that sets **Gravity** to 3 in **Direction** 270.

 10. Add an **Other, Outside Room** event and include a **Test Variable** action (**control** tab) that tests if falling is **equal to** true.

 11. Include a **Start Block** action.

12. Include a **Set Variable** action that sets falling to false.

13. Include a **Set Gravity** action (**move** tab) that sets **Gravity** to 0 in **Direction** 270.

14. Include a **Set Variable** action (**control** tab) that sets speed to 0. This is another way of stopping an instance dead.

15. Include a **Set Alarm** event (**main2** tab) that sets **Alarm 1** to 300 **Steps**.

16. Include an **End Block** action (**control** tab).

17. Add an **Alarm, Alarm 1** event and include a **Jump to Start** action (**move** tab).

At this point, you should now be in a position to create the final layout of your test level including all of the enemies, platforms, and collectibles. You can either take some time to do this for yourself or load the file zool13.gmk from the Chapter06/Games directory on the CD.

Parallax Universe

Parallax scrolling can help to add depth to the look of a 2D platform game by making the background appear to move at a slightly slower rate from the foreground. You can use multiple layers of parallax backgrounds to represent objects from the near to far distance to amplify the 3D effect. Some versions of the original Zool game applied this technique, so we're going to add it to ours next. The spr_clouds sprite (Misc group) contains seven images that are designed to represent background objects from the near distance to the horizon (see Figure 6–7). Notice that each of these is designed to be repeated horizontally, so the right side of the first image has a small piece of the purple blob from the left side of the image. They are also all 512 pixels wide, which is the width of our screen view into the room, and all but the first image is 32 pixels high.

When you normally assign a background to a room, it automatically appears to move as the view scrolls around the screen, but of course it is actually the view that is moving and the background is staying still. Parallax backgrounds are more complicated, as the backgrounds themselves need to move relative to the view position, and the amount they should move is different depending on how far away each background layer is supposed to be. This mimics the real world, where if you are walking along on a hilltop path looking at a town in the distance, then the position of that town appears to remain fairly static while nearby objects along the path seem to move by much more quickly.

To keep the work Game Maker has to do to a minimum, we're only going draw the clouds around the view itself (see Figure 6–8) and adjust their position as the view moves around the level. This may sound tricky, but it can be done using just one object.

Figure 6–7. *The parallax scrolling background sprite and its subimages*

Creating a Cloud Object:

1. Create a new object called obj_clouds, (Misc group) give it the spr_clouds sprite, and set its **Depth** to 10000 (behind everything).

2. Add a **Draw** event. Next, we're going to create some variables that aren't strictly necessary, but will aid in your understanding. The first four of these provide the left, right, top, and bottom boundaries of the view in the room.

3. Include a **Set Variable** action (**control** tab) that sets view_left to view_xview[0]. The variable view_xview[0] holds the x position of **view0** in the room. This is the left boundary of the view area the clouds need to cover.

4. Include a **Set Variable** action that sets view_right to view_left+view_wview[0]. The variable view_wview[0] holds the width of **view0**. By adding the width, we get the right boundary of the view area.

5. Include a **Set Variable** action that sets view_top to view_yview[0]. Yes, the variable view_yview[0] holds the y position of **view0** in the room, making it the top boundary of the view area.

Figure 6–8. *The clouds will actually only be drawn behind the view area that the player can see and not behind the rest of the room*

6. Include a **Set Variable** action that sets view_bottom to view_top+view_hview[0]. By adding the height of the view, we get the bottom boundary of the view area.

7. Include a **Set Variable** action that sets x to view_left. This makes the cloud object's horizontal position follow the view's horizontal position.

8. Include a **Set Variable** action that sets y to `view_bottom-80`. This makes the cloud object's vertical position follow a position 80 pixels above the bottom of the view. This will become the vertical position of the first cloud layer.

9. Include a **Set Variable** action that sets `parallax_y` to 0. This will eventually be used to provide some vertical parallax movement, but for now we'll set it to 0.

10. Include a **Set Color** action (**draw** tab). Click on the menu next to **Color** and select **Define Custom Colors** to define a new color with **Red**=224, **Green**=224 and **Blue**=248.

11. Include a **Draw Rectangle** action that draws a **Filled** rectangle from **X1**=`view_left`, **Y1**=y to **X2**=`view_right`, **Y2**=`view_bottom`. This colors the lower area of the view below the first cloud layer in a light blue color that matches its bottom edge.

12. Include a **Set Variable** action (**control** tab) that sets `cloud_index` to 0. We will use this variable to move sequentially through the different cloud layer images as we draw them.

13. Include a **Repeat** action that repeats the following block of actions 7 **Times** (once for each image in the cloud sprite).

14. Include a **Start Block** action.

15. Include a **Set Variable** action that sets `parallax_x` to 0. This will eventually be used to provide some horizontal parallax movement.

16. Include a **Draw Sprite** action (**draw** tab) that draws `spr_clouds` at a **Relative** position of **X**=`parallax_x`, **Y**=`parallax_y` with the **Subimage** `cloud_index`. As we haven't done anything with the parallax values yet, this will just draw the sprite image at the cloud object's current position.

17. Include a **Set Variable** action (**control** tab) that sets y **Relative** to -32. In other words, move the y position up 32 pixels, ready to draw the next cloud layer sprite.

18. Include a **Set Variable** action that sets `cloud_index` **Relative** to 1. This moves to the next sprite before repeating the block.

19. Include an **End Block** action.

20. Include a **Set Color** action (**draw** tab). Click on the menu next to **Color** and select **Define Custom Colors** to define a new color with **Red**=40, **Green**=4 and **Blue**=72.

21. Include a **Draw Rectangle** action that draws a **Filled** rectangle from **X1**=`view_left`, **Y1**=0 to **X2**=`view_right`, **Y2**=y+32. This colors the upper area of the view above the last cloud layer in a dark blue color that matches the top edge of the last sprite image.

Hopefully you can see from this how we've used a **Repeat** action in combination with the `cloud_index` variable to draw the successive cloud layers on top of each other. Now place an instance of `obj_clouds` in the test room and run the game. This should provide you with a cloud background that appears to stay still as you run around the level, but of course the clouds must actually be moving in the room (following the view) in order to look like they are standing still. Next, we're going to add some parallax.

Adding Parallax to the Cloud Object

1. Reopen obj_clouds and edit the **Set Variable** action that sets parallax_y to 0 and set it to -view_top/2 instead. This parallax value gets subtracted from the vertical drawing position of the cloud sprites so it will draw them further up, as the view itself moves further down in the room. This is what you would expect: as your view moves up, the thing you are looking at moves down with respect to that view. However, as the value is divided by two, the clouds move up and down at half the speed of the view, giving the impression that they are further away than the foreground objects.

2. Edit the first **Draw Rectangle** action and set **Y1** to y+parallax_y, as we now need to take the parallax into account too.

3. Edit the **Set Variable** action that sets parallax_x to 0 (at the start of the repeated block) and set it to -view_left/(cloud_index+2) instead. This parallax value gets subtracted from the horizontal drawing position of the cloud sprites so it will draw them further toward the left, as the view itself moves further right in the room. This time, the value is divided by cloud_index+2, where cloud_index starts at 0 and increases by one for each cloud layer. So the first layer of clouds moves horizontally at 1/2 the speed of the view, but the second moves at 1/3 the speed, the third at one 1/4, and so on. In this way, we get multiple levels of horizontal parallax that move less, and thus appear to be further away as the clouds get higher up the screen.

4. Edit the final **Draw Rectangle** action and set **Y2** to y+parallax_y+32.

If you play the game now, then things aren't quite there yet. However, you can clearly see these multiple levels of parallax in action, as the cloud layers separate like a staircase as you move across the level because of their differing movement speeds. Of course, this isn't what we want, and there is one last problem to solve. Our cloud sprites are only 512 pixels long, but so is our view so we're going to need to repeat the sprite in order to make it look like the clouds are continuous. However, even with two lengths of cloud, we're going to eventually reach the end of them, so we also need to get them to wrap around. In other words, once the length of cloud disappears off one side of the view, it needs to jump back to the other side of the view ready to come on again. That way, the clouds can continue to scroll indefinitely.

Adding Parallax to the Cloud Object

1. Reopen obj_clouds. Directly before the **Draw Sprite** action, include a **Set Variable** action (**control** tab) that sets parallax_x to parallax_x mod 512. Recall that the mod operator divides the left value by the right value, and then provides the remainder, so it will always produce a number between 0 and 511. As soon as it reaches 512, it will return to 0 and start again, producing our wrapping effect for us.

2. Follow this with another **Draw Sprite** action (**draw** tab) that draws the spr_clouds **Sprite** again, but this time at a **Relative** position of **X**=parallax_x+512, **Y**=parallax_y with the **Subimage** cloud_index. This is just directly to the right of the other sprite.

And that's it— you should now have a parallax scrolling background that significantly improves the look of the game. If there is any problem with your version, then load the file zool14.gmk from the Chapter06/Games directory on the CD. If you're still a bit confused as to what is actually going on to achieve this effect, then take a look at zool14a.gmk on the CD as well. This version is set up to allow you to see much more of the room as Zool moves about the level and you can see the wrapping effect of the clouds in action. It looks very strange in this view, but the player is usually completely oblivious to what is going on to achieve this effect.

Keeping Score

All that remains to complete our version of Zool is a user interface and one or two housekeeping tasks relating to health and lives. We're going to create a range of different icon objects that handle their own **Step** and **Draw** events for whatever it is they are displaying on the interface. Many of these need to display numbers (score, lives, and so forth), but we're not going to use a Game Maker font for this. Instead, we will display our own numbers using the subimages of the `spr_digits` sprite to represent the digits.

Adding the Score Object

1. Create a new object in the `Icons` group called `obj_score`. Give it the `spr_icon_score` **Sprite** and set its **Depth** to -2000, so that it appears in front of everything in the room.

2. Add a **Draw** event. The first thing we're going to do is move the current position to the top left corner of the view. That way, whenever we draw anything on the screen, we can just check the **Relative** option and it will follow the view around and appear static on the screen as far as the player is concerned.

3. Include a **Set Variable** action (**control** tab) that sets x to `view_xview[0]`.

4. Include a **Set Variable** action that sets y to `view_yview[0]`.

5. Include a **Draw Sprite** action (**draw** tab) that draws `spr_icon_score` at a **Relative** position of **X**=30, **Y**=20. So that is 30 pixels across and 20 pixels down from the top left corner of the view.

6. Include a **Set Variable** action (**control** tab) that sets the **Variable** digit to the **Value** 6. Scores in the original Zool could go up to 100000 (6 digits) and lower values would be preceded by 0s, so that the value 500 is displayed as 000500. Doing this requires a bit of playing around with numbers and text strings. Remember that you can use Game Maker variables to store either, but that doesn't mean you can use a text string as if it was a number or vice versa. Fortunately, Game Maker provides a whole range of functions to convert between them.

7. Include a **Set Variable** action that sets `text_string` to `string_format(score,digit,0)`. This is a function that turns the first numerical value (`score`) into a text string that is made up of the number of characters in the second value (`digit`). The third value is used to specify the number of places after the decimal point, but we don't want fractional scores, so we set this to 0. So, for example, if `score` was 500 and `digit` was 6, then it would produce the text string " 500", which is a string containing 3 spaces followed by the character "5", and two of the character "0". Significantly, it is no longer a number but a piece of text containing the symbols representing the number.

8. Include a **Set Variable** action. This time we're taking the output of the last function and altering it. Set `text_string` to `string_replace_all(text_string," ","0")`. Note that there is a single space between the first set of quotation marks. This function looks for characters in the first string (`text_string`) that match the second string (the space character " ") and replaces them with the third string ("0"). So to continue the example, if `text_string` was " 500" to begin with, then it would become "000500".

9. Include a **Repeat** action that repeats the following block of actions digit **Times**. This loop of actions will draw each digit of the score in turn.

10. Include a **Start Block** action.

11. Include a **Set Variable** action that sets the **Variable** digit_string to string_char_at(text_string,digit). This function gets a single character from the first string (text_string) at a position determined by the second value (digit). So if digit was 4 and text_string was "000500", then it would get the fourth character in the string, which is "5". Note that this is still a string rather than a numerical value.

12. Include a **Draw Sprite** action (**draw** tab) that draws spr_icon_digits at a **Relative** position of X=44+(16*digit), Y=20 and a **Subimage** of real(digit_string). Notice that the horizontal position of the sprite will move across by 16 pixels (the width of the sprite) for each digit. The digit sprite contains the numbers 0-9 in sequential subimages. So the real function simply turns the string that contains the digit back into a numerical value so that it can be used to select the correct subimage of the sprite.

13. Include a **Set Variable** action (**control** tab) that sets digit **Relative** to -1.

14. Include an **End Block** action. There should now be 12 actions in the **Draw** event of obj_score, as shown in Figure 6–9.

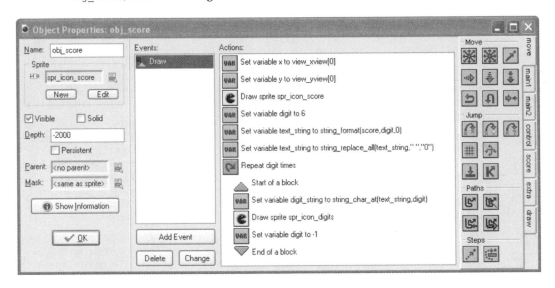

Figure 6–9. *The Draw event of obj_score*

15. Reopen obj_controller and select the **Create** event.

16. Include a **Create Instance** action (**main1** tab) that creates an instance of obj_score. There is no need to set position values, as the object will handle this itself.

If you run the game now, then you should see a score appearing in the top left corner of the screen. The original game also kept track of the high score on the top right. We're not going to take you through the steps of doing this, but if you want to then you can simply duplicate the score object and change the position and icons. The highscore_value(1) function will provide you with the top position on the standard Game Maker high-score table, but you'll need to integrate the table itself into the game too if you want to see this value update. In our version, you'll see that we've just made the high score display the score as well, for the time being. Next up is the timer object, which keeps track of the amount of time left to complete the level.

■**Note** For the remainder of this chapter, we're going to take you step-by-step through the implementation of the other user interface items: the timer, collection counter, health display, and lives counter. However, they all follow a very similar structure, so feel free to spare your mouse finger and just read the steps provided before loading zool15.gmk at the very end of the chapter.

Adding the Timer Object

1. Duplicate obj_score to create a new object called obj_time that uses spr_icon_time.

2. Add a **Create** event and include a **Set Variable** action (**control** tab) that sets time_allowed to 200. We have just hard-coded the default number of seconds to complete each level, but you could make this a global variable, or even a constant.

3. Include a **Set Variable** action that sets time_remaining to time_allowed.

4. Add a **Step, Step** event and include a **Set Variable** action that sets time_remaining to time_allowed-(global.step_count/room_speed). The room_speed variable stores the number of steps in a second for this room (as set in the Room settings tab).

5. Include a **Test Variable** action that tests if time_remaining is **smaller than** 0.

6. Follow this with a **Restart Room** action (**main1** tab).

7. Select the **Draw** event.

8. Edit the third **Set Variable** action for digit and replace 6 with 3.

9. Edit the fourth **Set Variable** action for text_string and replace score with time_remaining.

10. Edit the first **Draw Sprite** action for spr_icon_score and set it to draw spr_icon_time at a **Relative** position of **X**=230, **Y**=280.

11. Edit the second **Draw Sprite** action for spr_icon_digits and change the position to **X**=240+(16*digit), **Y**=280.

12. Reopen obj_controller and include a **Create Instance** action in its **Create** event that creates an instance of obj_time.

Note that obj_time actually includes the actions restarting the level when time runs out, so if you wanted to play the game without the time limit, then you can simply choose not to put obj_time in the room.

Next, we consider the collectibles. These items are closely linked with completing each level, as the exit does not appear until a certain percentage of them have been collected. Exits were often placed in hard-to-reach positions, so once activated, the interface also provides a kind of "compass" that points in the direction of the exit.

Adding the Collectibles Object and Exit

1. Create a new object (Misc group) called obj_exit and give it the spr_exit sprite.

 2. Add a **Create** event and include a **Set Variable** action (**control** tab) that sets image_speed to 0.5. This halves the animation speed of the exit sprite.

3. Select the obj_score object and right-click to **Duplicate** the object. Call the new object obj_collect_count and give it the spr_icon_collect sprite.

 4. Add a **Create** event and include a **Set Variable** action that sets image_speed to 0. This stops the sprite from animating, as only the first image of the sprite contains the initial collectibles icon and the remaining nine are the compass pointers used later on.

 5. Add a **Set Variable** action that sets collect_total to instance_number(obj_collect). This is a function that provides the total number of instances of a particular object on the current level, a bit like the **Test Instance Count** action.

 6. Include a **Set Variable** action that sets collect_percent to 0.

 7. Add a **Set Variable** action that sets obj_exit.visible to false. This hides the exit at the start of the level. Again, this is done in the collect object so that the exit only gets hidden when the user interface is turned on.

 8. Add a **Step, Step** event and include a **Set Variable** action that sets collect_current to collect_total-instance_number(obj_collect). In other words, the number of items collected is the total number to start with minus the number remaining on the level.

 9. Include a **Set Variable** action that sets collect_percent to (collect_current*100)/collect_total. This turns the number collected into a percentage from 0 to 100.

 10. Include a **Test Variable** action that tests if collect_percent is larger than 75. We have just hard-coded the percentage of items that need to be collected before the exit is revealed, but you could make this a global variable, or even a constant.

 11. Include a **Start Block** action.

 12. Add a **Set Variable** action that sets obj_exit.visible to true. This reveals the exit.

13. Add a **Set Variable** action that sets exit_direction to point_direction(obj_zool.x,obj_zool.y,obj_exit.x,obj_exit.y). Remember, this function provides the angle from one position toward another, in this case **X1**=obj_zool.x,**Y1**= obj_zool.y and **X2**=obj_exit.x,**Y2**=obj_exit.y.

 14. Add a **Set Variable** action that sets image_index to 1+round(exit_direction/45). The angle stored in exit_direction will be in the range 0-360, so dividing it by 45 will give a value between 0-8 that maps onto the appropriate compass image. The round function rounds fractions up to the nearest whole number.

15. Include an **End Block** action. The **Step** event for obj_collect_count should now have the eight actions shown in Figure 6–10.

VAR Set variable collect_current to collect_total-instance_number(obj_collect)

VAR Set variable collect_percent to (collect_current*100)/collect_total

VAR If collect_percent is larger than 75

△ Start of a block

VAR Set variable obj_exit.visible to true

VAR Set variable exit_direction to point_direction(obj_zool.x,obj_zool.y,obj_exit.x,obj_exit.y)

VAR Set variable image_index to 1+round(exit_direction/45)

▽ End of a block

Figure 6–10. *The actions that make up the Step event of obj_collect_count*

16. Select the **Draw** event.

17. Edit the third **Set Variable** action that sets `digit` to 6 and set it to 2 instead. We'll represent numbers under 10% with a 0 at the start.

 18. Follow this with a new **Test Variable** action that tests if `collect_percent` is **equal to** 100.

 19. Follow this with a new **Set Variable** action that sets `digit` to 3. We'll use an extra digit to represent 100%.

20. Edit the next **Set Variable** action for `text_string` and replace `score` with `collect_percent`.

21. Edit the first **Draw Sprite** action for `spr_icon_score` and set it to draw `spr_icon_collect` at a **Relative** position of **X**=25, **Y**=280 and **Subimage** `image_index`.

 22. Include a new **Draw Sprite** action (**draw** tab) immediately before the **Repeat** action that draws `spr_icon_percent` at a **Relative** position of **X**=56+(16*digit), **Y**=280.

23. Edit the final **Draw Sprite** action for `spr_icon_digits` and change the position to **X**=40+(16*digit), **Y**=280. The **Draw** event for `obj_collect_count` should now contain the 15 actions shown in Figure 6–11.

155

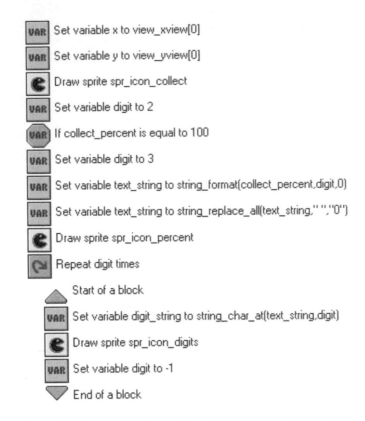

VAR Set variable x to view_xview[0]

VAR Set variable y to view_yview[0]

e Draw sprite spr_icon_collect

VAR Set variable digit to 2

VAR If collect_percent is equal to 100

VAR Set variable digit to 3

VAR Set variable text_string to string_format(collect_percent,digit,0)

VAR Set variable text_string to string_replace_all(text_string," ","0")

e Draw sprite spr_icon_percent

↻ Repeat digit times

△ Start of a block

VAR Set variable digit_string to string_char_at(text_string,digit)

e Draw sprite spr_icon_digits

VAR Set variable digit to -1

▽ End of a block

Figure 6–11. *The actions that make up the Draw event of obj_collect_count*

24. Finally, reopen obj_controller and include a **Create Instance** action in its **Create** event that creates an instance of obj_collect_count.

You can now place an instance of obj_exit in the room in a suitable position (in mid-air at the end of the slope perhaps?) and check that it works correctly. Of course, nothing will happen when you collide with the exit as we've not created an event for that. There's nowhere for Zool to go yet, so this is something you would need to come back to when you have more levels. Finally, for this chapter, we'll deal with health, lives, and the sad, but inevitable demise of the interstellar dweller we've come to know and love:

Adding the Health and Lives

1. Create a new object called obj_zool_dead (Zool group), with the spr_zool_die_left sprite, a **Depth** of -1, and obj_zool as its **Parent**.

2. Add a **Create** event and include a **Set Variable** action (**control** tab) that sets state to ZSTATE_DEAD. We handled the drawing of Zool in his dead state back at the start of the chapter (if you can remember back that far).

3. Include a **Set Gravity** action (**move** tab) that sets **Gravity** to 0 in **Direction** 0.

4. Include a **Set Variable** action (**control** tab) that sets speed to 0. These actions should bring Zool to a complete and permanent halt.

 5. Include a **Play Sound** event (**main1** tab) that plays snd_die.

 6. Add an **Other, Animation End** event and include a **Set Variable** action (**control** tab) that sets visible to false. This hides Zool once his dying animation is complete.

 7. Include a **Test Variable** action that checks if lives is **equal to** 0.

 8. Include a **Start Block** action.

 9. Include a **Set Variable** action that sets lives to 3.

 10. Include a **Restart Room** action (**main1** tab) that uses **Fade out and in** to imply that it is "Game Over."

 11. Include an **End Block** action (**control** tab).

 12. Include an **Else** action.

13. Include a **Start Block** action.

 14. Include a **Set Variable** action that sets lives **Relative** to -1.

 15. Include a **Restart Room** action (**main1** tab) that uses **Interlaced from bottom**.

 16. Include an **End Block** action (**control** tab).

 17. Reopen obj_zool and add an **Other, Room Start** event that includes a **Set Variable** action to set health to 3. Zool will have three bars of health for each life.

 18. **Create an Other, Game Start** event that includes a **Set Variable** action that sets lives to 3. He will have three lives to begin with.

 19. Create a new object called obj_health (Icons group), give it spr_icon_health, and set **Depth** to -2000.

 20. Add a **Step, Step** event and include a **Test Variable** action to test if health is **equal to** 0.

 21. Follow this with another **Test Variable** action that tests if obj_zool.state is **NOT equal to** ZSTATE_DEAD (if you are using Game Maker Lite, then replace ZSTATE_DEAD with 10).

 22. Follow this with a **Change Instance** action (**main1** tab) that **Applies to** the **Object** obj_zool and changes into obj_zool_dead while performing events. We're handling this in the health object rather than Zool again so that he only dies when a health object is in the room.

 23. Add a **Draw** event and include a **Set Variable** action (**control** tab) that sets x to view_xview[0].

24. Include a **Set Variable** action that sets y to view_yview[0].

25. Include a **Set Variable** action that sets unit to 0.

26. Include a **Repeat** action that repeats the following block of actions health **Times**.

27. Include a **Start Block** action.

28. Include a **Draw Sprite** action (**draw** tab) for spr_icon_health at the **Relative** position of X=224+(32*unit), Y=20.

29. Include a **Set Variable** action (**control** tab) that sets unit **Relative** to 1.

30. Include an **End Block** action.

31. Create a new object (Icons group) called obj_lives, give it the spr_icon_lives **Sprite**, and set its **Depth** to -2000.

32. Add a **Draw** event and include a **Set Variable** action that sets x to view_xview[0].

33. Include a **Set Variable** action that sets y to view_yview[0].

34. Include a **Draw Sprite** action (**draw** tab) for spr_icon_lives at the **Relative** position of X=490, Y=280.

35. Include another **Draw Sprite** action for spr_icon_digits at the **Relative** position of X=460, Y=280 and **Subimage** of lives. This will draw the appropriate digit for the number of lives Zool has left.

36. Finally, reopen obj_controller and include a **Create Instance** action (**main1** tab) in its **Create** event that creates an instance of obj_health.

37. Include another **Create Instance** action that creates an instance of obj_lives.

Zoolaphobia

Unbelievably, there is just one final action to add to our game to complete it—so what are we missing? Well, the original Zool had some brilliantly wacky music tracks to accompany the game that were ably composed by Patrick Phelan on the music tracker systems of the day. Patrick's auntie actually worked at the Bassets sweet factory in Sheffield, so it's nice to think that this music might have been written after consuming a particularly large amount of free Jelly Babies. It fits the game perfectly and brings our current journey to a fitting conclusion.

Adding Music to the Game

1. Create a new Sound resource using the file snd_music from the Chapter06/Resources directory on the CD.

2. Reopen obj_zool and select the **Game Start** event. Include a **Play Sound** action (**main1** tab) to play snd_music with **Loop** set to **true**. Enjoy!

Programming Memories

We began our journey with the reflections of the game's artist on designing the Zool character. So it is only right that we finish with the reflections of George Allan, the programmer of the original Amiga version of the game. These days, George has his own indie game-development company called Pi Eye Games, and even does his own graphics!

The best thing about working on Zool was the small team size. It was just Ade as the artist and me as the programmer, with Tony Dawson coming in to design the maps later on. We didn't know what a design document was, so most of the game's features came from playing (erm, I mean researching) 16–bit console games. Most of the baddy types were influenced by Mario, and the obsession with speed, naturally came from playing Sonic (a parallel which the marketing department had fun with when the game was released). The slopes and climbing actually came from the Strider arcade game, which I once completed on a single credit!

You can take things like scrolling for granted in Game Maker, but a lot of my programming effort went into achieving smooth scrolling in Zool. I'd come up with a nice scrolling routine for Switchblade II (the previous game I worked on), which was a blend of co-processor trickery, some nice hardware scrolling registers and on the fly map decompression. That game was quite slow paced however, so I wrote a demo with a block zooming around a map and within a week or two, that block had become the Ninja alien from Ade's imagination.

To keep the game's speed up at 50 frames per second on the Amiga, Zool had to be made up of three separate sprites. This is because hardware sprites could only be 16 pixels wide, but were much faster because they were handled by the graphics hardware. This means Zool could be updated every frame along with the scrolling routine. The rest of the level was updated every second frame as it needed to be drawn into a buffer and then swapped onto the screen display (double buffering).

All this use of hardware sprites meant that there weren't many left for anything else. The overlaid score panel had to be created using just two hardware sprites and multiplexing them horizontally across the screen. Multiplexing is a technique where you move a sprite during the update of the screen so that it appears in two positions at once! Unfortunately this led to a timing issue on the final day which made the whole screen occasionally jump 16 pixels to the right. It was fixed the day after the initial release, which was a shame as the game had been held back a couple of months waiting for the summer, and a mountain of lolly pops!

Looking back, I think small teams of dedicated people will always come up with the most interesting games. We developed Zool by trying stuff out and then tweaking it until it worked, just like you have in these chapters. So read this book, play around with Game Maker and go create some great games!

Congratulations—100% Complete!

So that's it! You can now consider yourself a battle-hardened platform game developer, as you have created a fully playable version of a classic nineties game. There is no doubt that it will have presented you with some real challenges, but you've made it through and you can rightly be proud of the result. Give your game a thorough play test to make sure everything works just as it should, and if you find any problems, then compare your version to zool15.gmk in the Chapter06/Games directory on the CD.

We hope that you're pleased with the result and that you have been able to get your head around the finer technical points of the chapter. However, more than anything, we hope we have given you the experience of creating and refining the basic game mechanics of a platform game. We have achieved our goal of producing a fluid and empowering movement mechanic by continually layering and refining the individual game mechanics. If you read the foreword to *The Game Maker's Apprentice*, you may remember this quote from Phil Wilson of Realtime Worlds (creators of *Crackdown*):

"The initial idea is simply the seed from which the game grows, or the stone from which the pillars are hewn. The role of a designer is to fully realize the vision: conceiving and continually refining the various supporting mechanisms to make them mesh like the components of a Swiss timepiece."

This is exactly what we have been trying to model in this chapter. You probably thought this was a purely technical exercise, but gameplay programming is as much about game design as it is about programming. Good gameplay programmers have a natural feel for creating and honing game mechanics, and their influence on the success of the final game is often as great as that of the designer who came up with the idea in the first place.

So before you continue, why not play around with some of the settings again and see if you can make the game even more appealing. Simply changing the values of some of the constants that we have defined can have a huge effect on the gameplay. If you're feeling brave, then you might even like to add some more features or enemies. There are a range of different sprites (created by the original artists) in the Chapter06/Resources directory to help you do this.

In the interim, it's time to take a bit of a break from programming as we start working towards the next project in the book. This time, we're going to create a completely new concept that relies on its storyline and characters to drive the gameplay forward. It's time to test your sea legs, land-lubbers, because there are some eerie-looking shadows on deck....

PART 3

Shadows on Deck

Making a game using existing characters and worlds can be a lot of fun, but game developers always aspire to create original concepts. Breathing life into a new game idea is hard work and to be successful, it needs to harness the talents of designers, artists, and programmers. We're going to take you through this process by designing and creating a "vertical slice" of game play for our own original concept; a game based on everyone's favorite anti-heroes: Pirates.

CHAPTER 7

■ ■ ■

Game Design: "Shadows on Deck"

Lots of people think they have a great idea for a game, a film, or a novel. What they actually have is the first spark of an idea that sets the imagination going, but a lot more is needed before you can say you have a complete game concept. Take for instance our Fishpod game in the earlier section. The first catch was—what if you played a fish that had to move to land and learn to live there? Our game description was as follows:

You play the role of Fishpod: a sea creature whose life is threatened by the eruption of a volcano. He is forced to flee the sulfurous, boiling waters that he once called home, for the relative safety of nearby caves. Unused to surviving on land, he must navigate his way through a series of perilous underground tunnels in order to find his way to a new home. To survive, he must learn how to make the most of his primitive limbs in order to avoid lava flows, sulfur gas, and poisonous pansies.

The left and right arrow keys will move Fishpod horizontally to the right or left, and the spacebar will make him leap diagonally upward in the direction he is currently facing. Fishpod can stand, walk, and jump on horizontal rock platforms, but will automatically fall down the screen when he is not supported by one. The level restarts if Fishpod comes into contact with any of the hazards.

It sounds like a great idea, but the description actually raises more questions than it answers.

- What does it mean to play a character that starts living on earth instead of water?

- What would be a successful outcome in the game? When he found a nice new lake to live in far from any volcano or when he had managed to grow legs and could live in a tree?

- How would he go about finding a lake or a tree?

- If he is the first creature to come out of the water, does that mean we can't throw any monsters in his way?

- Will it even be fun to control a lumbering "fish out of water" in the long-term?

For the small, fun games we have been making up until now, a short description is sufficient, but if you want to build bigger games, it requires a design with a lot more detail. To show you how, we will introduce you to Shadows on Deck. This will be a story-driven platform game that we will be creating in the remainder of the book. The next three chapters will concentrate on the design aspects of this project and once those are in place, we will begin to implement the levels.

The foundations of a good game are in the design. In this chapter, we will begin by defining an initial framework for the game, as once this is in place, it will be easy to flesh out with all the details. We will go from the basic idea to defining the game play and mechanics, the player character, his story in the game, the monsters he will meet, the levels he will overcome, and how the challenges flow and grow through the game.

A Good Beginning

Fishpod started with a question: **What if**? That's a very good way to start a game, but certainly not the only way. Here are some other approaches:

- **The visual style or feel**. For instance, *"I want to make a game that looks like the inside of a computer"* or, *"my game takes place in a world where everything is transparent."* Begin thinking about what kind of creatures live in such a world and what they would do.

- **A specific mechanic**. You've discovered that a ball you scripted in Game Maker moves and responds to the controls in a fun, satisfying way and want to make a game out of it. Start exploring what challenges you could set for a player who is controlling a ball.

- **Story**. *I want to make a game based on Puss in Boots or Last Recall.* Look closely at what happens in the story. Is the main character one that would prefer to think his way through challenges or should there be lots of fighting? What elements of the original story cry out to become a game play feature?

- **A character**. A game starring Thor, the god of thunder, or Bart Simpson. What is that character admired for, what is he good at, what are his dreams, and does he have any natural enemies? Does he have any special moves that could be used in the game?

- **A set of rules**. These could be from your favorite board game or indeed a genre that you like already. For instance, *I like the way you fit blocks together in Tetris, but it would be cool if you were actually building something out of the blocks.*

- **An existing game.** You could be building a sequel to a game you already made or one you admire, but would like to improve upon. Which parts were you really happy with and why? Which parts would you like to change?

There are other good starting points—anything that gets you excited and your ideas flowing. Our own starting point for Shadows on Deck was a visual style (see Figure 7–1). Back in the days of the Amiga, there used to be a truly atmospheric game called Blade Warrior. The game was set in the dead of night, and all the game play took place in silhouette. This often made it difficult to tell the difference between a harmless bit of scenery and some terrible creature waiting to pounce on you. Combined with an assortment of eerie sound effects, this produced some of the most intense game play available at the time. This atmosphere is part of what we would like to be able to recreate with our own game.

Figure 7–1. *This original mock-up shows how a silhouetted style can give a great atmosphere and a feeling of mystery*

So basically that is our starting point: a story-driven platform game in a silhouetted style.

Time to think. What looks good in silhouette? Well, normal people might be hard to distinguish from each other. If we have humans in this game, then they need to have some extravagant clothing to help recognize them. Aha! Pirates! Pirates have hats and scarves and wooden legs and sabres and hooks for hands. Not to mention, pirates have a broad appeal, which always helps in a game.

We could even have skeleton pirates, which make them look even better in silhouette.

Okay, so now we have some fierce pirates in our game. But who will the player control? We must have a hero and a good story to throw him into.

The Hero

The player's character should be designed with great care. Clearly, it must be someone that the player actually identifies with or it will put them off the game. In Chapter 8, we'll discuss how to build characters in more detail, but for now, let's look at a few approaches to creating the main character.

Make Him Invisible

We can make the character quite anonymous. The avatar won't say much and won't show personality in any way. That allows players to actually be the character. The players bring their own personality to the character and we interfere as little as possible with their choices. This is how most first-person shooters function; most of the time, you never actually see the character that the player is supposed to be playing. The player is experiencing the game first-hand, not through someone else's eyes. With an anonymous character, it is quite hard to tell a good story, and indeed many first-person shooters don't really need an elaborate story. That said, Valve still managed to tell a great story in *Half Life*, with *Gordon* being just such a hero.

Make Him Fantastic

Another option is making a character that players admire and aspire to be, or whose company they would enjoy. A strong, muscular warrior hero, for example. Someone the player looks up to and finds fun to play, because he can do all the things the player dreams of doing. This one is harder to get right, because you might end up choosing something that the player doesn't actually admire. What if the player thinks that muscular warriors are actually quite stupid and they would rather be a cunning wizard? What if the player is a girl and she would much rather be a strong female character? Lara Croft is a good example of a character that players can admire. She is good-looking, clever, and strong. A boy playing *Tomb Raider* might not want to be Lara, but he can certainly admire her.

Make Him Mortal

The third option is to go for someone that players can like and sympathize with. They might not want to be him, but they will want to help him, and will care what happens to him. To make such a character, he or she has to have more depth and personality. He has to have traits that players can recognize from themselves and sympathize with. That means that we aim for a character who is not a perfect hero, just an ordinary guy with talents and flaws like everyone else, but the adventure he is about to embark upon makes him (and the player) special. Games that use story to drive them usually have a character like this; April in *The Longest Journey* and Ratchet in *Ratchet & Clank* are good examples.

Flynn

So in our game, we'll go for the third option because it allows us to tell a rich story with the player character taking center stage. Our hero is a very ordinary boy, called Flynn, about 15 years old (Figure 7–2). He has never known his mother, doesn't know quite what he wants to do with his life, and feels like he is an outsider among the other boys on the island that he lives on.

Flynn has all that we need in a player character. He is basically a good guy, making it easy for us to like him. He doesn't quite fit in, and who hasn't felt like that at some point? We can understand and empathize with him. He is also restless; aching for something to do, to find a calling. And he has a bit of mystery–he doesn't know who his mother is. So now we need to give him a story: what will happen to Flynn?

Figure 7–2. *Flynn is our hero–a young boy from a fishing village*

The Beginnings of a Story

This is another subject that we could spend a lot of time on. There are plenty of ways to build up a story and some very good models that we can use to help with the structure. Chapter 8 will go into that in lots of detail, but for now let's simplify.

In the most basic form, you could say that a story is a problem that gets solved. You have to have a problem or you will have no tension. And tension makes a story. If they all live happily ever after already, then what will the story be about? Playing ball in a field and coming home for dinner? It doesn't work. What we need is a start, middle, and an end. Then we have a story.

- Start: We introduce our hero.

- Middle: Our hero goes on an adventure and overcomes some obstacles.

- End: Our hero overcomes a final battle and returns home stronger and wiser.

For this stage in the game design, it is enough to roughly outline how the story is going to pan out. In fact, a rough plan is better than a full story as you will see when we come to plan the game play. Here's the basic outline:

We start with Flynn on his home island where he is living with his dad. He is bored and slightly troubled. Then a problem arises. The island is threatened by a poisonous fog creeping in from sea. Flynn gets his opportunity for adventure; a chance to save his home and maybe discover who his mother is. Just as Flynn is starting to worry about the fog and what to do, a parrot appears (we need a parrot in a pirate game). The parrot–we'll call him Archie–lets Flynn know that his mother is in danger. He sets off on his adventure with the parrot as a companion and guide. He finds his mother and the cause of the evil, but then there's a twist. His mother has been kidnapped by an evil pirate and Flynn has to do what he is told to keep her safe. So he sets off to find a treasure for the evil guy, hoping that his mother will be freed afterwards. But the pirate tricks him; he intends to invade Flynn's home island and will probably kill Flynn and both his parents if his evil plan succeeds. In the end, Flynn finds a way to best the bad guy and we have our happy ending. Flynn has saved the island and found out something about who he is and something that he is good at.

If we were just writing a story, this is where we would start fleshing out all the details of the journey we just described. But this is a game, not a book or a film, and so before we can finish the story, we need to look at the game play.

Game Play

In a game, the game play is the most important thing. The story will help make the game more interesting and immersive, but first of all, the game play has to be fun. So it is time to look at what we are actually going to do in this game and what levels we will have.

Game play is a very broad term and not always easy to understand. It encompasses all the features in the game that are interactive, and it is this interactivity that distinguishes games from other forms of media such as films or books. A book is not interactive, because although the reader is affected by the words they read, the book is not affected back. It doesn't change depending on who is reading it.

Games also provide challenges to their players in the form of objectives or goals. Pre-defined challenges distinguish games from simple toys. You can create your own challenges using toys, but they do not impose them on the player in the same way as a game.

So the game play is how the game responds to a player's actions (interactivity) in pursuit of the objectives of the game (challenge). In essence, these are all the elements that affect how the player plays the game. We can divide these elements into three areas, each of which requires careful consideration: actions, rules, and challenges.

Actions: What Can the Player Do in the Game World?

By actions, we mean the controls and moves the player uses to play the game with. Can we jump, shoot, talk? Squeeze giant squids to produce ink splotches? Do we use the mouse pointer to choose troops or press "I" to bring up the inventory?

It's important to not confuse the player with too many moves and key combinations to remember. As a rule, the challenge of a game should never be the controls. It should be hard to beat the bog-eyed monster at the end of the level, but easy to remember where the jump key is.

Rules: What Restrictions Are We Imposing on the Player?

Gravity is a rule. If the player misses a platform, the character will fall down and maybe take damage or restart the game. Does the player have a certain number of lives or tries? Is there a limit to how many things he can pick up?

The rules define the world in which the game exists, and even the designer must be careful to follow those rules. If we say that there is gravity in the game world, then the monsters must be able to fall too, and anything that doesn't fall must have a very good reason not to (have wings, for example). Consistency is the key.

Challenges: What Are the Objectives and Goals We've Set for the Player?

What do players have to do to win? Which subgoals do we give them to conquer along the way? Challenges are what players are here for. They learned the moves, now they want to use them to win the game. A game must have clear goals to aim for and nice rewards when the player reaches them. The challenges must also be arranged, so that they steadily get harder as we travel through the levels.

Together, actions, rules, and challenges are what we call the *mechanics* of a game.

Mechanics of "Shadows on Deck"

We've already established that this is a platform game, and a story-driven one at that. A platform game means jumping will be involved somewhere down the line, but beyond that there aren't any restrictions on what we can do. But we need to be clear on what we consider to be the most important elements of our game.

Storyline

To support the story, we want to make beautiful cut scenes and be able to talk to people along the way. These will not be a major part of the challenge of the game, but they will be key to maintaining the player's motivation and interest in the game.

Nimble and Clever

For the game play, one particular aspect is important to us: we don't want to take the obvious combat option, and would prefer Flynn to use his wit and agility to beat the bad guys. That means we've got to make him faster than the lumbering skeletons and give him the ability to jump higher and use traps and distractions any way he can.

Sidekick

We've already given Flynn a companion (Archie the parrot), so let's put him to good use. The sidekick should be used both as a game play mechanic and important tool, but also as a guide Flynn can talk to and get good advice from. Archie will be a great help in making sure the player knows what the current objective is.

So with these in mind, let's flesh out the actions, rules, and challenges of *Shadows on Deck*.

Actions

Flynn can of course jump. To make him even more nimble, we'll give him a double jump to let him avoid and beat monsters more easily. He will also need to be able to duck out of harm's way. Because we won't be giving Flynn any weapons (besides Archie), he will need more moves to outwit the bad guys. We'll allow him to climb vertically and give him a charge so he can push monsters off platforms.

Flynn can send the parrot out to distract the pirates so that they briefly look the other way. Flynn can then charge them from behind and avoid their weapons altogether. So let's say that the player can tell Archie where to fly by clicking on the screen with the mouse pointer. Any pirate that is close to Archie will move toward the parrot and try to catch him. Flynn can then approach the pirate unnoticed and charge him so that he falls off the platform (Figure 7–3).

Figure 7–3. *Flynn sends Archie out to distract a pirate so that he can charge him from behind*

Other ways of dealing with the monsters will be to lure them into the booby traps that Flynn has to avoid himself. Say we're moving in the jungle and discover an old mechanism that makes a poisonous arrow shoot out of a hole. When Flynn triggers the trap, there will be a warning sound or animation warning him to get out of the way. But if a monster is following close behind, he can get caught in the crossfire (Figure 7–4).

Figure 7–4. *The baddies can be tricked into traps*

Main Moves for Our Hero Will Be:

- Run
- Jump
- Double jump
- Charge
- Climb
- Duck
- Send out the parrot

Besides his moves, Flynn will be able to talk to people along the way and help people in exchange for information and other favors.

That means we need a dialog system to be able to ask questions and give answers. The speech system will be closely related to how we tell the story, so we won't plan it until we've written more detail into the story. We'll go through dialog and cut scene techniques in Chapter 9.

Rules

Game World

We definitely have gravity in our game, but we will bend it in favor of our hero. Flynn can jump higher and further than his enemies. This is because he is nimble and small. Big enemies can't jump as high and they take more damage when they fall. In exchange, the monsters get to carry weapons. Flynn takes damage just by coming into contact with a weapon, be it saber or claw. When he does, he is pushed back slightly. This is both to make it obvious that he hit something bad and to make sure he doesn't repeatedly take damage from the same thing before he can move out of the way. As he is pushed back, he might fall off a platform. That means the player needs to be extra careful if he is on a high platform, which seems fair enough.

The parrot should be useful as a tool, so he is a clever bird. Flynn can talk to him and get important hints. When the parrot is sent as a distraction, he will always get the attention of the bad guys, but he is always clever enough to avoid their weapons. That way, Flynn can never lose his only weapon.

Main Rules in Our Game World Will Be:

- We have gravity, but modified in our hero's favor.
- Flynn can jump higher than any enemy.
- Flynn can fall further than enemies without taking damage.
- The parrot is always more "interesting" to enemies than Flynn.
- The parrot cannot take damage.

Monsters and Hazards

Monsters and hazards are essential elements of a game, particularly a platform game. They are there to provide challenges, add spice, and to populate the world that would otherwise seem very empty. For a long game like ours, we need a wide array of different hazards we can throw at the player.

The monsters we will encounter are of course the skeleton pirates, but lots of different ones can be introduced, depending on the level they are in. When coming up with these, it is a great help to already know which environment we will find them in. So, for instance, up in the masts of the ship, we could add some diving sea gulls with sharp beaks; in the dark cave, there should be bats and poisonous glow worms; in the hold of the ship, we could find crabs, rats, and even snapping barnacles. We should have several kinds of behaviors, too, so some patrol and will chase Flynn, some will stand and block the way, and some will pop out as a surprise and try to grab Flynn.

Figure 7–5. *Why are pirates cool? Because they arrrr!*

Monster and Hazard Rules

- **Wandering monsters**. The player has to deal with these when they're blocking the path and can otherwise be avoided. See Figure 7–5 for a first sketch.

- **Wandering beasts.** These are smaller than the humanoid baddies. They will die from a smaller fall, but have just as sharp weapons; rats with teeth, crabs with pincers, and so on. The player can also outwit or avoid them.

- **Stationary monsters.** These are actually small hazards such as seagulls and bats that dive from the sky. They will only attack at one spot, so that the player can avoid them with a bit of timing. Let's add spiders to this category. They can go up and down on strings. Poisonous glow worms in the caves can pop out of holes in the ground.

- **Traps.** These are stationary hazards, which won't move but that the player should avoid. The hidden ones will act with a bit of a delay, so you step on them, then a warning sound will indicate something is happening, and then SNAP. These can be meat-eating plants, poisonous arrows, bear traps, and so on (Figure 7–6). We can use quicksand, too. If the player pauses on a spot with sand, Flynn will slowly start to sink. He can move past these hidden traps, including the quicksand, if he keeps up a good speed. As mentioned earlier, these traps can also be used to defeat monsters.

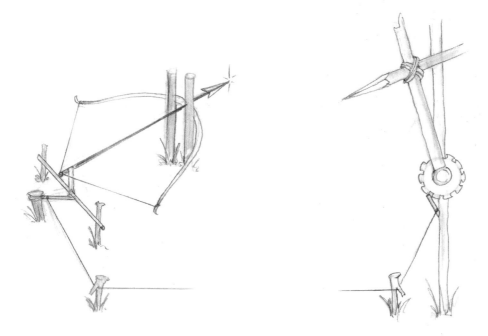

Figure 7–6. *Some of the many booby traps Flynn could encounter in the harder part of the game*

Boss Fights

Bosses are traditionally extra bad monsters that wait for the player at the end of a level; a big challenge to finish off and make the player feel like they've really achieved something. And besides, bosses are fun.

Bosses are usually set up so that they have their own unique kind of game play to really challenge the player. But here's the important bit: they usually test if you've mastered an ability you've been given in this level. Say we let the player learn the climb ability in the ship level. Well, then we've got to come up with a way to fight the boss that uses that ability. The Zelda games are very clever at doing this. We don't always have to stick with this pattern, but it's a nice idea. The rules for boss fights are a bit different, then, and we'll consider these once we know the levels and their challenges a bit better.

Challenges

In a story-driven game, the challenges and objectives are usually set up through the storyline. Therefore, the flow of the story that we've already outlined will help to determine the flow of the objectives in the game. Not all games are made this way, and sometimes the story isn't actually written until the game play is already well formed. It's not ideal from the perspective of the story, but it is not uncommon for games to reverse-engineer their storylines to fit.

In our case, we have a story structure that we will use as inspiration for the game play. First, let's see if we can sort out the levels of the game and what theme they will have. It's good to try to think of levels that are very different from each other, to add spice and variety to the game, and keep in mind that we want to start off easy and gradually get harder as the player gets better at jumping the platforms and overcoming the obstacles.

Level 1: Flynn's Island

We start on a small island. What would people be doing there? Fishing, most likely. So this is probably a little fishing village (Figure 7–7). Because we are making a platform game, we need something to **jump** on and a goal to aim for.

The roofs of the houses will make a good start. They will make wide and easy platforms, perfect for a first level of the game. Let's say that Flynn is down at the beach when the fog starts creeping in and he rushes home to tell his dad. He needs to be high up to avoid the low creeping fog. The parrot is already here, functioning as a guide, and keeping up with him can be a challenge in itself.

Remember the three stages we need for our story? Beginning, middle, and end. Level one is of course the beginning. This is where Flynn gets introduced in his own world.

Figure 7–7. *Flynn's home. Quick sketches help you clarify your ideas for yourself and others, and even help generate new ideas; maybe that fishing net can be used in the game play somehow?*

Level 2: Aboard Ship

Next, he sets off on his adventure. Where does he go? Well, he is on an island, so to get away he would need a boat. So let's set the next level on a ship. Flynn can be jumping the masts and help tighten the sails, and so on. This level is still at the beginning and shouldn't be hard, but jumping up and down masts is very different from roofs and should be fun. We will throw in a little **hazard** here to watch out for, nasty diving seagulls, and teach Flynn how to **duck**.

We now enter the middle of the story. The middle is all about putting obstacles in the hero's way and to give him challenges to overcome.

Level 3: Stowaway

Now trouble can arrive. Let's finally throw in those pirates. The ship is being attacked and Flynn has to get to safety. Archie suggests that he jumps his way across to the other ship and hide in their crow's nest (the lookout post in the top mast). Archie also teaches Flynn the **double jump** here, and we'll introduce the skeleton pirates. So now that Flynn has learned to jump, he needs to learn how to deal with **wandering monsters** without the benefit of a weapon, and we give him the **climb** ability.

This is also a very good point in the game to throw in the first boss fight, so let's design one for this level.

Level 3 Boss Fight: Crow's Nest

Flynn has managed to get to the other ship and he and Archie are almost at the crow's nest, but as they reach it the skeletons are closing in and surround Flynn.

Then a horrible laugh rings out and from high above; a skeleton, much larger than the others, thumps down onto the ropes.

"Hah! What's this, me hearties? A ship's boy who hasn't even got his sea legs yet? Is *HE* giving you trouble? Get out of my way. I will handle this."

This skeleton seems to have more limbs than are good for him. He has three arms and three legs-each with a hook on the end. He uses four limbs to hold on to the netting securely, while the other two hurl wooden pegs at Flynn, knocking him backward and off the platforms if he is not careful. Using the new climb ability, Flynn can clamber vertically up the various masts. He must unhook the pirate's limbs one by one until the pirate finally falls into the sea.

Level 4: Pirate Town

Now he must be getting close to that evil guy. Let's put him in a pirate town full of baddies and prisoners where he can look for his mother and the evil Pirate King. To make this level very different from the fishing village, we'll make this town sit on a cliff face; the pirates live like seagulls in nooks and crannies in the cliff, and all the makeshift huts are connected by loads of rope bridges and rickety ladders. This level will also feel different because Flynn now has to talk to a lot of people to get the information he needs. Let's give him the **charge** ability and teach him how to **send out the parrot**.

Level 5: Dark Caves and Tunnels

We've had roofs, masts, rope bridges, and cliff faces. Let's now have a dark ominous cave. Just for fun. Let's say Flynn has to go through a tunnel network of caves to finally get to this nasty pirate boss and free his mother. In here, we can have all sorts of new monsters for him to fight; **wandering and stationary beasts** like bats, worms, mushrooms, and rats.

Level 6: Jungle

Flynn has all that we need in a player character. He is basically a good guy, making it easy for us to like him. He doesn't quite fit in, and who hasn't felt like that at some point? We can understand and empathize with him. He is also restless; aching for something to do, to find a calling. And he has a bit of mystery–he doesn't know who his mother is. So now we need to give him a story: what will happen to Flynn?

When he finally reaches the Pirate King, he also finds his mother in danger and has to do what the pirate says: find a treasure. Where would he send Flynn to dig up treasure? Let's send him to the jungle; a nasty swamp jungle full of creepy crawlies and cannibals (Figure 7–8).

Figure 7–8. *Jungle sketch. Notice the hints of the booby traps and cannibals*

In the jungle, he has to find a treasure in a very Indiana Jones-like way. Let's put in some **traps** and quicksand to make it even harder. The boss at the end of this level could be a big mechanical door full of traps that Flynn has to open.

Next, Flynn returns with the treasure, but the pirate tricks him. He is locked up in the hold of a ship as the Pirate King sets sail for Flynn's home island.

Level 7: Ship's Hold

We're back on a ship level, but this time we are inside, so it should be nicely different from the mast level and, because this is a pirate story, we have to have more ships in it. Flynn should try to escape the hold and go warn the islanders of the coming danger.

Level 8: Back Home

As the final level, we should have a big battle of some sort. It should be on Flynn's island, but a flat beach or a small village sounds a bit boring for the final level. Let's put them all in a sea cave with deep water and waterfalls cascading over the sides. Flynn should fight the pirate boss all on his own while the villagers take care of the crew.

This is the end of our story and should have a big fight to show that the hero has learned a lot and is now stronger.

Can you see what we're doing? Instead of building the game play alone and the story separately, we're building the two elements up together, using them as inspiration for each other and molding them so that they fit perfectly together.

Difficulty

We've been careful to keep an eye on the difficulty of the challenges all along when designing the game. We want to balance the game play so that it slowly gets harder as the player gets better at the game. It is important not to flood the player with new mechanics and hazards all at once.

We'd like to remind you of a few game design principles that were discussed in *The Game Maker's Apprentice: Game Development for Beginners*.

The Game Maker's Apprentice

When you design a game, you are not trying to beat the player but to help them overcome the challenges you set for them in a satisfying way... the player is the game maker's apprentice!

It is your job to be the teacher; teach the player how to win in your game.

Learning Curve

The more time we spend on a task, the better we usually get at it. This is an important point to remember. When you first introduce a new ability, give the player time to get familiar and better at it, before you make the challenge harder. But don't overdo it. If the task becomes too easy, it also becomes boring.

Difficulty Curve

To avoid the player getting bored, we introduce new abilities and features along the way, to build on top of the tasks already mastered and to keep the game challenging and engaging. The difficulty curve gets steeper as we progress through the game, until we reach the final challenge, which is the most difficult of all.

To use Shadows on Deck as an example: in the first level, it is enough that Flynn has to jump from roof to roof trying to keep up with the parrot. In the next level, it will be more dangerous to fall–it's a long way down from a ship's mast, and we can introduce the seagulls here as something extra to look out for.

When the pirates attack, we are into the third level and it is time to introduce some harder monsters, namely the pirates, and we will also give Flynn the ability to climb. We continue in this way to make the game harder in a steady way that won't suddenly frustrate the player. We want them to feel like they're getting better, but make sure it never gets so easy that they get bored with the game.

This is what game designers call *balancing a game*, and it's by no means an easy task!

To check that we have thought it through carefully, let's draw up the flow of the challenges (see Figure 7–9).

First thing you'll notice is that no new monsters and hazards are introduced in the last two levels. This is not because we got lazy. It's not a good idea to keep adding new abilities right up until the end; too many new features could end up being very confusing. We want the player to be well-versed in all of Flynn's abilities by the time he faces the worst of the monsters. Besides, if you spend time and effort getting an ability just right, you want it to be used a lot, not just at the very end. Again, the Zelda series is a brilliant example of how to execute this well.

Another thing stands out from the chart. Notice that there are no boss fights for the first two levels. This is because boss fights are considered to be harder than the normal game play and, as we pointed out earlier, it is important not to flood the player right at the start but allow them to get used to your game and the mechanics.

On the other hand, the final level is nothing but a boss fight, but the hardest one in the game. We want an exciting challenge right at the end of the game.

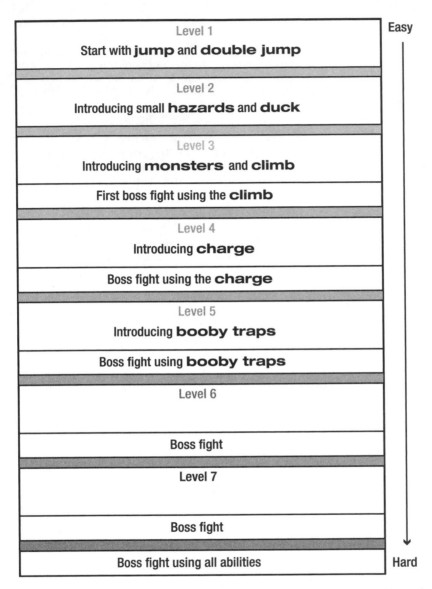

Figure 7–9. *This chart shows how the difficulty increases as new abilities and hazards are added to the game*

Conclusion

So there we have it. The bones of the game are now in place. We have a player character and a rough idea of the story we will tell. We've planned out the levels we'll go through, how the player will move, and the challenges and monsters they will face. There are still lots of details to sort out before this could be called a full game design, but now we are starting to get a good idea of what the game is about.

As ours is a story-driven game, it is now time to devote some serious attention to the story.

CHAPTER 8

■ ■ ■

Storytelling in Theory

When people told themselves their pasts with stories, explained their present with stories, foretold the future with stories; the best place by the fire was kept for the storyteller.

Jim Henson's Storyteller

Since the first campfire was lit, humans have told each other stories. There is just something magical about them. They allow us a glimpse into other lives, other situations than our own, and provide us with a better understanding of everything around us. Just like playing is a form of practice in agility and in hunting and surviving, so stories offer mental play to allow us to prepare for situations that might possibly arise. Stories are just naturally fascinating for us and we are drawn to them.

They are also lots of fun to write and there is plenty of knowledge out there to help us make great stories. Let's take a look at how to build stories, and how to structure them. Game stories are different from other stories because they are interactive, which means different rules to play by. But that doesn't mean we can't learn from books and movies along the way.

What Can a Story Do for My Game?

Some people argue that games don't need stories and they work perfectly well without them—just look at *Tetris*. Stories only get in the way of the game play and players actively avoid them by hitting the skip key until they're allowed to play again.

Consider, however, that photographs don't need colors, either. In fact, some of them are much stronger in black and white, but a lot more of them are enriched by the use of color. Likewise, a story can help to make the gaming experience richer, making you care for the character you control, immersing you more deeply in the experience, and making it more memorable.

Even a single line of story can enrich a game:

"Oh no, a band of demons have kidnapped all the dragon hatchlings. Help the mother free them!"

Other games call for a more elaborate story; "Shadows on Deck" is one of them.

A story can help clarify what the player is doing in the game and give them motivation to continue. All the challenges and objectives can be tied into the story, which means the game will flow more easily from objective to objective. The story adds backbone to the game, which might otherwise just be a series of unconnected challenges.

Even though the player has to focus on the short-term goal, the story will give them a sense of the journey ahead and a desire to see what's around the next corner, not to mention to know how it all ends. If we can hook the player at the start of the story, there's a good chance they'll stick around to the end.

Little or Big Story?

But first of all, you must decide whether your game needs a long story at all. What will fit the game? Mr. Driller, Namco's popular series of arcade games, had a story that was short and sweet:

A monster has burrowed beneath the city and threatens to destroy it. Mr. Driller must use his drill to get down there and defeat the monster.

That's all the story this game needs. The player gets a noble quest to save an entire city from a monster. Mr. Driller is all about speed and a sense of urgency as he has to get to that monster quickly. He is constantly in danger of running out of air and blocks fall on his head if he doesn't keep moving. If there was a longer story, the game would have to pause between each level and explain some more, maybe show houses falling down from the tremors underground. Maybe Mr. Driller would have to stop to talk to a character that just happened to be underground. So in this case, a detailed story slows the pace down and gets in the way.

Our pirate game, on the other hand, will definitely improve with a more elaborate story. Though Flynn is fast and agile, he is also clever and has to use his wit to outsmart some of the bad guys. That means we have to give him information along the way, and a story can help structure that information and make it relevant. We want him to search for his mother. We want him to save his home town. Without the story, he might wander around aimlessly and not be sure what exactly he is supposed to be doing.

So how do we go about structuring a longer story?

Story Structures

There are many ways to structure a story, and you could fill a library with the books written on the subject—all trying to find the perfect formula for a good story. Although some very good patterns have emerged, the truth is that there is no such thing as a guaranteed formula for creating a good story, just as there is no such thing as a guaranteed formula for creating a good game. But these ideas and patterns can still help us when building the stories for our games, particularly when you are new to storytelling. So think of them as forms, not formulas. They are guidelines to help us along, not a strict rule set we have to follow.

We will go through two very popular forms here, which actually work well in unison:

- The Three-Act Structure
- The Hero's Journey (also known as the Monomyth).

For the rest of the chapter, we will use these two structures to show you how they can help build up your story from loose idea to finished narrative. They teach some valuable lessons about storytelling, but you should never let them restrict your imagination. Once you know the rules; don't be afraid to break them. It can be a lot of fun and lead to new astonishing stories.

The Three-Act Structure

There's a classic pattern that you will have seen, perhaps without even realizing it, a hundred times. It is called the *Three-Act Structure*. This form dates all the way back to the ancient Greek amphitheatres with its tragedies and comedies, and Aristotle (a clever Greek philosopher type) was the first to formulate this idea. Most books, films, and theater plays follow this structure and it can be used in games with good results, too.

Act 1

This is where the story begins. The main character is introduced, establishing who he is, where he comes from, and so on. Usually, this is also were the problem is presented, something that makes it impossible for the hero to keep living his normal life. We call it the point of no return. The hero has now lost his normal life and must go on; straight into Act 2.

Act 2

Here, the challenges begin in earnest. This is usually the longest act and can easily take up half the story. The hero sets out on his journey with a clear goal. He is put through a series of challenges and trials and he will meet new friends and enemies. At the end of the act, the hero finally reaches his intended goal, what should be the climax of the story, but then there's another turning point; a twist, the hero discovers that he has been wrong, or that things have now changed. What he has been seeking turns out to be either not what he believed it would be, or no longer what he desires. So right after the high point, we see disappointment, a low point. It was all in vain.

Act 3

The hero must now show what he is really made of. He has been tried and tested in Act 2. He now truly understands what is at stake, and with new strength, he sets out to conquer a harder set of challenges and a last final battle in which he proves he has grown since the beginning of the story. The true climax comes here, close to the end, and the last bit of the story is about tying up all the loose ends and explaining what just happened. We often get to see the hero in his new normal world, which can be the same one he left in the beginning, only now he sees it with entirely new eyes.

The Hero's Journey

Another useful guide is a structure called the Monomyth, put together by Joseph Campbell in a 60-year old book called *The Hero of a Thousand Faces*. Campbell's book isn't actually a storytelling guide, but rather an exploration of myths from all over the world and how they share the same structure. He called it the Monomyth and also explored how archetypical characters (child, hero, mentor, sage,and so forth) fit into this structure. Many years later, a man named Christopher Vogler read this book and realized how useful it was as a guide to scriptwriters. He wrote a simple leaflet briefly outlining the structure and it became so popular in Hollywood that he later expanded it to a complete book called *The Writer's Journey: Mythic Structure for Writers*. Vogler extracted 12 stages of a story from the Monomyth and called it *The Hero's Journey*. Some stories have all of them, some miss a few out, some jumble up the order of them, but if you find that your story loses its momentum in the middle or the ending doesn't feel quite right, then going through these stages can help you spot what might be missing. The 12 stages are:

- The Ordinary World

- Call to Adventure

- Refusal to the Call

- Meeting with the Mentor

- Crossing the First Threshold

- Tests, Allies, and Enemies

- Approach to the Innermost Cave

- The Ordeal

- Reward

- The Road Back

- Resurrection

- Return with the Elixir

Let's go through each of these to learn a bit more about them. We'll use *Toy Story* as an example to see how the structure matches a story you probably already know well.

The Ordinary World

We start in the ordinary world and show our hero in his everyday environment, before anything has happened to him. Why start before the adventure actually begins? Well, we want to get to know our hero a bit before we plunge him into danger, and to do that it helps to see his background. This is the time to show him at his best, to let the audience start to like him. Hopefully, we will then be as shocked as the hero is when we plunge him into change, and the player will share his motivations.

This is also a good stage to introduce little teasers of what is going to happen later. We're sort of saying to the player, "Yeah yeah, this is ordinary and boring, but stick around, something is about to happen." This is called foreshadowing. In our pirate story, that could be two kids playing on the beach where Flynn is watching the sea. They are playing with swords and one of them is wearing a skeleton mask.

The Ordinary World is a stage that can be missed out altogether or appear later in the order. For example, the story could begin in the middle of the action, and then in a quieter moment later on, the hero can sit back and tell someone else where he came from. Alternatively, we can leave it as a mystery and never explain who this hero actually is. That would work well for the games using an invisible hero (see Chapter 7) as the player character.

In *Toy Story*, this part of the movie shows Andy playing with Woody in a lovely sunny room. Woody is Andy's favorite toy and Woody loves Andy right back. Woody is also regarded as something of a hero by all the other toys and he takes good care of them all. The foreshadowing here is threefold. First, the birthday party is mentioned, and then the house move, and lastly we get a good look at nasty Sid, the horrid neighbor kid who likes to torture toys.

The Call to Adventure

This stage is where the hero, or sometimes just the audience, realizes that something is about to happen. It is the event that starts the ball rolling. In our pirate story, this is the poisonous fog that comes creeping in as Flynn watches.

In *Toy Story*, it's the birthday party. We see that although all the toys seem happy, they are all living with one fear—to be scrapped because newer and better toys enter their owner's life. Woody himself does not seem worried and spends a lot of time calming the other toys down. He is confident in his role as Andy's favorite toy. He begins to realize his mistake when he is knocked off the bed (his personal throne) in favor of a cardboard spaceship. Buzz Lightyear has arrived.

Refusal to the Call

This stage is less straight forward. It deals with the fears and reluctance that the hero might feel when first faced with the prospect of adventure. Lots of games miss this. After all, the player has come for adventure. If he doesn't go on it, then there's no game to play. But it can be quite an important stage. It is another opportunity to show that the hero is just an ordinary guy like us, and the fact that he doesn't rush in without thinking could actually be to his credit. Another reason could be that he has a fear of change and doesn't believe in himself (a deliberate flaw we have given him—more on that later). This small hesitation makes him more likeable and makes the audience consider equally what is at stake here, and what he could lose by accepting the challenge.

If a call is refused for too long, it could have a drastic impact on the story. The hero might miss his opportunity altogether. In some stories, you see these tragic heroes as supporting characters in another hero's tale, like Gollum in *Lord of the Rings*.

In *Toy Story*, this stage shows Woody refusing to see the truth, while Buzz takes the other toys by storm and slowly all the cowboy motifs in Andy's room gets replaced with space motifs. Woody is even made to be the villain in one of Andy's games. But Woody denies it; "I'm still Andy's favorite toy…."

Meeting with the Mentor

The mentor is a powerful character and someone we'll hear more about later. This is a character that gives the hero information and helps him make the right decision. We don't have to take this literally. It doesn't have to be a character. It can be a telephone call, a book, or even something that the hero suddenly remembers. For Flynn, both the parrot and his dad perform this role by giving him information about his mother.

In *Toy Story*, Woody finally understands that he is being replaced; he sees the poster on the wall has changed, Andy's bed is covered in a Buzz blanket, and Andy has scribbled his name on Buzz's foot. All these little things come together to perform the mentor role. Woody decides that he has to do something.

Crossing the First Threshold

This stage is where the hero actively steps into the new world. Sometimes he does so unwillingly or even inadvertently, but all the same, he has crossed into the new world. In the three-act structure, we called this the point of no return. As already mentioned, the hero himself can show fear or unwillingness, but here he can also meet a lot of resistance from other people serving as "threshold guardians." This can be friends advising against the new adventure or characters from the new world trying to stop the hero entering, as Cerberus guards the underworld. It can even be something as simple as a locked door.

In *Toy Story*, Woody is spurred into action when Andy's mother tells Andy that he can only bring one toy to Pizza Planet. Woody decides to get rid of Buzz by knocking him down behind a piece of furniture out of sight when Andy comes up to choose his toy. The plan goes wrong, Buzz is knocked out of the window instead, and the other toys turn against Woody in outrage. Andy arrives and chooses Woody, as he can't find Buzz. Woody is launched on his adventure, knowing that if he comes back without Buzz, the other toys won't take him back.

Tests, Allies, and Enemies

This stage is probably the biggest one in the story. In games it certainly takes up a huge chunk of the time. It's the training ground for the hero, practice for facing the big ordeal at the climax. The hero meets friends and enemies, not always knowing which is which. He faces lots of challenges that will give him the opportunity to learn and grow. In Flynn's story this is everything that happens from first setting out to finding out where his mother is being held.

In *Toy Story* this stage is the longest too. It starts as Woody and Buzz are left by Andy at the gas station and covers their trials at Pizza Planet and Sid's house of horrors. They are forced to work together to plan their escape past Sid, his terrible dog, and weird sister, not to mention some very creepy cannibalistic toys.

Approach to the Innermost Cave

The approach gets its name from old myths and fairy tales. This is when the hero arrives at the dragon's den. The big ordeal is almost at hand. The approach can be full of action, as the hero frantically prepares for the big battle, or it can be a quiet moment, where he contemplates what has happened and what will happen. Here, we can foreshadow the second turning point. What will happen when the hero reaches his goal? Is it really all he had hoped it would be?

In *Toy Story*, we see Woody quietly thinking, coming to terms with the fact that he might never get home. On the table, the alarm clock counts down the minutes until Sid will launch Buzz and blow him up. Without Buzz, Woody can never go home. He makes up with Buzz here in the "quiet before the storm," and helps him see that being a toy is not a bad thing. They finally become friends.

The hint that the goal might not be enough here is a scene showing that Andy's toys are actually already packed up. Even if Woody manages to get back home against all odds, it might be too late.

The Ordeal

Time's up. This is what the hero has been trained for. He now faces the last great obstacle to reach his goal. A great battle ensues—the ultimate test. In movies, they make sure that the hero is almost defeated here, but then comes back against all odds. In a game, we have to make sure this stage feels very hard, but isn't impossible.

In *Toy Story*, having revived Buzz's fighting spirit, the toys make a last bid to get out of Sid's room before he wakes up. But it's too late. Buzz is taken out to the garden for the big launch. Woody prepares a plan with the creepy toys, now turned allies, to free himself and pacify Sid forever. The plan goes well, and they manage to lock up the dog, but then Woody is suddenly caught by Sid. He is put on the grill with the promise of being fried later. He has to improvise. He starts talking, although that is not allowed in front of humans. The other toys rally up around him and Sid gets the scare of his life.

Reward

The hero has reached his goal and now reaps his reward. We could end the story here, and in fact a lot of games do. We have reached the goal we set out to reach. But here is also the chance to add the second turning point—a twist in the tale and a chance to surprise the audience (although the clever ones will have understood the foreshadowing we gave them in the approach). The goal turns out to be fake or not enough. The hero has been tricked or the journey has changed him so that he no longer desires the reward.

In *Toy Story*, the other toys have been freed from Sid's tyranny and Woody and Buzz are free to go home to Andy. But just as they are celebrating, they see the moving truck move away from

Andy's house. They are too late. If they don't catch it, they will never be home again, as they don't even know where the new home is.

The Road Back

Depending on the story, this stage can take very different forms. If we didn't add an extra twist in the reward, then this is a slow wind-down where there is room to show how the hero has been changed by his journey. If we added a twist, there will be more challenges on this road. For Flynn, he has barely reached half-way; he has to complete a quest for the evil guy to get his mother back. The journey still seems long.

In *Toy Story*, the twist means that Woody is still fighting to get home. The goal post has moved and he now has to reach the truck and not the house next door. Using their newfound friendship, Buzz and Woody help each other overcome the chasing dog and catch the truck.

Resurrection

This stage is named resurrection because traditionally this is where the hero is "reborn" and restored to everything he might have lost when he first got the call to adventure. He is reborn as a new, better person.

Time to resolve all the plot threads. There might be a final challenge here. We can also add yet another twist here, like the villain not being dead at all. Incredibly, he rises again to continue the fight. There might be a revelation here the audience will not have foreseen ("I am not really your father"). This twist might also have been foreshadowed earlier.

In *Toy Story*, this stage is actually merged with The Road Back. Buzz and Woody fight to catch up with the truck. The other toys work against him thinking that Woody has killed Buzz and is now coming back to do more evil deeds. But they now all see with their own eyes that he has been rescuing Buzz all along and his hero status is "resurrected."

Return with the Elixir

The name of this stage also harks back to fairy tales. The hero returns with the potion that will make his sick father better, or make the princess wake from her enchanted sleep. It signifies the end of the story.

In this final stage, we get to see the hero return to glory. We get a chance to compare the hero as he was at the start of the story with this new greater hero. He has his ordinary world restored, or the new world becomes his ordinary world. If you plan to send him on new adventures in the future, this is the perfect place to foreshadow these new events and leave the audience wanting more.

The end in *Toy Story* sees Woody and Buzz both being Andy's favorites and the new wiser Woody gladly accepts this, where the old one would be jealous and hateful. There is a sense that whatever Christmas and birthday parties may throw at them, they can overcome the problems together.

So there we have it; the journey returns to its starting point, ready to start again.

Of course, all of this is not meant to be taken too literally, not even the journey itself. Not all stories are about journeys, but metaphorically we could say they are. It could be an inner journey. The story could be about a girl who gets a new step-dad and has to learn to live with this new person in her family whether she wants to or not. She won't go traveling, but her ordinary world is still turned upside-down. Or it could be about a man who finds out that his boss is actually working for the mafia and counterfeiting money. The police ask him to be a spy in his own company. Again, the hero is not going anywhere, but still the journey begins.

The Structures Working Together

The monomyth and the three-act structure have a lot of similarities and if we mesh the two together we get some sound waypoints that can help us find a way through our story.

- Act 1

    Ordinary World

    Call to Adventure

    Refusal to the Call

    Meeting with the Mentor

    Crossing the First Threshold

- Act 2

    Tests, Allies, and Enemies

    Approach to the Innermost Cave

    The Ordeal

    Reward

- Act 3

    The Road Back

    Resurrection

    Return with the Elixir

Pace

As well as structure, pace is extremely important for a story. By pace, we mean the rhythm and tempo of the story, the way that the action increases and decreases along the way. The three-act structure comes with directions regarding the pace as well. It looks something like Figure 8–1:

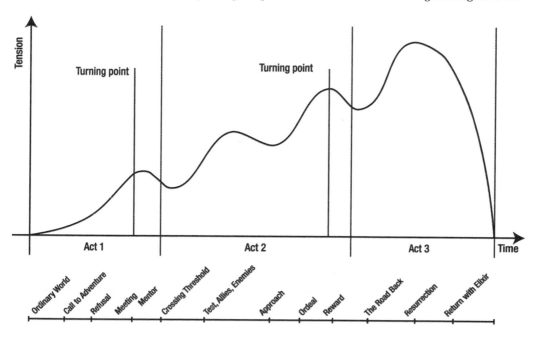

Figure 8–1. *The pacing of the three-act structure. The tension/pace of the story gradually builds.*

You'll notice that it's not a steady rise to the climax, but a series of bumps along the way. That's because it is important to vary the pace a bit, or the audience will get used to the intensity. If the pace becomes too predictable, people will start to feel bored. We want to keep them alert and on their toes. So we give them breathing spaces in between the action. If a fast car chase in a movie went on for an hour, you can imagine that it would start to get boring even though car chases are usually high adrenalin and intense. The structure can vary quite a lot depending on the story you tell. You can stretch certain parts to fit the story you want to tell. Remember, this is a guide, not a strict rule.

In games, the structure tends to look a bit different. See Figure 8–2. Act 1 becomes very short, often it is just the intro cut scene and when the player gets control, we are already in Act 2, starting the journey. Act 2 in games tends to be very long, because this is where most of the game play is. Act 3 also holds a series of challenges, but in games, the wind-down is very short as we don't need the same resolution to a game. We beat the end boss and are in effect done with the game, so the end cut scene is usually short, acting mainly as a reward for the player.

In fact, if you are planning to make more than one game, it's quite handy to leave a few ends untied, to make the player wonder what happens in Episode 2.

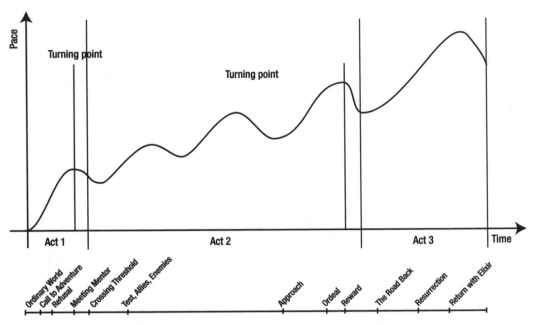

Figure 8–2. *The game version of the three-act structure. The tops of the curves usually correspond to the final challenges at the end of each level.*

■**Note** Remember that these forms are only guidelines and need not be followed to the letter, but can help point out what might be missing from your story or how you can tighten it up.

Characters

Of course, all stories have characters in them and there are tricks to getting them right, too. Adding convincing characters to your world will really help to make it come alive. You should try to avoid stereotypes like the dumb blonde, the lazy plumber, or the Italian mobster. If your characters are too predictable, they become boring, stupid, and maybe unintentionally funny (stereotypes are often the butt of jokes).

The monomyth covers characters, too. It describes characters in terms of archetypes that illustrate the function of a character rather than their personality. Initially, you may find it hard not to think of them as stereotypes, but they don't focus on superficial traits like stereotypes do and a hero archetype can just as easily be a mouse as a muscle-bound warrior. This is extremely useful for a storywriter, as it means we can start populating our world in a way that serves the story first and concentrate on giving those roles some color and personality afterward. Let's take a look at the most useful archetypes in storytelling. Even if you decide not to use the monomyth, archetypes can still be useful for creating your characters.

Hero

The hero is of course the most important archetype. This is the central character that the story revolves around. The word *hero* is Greek and means "to protect and to serve" and this implies that a hero is one who is willing to sacrifice his own needs in favor of the common good. In games, this is usually the character that the player controls and so needs to identify with the most. The hero is the epicenter of the story and as he travels through the 12 stages, he grows and changes on an inner level just as much as he changes the world around him.

There are several types of heroes from which to choose. Choose a type of hero that fits nicely into your story and then, with the help of that type, you can define his character traits. A few that are really useful to know in games are as follows.

Willing Hero

This guy steps up to the challenge. He knows what is expected of him and is eager to fulfill his fate. Good examples would be King Arthur or Buzz Lightyear (he is the hero in his own story).

Unwilling Hero

This hero is being dragged kicking and screaming to perform. He doesn't want the role, but circumstances force it upon him. Bilbo from *The Hobbit* is an unwilling hero.

Cynical Anti-Hero

He has given up on the world and usually works purely for his own interest. This hero can still do great deeds, but his motivation is to help himself first of all. The player characters in *Grand Theft Auto* are usually anti-heroes, and so is Han Solo from *Star Wars*.

Loner Hero

This is a very common one in games. The loner sets out to right the world. He is usually a bit of a misfit, but can nevertheless have a heart of gold. Good examples are Guybrush Threepwood from *Monkey Island* or John McClane from *Die Hard*.

Catalyst Hero

The catalyst breaks a few of the rules of the myth. He doesn't actually change himself as the story progresses, but acts as a catalyst for changes in the people around him. We most often see this hero in serial stories. Sherlock Holmes is a catalyst, not changing much himself. The catalyst is very useful in games too. In fact, you could say that all the games that do not focus heavily on story have a catalyst hero. Mario never changes, and neither does Crash Bandicoot.

The Rest of the Crew

Usually there is only one hero. They often have friends and allies with them on their journey, but one person takes center stage. When looking at the rest of the cast, bear in mind that you do not have to confine each character to a certain role. Think of the different archetypes in the next few sections as masks that the characters can wear when they're needed in the story.

The Mentor

The mentor serves the role as advisor, teacher, friend, and ally. He gives the hero the knowledge he needs and often other gifts to help him on his journey. Mentors are hugely important in games, as they show the player how to play the game and point him in the right direction.

In *Toy Story*, the shepherdess is a mentor, trying to make Woody see that there is room for both him and Buzz and that Andy still loves him.

Herald

The herald is the giver of the challenge. He brings the news of trouble ahead. He usually appears in the "Call to Adventure" stage of the story, because that is exactly what he does. He is the catalyst for changes and brings news that is impossible to ignore. The herald doesn't have to be an actual person. It could be a letter or an earthquake even.

In *Toy Story*, Andy plays this part when he lets Woody know that the birthday party is brought forward. But the biggest herald is Buzz Lightyear himself, announcing a serious change in Woody's life as he lands on the bed and amazes all the other toys.

Threshold Guardian

A guardian is simply anyone or anything that stops the hero from going where he wants to go. Think of the bouncer by the red carpet or the ticket collector in a cinema. He is there to test whether the hero is worthy enough to pass. The guardian need not be evil, but can have good intentions too, such as a friend advising the hero against danger, or locking her up to keep her safe. In games, the most notorious guardians are the end bosses in a level, guarding the innermost treasures.

In *Toy Story*, Sid's dog is a worthy guardian, barring the way to freedom as Woody and Buzz try to escape the house.

Shapeshifter

The shapeshifter is a sneaky customer. Sometimes they will appear to help the hero, sometimes they work against him. We're not quite certain which side the shapeshifter is on. Shapeshifters can be dangerous enemies but also very useful allies. A good example even in a very literal way is Sirius Black in *Harry Potter*. When he first appears in the story, he is presented as a mad murderer and a dangerous wolf, but turns out to become one of Harry's best friends.

In *Toy Story*, Woody believes that Sid's toys are evil, but finds out that they are friendly and helpful. To some extent, Andy's own toys are shapeshifters too, as they turn on Woody for what he did to Buzz.

Trickster

The trickster is easy to confuse with the shapeshifter. He can trick and lie and pretend to be someone else, too. But usually the shapeshifter believes what he does is right, whereas the trickster is mischievous and often does harm just for the fun of it. He can turn out to be an accidental ally sometimes, but often he steps in to disrupt the hero's plans purely for his own amusement. The Cheshire Cat in *Alice in Wonderland* is such a trickster.

In *Toy Story*, Sid's sister plays the trickster. She holds Buzz prisoner, forcing him to play the part of Mrs. Nesbitt and prevents his escape, but later actually helps the toys by scaring Sid with a doll.

Shadow

The shadow represents all that the hero is fighting against—even his own inner flaws and insecurities. Games are full of shadows usually, as they are all the monsters and enemies the player has to fight. Without the shadow, there would be no conflict and no story. Some shadows are purely evil and must be fought; others are more sophisticated and represent some aspect of the hero that he would rather be rid of. Darth Vader represents the dark side that tempts Luke Skywalker, while the Emperor is just pure evil.

In *Toy Story*, we have both types. Sid is a pure shadow, while Buzz merely represents one. He threatens Woody's ambition about being the favorite toy and the shadow that must be fought here is not really Buzz but Woody's selfishness.

Filling Roles

As you can see, a character can play several roles in a story. Buzz plays the herald and a shadow at first, but turns out to be a very strong ally in the end. Even the hero can take on different roles for the people around him. When Buzz realizes he is just a toy, Woody takes on the role of mentor and teaches him that being a toy is an amazing thing. Take a look at your story and figure out what roles need to be filled and use that as a starting point.

Traits

Once a character in your story has a role in the game, you can then add some traits to his personality to really make him come alive. Let's talk about the hero first.

As mentioned earlier, we want him to be likeable and someone that the player can identify with. The first thing we need to do is to make sure he is not perfect. Perfect people are not loveable. They are annoying. They do everything just right and have no dilemmas. They always know how to act and what to do. Kind of boring, really.

If we give our hero a flaw, something that he struggles with every day, then we instantly make him more likeable. Why? Because that makes him one of us. We all have flaws, things we don't like about ourselves and would like to change. Alice didn't sit and listen to her lecture like a good little girl. She got bored, stopped paying attention, and went on an adventure instead. That is something we can all understand. Who hasn't sat in class and wished they were somewhere else?

The same goes for the rest of the characters. Try to give them all a couple of traits that make them more real. If you want to make them more interesting, give them two traits that don't normally go together. For instance, a girl who pretends to like dolls but would really rather play football with the boys. Or a thief who takes in stray cats. These traits let you know your characters better and even if the player never knows about these traits, they will help you figure out the dialog and how the character would react in certain situations.

A fun way to assign traits is to write one trait each on a bundle of small paper scraps.

- Smart
- Devious
- Charitable
- Has a limp
- Hates his brother
- Color blind
- Has no confidence
- Day dreamer

And so on. Then pull them out of a hat, no peeking, and give each character two or three traits. The result might surprise you and you certainly avoid the clichés this way.

Interactive Stories

When people first started making motion pictures, they started out with filming a theater stage. That was a way of telling stories that they understood. Then pretty soon they discovered all the different things you could do with movies that you hadn't been able to do on stage. The old lessons learned on the stage still applied, but new techniques blossomed with the new media. So it is with games and interactive stories now. We can learn a lot from the structure of books and films, but there are also new things to consider. Interactive stories are still a very new medium and we are still developing new methods to explore their full potential. Here are a few considerations.

First of all, we can allow the player to influence the story. Let them have a say in what will happen. This is actually similar to how stories were told in the old days. The storyteller would listen to the response of his audience and alter the story to fit the mood of his listening crowd.

Because the players are actively participating in our story, there is a lot of opportunity to let them have a real impact on how the events unfold.

Let's look at a few new tricks we can use in a game and try them out on our own game *Shadows on Deck*.

Branching

One way is to let the player make the choice (rather than the player character) at certain key points in the story. Depending on what the player chooses, he will see a different story.

If, for instance, the player didn't trust Archie the parrot in our story, he might not take his advice to hide on the pirate ship once they attack. He could instead choose to fight alongside his friends on the merchant ship. If we let the player choose this action, then the story has now branched out and from here on there are effectively two stories running; one where Flynn hides and gets to the pirate town and one where he stands and fights. That story could either end in his death, or the merchant ship could go on to its destination or it could even go back home if it was damaged badly.

If Flynn *did* trust the parrot and got to the pirate town, then we could now give him a different choice. He could either help the prisoners escape and get information that way, or he could try to make friends with the pirates by behaving as badly as they do. One option makes him law-abiding and good, and the other makes him a rascal and a pirate. Depending on which, the boss at the end could either fight him or help him willingly.

As you can see, this way of branching stories to give the player more control can quickly mean that you have to write a lot more story than you first intended (see Figure 8–3). We now have several stories to write and they all have to be interesting and have a satisfying ending.

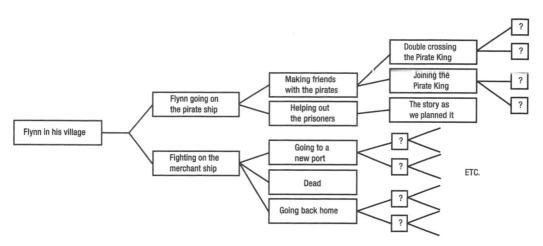

Figure 8–3. *Branching out your story can quickly get out of hand.*

There are different ways of tackling this problem. One obvious one is to kill the player every time they make a choice we don't want them to. But that's a poor solution and not very fun for the player.

Another way to do it is to write the branches so that they meet every now and then. Say Flynn had stayed on the merchant ship and gone to a different port than the pirate town. He still has to gain information to find the Pirate King. So we let him find it in this other location and then send him to the entrance of the cave. Now we have a point where the branching stories have come back together and that makes it a lot more manageable to write the different versions of the story. Instead of a tree structure that branches outward forever, we now have something like the structure shown in Figure 8–4.

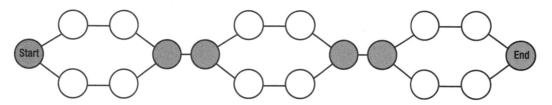

Figure 8–4. *The branching is now under control even though the player can still get a vastly different game depending on his choices.*

This structure is a lot easier to write a satisfying story for and the player is still allowed to influence the story.

These are two examples of how the story can pan out interactively. There are plenty of other structures that you can use. But they all have three problems, or challenges, that are worth considering when you make a game:

- Did I miss out?

- Interesting choices

- Wasted content

Did I Miss Out?

When the players are asked to make a choice, they will often start to worry whether they made the right choice and whether they missed something fantastic by taking the right-hand path. If they start feeling worried, then the spell is broken and they are not as immersed in the game as they could be, because now they are wondering what happens in the other version instead of paying attention to the story they do have.

Some game designers think this is fine because it entices people to play the game again to see what they missed, but we don't think that is a good excuse to break the player's immersion in the game. A way to deal with this is to make it clear to the player what they missed. Show them that if they stay in the inn, the pirate ship will take off without them or that because they didn't sleep at the inn, they didn't get caught in the fire.

Interesting Choices

In some cases, however, most often seen in role-playing games (RPGs), this missing out is a main feature of the game. If you chose to play a dwarf, for instance, you might not get the choice of becoming a mage, but would gain extra stamina that would be great for a warrior.

In this case, the challenge is to balance the choices so there is no right or wrong, only preference. The choices should be real dilemmas and not have an obvious right version. If you make a choice that loses you a weapon, then some advantage should be gained. It is hard to get right and often the game designer can't help but hint at the choice they think is the best.

Wasted Content

There is a third quite serious problem, and the greatest reason why most games never branch out or save it for the very end. If you look again at Figure 8–4, you can see why. Imagine all the bubbles are levels. The game consists of 18 different levels, but the player only sees 12 of them on a playthrough. That is a whole third of the game that the creators have to make but the player never sees. And they still have to pay for it. When you go through the effort of making a great level, you want the player to see it, right? That means we usually like to make sure that the player has to go through all the levels, and make every bit (and byte) in the game count toward the player experience.

Modifying Non-Player Character Behavior

Instead of branching out the story, there are other ways we can make it feel different depending on how the player plays the game. We can tailor the conversation so that the non-player characters (NPCs) react differently according to the player's actions. This also means a bit of wasted content, but it is easier to keep at a minimum.

We could, for instance, give Flynn the choice of helping or threatening an old pirate to get information. Depending on the strategy the player chooses, the NPCs will reflect it in their speech. The information the player gets is the same, but how he gets it will be different.

If Flynn continually uses threats to get his way, the NPCs will get increasingly hostile, but the pirates will get friendlier. If he helps people a lot, they will tend to help him more, too.

The game *Fable* does this well, making a player's reputation a vital part of the game play.

Changing Character Appearance

We can also change the appearance of Flynn to reflect the player's choices. The following offers an example:

Flynn has been given the task to get a grapple hook for a particular puzzle. The shop keeper selling them wants him to do a number of tasks as a fair trade. But we also give Flynn the option to steal the hook. If he chooses to steal, he will get caught and have his hand chopped off, but another NPC helps him fit a hook instead of a hand. If he chooses to do the tasks, he will eventually get the grapple hook from the shop keeper. Either way, the story goes on just the same. Flynn now has a grapple hook, but if he stole he will look more piraty and threatening–reflecting the choices he has made.

Cosmetic Changes

Yes, it sounds boring, but sometimes players like these options, too. What we mean is if you make a racing game, let the player choose the color of the car. When you make an RPG, you can let the player choose the outfit and gender of their avatar. These choices let the player customize their experience in the game without those choices having an impact on your game play or story. It's an easy and popular way to let the player influence the game.

Be wary of giving the player too many choices like this when building a game in Game Maker, though. Remember that all the different costumes and outfits require resources that could make your game quite bulky.

Tools to Tell a Story Inside a Game

When we do take the trouble to tell a story in a game, we should also make sure it ties in well with the game play itself. If the story doesn't relate to the game play at all, it is hard to see any reason why it is there and it becomes irrelevant to the player and just an interruption of the game play. If at all possible, make sure the story fits the game play well and works with it to enhance the experience. It helps a lot if you are able to work on both story and game play at the same time, like we did with our pirate story. We built the story with the levels so that everything ties nicely together. The story is about pirates and the game play is about pirates. The places Flynn travels to have a relevance to the story and the story gives purpose to the game play.

For *Shadows on Deck*, there are still decisions to be made about how to tell the parts of the story that are not game play; which tools to use.

Cut Scenes

The most common tool used to convey the story in a game is cut scenes. Cut scenes are effectively little snippets of movies played in between the game play. They can be more or less elaborate. The *Final Fantasy* series puts great store in cut scenes and have more people creating those than the rest of the game. Special art, cameras, lighting, characters, and sounds are created for the cut scenes alone. However, they don't have to be that complicated to make. A simple shot with two characters talking can be enough to relate the story to the player.

During cut scenes, the player generally doesn't have control of the character and they are as such an interruption of the game play, which is why many dedicated designers (and players) hate them. The trick is to keep them short and relevant. Make every word the characters say count. Don't have them go on about the weather (unless surviving an oncoming storm is the next bit of game play).

If done well, they can be a special treat to watch. The cut scenes serve as reward and payoff for objectives the player has achieved and provides the motivation for the next challenge.

Dialog

Speech is our main tool for conveying the story. As the player character talks to NPCs to get information and help, what they say can greatly help advance the story and give a nice flavor to everything. How the hero responds can show a lot about his character. Dialog can be put in the player's way without interrupting the game play. When he talks to NPCs to get information, make sure he also gets a bit of the story. As mentioned earlier, you can also have the NPCs react differently according to how the player has made his choices in the game. Remember the traits you assigned to the characters and let them show through the words they say.

Lengthy dialog can be just as annoying as cut scenes, so again, keep it to the point. A nice trick used in *Dragon Age Origins* is to have your companions chatting as you go along your business. It doesn't force the player to stop and listen, but still provides extra depth to the characters.

NPCs along the way could also be chatting amongst themselves, providing atmosphere. The players can stop and listen to the gossiping townsfolk or run past as they prefer.

Clues

The game world should support the story you are trying to tell. If the hero is in a hostile new place and he is scared, you can make the surroundings reflect that mood; perhaps darker corners, harsher colors, and ominous music. Put things in the player's way that give hints and clues to the story. In Flynn's case, for instance, he could find his mother's hat in the pirate town to show that she has been here. He could read some graffiti in the ship's hold that tells us that the Pirate King has always been ruthless. At home, Flynn could find a letter from his mother to his father revealing more about their relationship. We can put hints like these in the game world for the player to explore. They support the story and the characters and help the story come alive.

Adventure games do this a lot—including extra items to examine that will reveal a bit more about the characters and their world. Players who would rather not waste time on more story are free to move on, but the more exploring, more thorough players can get the information if they look for it.

Conclusion: Where's the Skip Button?

So that's the story and how we build it. Using the guiding form of the *Hero's Journey* and the archetypes for our characters, we can structure the story so that it fits within the game.

As we've already said, the *Hero's Journey* is just one form to use as you build a story. Experiment and find a way that works for you. The guidelines are here to help, not to dictate how your story should be told.

Let us remind you once again that even though stories make games more exciting, the most important thing to remember is that in a game, the player is there to play, not to sit passively and listen to a story. The game play always comes first. The story is there to enhance the game play, not the other way round.

If you do have sections where you take away the player's control to tell a bit of the story, make sure the cut scene is relevant and that it isn't too long. Don't bore the player with long cut scenes where they can do nothing and, if possible, allow them to skip past your story scenes if they are not interested.

In the next chapter, we will go through our pirate story and see how all this applies to the story we want to tell in our game.

■ ■ ■

CHAPTER 9

Storytelling Applied

Now that all the theory is in place, it will be useful to see it all in action. It is time to look at our story in *Shadows on Deck* using the tools we've been examining. We'll go through the 12 stages of the Hero's Journey and see what we still need to do to our story to make it better. We also need to flesh out all the characters and decide which storytelling tools we will be using in our game and how.

Applying the Theory to *Shadows on Deck*

On our way through the Hero's Journey, we saw that Flynn's story definitely has some holes that need filling out, which is no wonder really, as so far it is only a paragraph long. This is what we have so far:

> We start with Flynn on his home island where he is living with his dad. He is bored and slightly troubled. Then a problem arises. The island is threatened by a poisonous fog creeping in from sea. Flynn gets his opportunity for adventure; a chance to save his home and maybe discover who his mother is. With the fog comes a parrot—we'll call him Archie. The parrot lets Flynn know that his mother is in danger. He sets off on his adventure with the parrot as a companion and guide. He finds his mother and the cause of the evil, but then there's a twist. His mother has been kidnapped by an evil pirate and Flynn has to do what he is told to keep her safe. So he sets of to find a treasure for the evil guy, hoping that his mother will be freed afterward. But the pirate tricks him and sets off to invade Flynn's home island and will probably kill Flynn and both his parents if his evil plan succeeds. In the end, Flynn finds a way to best the bad guy and we have our happy ending. Flynn has saved the island and found out something about who he is and something that he is good at.

Let's go through it stage by stage and fill out as we need. When we have all of *what* will happen, we can begin to think about *how* to show it. While the first outline helped us while we were planning the levels of game play, so the levels will now help us in elaborating on the story.

The Ordinary World

Flynn is from a little fishing village. We'll show this by introducing him down at the beach where all the boats are busy hauling in the day's catch. We need to show his personality somewhat here, so what do we want to get across? He is a bit of a loner, so he is set apart in this first scene from the other boys on the beach. They are laughing and having a good time. Let's have them play at being pirates, as mentioned earlier as a kind of foreshadowing of what is going to happen. We'll also show that he has something on his mind. He is staring out to sea wondering if there isn't something more exciting he could be doing than living his life in a sleepy little village.

The Call to Adventure

The fog starts creeping in. People start to panic and one of the smaller boys cries out for his Mum. Flynn watches him as he is scooped up by his mother and carried home. Is that a bit of envy in his look? A little indication that Flynn doesn't have a mother? Soon the beach is completely covered in mist. A dog barks in fear and one of the fishermen collapses and has to be carried to safety by his friends.

The Refusal to the Call

Flynn can barely see his feet and decides he better go home to his father and away from the fog.

We want Flynn to be eager for adventure, so we'll downplay this stage of the structure. Flynn is not a reluctant hero, but we can still show him shying away from the fog. He might long for something to happen, but he's not about to do something completely stupid like running headlong into the fog. His father will be the one really refusing the call, as he does not want Flynn to get into any danger.

The Meeting with the Mentor

This one we can do very literally. The parrot lands on his shoulder. Archibald, Archie for short, will serve several purposes throughout our story, but one of the important ones is as a mentor showing Flynn what to do. The parrot shouts the first mysterious words about Mary. "Save Mary!" Let's also have him suggest to Flynn that he uses the rooftops to stay above the fog and get home safely. That's the first easy level, remember?

We want Flynn's father, Ben, to act as a mentor. Fortunately, we can have several of those. He will tell Flynn about Mary, his mother. He recognizes Archibald as being Mary's parrot. This is an important vouchsafe for the parrot, because here in the beginning we want the player to completely trust the parrot and follow his advice. Ben explains that he first met Mary when her ship came into port, barely afloat. They fell in love as he helped her repair it. At first, Mary did make an effort to stay with Ben and be happy on the island. They had a baby boy, Flynn, and all seemed alright, but eventually Mary's heart called her out to sea again. She was captain of her own ship, and a pirate at that. "Why didn't you go with her, Dad?" asks Flynn. But Ben loved his island and his job and besides didn't think it would be any good to go sailing the seas with a small baby to take care of.

Here, we provide the player with a bit more of Flynn's story. We also help Flynn understand why he is so restless on the island. His mother is a pirate captain! No wonder he longs for adventure, it must be in his blood. But he is also hurt that she would leave her own son just like that. He wishes that Ben had gone with her. In fact, he is disappointed with his dad for being so boring.

Archie now pipes up, saying that Mary is in danger, captured by the Pirate King. He says that the king is responsible for the weird fog that now engulfs the island. Ben is deeply distraught, but doesn't believe he can do anything about the situation and he doesn't want Flynn to try either, it would be too dangerous.

Together, the two mentors have now provided Flynn with information to act on. Mary is in danger and so is the whole island. If he goes off on this adventure, he might find his mother and even though Ben doesn't want him to go, it is clear that he can't just stay. Something needs to be done or the fog will poison them all. He decides to go find his mother with Archie acting as a guide. He finds a fishing boat that takes him to a merchant ship, on which he gets the post of ship's boy (our second level).

Crossing the First Threshold

Flynn crosses the threshold in the third level. As the pirates attack, he crosses over to their ship to hide and to let them take him to the Pirate King. Before then, he would have been able to go back on the merchant ship, but this is the point of no return and now he can no longer go back. He has to stay hidden. The fog also stops him from going home. Even if he did manage it, his ordinary world is now no longer the same, as it is being poisoned.

Tests, Allies, and Enemies

Here's the fun part of our story. We'll have plenty of scope to throw baddies and challenges at the player. Flynn arrives at Rogues' Rendezvous, the pirate town, and has to find his mother. He rescues several prisoners (unexpected allies) in an attempt to get the right piece of information. Finally, he is led to the town sheriff, who is a major baddie himself. Flynn defeats him and he promises to show the way to the Pirate King and Mary. He takes Flynn to the entrance to the caves. As Flynn enters, the sheriff chuckles to himself; although he is actually telling the truth about the Pirate King's lair, he thinks that there is little chance of Flynn surviving the journey. The scary path is full of poisonous spiders and maggots. Even if he survives that, there is the guardian at the other end to consider.

Let's have the sheriff talking to himself as he walks away from the cave. Flynn doesn't hear him. "Heh, good luck tackling the guardian, my young fool." This is another bit of foreshadowing and it helps us instill a bit of caution and fear in the player. Who exactly is the guardian?

Approach to the Innermost Cave

Flynn survives the cave, of course, and at the end there is indeed a giant monster. The boss of the cave level waits here as a final test before the innermost cave. This could be a huge fire-breathing dragon. As it breathes fire, it sets alight some of the poisonous mushrooms, which then explode in a rain of acid. Flynn has to trick the dragon to set fire to mushrooms that explode near its own body. Archie will here be extra helpful, so that what happens in the next stage is more of a shock. As the dragon is defeated, Flynn takes a deep breath as he steps through the door. He is about to see his mother for the first time, and he is nervous. Behind him, Archie follows with a guilty look on his face.

The Ordeal

Here, we arrive at the first twist in our tale. Flynn manages to get past the guardian and is allowed an audience with the Pirate King.

But what's this? He is actually expecting Flynn. "Well done, Archie! Who knew a stupid parrot could be that useful?" Archibald is revealed as a trickster! He has taken Flynn through thick and thin to deliver him into the hands of the Pirate King. To his defense, he looks slightly ashamed of it. The Pirate King has plans for Flynn. He has Mary locked up, but hasn't been able to get the information he wanted from her, even though he has tried every nasty piece of torture he could think of.

He calls for Mary and the guards carry a bedraggled woman in and throw her to the floor. The Pirate King explains that this little lady stole his treasure 17 years ago and made off with it.

The first time Flynn sees his mother, she is presented as a thief.

The King's scheme works. When Mary sees her son at the King's mercy, she immediately gives in.

She explains on which island she hid the treasure and how she placed booby traps around it to keep it safe. The Pirate King doesn't trust her. She's always been a cunning rogue, even when they worked together. Flynn is shocked. She used to work for the Pirate King?

The King comes up with a plan: he'll send Flynn to get the treasure for him. If Mary is telling the truth, he should be able to retrieve it safely. Mary cries out in agony but there's nothing she can do.

The King orders Archibald to accompany Flynn. "Make sure he comes back!"

The two of them set off into the jungle to retrieve the treasure. The mood is ominous. Flynn is furious with Archie for setting him up and Archie tries to explain he only did it to save Mary, but Flynn doesn't believe him. He doesn't know what to think about his mother either. Apparently, she lied to Ben all along. She never intended to stay and never told him about the treasure. And here Flynn is, traveling through a deadly jungle to try and save her. Does he even want to rescue her?

But the King has promised him that if he returns with the treasure, not only will he free Mary, he'll bring them all safely home and even get rid of the fog.

Flynn can only hope that he will keep his promises.

So this is the ordeal. Flynn still has a lot of work to do to claim his reward, and already we suspect that the reward might not be that easy to get or even worth having. Mary is just a mean thief who lied to Ben and abandoned Flynn as a baby. Flynn still goes on, though. What else can he do? He finds the treasure in the jungle level and returns to claim…

The Reward

As we suspected, the reward is unfortunately not worth having. The Pirate King cheats again. He says he will bring them all home himself, secretly planning to get rid of everyone in one go. The King needs to go to the island because the treasure that Flynn brought home from the jungle turns out to be a map. The little island where Flynn was born has a bay with a cave, but no one ever goes there because it can only be approached by sea and the bay is full of reefs that will tear the hull of any ship that tries to get past.

But Mary has mastered it. During her time on the island, she explored the reef and found her way to the cave. She buried the treasure there and drew the map so that she could find her way back.

The Pirate King drags them all to his ship and locks them up in the hold, even Archie who he also tricked into cooperation. They are headed for Ben's Island.

The Road Back

In the hold, Mary explains to Flynn that she only left to throw the King off the scent and always intended to return, but the King caught her before she managed to be rid of him. She begs Flynn to escape and go warn Ben and the other islanders that trouble is coming. As they anchor not far from the island to wait for the tide in the early morning, Flynn escapes the hold, but up on deck he is confronted with the King himself. A great fight takes place and Flynn wins with the help of Archibald. Or so it seems. The fog slowly dissipates.

He frees his mother and the forgiven parrot and off they go to meet Ben. All is well and they celebrate with all the islanders. The village boys refuse to believe Flynn's tall tales of adventure. Flynn tries to convince himself that it doesn't matter.

We have a fake ending here. But in the morning, oh dear…

The Resurrection

As the sun rises, the little family takes a boat out to the bay to bring up the treasure.

But oh no! The Pirate King is not dead after all. He has taken on his true form and stealthily follows the boat through the reef.

As Ben and Flynn are carrying back the treasure chest, the King rises from the sea. He is a kraken!

This is the final challenge. Flynn takes on the Pirate King, and with a bit of help from Ben and Mary, he wins. Flynn realizes his own worth as he claims the kraken's claw. He can return proudly to his home, having achieved all he set out to do; he found his mother, he saved the island from disaster, and he learned something about himself and who he is.

Return with the Elixir

Along with the treasure chest, he brings back the kraken's claw and the village boys finally believe his story.

The family shares the treasure amongst all the islanders and we have our happy ending.

But as a last shot, we see Flynn staring out to sea again. He has the admiration of all the other boys and is no longer an outsider, but greatly admired. He has found his mother too and made his father a very happy man. But his blood still yearns for adventure. Archie sees it and feels the same.

We're rounding off with a happy ending, but also leaving room for a new adventure. Will Flynn go off again? Almost certainly.

Archetypes for Our Story

We already have an indication of what characters we might populate our world with, but we would do well to look closer at all our characters, good guys and bad guys, helpers and enemies, protagonists and antagonists alike.

The cast of *Shadows on Deck* fits neatly into the archetypes we've already been through. They were:

- Hero
- Mentor
- Herald
- Threshold Guardian
- Shapeshifter
- Trickster
- Shadow

Let's go through the most important characters.

■**Note** You will notice that the sketches are not in silhouette style yet. For first sketches, the important thing is to get the first idea down fairly quickly without having to worry about fitting it into a certain style. That can come later, when we have a clearer picture of the whole game.

Flynn

Our player character, Flynn, is a boy of 15 who longs for adventure. See Figure 9–1 for a first sketch.

Figure 9–1. *Flynn, our hero, with Archibald the parrot.*

He doesn't know what to do with his life yet, and is torn between doing what his father expects and joining his shipwright business, or to catch a boat out of here away from the island. He is also very curious about his missing mother. Who was she, and why do the other village boys jeer and snigger whenever she is mentioned?

Archetype: Hero

Flynn is our archetypical willing hero. He is smart enough to be afraid of the Pirate King, but he is yearning to test his own mettle and find out more about his mother.

Father

Ben is a stout sort of fellow, as shown in Figure 9–2.

Figure 9–2. *Flynn's father, Ben.*

He seems like the picture of a good responsible citizen and father, but once he was just like Flynn, dreaming of other shores and big adventures. That's why he fell in love with Mary, the pirate, but having an unexpected baby sobered him up, and as Mary would never be a good mother to the baby, he chose to stay and do his best for his son. He tells himself he doesn't regret the choice, and most of the time, he doesn't.

Archetype: Mentor

Ben acts as a mentor in our story. He gives Flynn information about his mother and some good advice. He serves as a threshold guardian as well, as he is afraid for Flynn and doesn't want to let him go. He is the one who really voices concern in the stage "Refusal to the Call."

Mother

Mary (Figure 9–3) has always been a wild girl. She has always done exactly what she wanted. She stole the Pirate King's treasure, got caught, and ran her ship aground while fleeing. She seduced the local shipwright, Ben, to get him to fix her ship, meanwhile hiding her treasure and keeping it from him.

Figure 9–3. *Mary, pirate and reluctant mother.*

She hadn't planned on actually falling in love. She never liked the prospect of settling down on a small boring island, but in fact she would have done it, were it not for the threat of the Pirate King. She chose to travel on to keep Ben and her baby son safe, but the decision gnaws at her conscience. She never told Ben why she left, and often wonders whether there could have been another way. She has been dreaming for a long time about returning to the island.

Flynn doesn't quite know how to trust her, especially since she has abandoned him before and he learns that she once worked for the Pirate King.

Archetype: Shapeshifter

Mary is a classic shapeshifter. At the start of our story, Flynn isn't sure whether she is good or not. She left him as a baby, so she must be bad, mustn't she? But as he gets to know her, he realizes that it isn't that simple; life rarely is. Mary loves Flynn and has only his best interests at heart, but she has her own ideas about what is best for Flynn, which might be very different from what he wants himself.

Even at the very end, Flynn doesn't know whether Mary will stay.

The Parrot Archibald

The parrot (Figure 9–4) is an extraordinarily clever bird. He speaks, often and loudly. Getting nowhere with Mary, the Pirate King started torturing Archie. He caved in immediately and told the King all about Ben and Flynn on the little island. The King believes that Flynn will be valuable as leverage and sends Archie on pain of death to bring him back. Archie agrees, not only to free Mary and his own feathers, but because he thinks it will serve his purpose. If the Pirate King should happen to kill Flynn, then there is no reason for Mary to return to the island and settle down.

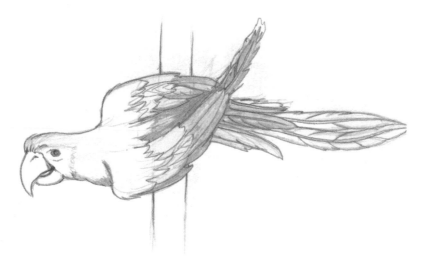

Figure 9–4. *Archibald, the sidekick parrot.*

The bird isn't actually evil; he just serves his own interests first and foremost. He loved his life as Mary's pirate parrot and is happiest when there is adventure around. Settling down on a little island would not suit him at all. But he never expected that he would start to care for the island boy he is sending into danger.

The parrot spans a number of roles, being a very useful guide and tool throughout the game.

Archetype: Herald, Mentor, Trickster

Archie is extremely useful in our story and takes on many different roles as we go through the story. First, he is the herald bringing the news that Mary is held captive; next, he takes on the role as mentor and guides Flynn through most of the game. He is the one informing Flynn of almost everything he needs to know along the way. He also teaches Flynn new moves.

But as they meet the Pirate King, Archie reveals himself to be a trickster. He has been serving his own agenda all along, and though he sounds like he is sorry about the deception, it is likely that he would do it again to save his own hide.

Sidekick

The parrot has another important role here worth mentioning. He is the Hero's sidekick, his companion and the one who asks all the silly questions. Sidekicks are brilliant tools. They give us an opportunity to use dialog to carry the story along. If the hero is alone, how will we know what he is thinking?

Imagine if Sherlock Holmes was always solving crimes alone. The spectators would never know what he was up to, unless he always spoke his thoughts aloud to himself. But because he has to explain everything to Dr. Watson, the audience is informed too.

Sidekicks can also bring humor to any story. We don't usually want the hero to be laughable; remember, we want the players to identify with the hero and if he is a laughing stock, they might not do so.

But the sidekick can be a clown or a bit stupid, and get into all sorts of scrapes.

The Pirate King

The Pirate King is the main bad guy and is actually not human at all. He possesses magical abilities and uses them all for purely selfish reasons. He is a necromancer. He has a crowd of human pirates at his beck and call, and anyone who disobeys will be killed and raised as a skeleton. He is like a gangster boss that you really don't want to cross, and of course, Mary did.

He thinks himself wholly justified in spreading his poisonous fog across the sea and torturing Mary to get his treasure back. No matter that he actually stole it all himself. He follows his own code of honor and is disappointed that one of his most promising students would turn against him like this.

Archetype: Shadow

The Pirate King (Figure 9–5) is not just a shadow; he is THE shadow; often referred to as the *arch-nemesis*. A good hero has a mighty enemy to conquer, one who is often just as strong as, or maybe stronger than, the hero, which is why defeating him is such a major achievement. The hero wins against all odds. It is therefore important to make the arch-nemesis formidable. They are also great fun to create, and to be honest usually much more interesting than the hero. Pure evil is FUN, isn't it? The bad guy can do whatever he wants; the hero usually has to be law-abiding or at least honorable.

Figure 9–5. *The Pirate King.*

Level Bosses

Besides being *shadows*, all the bosses found at the end of the levels are all *threshold guardians*. That is their sole purpose in the game, but it is still a very important role. They test whether the player is ready for the next level. One of those is the sheriff of Rogues' Rendezvous (Figure 9–6).

Figure 9–6. *The sheriff of Rogues' Rendezvous.*

Minor Characters

We have other characters too, of course, but their roles are more minor, and can be divided into allies and enemies.

Allies

- The villagers on Ben's island
- The sailors on the merchant ship
- The prisoners in Rogues' Rendezvous

Enemies

- Skeleton pirates
- Bandits
- Birds
- Bats
- Spiders
- All the monsters that we throw in Flynn's path.

Titles Tantrum

Thinking of a good title for your game is not easy. We struggled a bit with a good name for our game. When that happens, it's a good idea to get a few friends together and throw ideas around. Even the silliest name might jog someone else to think of a good one, so put them all on the paper.

We were trying for a title that was nice to say, easy to remember, and at least hinted at the story and the style of the game. First, we tried to think of keywords that might spark some good ideas, and then we started suggesting titles. Brainstorming like this is great fun. The only rule is that no idea is too stupid.

Here are some of the keywords and silly names we managed to come up with. Maybe you can tell that alliteration is one of our favorite approaches.

Keywords

Platform, Pirates, Jumping, Skeletons, Treasure, Silhouette, Contour, Cut out, Parrot, Sail, Bandits, Profile, Relief, Ship, Schooner, Port, Starboard

Titles

- *The Adventures of Peter the Irate Pirate!*
- *Where's Mi Booty? -A Pirate Escapade!*
- *Shiver Mi Timbers!-A Musical Pirate Adventure!*
- *Hard-a-Starboard*
- *Ship-Shapes*
- *Pouncing Platform Pirates*
- *Pirates Ahoy!*
- *Parrot Ahoy!*
- *Platforms, Pirates and... A Parrot*
- *Peg Leg Polly and the Parrot Ultimatum!*
- *Here Be Pirates!*
- *Here Be Parrots!*
- *Parrots Be Pirates!*
- *Pirates be Pa... you get the idea....*
- *Pieces of Eight*
- *The Adventures of Hercules Parrot, the Feathered French Pirate Detective.*
- *The Pickled Pirate Pontiff of Pontefract*
- *AAAAAAAAAR!*
- *Blackbeard Cyril and the Runaway Crossbones!*
- *On Deck 'Til Dawn*
- *From Dusk 'Til Dawn*
- *Shadows on Deck*
- *Stowaway*
- *Ant and Deck's Saturday Night Pirate Adventure*
- *The Pesky Problem of Putrid Pirates*
- *Twilight Pirates*
- *Shady Pirates*
- *Dusky Journey*
- *Flynn's Nightmare Adventure*

In the end, we settled for *Shadows on Deck*. It has a nice ring to it, sounds mysterious, and hints at both silhouettes and ships.

Storytelling Tools for *Shadows on Deck*

We now have a good story and a nice wide cast for our game. We need to decide how we will convey that story in the game. When we decide on which tools to use and how, it is important to remember what type of game we are dealing with. This is a platform game, so the cut scenes should never be too long. We don't want to slow down the pace of the game. The game play of a platformer is quite fast, with the player mostly running, jumping, and dodging. With that in mind, let's have a look at the options.

Clues

Unlike a lot of adventure games, we won't let Flynn investigate objects lying around in the game. If we did that, we would slow the game down too much. Instead, we will use the environment to emphasize the feel of the story. It would, however, be nice to actually let Archie betray his sneaky intentions while Flynn's back is turned, so that the player gets a definite sense that he is up to something, without letting Flynn know the same.

That could be one of the skeleton crew actually stopping to wave familiarly at Archie, and the parrot frantically trying to get him to stop, or Archie could be triggering a secret lever that opens the right way through the tunnels.

Dialog

We will definitely have dialog in our game. Flynn will be talking to the people he meets and will get information that way, which means we will need to set up dialog options. When the player clicks on a character in the game, he will sometimes have the option to select different things to say. He will also be able to talk to Archie.

Minor characters who do not have an important role will just deliver a one liner, without actually engaging in a full conversation. There are two good reasons for this; firstly, we don't want to write too much dialog if we can help it; secondly, we don't want to bore or mislead the player. If you fill your game with too much talk that isn't relevant to what the player needs to do, you end up both confusing and boring your audience. Remember, they are here first and foremost to play the game, not listen to a story.

For the more important characters, we will set up dialog trees. They are a way of structuring conversations in the game. If Flynn chooses to talk to Ben, for instance, it might look something like Figure 9–7.

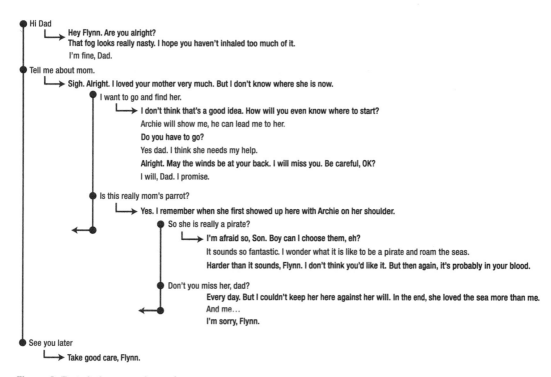

Figure 9–7. *A dialog tree planned out.*

A tree like this shows you, the game programmer, what to write in your script to make the conversation take place. Where the tree branches out, the player has a choice of responses. When it doubles back, it means that the line of enquiry is finished and the player can now go back to ask about something else.

When you plan these out, remember to think about what your characters are like and what they are likely to say. Again, we have to stress that dialog should always be kept tight. Make sure your dialog has a purpose in the game; a lot of players don't like to read extensive text. Every sentence in the tree in Figure 9–7 has a purpose, either in the story or in the game play. For example, the line: **Archie will show me, he can lead me to her** is important information to the player that the parrot will act as a guide, and Flynn accepts the call to adventure with the line: **Yes dad. I think she needs my help**. Even if they do all have a purpose, all these lines might be too much. With dialog in games, less is always more.

Cut Scenes

We will also be using cut scenes, mostly as introductions to new levels and as rewards after defeating end-level bosses. It would fit in nicely with the cut out style if we drew the cut scenes as comic book pages. The camera will pan down the page, letting the player read the cut scene. What we need to do then is to plan them out carefully and this is usually best done using a rough storyboard style.

Storyboards are almost comic books anyway, telling the story they need to tell in images as well as words. Each "camera view point" gets a quick sketch along with a description. This is a technique often used in both games and films when the director wants to show the cameraman and the rest of the crew what he is planning for the scene they're about to shoot. Let's look at the very beginning of our story as an example (see Figure 9–8). We start our game on the beach where Flynn is daydreaming.

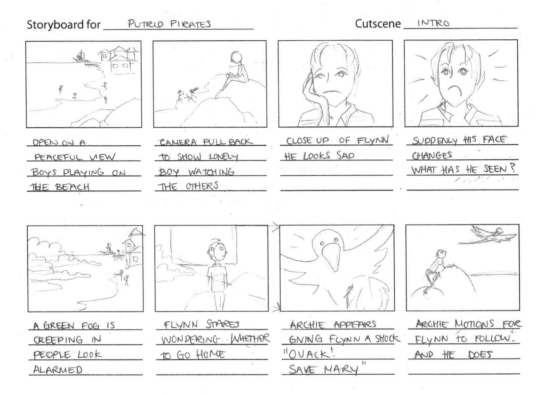

Storyboard for ____PUTRID PIRATES____   Cutscene ___INTRO___

OPEN ON A PEACEFUL VIEW BOYS PLAYING ON THE BEACH

CAMERA PULL BACK TO SHOW LONELY BOY WATCHING THE OTHERS

CLOSE UP OF FLYNN HE LOOKS SAD

SUDDENLY HIS FACE CHANGES WHAT HAS HE SEEN?

A GREEN FOG IS CREEPING IN PEOPLE LOOK ALARMED

FLYNN STARES WONDERING WHETHER TO GO HOME

ARCHIE APPEARS GIVING FLYNN A SHOCK "QUACK! SAVE MARY"

ARCHIE MOTIONS FOR FLYNN TO FOLLOW. AND HE DOES

Figure 9–8. *A storyboard template, filled in with our first cut scene.*

We've planned out the levels of the game already in Chapter 7. Now all we have to do is add in the cut scenes so we know where they occur and what they should contain (see Figure 9–9).

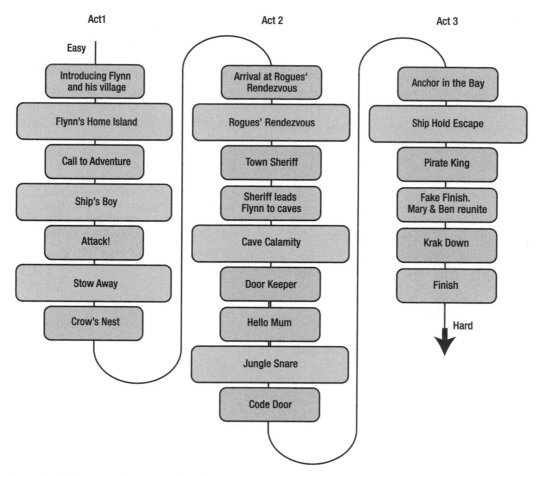

Figure 9–9. *The game shown as a flowchart containing all the levels, boss fights, and cut scenes.*

Turns out we have quite a few cut scenes, but then, this is a story-driven game we are creating.

We won't draw storyboards for all the scenes here, but instead show you what the script might look like for a few of these, with the dialog planned out.

To see how we progress to the next cut scene, we'll have a quick description of the game play that follows each one. This will give you some context so you can see how to lead in and out of a cut scene, which is an important aspect of cut scene design.

Cut Scene: Attack!

Flynn has just come from the masts atop the trade ship to receive praise for his first efforts up there. He did well... for a landlubber. The crew is teasing him good-naturedly, when a cry rings down from above; Pirates Ahoy! The crew rushes to the side of the ship to take in the ominous sight of the huge pirate ship. "Alright, men. Arm the guns. We've dealt with scum like this before," the captain shouts.

But Archie shakes his head and whispers to Flynn. "They're not ordinary pirates. They are sent from the Pirate King himself. I'd bet my remaining tail feathers on it."

The ship looms closer and some of the crew cry out in fear as they realize the pirate crew is all skeletons. The captain shouts frantic orders, trying to keep his crew calm and to get away from the other ship, but it is too late. Heavy grappling hooks thud into the wood as the crew, frozen with fear, looks on. Flynn is stunned himself, but the parrot stirs him into action.

"Get aloft again, boy. We stand a better chance up there. Keep moving and see if you can get to the other ship. If we can hide on their ship, they'll take us straight to the Pirate King with any luck."

Game Play

Flynn jumps for his life and gains some height in the masts. Below him the battle rages on. If he talks to any crew member, they urge him to get out of the way and stay out of trouble. At one point where he looks stuck, the parrot will tell him how to climb to the other ship. Flynn has a new move and needs to use it a good few times to get near the crow's nest on the pirate ship.

Birds are snapping at him from above, so it's safest to keep moving. He can duck the birds.

Cut Scene: Introduce Boss in Crow's Nest

The parrot has steered Flynn towards the crow's nest throughout, but as they reach it, the skeletons are closing in and surround the boy. Then a horrible laugh rings out and from high above, a skeleton, much larger than the others, thumps down onto the platform. "Hah! What's this, me hearties? A measly little boy who hasn't even got his sea legs yet? Is *HE* giving you trouble? Get out of my way. I will handle this."

Boss Fight

This skeleton seems to have more limbs than are good for him. In fact, he climbs the netting like a six-legged spider. Using the new climb ability, Flynn must unhook his limbs one by one till the pirate finally falls into the sea. The skeleton moves between three different positions–all of which he can reach by climbing vertically. The pirate hurls wooden pegs at Flynn, knocking him backward and off the platforms if he is not careful.

Cut Scene: Arrival at Rogues' Rendezvous

With the lookout out of the way, Flynn hides in the crow's nest. The battle that had been going on so fiercely down below suddenly stops; the skeletons withdraw and leave the other ship. Baffled, the captain looks his crew over. Is everyone alright? Where's Flynn?" The sailors look at each other, but shake their heads sadly. No one knows.

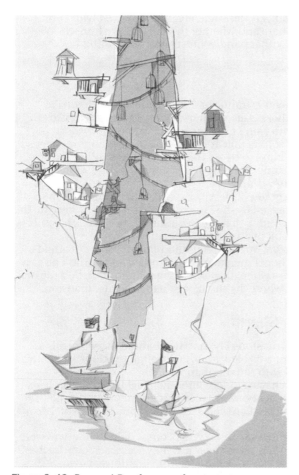

Figure 9–10. *Rogues' Rendezvous, the pirate town.*

The pirate ship sails with all speed now. Flynn wonders why nobody notices that the lookout is missing (*Shh, Flynn is being lured toward the Pirate King, remember?*), but is relieved to be left alone.

After days at sea, the ship reaches a hostile-looking island. Huge cliffs loom out of the ocean and the captain seems to be steering the ship right into the rocks. But then at the last minute, a small inlet is revealed and the ship slowly negotiates the narrow channel into an inner pool, completely hidden from the sea (see Figure 9–10). Flynn looks up in awe. A sprawling town inhabits the cliffs. Makeshift houses and huts made from what looks like driftwood fill the gap above the ship. Rope walkways connect the different buildings and pirate flags are flying proudly everywhere.

"Welcome to Rogues' Rendezvous," whispers Archie. "This is where all the pirates meet and barter their newly stolen goods. I don't know if the Pirate King is here, but there must be someone here who can tell us more." Flynn spots a dangling cage hanging high above. A skeleton foot pokes out from the bars. "What's that?" he asks with dread. "Oh that," Archie says with a chuckle, "is a captive held ransom for money. I guess his family didn't raise the money in time."

Flynn looks sideways at the parrot. He seems very much to be on the pirates' side; laughing at a poor prisoner. And this is his mother's pet? Does that mean that Mary is as ruthless when it comes to making money? He hopes not. The skeletons tie up the ship and, except for a grumpy-looking crew member left as guard, the ship is quickly deserted. Flynn sneaks past with ease. Archie says: "Let's go find out if Mary has been here and whether the King is here himself. We better avoid the skeleton crews, but some of the other bandits must know something."

Game Play

This level is a slight change of pace from the previous frantic one. There are still skeletons to avoid and push over the side of platforms, but there is also a lot of talking. Flynn can talk to unfriendly bandits who won't attack him but who won't give him any information, either.

The best shot Flynn has got is to ask the prisoners that are locked up in the hanging cages. They all want one thing in exchange for information; to be set free. Flynn must explore the level to find keys for the cages (all keys fit all cages). Some can be found just by exploring, some by knocking over particularly grumpy bandits so they drop a key.

Several cages have to be opened and Flynn gradually learns that Mary has indeed been through Rogues' Rendezvous. She was being dragged by the Pirate King's skeletons. Where to, the prisoner doesn't know. Another has overheard rumors that the town sheriff, as he calls himself, is famous for selling information. He even looks a bit like a rat.

The sheriff imposes a kind of order on the town, but only as it suits him and he is not afraid to break the rules if it lines his pockets. He has two henchmen that keep him safe and it won't be easy to get information out of him. But if anyone knows where the Pirate King is hiding out, he's the one. Flynn makes his way to the very top of the town, where the sheriff is said to have his "mansion."

Cut Scene: Introduction to the Town Sheriff

Outside the door of the shanty mansion, the parrot stops Flynn. "Hide behind those barrels a minute and I'll take care of the henchmen. As soon as I am gone, go through the door and bolt it from the other side. Then you only have to deal with the sheriff himself."

"Only..." mutters Flynn. "Well, it's better than having to fight three men, right? Right. Wait here."

Archie lands by the door and starts yelling in a booming voice that doesn't sound at all like his normal voice: "Raffi, you great big lout, come out here and show what you're made of. I've a score to settle with you!"

There's some shuffling inside and a scared voice answers. "Why, Tony, I didn't know you were in town, how nice, how nice. Unfortunately I'm really rather busy just now. Can you come back later?" The parrot roars, "Come out here you great yellow belly or I'll tear your house down."

More shuffling inside. Flynn is wondering how on earth Archie knew that the Sheriff was scared of someone called Tony?

Finally the door opens and two rather uncomfortable-looking bulky guys are pushed outside. "I said deal with him, NOW! That's what I pay you for."

Archie takes off and lands on a platform further down. He shouts again. "Are you coming, Raffi?" The two henchmen reluctantly follow the voice and Flynn quickly grabs the door before it shuts. He slips inside.

Conclusion

We'll leave the storytelling here. You get the idea, no doubt. We hope you find it as much fun as we do, and that you'll try to write some of the cut scenes we missed out.

So, we have a story. A fast-paced tale that suits our little platformer well and some interesting characters to fill our game world with. Using the Hero's Journey as a general guide, we've mapped out the whole game and know which tools we'd like to use. That's enough planning, don't you think? It's time to start building the game, and that begins with the art resources.

CHAPTER 10

■ ■ ■

Of Mice and Pen: Pirate Art

So, we have a game design, we have characters, and we have a story. Broadly speaking, these are the bare bones over which the body of the game is built. The design and story dictate to some extent the direction the programmers might take, and of course the same is true for the artistic style, which is where the job of a concept artist begins.

In this chapter, we'll explore the different parts of the art production process for *Shadows on Deck*, from first ideas through to implementation of the finished art. Along the way, we will encounter various problems and explore the methods of solving them, and throughout there will be lots of advice and tips about creativity and the art process in general.

A Little Art History

The video game artist's job has certainly evolved over the past 20 years. In the 1990s when Zool was made, it was possible for a team of three people to create a game from scratch and get it onto the shelves in under six months! Back then, most of the game graphics still involved sprites that moved against layered 2D backgrounds, but since then, games have become far more elaborate and complex to develop. This meant the job of the artist expanded to include many roles, such as concept designers, character modelers, animators, 2D texture artists, and HUD/ front-end designers. As a result, it became impossible for one artist to perform all the tasks required within a game's development.

Happily, however, our game *Shadows on Deck* is to be presented as a classic style of game: an homage to how games used to be made, which means most of the graphics and art comes from the hand and mind of a single artist. By the end of this chapter, you should be in a position to pick up that role and take the game to new places from your own imagination.

Shadows On Spec

Everyone loves a pirate story. As a theme, these swarthy bilge rats have persisted for centuries, thrilling generations of children and adults alike with their outlandish costumes and the romance of high-seas adventure. Pirates are perfect computer game material, and a gift for any artist lucky enough to work on such a game.

As described in the previous chapters, our game is to feature backgrounds and characters presented in an intriguing silhouetted style. Producing art of this type might seem straightforward—after all, we don't have to worry about color or the finer aspects of costume design or the surface detail of the environment. However, presenting everything as a flat, single-colored shape comes with specific problems of its own:

- How do we make the characters stand out from the backgrounds?

- How do we prevent a collection of shadowy shapes looking obscure?

- Can we include a little detail on the characters, and how could this be achieved?

- What methods can we use to add depth to the levels?

- How many layers should we use for the backgrounds?

- Will it be possible to tell the story effectively in a silhouette style?

- What tools should we use to design, create, and animate the artwork?

These are kinds of questions that we will try and address in the remainder of this chapter as we take you through a standard art process that might take place for a game like this.

The Art Process

Just as the story for the game has a beginning, middle, and end, the whole art process must progress in a similar way. Some of the issues identified in the last section can only be addressed as the game develops, so in the first instance, we'll cover a stage in the art process called conceptual design. Once that's over, we'll move onto the serious business of asset creation, and finish up by touching upon art integration, bringing us neatly back into the implementation side of the game. We'll take each of these in turn to provide an insight into how the whole process fits together when you create a game.

Phase 1: Conceptual Design

The conceptual design phase is all about trying out as many ideas as possible in order to come up with something that works. This initial period spent sketching, gathering reference material to inspire ideas, and the imagination is quite an in-depth process, requiring a great deal of detailed thought, as you shall see!

There is a saying: "measure twice, cut once." This basically means that you pay a lot of attention at the start of a job, thinking carefully about what you want to achieve and what you need to do to make sure it goes smoothly. While the burden of this task is very much on the concept artist, it's important to stay in close contact with your creative colleagues to avoid going off in the wrong direction and having to throw away your hard work.

Figure 10-1. *Some initial pirate concept sketches from Kevin's sketchbook*

The Art of Communication

To begin, the designer, programmer, and artist get together to discuss the art style and design aesthetic, as well as brainstorming lists of things the game might feature, including characters, enemies, objects, and environments. Although it is too early in the process for this list of assets to be definitive, by the end of the meeting, you should have a plan of action that helps to guide the initial direction for the artistic content of the game.

It may seem strange to sit down with a programmer to discuss the art style, but there are usually technical constraints to consider, which designers and artists might not be fully aware of. There may even be technical concepts that need trying out in order to discover whether a particular style or visual technique is feasible on the target platform.

A Pirate's Brew

I met up with Jake (the programmer) and Nana (the designer) in a coffee shop to discuss the initial idea for the game. Back then, it didn't even have a name, but Nana had a clear idea of what she'd like to achieve with the game play and story, and Jake was keen to keep a handle on the technical and time constraints. I made some notes in my sketchbook as we threw ideas around and by the end of the meeting, I had some initial ideas for some styles that I wanted to play around with. You can see some of my initial scribbles and notes in Figure 10–1.

Gaining Inspiration

Inspiration can be a tricky thing to pin down, but it's also a very good excuse to watch lots of DVDs. One absolutely essential requirement for any artist (or would-be artist!) is a good selection of books, comics, magazines, and DVDs. As you work through different projects, you tend to acquire new reference materials along the way, and eventually you'll be the proud owner of a fantastic selection of imagination-inspiring things. But where do you start such a library in the first place?

Your house very probably has many interesting books, objects, or DVDs in it to start with, just have a good look around and see what you can find that looks interesting or that gives you cool ideas to work from. You might want to tailor your collection according to what you have in your game design. If you have creatures and natural environments in your game, then watch some natural history documentaries, look up such subjects online, or get a hold of some cool natural history books. The same goes for buildings or vehicles. Check out your local library, too; there are always lots of interesting things to discover there, just remember to take your notebook with you! Postcards, weekend newspaper supplements, cereal boxes, pizza flyers dropped through the letterbox; absolutely anything could spark some amazing response in the imagination receptors within your brain, so learn to see the potential in everything you come into contact with.

After a while of reading and studying, your head will naturally fill with all sorts of knowledge and facts, and it'll stay up there even though you might not realize it! Then, when you're thinking hard about some design problem, you'll find that stored knowledge will inspire all sorts of ideas to come flooding out!

Phillip Pullman said the way he approaches writing is "to read like a butterfly and write like a bee. Any honey in my writing is due to the nectar I found in the work of better writers." This is a wonderful sentiment and is as true for art or music as it is for writing. So read, look, listen, learn. Remember, you get out what you put in, so cram as much cool stuff into your head as you can!

Reference Material

Nana's starting point for this game was to create a platform game in a silhouette style. The problem of selecting environments and characters that would "read" well as silhouettes became the inspiration that ultimately suggested a pirate-themed game. Once they were in the mix, there were a number of obvious, and not so obvious, places for me to look for further inspiration. Watching *Pirates of the Caribbean* and other pirate films was a natural place to start, and helped to generate numerous drawings in my sketchbook. I also spent some time studying old sailing ships, familiarizing myself with the way the masts are constructed and gathering ideas for objects I could produce for the game levels. I even browsed online for fancy dress stores; pirate costumes are as popular as they ever have been, it seems!

However, the game is not solely restricted to a pirate ship. There are two other levels I had to design assets for, one is based in a swamp, the other is a village built onto the sheer walls of two facing cliffs.

For these environments, I wanted to come up with as many ideas for plants, trees, houses, and platforms as possible, and so natural history DVDs and books on botanical subjects became my next port of call. In particular, I drew huge inspiration from fungi for some of the strange plants and growths that rise from the swamp and cling to the cliff faces, as their fantastic shapes and forms are nearer to fantasy than reality, distinctive shapes and outlines that lend themselves effortlessly to our game's requirements!

Other inspirational avenues include browsing through my collection of art books. In particular, my 'Art Of...' video game books and guides, plus movie and animated film art books. Titles as diverse as *Monsters, Inc., Super Mario Galaxy, The Legend Of Zelda: Wind Waker, Avatar, The Lord of the Rings,* and *Aliens vs. Predator* all offer a little something to the mix.

Getting Warmed Up

With this philosophy in mind, you can set about developing the sketches and doodles you have made so far into a series of more detailed exploratory drawings. This artwork should be experimental; a series of tests just to see how characters and environments might look and work together, but it is also an opportunity to get a feel for the project and continue the creative flow.

This is all about the creative exploration of ideas, and taking those ideas as far as possible. Unbridled artistic creativity early in game development is responsible for the way the game will eventually look, so you want to allow those ideas to be as wild, silly, and outlandish as possible! In so doing, you may well come up with some unusable stuff, but there will be plenty of material you can then develop and build upon.

Drawing Tips

My earliest memories involve drawing *Daleks, The Incredible Hulk,* and *Dinosaur-Cybermen* on my bedroom walls with wax crayons. In a bid to save the wallpaper, my mother bought me paper and pencils and from then on I was hooked. But even though I have been drawing since I was little taller than those pencils my mother bought for me, it is still difficult on occasion to get myself into a frame of mind where the work flows. Sometimes it can be a little… sluggish. The ideas just refuse to come, that blank page is just too intimidating.

Such times happen rarely these days, thankfully, but when they do there is a simple exercise I use to get going, and all it requires is a bit of faith in your own imagination. With pencil poised over a blank sheet of paper, close your eyes and make a few marks or scribbles on the page! It may seem like madness, but the paper is no longer blank, you've made a start! And the best part; those random lines you've made can become absolutely ANYTHING. Just let your mind relax and allow your pencil to build upon the marks on the paper!

The More the Merrier

No matter how concrete your initial game idea seems, it always evolves from its original form, so during this early stage, we try to include as many eventualities as possible. One such strategy is to aim to produce more concepts than are actually required.

Let's say, for example, that in your finished game you want to have ten different bad guys with three boss characters ranged over eight levels. It's a fair target, but it might be a good idea to increase those numbers a little; perhaps 15 different baddies, 5 bosses, and 12 levels. With luck, you won't need to use all of these, but it is always better to have too much content at the start than not enough. Often, the original ideas turn out not to work as well as everyone thought and the extra ideas take their place, perhaps even opening up new avenues for the game design in the process. So, make a list of everything your game might feature, and then add a little more, just for luck!

Figure 10–2. *Variations on a design for a spaceship*

Idea Building

Once you're ready to get stuck into designing characters and environments, you'll want to come up with as many ideas as you possibly can. Remember, at this stage, it's always better to have too many ideas to choose from than too few.

One method I sometimes use to get those ideas flowing is to "invent" a game and explore concept designs for it. Let's imagine we need to design a space ship for a video game. We all know one when we see it, but there are so many different design choices that can be explored:

- How many engines does the ship have?

- How many wings, fins, and other such features are there?

- Are there weapons? Where are they situated?
- What is the configuration of the ship?
- How large is it?

I begin this exploration process by filling a page with drawings of ships, simple sketches from a top-down perspective, experimenting with different outlines and silhouettes, moving engines around, and positioning weaponry in different places (see Figure 10–2). I then choose the best examples from this page, and set about producing another page of ideas with these as a starting point. While it might seem excessive to produce so much artwork when so few will ever be used, the sheer number of variations means there is a greater chance of finding that killer design, and some of the other designs can of course be used elsewhere in the game, or used in a future project! Finally, I chose an image from the last page of variations and rendered this up as a finished design (see Figure 10–3). The player won't know how many different designs were explored in order to reach this point, but the result benefits from all that hard work.

Figure 10–3. *The final spaceship*

Silhouetiquette

It was during this phase that the issue of silhouette legibility came to the fore. The initial sketches for the levels made it clear that some objects were either a little obscure, such as the featureless squares of boxes and crates, or just messy in the case of bushes and trees. The solution to these problems also answered another issue, that being whether or not to include certain amounts of detail in the artwork. So, a featureless box becomes a crate by the use of erased lines to define the planks of wood that make it. A messy bush gains some definition via a little trimming and erasing leafy shapes into the silhouetted mass (see Figure 10–4). Once the decision is made to add this sort of detailing, then the flat-colored shapes that will define the game environment become a little less intimidating to tackle, and a lot easier to visually read.

Figure 10–4. *Boxes and bushes with and without detail*

Complementing the Code and Design

If there is one truly unique aspect about video game development, that has to be the relationship between the very different disciplines involved in the production. Coders (or programmers), artists, and designers each do very different jobs involving very different skills and abilities, and yet they can work together in amazing ways while making video games.

Sometimes this relationship can result in something extremely cool happening in the evolution of the game's design. This happens when one member of the team interprets the output of another in ways that they had never intended, but the game becomes much better as a result. Designers sometimes refer to players finding cool solutions to their games that they never intended as *emergence*. This is just another kind of emergence, but one that happens at the design stage rather than after the game has been released.

Emergent Design

The very first game I worked on was a racing game called *Fatal Racing*. My responsibilities included designing and building the race courses using a software engine coded by one of the programmers on the team. The engine initially allowed for rather straightforward race tracks that were flat and went around bends, with the ability to make the road surface tilt a little. I soon started experimenting, and realized I could not only tilt the road, but make it spin almost completely around, allowing the cars to drive upside-down on "corkscrew" sections of track. It didn't work very well at first, but I showed my ideas to the programmer who was amazed! He'd not anticipated his engine being used in such a way, and he went away for an afternoon to write some extra code to allow my ideas to be incorporated in a more robust way. Within a few weeks, we were building race tracks with loops, corkscrews, moving ramps, bridges, and extreme jumps! None of which had been a part of the original game concept, but they went on to become the defining features of the game. It was a great example of artist and programmer achieving more together than they could alone, and the resulting game was great fun because of it.

In a similar way, the artist can expand upon the elements set down in the game design by the designer. The *Shadows on Deck* design calls for enemies in the form of pirates and skeletons, chosen for their striking silhouettes. During my initial sketching (and indeed throughout the game development), I expanded this baddie list to include all sorts of monstrous variations the designer hadn't considered (whelks for heads, eyeballs on tentacles, snake bodies, flying winged skulls, bee-hive-headed pirates, and so forth). I then began to think about other creatures, such as hermit crabs, lizards, spiders, and bears, and wondered if I could make some of those work in the silhouette style of the game. As a result, the finished game should look a little more varied, and greater variation makes for a more interesting game!

By the end of the conceptual stage, we had concept sketches for Flynn (see Figure 10–5) and many, many enemies (Figure 10–6). The three level environments—Pirate ship, Cliff village, and Swamp—are all roughly sketched out (for example, Figure 10–7). The first stage of the art process is over, and so the middle section of the art "story" begins!

Figure 10–5. *Concept sketches for Flynn*

Figure 10–6. *Sketches of enemies*

Figure 10–7. *Sketches of the Swamp environment*

Phase 2: Asset Creation

Generally, the artist and designer would maintain close contact during the concept stage, but at the end of it, the whole team gathers together again to review the direction of the style. These first drawings offer a visual starting point from which we develop a more specific idea about how the game will look. A further list of requirements is drawn up, including ideas for level content and characters, plus storyboards for cut-scenes. All this feeds into the evolving plan for the game that begins to solidify as the style is signed off and the process of building the first set of game assets begins.

Art Pipeline

The *art pipeline* is the process by which raw artwork ends up in the finished game, and it is an important thing to start to nail down at this stage. *Shadows on Deck* calls for a lot of outlined shapes for monsters and swash-buckling environments; something that lends itself well to a traditional approach that starts with a sketchbook, pencils, and drawing pens. From here, these can be digitally scanned and cleaned up in a package such as Adobe Photoshop (see Figure 10–8).

There are numerous software art packages you can use, but Photoshop is the industry standard. It is an incredibly versatile piece of software that allows you to easily manipulate photographs or scanned-in pencil artwork as well as providing numerous drawing tools to create your own artwork from scratch. With layers and the life-saving undo function (Ctrl Z shortcut fans!), you can be confident you are producing great artwork without any mistakes.

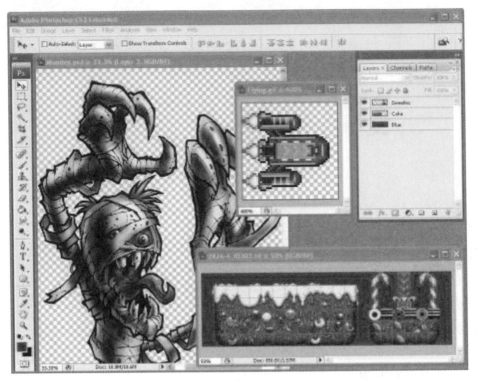

Figure 10–8. *Photoshop CS3 is a serious artist tool. Paint.NET and Gimp are free alternatives that contain some of the same features*

Animations

The mechanics of character movement and animation need to be considered at this point, too. This is going to be a 2D game with a retro feel, but we want it to be a lot more crisp than the low-resolution games of the past. Sprites were traditionally drawn by hand, pushing pixels about in a 2D art package such as Deluxe paint, but animating higher-resolution characters in this way is a job for an army of Disney animators, not a small team of game developers. That's why we decided to use Anime Studio (Debut edition) to create our animations. Anime Studio provides a hierarchical animation system similar to the ones in 3D animation packages used in modern films and games (see Figure 10–9). That means you can create animations by posing the character in different positions and the package creates the frames in-between for you.

So working back from our animation technique, we know that the characters will need to be created from separate body components: torso, upper and lower arms, upper and lower legs, and heads. These parts will be linked together in an intuitive biological way; lower arm connected to the upper arm at the elbow, upper arm connected to the torso at the shoulder, and so forth. Therefore, we must split character art into all these composite parts. These are all scaled to ensure all arms and legs and other parts are proportioned correctly, before being saved as separate pieces of art. We can then pass them onto the animator to be "rigged" (attaching the animation hierarchy to the images) and animated in Anime Studio.

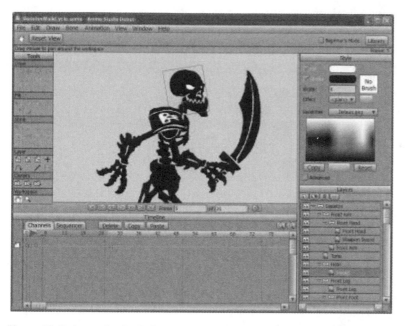

Figure 10–9. *Anime Studio Debut version 7 provides a cheap way of creating great-looking 2D animations*

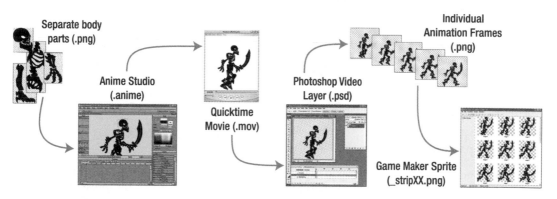

Figure 10–10. *The animation pipeline for Shadows on Deck*

Anime Studio renders each animation as a movie file that you can then import back into Photoshop and render it out again as a sequence of `.png` images compatible with Game Maker. Figure 10–10 gives an overview of the overall process, but we show you how to do it step-by-step in the section on Art Integration.

Environments

The asset pipeline for environment art is a little more straightforward than for animated characters. In fact, you can just resize some of the artwork and export it as `.png` files that will load straight into Game Maker. Nonetheless, a significant portion of the background artwork needs to be put into a format that is compatible with Game Maker's tileset system. This means breaking down objects into a set of square sections that you can arrange into different configurations. The exact number and choice of tiles depends entirely on the situation. For the rocks on the Rogues' Rendezvous section, we needed to consider all the different combinations of full- and half-sized tiles (see Figure 10–11). This can be quite fiddly, but it's worth it to give the maximum scope for the level designer to work with.

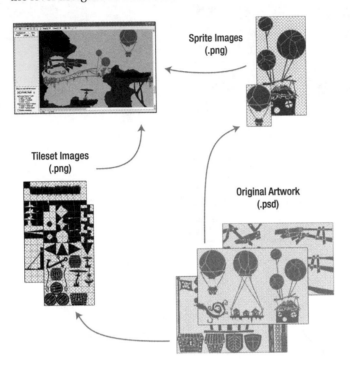

Figure 10–11. *The environment asset pipeline for Shadows on Deck*

Character Building

We have a good starting point for Flynn thanks to the sketches provided by the designer (see Chapter 7). An ordinary boy, 15 years old sounds simple enough, but it actually presents some interesting problems:

- Can such a seemingly unremarkable character work as a silhouette?

- How do we ensure he stands apart from all other characters and enemies?

- How can we make his silhouette interesting without over-embellishment?

- How extensive should the cosmetic changes to the character be, as the player progresses through the game?

You can see the initial side-on pencil drawings of the character in Figure 10–12. Based on the original sketches, numerous drawings were made with variations of hair style and clothing. These were then tidied up and inked using a black drawing pen, resulting in a set of black outlined drawings. Rather than using a brush and ink to block in the color, it is easier and quicker to scan the line art into the computer and finish it up digitally.

Figure 10–12. *The original charater sketches for Flynn*

Photoshop is great for tidying up any blotches or stubborn pencil strokes and ensuring the outlined shapes don't have any breaks in them. This is important when using the Paint Bucket Tool. Using this tool, you can instantly fill a selected area, or an area bound within another color. With any gaps filled in, the Paint Bucket Tool will fill the inside area of scanned line drawings, turning them into the solid, flat black shapes required (see Figure 10–13).

Figure 10–13. *The cleaned-up outline shape for Flynn*

The question of detailing and how to add things like facial features must now be addressed. It is important that Flynn's features are not overly expressive, which will set him apart from anyone or thing he might encounter during his adventures. His spiky hair and slight, boyish frame will also help to make him a distinctive counterpoint to the various villains and monsters he will meet, but perhaps a face might imbue him with a little more character that will bolster his unique personality. Using the Eraser Tool in Photoshop, features such as eyes, nose, ears, and hair-line are suggested by simply deleting appropriate portions of the head, using the original inked drawing as reference. Details are added to the torso and the other body parts in the same way. (This process is also applied to the various monsters and enemy pirates). Obviously, this method of detailing will need to be tested against the level environments, but as this cannot be further investigated until the Integration part of the process, the art components of Flynn and the other *Shadows on Deck* characters are signed off, for now.

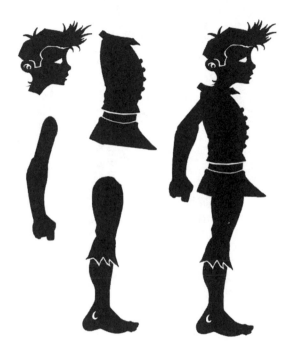

Figure 10–14. *The final version of Flynn with added details*

Ssssh: Character Design Secret!

A handy and time-saving technique I use to produce multiple variations on a theme involves making a basic line drawing of a character pose, side or face-on. This drawing needn't be too detailed, as long as the arms and legs and body and head are all proportioned correctly and the features of the face are very loosely suggested with sketched marks. You can make this drawing in pencil and scan it into the computer or you can draw it using Photoshop or another such program. You can then print the drawing out as many times as you need, and on each you can make a character concept drawing featuring as many different variations as you like, without having to work out the body shape every single time. It might seem like a bit of a cheat, but when a deadline is looming, you need every trick you can use to get as much work done as possible in as little time as possible!

Let's Get Environmental

The characters are coming along nicely, so it's time to start producing some levels for them to inhabit. In most games, different levels offer a wide range of variation defined by time of day, weather, and quality of light. Variation is also found in details such as location and the materials objects are made from.

In the case of our pirate game, the silhouette aspect meant the environments had to be distinctive in ways not reliant on color and other atmospheric details. Also, in some cases, to ensure objects work as a single flat color, a little simplification of form is required (see Figure 10–15). This is particularly applicable for some deep background objects where finer detail could be lost, or make it harder to recognise the shape. For example, a bush or tree that is used as a foreground object might have some leafy definition added within its mass (added using the same Eraser/ deletion method as employed with the characters), but these details are not required if the tree were to be used as a distant object. Any excessive detail in a piece of the deep background would serve only to distract the eye of the player. Even if this distraction were slight, after a while of playing, the cumulative effect of this "messiness" in the background environment would become tiresome, and this is the last thing a game should be. As with any piece of art, knowing when to reign in the detail is of paramount importance.

Figure 10–15. *Simplifying form for background objects*

Luckily, the themes and objects associated with the pirate concept lend themselves very well to the art style arrived at during the concept phase. Boxes, rigging, masts, barrels, treasure chests, and all the other things you are likely to find on a pirate ship can all be rendered legibly in silhouette, as can the wooden huts, trees, and various other plants and platforms that inhabit the different level environments.

The process involved in building the raw art for the levels is the same as that used to create the characters: pencil drawings are touched up with ink, scanned into Photoshop, and turned into solid black shapes. The detailing process is similar, too. The Eraser Tool is used as before to define textures and add some identity to the shapes, such as the planks of wood that make up barrels and crates, or patches on the caps of fungi. Although most of the in-game art was traditionally drawn and "inked", then scanned and finished digitally, it was easy to use Photoshop to produce further unique or location-specific objects, using the existing material as a jumping-off point. In this way, a broken crate can be produced by taking an existing whole crate and manipulating the planks using the Selection, Erase, and Transform/Scale Tools until they look battered and split. Several new assets were produced from existing platform elements by scaling and rotating them. In this way, you can produce enough material to ensure a level has lots of uniquely interesting components within it (see Figure 10–16).

Figure 10–16. *Breaking up and recombining objects*

The environments must also feature interactive components; these are the platforms and objects Flynn can walk on or use to traverse otherwise impassable areas (see Figure 10–17). Such objects must look clearly and distinctly as if they can be walked upon, which for the most part means they have flat upper surfaces, and are arranged in such ways as to suggest a route across the environment toward a target area or objective. These are an integrally important part of the game environment, and will require substantial testing during the Integration phase of the art process. As with the characters, the different elements of each level are arranged into separate .psd files for backgrounds, objects, and interactive objects.

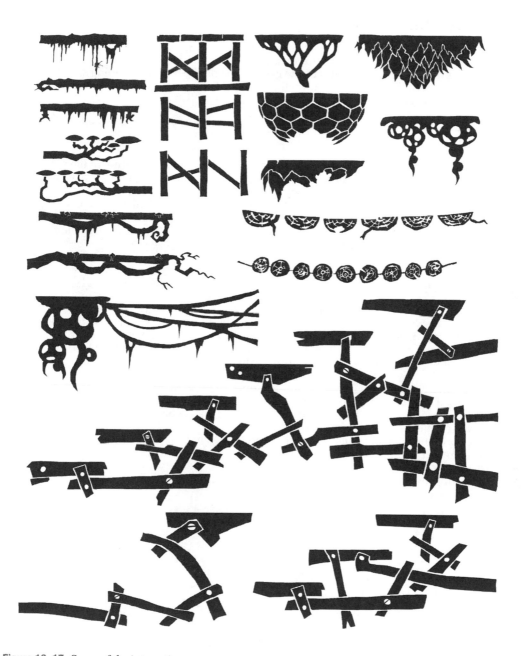

Figure 10–17. *Some of the interactive components*

By the end of the Asset Creation phase, we have components for Flynn, the pirates, and their various allies as well as interactive and background elements for the levels. These assets are presented in a format ready to be used within the game, and so begins the final phase in which the art is integrated into the game.

Phase 3: Art Integration

The Integration phase, as the title suggests, is when the environment and character art can finally be seen working in the game. This does not mean that the job of the artist is over, however, for although the art puts flesh on the bones of the game concept, the very act of doing so will reveal any problems with how that art works within the game, and any such problems that might arise will need to be rectified.

Art Therapy

When a level is constructed using the art assets, previously static graphics come to life as the first living, breathing version of the game is born. Although it is undeniably exciting to be able to glimpse how the game might look when completed, it is while playing this "first skinned" version of the game that any problems with the art assets will need to be identified and solved. (Objects might need redesigning, or further objects might be required). The artist must therefore be on call to help with the troubleshooting, making amendments to the art where required, as many times as necessary until each issue is resolved satisfactorily.

Shades of Grey

During the initial level construction, one of the first problems to arise involved the backgrounds. Because the objects that made up the background were black, they threatened to obscure the characters, and in turn became obscured where different background layers were positioned over one another. Also, there was a more fundamental problem in that it was impossible to differentiate interactive objects such as platforms from non-interactive elements (see Figure 10–18).

The solution involved changing the default color of all background level components to 50% grey. These could then be altered to a lighter shade if they were to be in deep background, or darker if they were closer to the foreground, but they would never be true black to ensure the characters were well-defined against them.

In the case of the interactive platforms, they too needed to be clearly separate from the non-interactive elements of the levels, and so were all colored black, making it clear to the player on which areas they could walk.

The resulting level environments have a depth and clarity they previously lacked, and won't obscure the characters in front of them.

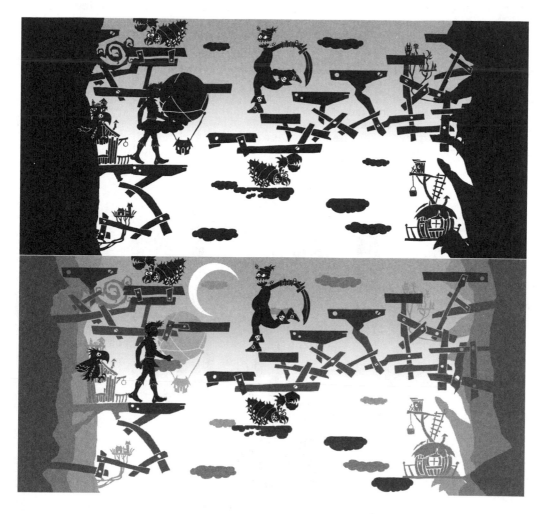

Figure 10–18. *Two game screens, first with everything solid black, second with levels of gray introduced*

The Devil Is in the Detail

Now that the environment art is in place within the levels, and a villainous rabble of baddies is in residence, we can test how the characters actually work against the backgrounds. This includes appraising how the detailing on those characters looks in game, and addressing any problems that might arise.

The final method of detailing the characters is decided by a process of trial and error. Initially, during the Asset Creation phase, facial features and buttons, studs and other features of clothing were created by simply erasing portions of the character elements. Now that the characters can be tested against the level backgrounds, it becomes clear that the see-through aspect of these details became easily confused or obscured by the background visible behind them.

To rectify this problem, these see-through areas are filled with white, and the results are immediately much better. It might take the characters a step away from being true silhouettes, but it does allow them to show a little more detail, and in doing so a little more personality is added (see Figure 10–19).

However, our hero Flynn became an interesting exception to the rule. He was given detailing and features just like every other character, but we found we didn't like the result. Giving Flynn eyes and nostrils gave him a very fixed expression, which didn't always suit the conversations or situations he was in, so we decided to keep him all black. We think it works better this way as it is now easy to imagine different emotions on his face, without the fixed one getting in the way.

It is worth noting that this legibility issue was not so important for the environments as it was for the characters, so any "erased" detailing in the environment elements were not filled with white. This also sets the backgrounds apart from the characters quite nicely.

Figure 10–19. *A comparison of Flynn, Archie, and the pirates with and without detail*

We've Got It Covered

It was during the final art phase that artwork for the cover of *The Game Makers Companion* was completed. Although this doesn't implicitly relate to the in-game material, it was developed from sketches made of Flynn during the Concepting stage, and is an interesting addition to the art story (see Figure 10–20).

Figure 10–20. *The stages in producing the cover artwork*

The initial sketch was quite loose and ill-defined, but was a great starting place from which to develop a new, tighter pencil drawing. This featured a great, dynamic pose as well as other content such as the parrot and the bat-skulls!

An inked version of this drawing is made, before being scanned into Photoshop. The inked image is tidied up digitally, and the outlines of the various elements are thickened slightly. Next, a new layer is created above the line drawing, and the blending mode is set to Multiply. This will allow the ink beneath to show through. Flat colors are carefully added into this layer using the Paint Bucket Tool, with the Lasso Tool defining the boundaries of all the different areas in turn.

Finally, a little shading and highlights are added using Dodge, Burn, and Hue/Saturation. The final result is a clearly defined image that should prove a striking addition to the cover!

Pirate CD

We've deliberately created far more artwork for *Shadows on Deck* than is actually required for the version of the game we'll be making in the book. If you explore the Chapter10 directory on the CD, you'll find many more examples of monsters, environments, and objects that you can use to build completely new levels and scenarios. We've tried really hard to make it easy to mix and match artwork to fulfill your own wild ideas. How about flying ships, upside-down swamps, or levels made entirely out of skulls and bones? Perhaps you'd like to make a skeletal centipede dragon? How about cannon-headed pirates or skeletons with spider legs? Well, if you want them, then it's now within your power to create them. The beauty of the silhouette style is that it's really easy to modify, recombine, and incorporate bits and pieces of other artwork. In this section, we'll give you a brief crash-course in how to modify these resources for yourself. This is not intended as an in-depth tutorial of any kind—more of a quick bluffer's guide to creating and animating graphics for *Shadows on Deck*.

Paint it Black

Although we realize that not everyone will have access to Photoshop, it's certainly worth investing in if you're serious about artwork. We're going to focus on Photoshop CS3 for this tutorial, but any of the more recent versions will do just as well. Before you fire it up, take a moment to explore the contents of the Chapter10/Environments/Cliff directory on the CD. Here, we have a huge range of objects, scenery, and platforms that are designed to be used in the Rogues' Rendezvous level. These are all high-resolution images colored in a mid-tone grey so that you can easily adapt them to the needs of different levels and situations.

You should be familiar with the idea of using RGB (red, green, blue) values to specify colors, and we're going to use absolute black for foreground objects (R=0, G=0, B=0), and a very dark blue for objects in the near background (R=35, G=37. B=53). This slight difference is enough to give a visual cue to the player about what to expect to be collidable within the environment. Getting the artwork in these colors is very easy.

Adjusting the Color of the Environment Artwork

1. Load one of the .psd files into Photoshop and double-click on the main layer to open up the **Layer Style** dialog.

2. Now select the **Color Overlay** option within the dialog. A check mark should then appear next to this option and the layer should turn bright red, as shown in Figure 10–21.

3. Click on the smaller red rectangle and a color picking dialog should appear. You can now select the color you require. Try both absolute black and the dark blue value (R=35, G=37. B=53) to see what it looks like.

4. Now use the Crop Tool to select the rectangular area of the image that you're interested in and then press **Enter** to crop.

5. Next, use the **Image, Image Size** option to rescale the artwork to an appropriate size, bearing in mind that the entire game screen is only 1024x600 pixels.

6. Finally, use the **File, Save As** option to save the file as a .png format file, which is compatible with Game Maker and preserves the transparency of the image. Don't worry about doing this for now, as this is a hypothetical exercise.

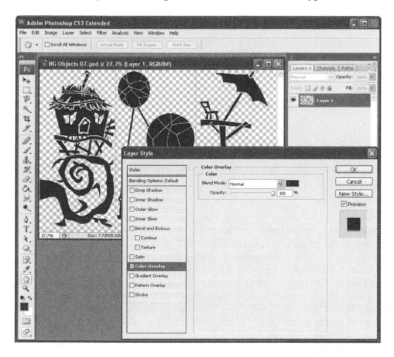

Figure 10–21. *Using the Color Overlay layer effect to color the environment art*

Of course, you don't just have to stick to using the artwork we've provided and it's quite easy to turn a photograph into a silhouette using the same **Color Overlay** option. You'll need to cut out the shape of the image from the photograph first, but if you take your own photographs of objects against a single-color background, then it's child's play to use the **Magic Wand** Tool to highlight and delete the background. Figure 10–22 shows a children's toy turned into a spooky-looking church by applying this technique. Just think how easy it is to realize your craziest ideas with all the images of the internet at your disposal.

Figure 10–22. *The Color Overlay effect can work wonders on photographs, too*

Make it Move

Now explore the contents of the Chapter10/Characters directory on the CD. Here, you'll find all the various body parts that are available to you to create all the different characters and monsters in the game. Making your own characters is a little more involved than creating environment art and will also require a copy of Anime Studio Debut, which costs about $50. However, it doesn't necessarily require animation skills, as we've provided a whole range of animations for you in the Chapter10/Animations directory and all you need to do is swap out the body parts to create a new animation for your character. In this section, we'll take you through the process with a simple example: creating a new pirate walk-cycle animation for a pirate with a clam for a head.

Making a New Pirate Walk-Cycle Animation

1. Load Mad Pirate Heads.psd into Photoshop from the Chapter10/Characters directory.

2. Use the Crop Tool to select the area enclosing the clam head in the top left corner of the image and press **Enter** to crop.

3. Now, save the image in .png format to somewhere on your PC using the file name PirateHeadClam.png. You can now minimize Photoshop.

4. Launch Anime Studio and select **File, Open** to load PirateWalkCycle.anme from the Chapter10/Animations directory on the CD. If you are asked whether you want to use the basic version, select **No**, as we will quickly need to access one of the features that isn't available in basic mode. The interface should now look like Figure 10–23.

5. If you press the small Play button beneath the pirate image, then you will see the walk-cycle animation playing. Notice the moving red vertical line within the timeline beneath the pirate. This shows the current frame.

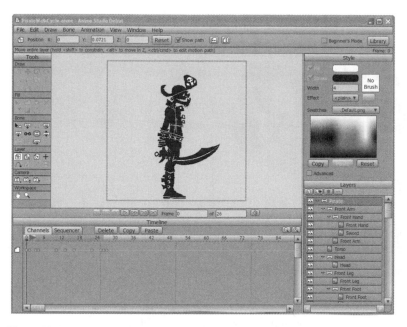

Figure 10–23. *The pirate walk-cycle animation loadeed into Anime Studio Debut version 7*

6. Stop the animation and drag the red line back to frame 0 at the start of the animation. This is critical before you perform the next steps, otherwise the changes you make may be treated as part of the animation and not a global change to the hierarchy.

7. In the Layers section on the bottom right, find the two Head layers. There is one with a bone icon next to it and one with a picture icon. Double-click on the one with the picture and a dialog should appear. Select the **Image** tab and click on the **Source Image** button.

8. Select the PirateHeadClam.png file you created earlier and select **OK**. The pirate should now have the clam's head, but it will be a little bit off-center.

9. Select the **Translate Layer** Tool from the **Layers** Tool section on the left-hand side of the interface. Now, drag the clam's head so that it fits neatly within the pirate's neckline. as shown in Figure 10–24.

Figure 10–24. *Setting the rotational origin of the clam pirate head*

10. Next, select the **Set Origin** Tool from the **Layers** Tool section. The origin determines the rotation point of the head image, which is currently positioned at the red cross shown in Figure 10–24. Move its position by clicking somewhere near to the position of the blue cross shown in Figure 10–24 instead. This will not make a huge difference for this example, but it can be essential to reset the origin for some combinations of body parts.

11. Now, play the animation and it should look fairly reasonable (for someone with a clam for a head, anyway). All we need to do now is render it out as a movie file.

12. Go to **File, Project Settings** and click on **Background Color**. Make sure this is set to absolute black (R=0, G=0, B=0) before continuing. If you don't do this, then the edges of your animation images will have a faint color to them (the color of the background).

13. Select **File, Export Animation** and click **OK** to accept the default settings offered. Choose where you want the movie saved to and call it `PirateClamWalk.mov`. The **Compression Settings** dialog should then appear, as shown in Figure 10–25. Change the **Compression Type** to **PNG** (we know where we are with `pngs`) and **Depth** to **Millions of Colors+**. The plus is important, as it indicates that you want to include alpha so that the background can appear transparent. Now, select **OK** and you should now see the animation rendered in front of you. This may take some time, but once it has finished, you can close down or minimize Anime Studio.

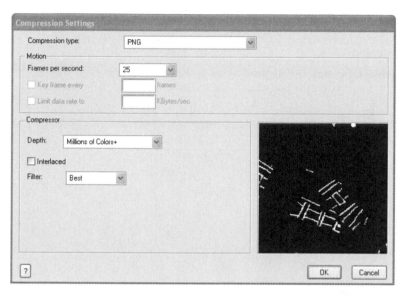

Figure 10–25. *The compression settings for exporting the video from Anime Studio*

14. Maximize Photoshop again and load in the `PirateClamWalk.mov` file you just created. Go to the **Window** menu and enable the **Animation** window (see Figure 10–26). This window allows to you play and view the animation from within Photoshop.

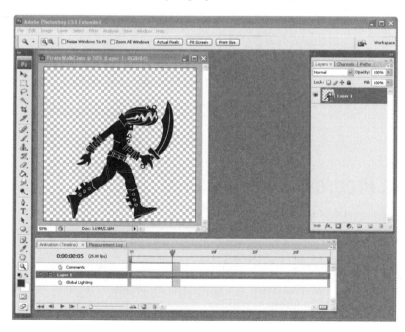

Figure 10–26. *The animation now in Photoshop*

15. The first thing to do is to scale down the dimensions of the animation to something compatible with the game. Go to **Image, Image Size** and set the image dimensions to 210x210 pixels. Select **Convert** when you are asked if you want to convert the video layer into a smart object layer.

16. Now go to **File, Export, Render Video** and the dialog shown in Figure 10–27 should appear. Make sure that your settings are the same as these before clicking **Render**.

Figure 10–27. *The render settings for exporting the animation as a png sequence from Photoshop*

17. After a short period, you will have a new directory filled with sequentially numbered .png files corresponding to each frame in the animation (there should be 24, numbered 0-23). These are now ready to import directly into Game Maker as new animated sprites.

So that's it. You can now let your imagination run riot, creating bizarre combinations of pirates using all the limbs, heads, and weapons provided on the CD. If you get into Anime Studio a bit more, you can soon begin to create your own animations, too. We look forward to seeing what you come up with.

Conclusion: Save Progress and Continue!

Rick Wakeman said: "Success is found buried in the garden of failure. You have to dig a lot before you find it!" The *Shadows on Deck* art process threw up some interesting problems, but through generous portions of trial and error, and a lot of sustained effort, we managed to find some interesting ways to address them.

In doing so, the team witnessed *Shadows on Deck* evolve from a story into a living, breathing entity, perhaps the likes of which even they hadn't quite envisioned, but this is the role of the artist, after all! The art process doesn't quite end here, though; as the programmer implements the art into the game, there are bound to be one or two further issues that arise, but creating something isn't as much fun if it's too easy!

CHAPTER 11

■■■

GML: From Ninja to Pirate

Designers and artists often have to begin projects by facing the daunting prospect of a blank page, but programmers rarely have the same problem. That's because it is nearly always possible to reuse at least some code from previous projects. No matter how different your new game is from your last, there are always similarities you can draw upon. In fact, some of the "skill" of an experienced programmer can actually be the large archive of existing code they have to borrow from in order to make new software! You'll soon find that using a text-based programming language such as Game Maker Language (GML) makes it much easier to reuse your code between projects in this way.

So we would need to be mad to start from scratch when it comes to making *Shadows on Deck*. Zool may not have much in common with Flynn as a character, but the games are both part of the platform game genre and so share many common behaviors. *Shadows on Deck* may look a lot different too, but by the end of the book, we will have transformed colorful Sweet World into something much more sinister and atmospheric. We certainly want to do our best to try and realize the creative vision set out in the previous chapters, but there's nothing wrong with taking a few shortcuts to get there.

GML Babel Fish

In the classic sci-fi comedy, *The Hitchhiker's Guide to the Galaxy* by Douglas Adams (Del Ray, 1979), there is a fictitious species of fish that can translate any language. That fish was called the Babel fish and right now we could do with one that understands programming, too. For we're going to begin by translating our *Zool* "engine" from the icon-based drag-and-drop actions (D&D) we used to create it, into the script-based Game Maker Language (GML).

The Zool game we've created has pushed drag-and-drop (D&D) programming about as far as it can go—and in fact some of the D&D approaches we've used in the game could be more elegantly achieved in GML. Using D&D programming to write a game is a bit like trying to tell a story using mime. It can be an effective way to quickly express certain things, but it lacks the precision and variety to tell the story in exactly the way you might want to. In contrast, GML programming is more like having the full vocabulary of a language at your disposal, giving you the power to take your story exactly where you want it to go.

We can assume by now that you're pretty good with D&D programming, but we'll also take it for granted that you've had *some* contact with GML before. You don't need to be an expert, but it will certainly help if you have done some basic tutorials in the past like those included in Chapters 12-14 of *The Game Maker's Apprentice*. We're not going to teach you GML from scratch in this book, but we will compare and contrast GML and D&D as we go through the process of converting the Zool game to GML. This is actually quite a good way to begin to understand the language, as it allows you to connect your existing understanding of Game Maker with this new way of programming.

■**Tip** If you own *The Game Maker's Apprentice* and feel a bit rusty on GML, then now would be a great time to go back through at least chapters 12 and 13.

So let's begin by opening the file zooldrag.gmk from the Chapter11/Games directory on the CD. It should seem pretty familiar, but open up one of the object resources and look at the actions list for each event. Instead of all the actions you might expect to see there, you will see a single action called **Execute Code**. This action allows sequences of GML instructions to be included in events as a direct replacement for lists of actions. Open obj_zool_air and select the **Collision** event with obj_solid. Double-click on the **Execute Code** action to open up the code editor and reveal the GML code (see Figure 11–1).

Figure 11–1. *The code editor for an Execute Script action with the equivalent drag-and-drop actions*

Here are a few basic reminders about working with GML:

- GML is written in a code editor, which is basically just a text editor similar to Windows Notepad. You have to type in the commands that you want Game Maker to execute, in the order that you want them to happen.

- Game Maker has to read and interpret the commands that you type into the code editor and (as in all programming languages) it doesn't tolerate mistakes! So if you mistype something or get the "punctuation" of the language wrong, then it usually won't work at all, or worse, may behave differently from how you intended.

- Nonetheless, Game Maker doesn't care about the number of spaces (or tabs) you put between different elements of its language. So, as far as Game Maker is concerned, x=xprevious is the same as x = xprevious and if (y == 0) is the same as if(y==0). However, that doesn't mean you can put spaces in the middle of the "words" of the language, so xprev   ious is not the same as xprevious.

- If you have the 10/01 button enabled in the code editor toolbar, then it will look for errors in your code as you type. Game Maker will tell you when it has spotted a mistake in your code by displaying an error at the bottom of the code editor window (see Figure 11–2). However, bear in mind that the error displayed may just be a result of you not having finished your line of code yet!

- The punctuation of GML consists of semi-colons (;), commas (,), colons (:), curly brackets ({ and }), parenthesis ((and)), square brackets ([and]), the single quote ('), and double quote ("). Semi-colons are used very frequently, as they provide a way of ending an expression (much like a full-stop in English); commas are used to separate arguments to scripts or functions; and colons are used more rarely. The others appear in matching pairs to mark the start and end of things. You'll also see the double-backslash (//) appear in front of any comments. Comments are just ignored by Game Maker and are there for the benefit of human readers of the code only.

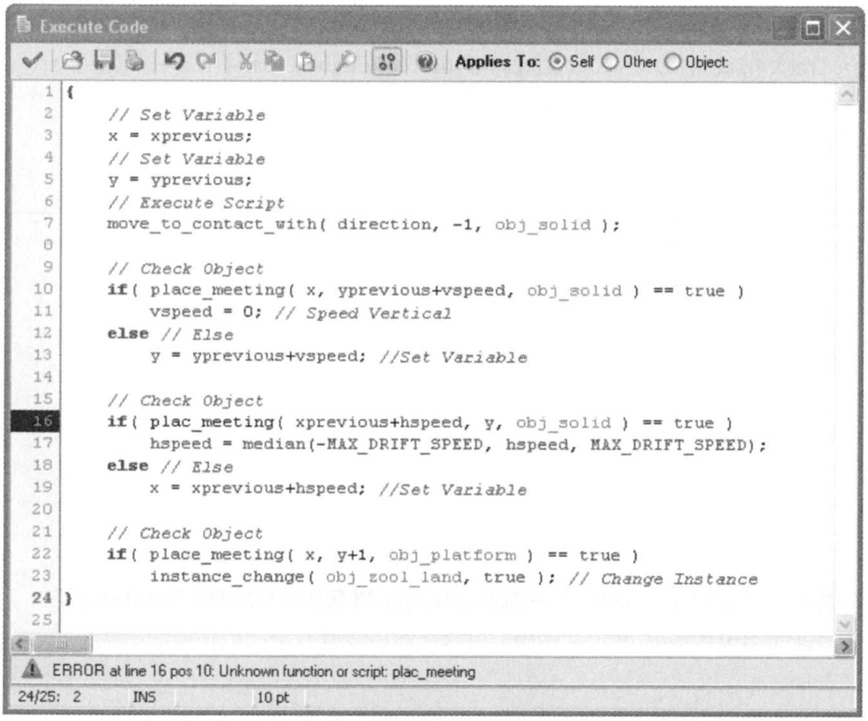

Figure 11–2. *The same code with an error in it: the function "place_meeting" has been mistyped without an "e". The line with the error in it is highlighted red and the error is listed in the panel at the bottom*

Literal Translation

Now look back at Figure 11–1 and compare the GML on the left with the actions on the right. It follows exactly the same structure as the original sequence of actions for this event. We've even added comments (in green) to show you the equivalent action for each line of GML code. In this case, there were 13 actions that have converted into 13 lines of GML, but this will not always be the case. In zooldrag.gmk, we have directly mapped each action sequence into the equivalent GML without taking any shortcuts to make it easier for you to relate the GML back to your previous experience with actions.

So for every action you can use in D&D programming, there is an equivalent piece of GML that does the same job. We've compiled a list of the most common actions from Zool and how they translate into sequences of GML instructions that have similar, or identical, results. Take some time now to look through the new GML version of Zool and see how the original actions have been replaced with code that creates a comparable outcome.

Actions and Their GML Equivalents

1. Include a **Set Variable** action that sets the **Variable** x to the **Value** 3.

    x = 3;   (standard)

    x = x+3;   (**Relative** option checked)

2. Include a **Test Variable** action that checks if the **Variable** x is **equal to** the **Value** 3.

    if(x == 3)   (**equal to**)

    if(x > 3)   (**greater than**)

    if(x < 3)   (**less than**)

3. Include a **Start Block** action.

    {   (**Start Block**)

    }   (**End Block**)

    else   (**Else**)

4. Include a **Change Instance** action to change into obj_dragon with **Perform events** set to **yes**.

    instance_change(obj_dragon, **true**);   (**Perform events** set to **yes**)

    instance_change(obj_dragon, **false**);   (**Perform events** set to **not**)

5. Include a **Speed Horizontal** action with **Hor. Speed** set to 3.

    hspeed = 3;

    hspeed = **hspeed+3**;   (**Relative** option checked)

6. Include a **Speed Vertical** action with **Vert. Speed** set to -4.

    vspeed = -4;   (standard)

    vspeed = **hspeed-4**;   (**Relative** option checked)

7. Include a **Play Sound** action to play snd_boom with **Loop** set to false.

    sound_play(snd_boom);   (**Loop** set to **false**)

    sound_loop(snd_boom);   (**Loop** set to **true**)

8. Include a **Set Alarm** action to set **Alarm 0** to 30 **Steps**.

    alarm[0] = 30;

9. Include a **Destroy Instance** action.

    instance_destroy();   (for **Self**)

    with(other)
          instance_destroy();   (for **Other**)

10. Include a **Set Friction** action that sets **Friction** to 0.5.

    friction = 0.5;

11. Include a **Set Gravity** action that sets **Gravity** to 1 and **Direction** to 270.

    gravity = 1;
    gravity_direction = 270;

12. Include a **Set Health** action that sets **Value** to 100.

    health = 100;

13. Include a **Test Health** action that tests if the health is **less than** the **Value** 0.

    if(health < 0)

14. Include a **Set Lives** action that sets **Value** to 3.

    lives = 3;

15. Include a **Test Lives** action that tests if the number of lives is **equal to** the **Value** 3.

    if(lives == 3)

16. Include a **Move Free** action that sets **Direction** to 180 and **Speed** to 10.

    direction = 180;
    speed = 10;

17. Include a **Reverse Vertical** action.

    vspeed = -vspeed;   (**Reverse Vertical**)

    hspeed = **-hspeed**;   (**Reverse Horizontal**)

18. Include a **Repeat** action with **Times** set to 10.

    repeat(10)

19. Include an **Exit Event** action.

    exit;

20. Include a **Check Object** action that checks whether the current instance would collide with **Object** obj_dragon at a **Relative** position of **X**=6, **Y**=5.

    if(place_meeting(x+6, y+5, obj_dragon) == true)   (standard)

```
if( place_meeting( x+6, y+5, obj_dragon ) != true )
```
(**NOT** option checked)

21. Include a **Test Chance** action with **Sides** of 150.

```
if( irandom_range( 1, 150 ) == 1 )
```

22. Include a **Wrap Screen** action that sets **Direction** to horizontal.

```
move_wrap( true, false, sprite_width/2 );
```
(**Direction** to **horizontal**)
```
move_wrap( false, true, sprite_height/2 );
```
(**Direction** to **vertical**)
```
move_wrap( true, true, sprite_width/2 );
```
(**Direction** to **both**)

■**Note** The move_wrap function does not provide identical results to the **Wrap Screen** action in all situations, but the code preceding will provide comparable results providing the origins of your sprites are centered.

---

23. Include a **Draw Sprite** action that draws the **Sprite** spr_dragon at **X**=66, **Y**=55, with a **Subimage** of 3.

```
draw_sprite( spr_dragon, 3, 66, 55 );
```
(standard)
```
draw_sprite( spr_dragon, 3, x+66, y+55 );
```
(**Relative** option checked)

24. Include a **Create Instance** action that creates an instance of the **Object** obj_dragon at **X**=66, **Y**=55.

```
instance_create( 66, 55, obj_dragon );
```
(standard)
```
instance_create( x+66, y+55, obj_dragon );
```
(**Relative** option checked)

25. Include a **Create Moving** action that creates an instance of the **Object** obj_dragon at **X**=66, **Y**=55, with a **Speed** of 3 and **Direction** of 270.

```
var instance;
instance = instance_create( 66, 55, obj_dragon );
instance.speed = 3;
instance.direction = 270;
```

Translation Tips

Here are some general observations about the relationship between D&D actions and comparable GML code. Try and see if you can find specific examples of each of these points in the Zool code as you continue to explore the zooldrag.gmk example.

- Setting the **Relative** option is generally equivalent to adding or subtracting a value from the previous value of a variable. So a **Set Variable** action that sets the **Variable** x **Relative** to the **Value** -3 is equivalent to x=x-3.

- A great many actions simply set or test variables that are predefined by Game Maker. **Set Lives** sets lives, **Test Health** tests health, **Set Speed** sets speed, and so forth (refer back to Chapter 1 for the full list of predefined variables).

- Most conditional actions (the ones with hexagonal icons) translate into if statements. These if statements are followed by brackets containing an expression; for example, if(a > b) or if(place_meeting(x,y,obj_object) == true). If the expression is true, then the next statement or block of statements is executed; otherwise, it is not.

- Blocks of statements are grouped within curly brackets ({ and }) and the code within them is indented to show which statements are part of that block (just like in the actions list). Note that this doesn't happen automatically in the code editor and you will need to manually add tabs to achieve the indentation.

- Selecting **Other** for the **Applies To** option of an action is equivalent to putting the statement with(other) in front of the code. This makes the following statement or block of statements act as if it is operating on the other instance in a collision instead. Likewise, selecting **Object** obj_dragon for **Applies To** is equivalent to putting the statement with(obj_dragon) in front of that code so that it acts upon all instances of obj_dragon.

- It is possible to set the local variables of another instance after creating it! This is because the GML equivalent of **Create Instance** instance_create(x,y,obj) returns the id of the instance that is created. This id can then be used to set its local variables. In fact, that's just what our GML version of the **Create Moving** action does (see point 25 in the previous section). It assigns a temporary local variable (called instance) to store the id and then sets instance.speed and instance.direction, accordingly. Using the period (.) in this way just means that we're referring to the local speed and direction variables of the instance.

The Power of Language

A direct translation of D&D to GML is a bit like watching a mimed performance and then writing down what happened. The result might be articulated in a different form, but it can't express anything more than the original. The power of GML is in its ability to "say" things that you simply can't in D&D. Our next task then is to take advantage of some of GML's additional power by making some improvements to our Zool code. This code will form the basis of our Pirate game too, so we're improving them both at the same time.

A Global Evil

Global variables are accessible to all objects in your games, and as such provide one way of sharing or passing information between them. However, generally speaking, global variables are considered particularly bad practice in most programming languages.

One of the great advantages of programming using objects (as in Game Maker) is that it keeps different parts of your code nicely separated from each other. It is easy to consider objects in relative isolation, and changing a piece of code in one object doesn't necessarily have any knock-on effects on other objects. The problem with using global variables is that they often have the opposite effect. They can create unnecessary links between objects that make it impossible to change one without affecting another (because they all make use of the same global variable). Changes in one area of code can easily have unintended effects on other parts of the game, leading to more errors and less reliable code. Global variables are therefore something you should try and use sparingly in your games, and we will attempt to address this in our GML version of the game next.

There was one use of a global variable in our original version of Zool, which is probably acceptable, and this was when we used it to create a global.step_count variable that kept track of the number of steps since the start of the game. Even so, this relies on an understanding that only the controller object should ever change this variable, and other objects should only ever get the value of it—otherwise, it could cause problems too.

On the other hand, there was another use of a global variable that was both ugly and no longer necessary in GML. This was where we used one to pass through the sprite of the dying enemy object, and this can now be removed.

For the following sections, you'll need to open two Game Maker files: zooldrag.gmk (which should already be open) and zoolgml.gmk, which is also in the Chapter11/Games directory on the CD. Launch Game Maker again (so that it is running twice) and open the new file as well. Refer to the headings before each set of instructions to tell you which file we're currently looking at.

Within zooldrag.gmk

1. Open up obj_beastie and select its **Destroy** event. Double-click on its **Execute Code** action and notice the following lines within the code:

   ```
   global.die_sprite_index = spr_beastie_die;
   event_inherited();
   ```

   This is the event called when the Beastie is killed and you can see that it sets up the global variable so that it contains the Beastie dying sprite and then calls the **Destroy** event of its parent (obj_enemy). So let's look at its parent's **Destroy** event next.

2. Open up obj_enemy and select its **Destroy** event. Double-click on its **Execute Code** action and find the following lines within the code:

```
1:       var instance;
2:       instance = instance_create( x, y, obj_enemy_die );
3:       instance.speed = 4;
4:       instance.direction = random( 180 );
```

3.   These lines are comparable to a **Create Moving** action and they get called four times to create four instances of obj_enemy_die. However, the instance_create function (line 2) also calls the **Create** event of obj_enemy die before it reaches lines 3 and 4, so we'll go there next to remind us what that does.

4.   Select the **Create** event of obj_enemy_die and observe these lines of code within its **Execute Code** action:

```
sprite_index = global.die_sprite_index;
image_index = random( image_number-1 );
```

This sets the sprite to be the same as the one held in the global variable and then randomly assigns a subimage (a random piece of the exploded enemy sprite). In this case, that would be spr_beastie_die, but each enemy object sets the global variable to an appropriate sprite before the instances of obj_enemy_die are created. In this way, each instance of obj_enemy_die can have a different sprite, but still share identical object behavior. It saved us from having to create a new dying object for each different kind of enemy in the game.

You can summarize this technique as using a global variable to provide information (the appropriate sprite to use) to a newly created instance. However, we can already see from lines 3 and 4 of step 2 that it is possible to do this in a more elegant way in GML—and avoid using global variables altogether!

■**Note** We will sometimes add line numbers to larger sections of code so that it's easier to reference different parts of the code in the text. These do not correspond to the line numbers in the .gmk file, and are purely for the purposes of the book, so there's not need to worry when they don't match up.

Within zoolgml.gmk

1.   Open up obj_beastie and select its **Destroy** event. Of course you can't, as there isn't one! The old **Destroy** event simply set the value of the global variable and we're not using that anymore, so there is no need for the **Destroy** event in obj_beastie at all. Open up the **Create** event of obj_beastie instead, and observe this line:

```
die_sprite_index = spr_beastie_die;
```

This time, we're setting a local variable (which we've chosen to give the same name as our old global variable) to hold the correct dying sprite for the Beastie enemy.

2. The beastie object will still inherit its **Destroy** event from its parent so open obj_enemy and select its **Destroy** event. Now observe the difference in the following lines of code:

```
1:      var instance;
2:      instance = instance_create( x, y, obj_enemy_die );
3:      instance.speed = 4;
4:      instance.direction = random( 180 );
5:      instance.sprite_index = die_sprite_index;
6:      instance.image_index = random( instance.image_number-1 );
```

This now extends the principle of the **Create Moving** code to change the sprite_index and image_index of the new instance as well. In fact, you could set any variables you like on a new instance in this way, but bear in mind that these are set after the **Create** event of the new instance is called. In other words the **Create** event called as part of line 2 can't rely on values that are not set until lines 3-6.

3. The **Create** event of obj_enemy_die now doesn't need to handle anything to do with the sprite—and we've avoided the use of a global variable.

Switching Sprites

It's understandable if the thought of opening the **Draw** event of obj_zool fills you with a certain amount of dread. Although it grew over a long period of time, the final event contained a quite ridiculous 53 actions! Moreover, this event only ever *drew* the correct sprite for the current state, and it never actually *changed* the current sprite (by using **Set Sprite** or setting the sprite_index variable). This meant that Game Maker wasn't actually aware that the sprite was changing, which could potentially have caused animation and collision problems. If Game Maker doesn't know how many frames there are in the sprite being drawn, then it might not loop the animation correctly, and it won't be using the correct collision mask either (although our masks were all the same for Zool, which is why it didn't cause a problem). We could have fixed this by adding another **Set Sprite** action for each condition, but this would have increased the number of actions to nearly 200 (because we would have needed **Start** and **End Block** actions, too). Clearly that wasn't a great alternative, but fortunately there are much better ways of doing this in GML.

Within zooldrag.gmk

1. Open up the **Draw** event of obj_zool and look at the code in the **Execute Code** action. The direct conversion of the D&D is still pretty long, but looks a little bit neater. You'll see variations of the following lines repeated over and over again:

```
if( state == ZSTATE_STAND )
    draw_sprite( spr_zool_stand_right, -1, x, y );
```

Nonetheless, it still doesn't set the sprite_index variable, so it remains vulnerable to the same animation and collision problems as the D&D version.

Within zoolgml.gmk

1. Now open up the other **Draw** event of `obj_zool` and take a look at the alternative code:

```
 1: {
 2:     if( hurt == true )
 3:         if( global.step_count mod 6 == 0 )
 4:             exit;
 5:
 6:     if( facing == FACE_RIGHT )
 7:     {
 8:         switch( state )
 9:         {
10:             case ZSTATE_STAND: sprite_index = spr_zool_stand_right; break;
11:             case ZSTATE_WALK: sprite_index = spr_zool_walk_right; break;
12:             case ZSTATE_JUMP: sprite_index = spr_zool_jump_right; break;
13:             case ZSTATE_FALL: sprite_index = spr_zool_fall_right; break;
14:             case ZSTATE_CLIMB: sprite_index = spr_zool_climb_right; break;
15:             case ZSTATE_CLING: sprite_index = spr_zool_climb_right; break;
16:             case ZSTATE_SLIP: sprite_index = spr_zool_slip_right; break;
17:             case ZSTATE_SKID: sprite_index = spr_zool_skid_right; break;
18:             case ZSTATE_KICK: sprite_index = spr_zool_kick_right; break;
19:             case ZSTATE_SPIN: sprite_index = spr_zool_spin_right; break;
20:             case ZSTATE_DEAD: sprite_index = spr_zool_die_right; break;
21:         }
22:     }
23:
24:     if( facing == FACE_LEFT )
25:     {
26:         switch( state )
27:         {
28:             case ZSTATE_STAND: sprite_index = spr_zool_stand_left; break;
29:             case ZSTATE_WALK: sprite_index = spr_zool_walk_left; break;
30:             case ZSTATE_JUMP: sprite_index = spr_zool_jump_left; break;
31:             case ZSTATE_FALL: sprite_index = spr_zool_fall_left; break;
32:             case ZSTATE_CLIMB: sprite_index = spr_zool_climb_left; break;
33:             case ZSTATE_CLING: sprite_index = spr_zool_climb_left; break;
34:             case ZSTATE_SLIP: sprite_index = spr_zool_slip_left; break;
35:             case ZSTATE_SKID: sprite_index = spr_zool_skid_left; break;
36:             case ZSTATE_KICK: sprite_index = spr_zool_kick_left; break;
37:             case ZSTATE_SPIN: sprite_index = spr_zool_spin_left; break;
38:             case ZSTATE_DEAD: sprite_index = spr_zool_die_left; break;
39:         }
40:     }
41:
42:     draw_sprite( sprite_index, image_index, x, y );
43: }
```

Notice the use of a switch and case statements for each state instead of if statements. Although the structure of a switch statement is a little different, it has the same effect as a series of if statements in most situations. Just like an if statement, the parenthesis of a switch statement contains the expression being evaluated. However, case statements are used to make different things happen when the expression evaluates to different values. Each case is followed by a colon (:) and then a number of statements, the last of which is a break statement to indicate the end of the statements in that case. You can also leave off the break statement, in which case the contents of the following case will be executed as well.

However, what's more important here is that we are setting the sprite_index variable in each case so that Game Maker knows which sprite we are using. Finally, on line 42, we draw that sprite_index sprite using the current image_index (subimage). This produces is a neater and more effective solution for controlling sprites in our game.

The Ninja Elbow Walk

You may have already noticed that the level design in the two GML versions of Zool is slightly different from the D&D version we made in Chapter 6. It has an additional green jelly ledge platform on top of the first set of ramps. This is just a little taller than the existing blue one (see Figure 11–3) and it reveals a problem with the way our existing code detects if Zool is standing on top of a solid platform.

At the moment, we use the place_meeting function in obj_zool_land to check if Zool would collide with an instance of obj_platform if he was moved down by a single pixel. However, our new platform creates a situation where Zool is still colliding with an instance of obj_ledge (which has obj_platform as a parent) if he is moved down by a single pixel, but it is his upper body that is colliding—not his feet! If you try this out in the zooldrag.gmk version, then you'll see that this allows Zool to run along the new platform when he clearly should not. We have avoided this happening in the past by simply not creating this kind of situation in our level design, but it is possible to fix this problem properly using GML.

Figure 11–3. *Zool is walking along the ledge supported by the collision with his upper body! Zool's collision rectangle is shown in black and the ledge's collision mask is shown in purple*

Within zooldrag.gmk

1. Open up the **End Step** event of obj_zool_land and look at the code in the **Execute Code** action. Toward the end of the code, we have the following lines:

```
1:  if( place_meeting( x, y+1, obj_platform ) != true )
2:  {
3:      if(place_meeting(x, y+max(speed,LIFT_SPEED+1), obj_platform) == true )
4:          move_to_contact_with( 270, -1, obj_platform );
5:      else
6:          instance_change( obj_zool_air, true );
7:  }
8:
9:  if( place_meeting( x+facing, y, obj_wall ) == true )
10:     instance_change( obj_zool_wall, true );
11:
12: if( place_meeting( x, y+1, obj_slope ) == true )
13:     instance_change( obj_zool_ice, true );
```

The first two calls to place_meeting on lines 1 and 3 are the ones that mainly need addressing here. It's not worth changing the call on line 9, as it is making a horizontal check for walls, which can't be affected by ledges.

Within zoolgml.gmk

1. Now open up the new **End Step** event of obj_zool_land and look at the alternative code in the **Execute Code** action for the three place_meeting tests:

```
1:  if( check_standing_on( obj_platform, 1, 0 ) != true )
2:  {
3:      if(check_standing_on(obj_platform, max(speed,LIFT_SPEED+1),0) == true )
4:          move_to_contact_with( 270, -1, obj_platform );
5:      else
6:          instance_change( obj_zool_air, true );
7:  }
8:
9:  if( place_meeting( x+facing, y, obj_wall ) == true )
10:     instance_change( obj_zool_wall, true );
11:
12: if( check_standing_on( obj_slope, 1, 0 ) == true )
13:     instance_change( obj_zool_ice, true );
```

Here, we've used a brand new script function called check_standing_on to check for specific kinds of objects directly below the instance. We'll cover the operation of that function in the scripts section coming up next. The place_meeting function was used in a number of objects to look for platforms beneath Zool's feet, so all of these tests have been substituted with check_standing_on in the zoolgml.gmk version.

Scripts

Scripts are just another form of GML, but they are independent from any specific type of object, which means you can potentially use them anywhere in your code. They act as functions that can take a number of inputs (*arguments*) and provide an output in the form of a *return value*. Let's begin by considering the brand new script check_standing_on as an example. You'll find all these scripts in the **Scripts** folder of the zoolgml.gmk file.

Staying on Top

The aim of the check_standing_on script is to provide an alternative test for standing on objects. Rather than checking for a collision with the entire object moved one pixel down (as in Figure 11–3), it will only check for collisions within a small rectangle beneath the object's bounding box (see Figure 11–4). Specifically, this allows us to prevent the problem caused by ledges that support Zool when they are intersecting his body.

The check_standing_on Script

```
 1: {
 2:     var stand_obj, vert_dist, xoffset, x1, y1, x2, y2
 3:
 4:     stand_obj = argument0;
 5:     vert_dist = argument1;
 6:     xoffset = argument2;
 7:
 8:     x1 = bbox_left+xoffset;
 9:     y1 = bbox_bottom;
10:     x2 = bbox_right+xoffset;
11:     y2 = bbox_bottom+vert_dist;
12:
13:     if( collision_rectangle( x1, y1, x2, y2, stand_obj, true, true ) > 0 )
14:         return true;
15:     else
16:         return false;
17: }
```

The script begins by using the var keyword to declare a range of temporary variables that are only required within this script (note the commas). These are not treated as local instance variables and their contents are discarded when the script finishes execution. Significantly, the first three of these variables correspond to the kind of object we want to be standing on (stand_obj), the vertical size of the rectangle we'll use to look for those objects (vert_dist), and an optional horizontal offset that moves the rectangle a bit to the left or right as well (xoffset).

In lines 4-6, these variables are then set to the value of argument0, argument1, and argument2, respectively. These special argument keywords correspond to the arguments passed in when the script is called. So for example, check_standing_on(obj_slope, 1, 0) would set argument0 to obj_slope, argument1 to 1, and argument2 to 0. In other words, it would check for instances of obj_slope one pixel directly beneath the bounding box of the current instance.

Lines 8-11 set up more temporary variables that are used to calculate the four corners of the rectangle we'll be checking within. To do this, it uses the local instance variables that store the top, bottom, left, and right positions of this instance's bounding box within the room (Game Maker automatically updates these variables as an instance moves). Whenever you call a script, it has the ability to access the local variables of the calling instance in this way, but you must be sure that your calling instance has those variables. Of course, every instance has these bounding box variables, so this is not a concern here.

Finally, in lines 13-16, the script uses the `collision_rectangle` function to check for instances of the object held by the variable `stand_obj` within a small rectangle beneath the instance's feet (as in Figure 11–4). The last two arguments of the `collision_rectangle` function specify that we want precise collision detection (which we do because we're looking for solid landscape, and that includes ramps and slopes), and that we want it to ignore collisions with itself (in case you wanted to check if a platform was on top of a platform). If it finds a collision, then the function returns the id of one of the colliding instances (a value > 0) and if it doesn't, then it returns a negative value. We don't care exactly which instance it is, so we return `true` from the script if it is greater than 0 and `false` otherwise. This return value can then be used to determine whether the script was successful in finding something to stand on.

Figure 11–4. Zool will now fall down in this situation (as he should) because we are only checking directly beneath his feet (in red)

■**Note** If you want to find out more about a Game Maker function like `collision_rectangle` or any of the others discussed in this book, then select **Contents** from the **Help** menu and type the name of the function into the **search** tab. Usually, the first search result found will contain the help page for that function.

Staying in Contact

Since Chapter 5, we've used the `move_to_contact_with` script as a way of ensuring that Zool stops when he comes into contact with a specific type of object, rather than **all objects** or just objects with the **Solid** flag set (which we wish to avoid using altogether). It does this using a "brute force" approach, moving one pixel at a time in the direction provided until it collides with an instance of the specified object. Let's look at how that works.

The move_to_contact_with Script

```
1:  {
2:      var dirn, max_dist, contact_obj, dx, dy;
3:
4:      dirn        = argument0;
5:      max_dist    = argument1;
6:      contact_obj = argument2;
7:
8:      if( max_dist == -1 ) then max_dist = 1000;
9:
10:     dx = lengthdir_x( 1, dirn );
11:     dy = lengthdir_y( 1, dirn );
12:
13:     dist = 1;
14:
15:     while( dist <= max_dist )
16:     {
17:         if(place_meeting(x+dx,y+dy,contact_obj) == true) then return true;
18:         x = x + dx;
19:         y = y + dy;
20:         dist = dist + 1;
21:     }
22:
23:     return false;
24: }
```

So just like before, the script begins in lines 2-6 by setting up temporary variables to hold the argument values. Doing this is by no means compulsory, as you could just use argument0 and so forth directly in the code. However, it does improve the readability of the rest of the script because numbered arguments are pretty meaningless.

Line 8 checks to see if the distance argument has been set to -1, as this is the value used in the original **Move to Contact** action to signify an "arbitrary" moving distance. That arbitrary distance turns out to be 1000 pixels, so we're doing the same.

Lines 10 and 11 use the lengthdir_x and lengthdir_y functions to convert a distance of 1 pixel in the angle dirn into its component distances in x and y (see Figure 11–5). This provides the separate increments required in the x and y axes to move the instance forward by a total distance of one pixel. Note that this means dx and dy will usually contain hypothetical fractions of a pixel, but this is fine as they eventually add up to whole pixels.

Line 13 initializes the dist variable to start at 1. This variable will be used to keep track of how far the instance has moved to ensure that it remains less than max_dist. Lines 15-21 now perform a while loop using this variable. A while loop is similar to a repeat loop, but rather than repeating a fixed number of times, it keeps repeating while the expression in brackets evaluates to true. Therefore, this particular while loop will keep repeating lines 17-20 while dist is less than or equal to max_dist.

Line 17 uses the familiar place_meeting function to check if the instance would collide when moved by dx pixels in the x axis and dy pixels in the y axis (hence x+dx and y+dy). If it would collide, then the function returns true, ending the while loop and exiting the script immediately. We don't add dx and dy to the current position until lines 18 and 19, so the instance will still be at its old position (just before the collision) if the script returns on line 17.

If there wasn't a collision, then lines 18 and 19 will move the instance forward one pixel and line 20 will add one to the dist variable, accordingly. We now return to the start of the while loop, which will keep repeating this process until dist is greater than max_dist or the script returns true as a result of finding a collision. Line 23 will therefore only ever be reached if no collision was found and it returns false to indicate that this is the case.

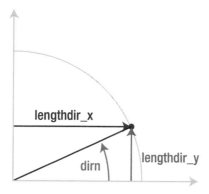

Figure 11–5. *In this diagram, the black line has a length of one pixel and is rotated by the angle dirn. The function lengthdir_x(1, dirn) provides the horizontal component of that line (in red) and lengthdir_y provides the vertical component of that line (in blue)*

Changing Lifts

There were also two scripts we created in Zool so that we could get hold of all adjacent lift instances and change them all into another kind of lift object during the same step. The check_object_returned script provided the id of adjacent instances and the change_instance_for script used that id to change those instances into another kind of object. However, both of these scripts can be simplified to a couple of lines of code in GML, so it isn't worth having them as scripts at all anymore.

You can write the check_object returned script as:

```
returned = instance_place( x+dx, y+dy, find_obj );
```

Where dx and dy are the offsets required and find_obj is the type of object we're looking for. Similarly, you can write the change_instance_for script as just two lines:

```
with( returned )
    instance_change( change_obj, true );
```

Where change_obj is the type of object we want the instance to change into. Both of these scripts have therefore been removed from zoolgml.gmk, and replaced with these lines where they were called. However, another script has been added to handle the entire process of switching lift instances called change_lift_instances and this uses both of these processes to handle the majority of the lift changing process in one place.

The change_lift_instances Script

```
 1:  {
 2:      var from_obj, into_obj, dx, returned, xpos;
 3:
 4:      from_obj    = argument0;
 5:      into_obj    = argument1;
 6:      dx          = argument2;
 7:
 8:      xpos = x + dx;
 9:
10:      do
11:      {
12:          returned = instance_place( xpos, y, from_obj );
13:
14:          with( returned )
15:              instance_change( into_obj, true );
16:
17:          xpos = xpos + dx;
18:
19:      } until ( returned == noone )
20:  }
```

You should be starting to recognize the structure by now, starting with assigning local variables to the argument values to make them more readable. There are only three arguments: a type of object to change from (from_obj), a type of object to change into (into_obj), and a horizontal spacing to look for the next lift instance (dx). The script also uses the temporary variables xpos to keep track of the position currently being checked for lifts, and returned to store the id of any object found.

The script is based around a loop of lines 10-19 until no more objects of the indicated type are found. However, this is a do, until loop, which works the other way around than a while loop. There's not much difference, but instead of evaluating the condition in brackets at the start of the loop, it does it at the end instead (on line 19).

Line 12 does the equivalent of our old check_object_returned script and lines 14 and 15 the change_instance_for script. Line 17 then advances the position to check for lifts, and line 19 continues the loop unless no object was actually found. In this way, all the adjacent lift instances of the same type are changed at the same time.

Delayed Lift

One last improvement we'll make to the GML-enhanced version is to fix the small delayed reaction in Zool's movement when he is standing on lifts. This happens because we update Zool's movement with respect to lifts in the **Begin Step** event, but the lifts themselves don't start or stop moving until the **Collision** events. We did talk about moving Zool's lift update to after the **Collision** events in the **End Step** event in order to fix this, but that could result in Zool being pushed through the landscape in certain situations. So to make this work, we need to make some additional checks to make sure that the lift isn't pushing Zool into the landscape. These checks have now been added to the new **End Step** event of obj_zool_land:

```
 1:  var returned, newx, nexy;
 2:
 3:  returned = instance_place( x, y+1, obj_lift );
 4:
 5:  if( returned != noone )
 6:  {
 7:      newx = x+returned.hspeed;
 8:      newy = y+returned.vspeed;
 9:
10:      if( place_meeting( newx, newy, obj_solid ) != true )
11:      {
12:          x = newx;
13:          y = newy;
14:      }
15:  }
```

This sort of code should be starting to make sense without too much explanation now, but you can see that we are using the `instance_place` function again to see if Zool is standing on a lift and using the `place_meeting` function to make sure the lifts movement wouldn't push him inside something solid. We only add the lift's movement if the result is safe, which now means Zool will fall off the lift when it pushes him up against something.

Goodbye Ninja, Hello Pirate

We have reached a very sad point in our journey, as it is finally time to say farewell to the interstellar cosmos dweller that is Zool. We have learned about as much as we can from him and it's time to trade up for a larger model—but this one only comes in black.

The scope of *Shadows on Deck* is much larger too, and although we'll cover some of the implementation step-by-step, it's simply not practical to cover the whole game in this way. We'll provide incremental versions of the game as usual, but you'll often have to load our version at the beginning of each new section—as there will be additions we have made for you. It will be more of a "steps and jumps" approach than taking everything step-by-step as we did for Zool. Nonetheless, it will be good for you to go through the motions of typing in some of the scripts when we ask you to, as it will familiarize you with the syntax and grammar of GML in a much more direct way than just reading this book.

The Problem with Giants

So we'll begin with a bit of a jump. Load `shadows0.gmk` from the `Chapter11/Games` directory on the CD. If you run this version of the game, you'll find we have already taken a number of steps toward converting the `zoolgml.gmk` framework into a fledgling version of *Shadows on Deck* (see Figure 11–6).

Figure 11–6. *Zool is a shadow of his former self, and quite a big one at that*

Changes Made to Create shadows0.gmk

1. **Sprites.** Zool's character sprites have been replaced with those of our new protagonist, Flynn. Flynn's sprites are much bigger: most being 128x192 pixels compared with Zool's 48x48. We've only made direct replacements at this stage (so no new animations) and we've removed sprites that Flynn will never have, like spinning, kicking, and skidding.

2. **Names.** If it was called Zool before, it's now called Flynn, everything from the names of sprites and object resources to the appended letter of state constants have been altered to reflect the name of the Pirate's son.

3. **Functionality.** We'd like to reuse as much functionality as possible, but there are certain things that are definitely surplus to requirements. All the ninja attack moves that Flynn doesn't need have been removed. All the enemies and user-interface elements that won't feature in the new game have also been taken out of this version. We've also removed the automatic drifting mechanic that maintains horizontal speed even after a horizontal collision. *Shadows on Deck* will not rely on a super-slick movement mechanic like *Zool* and this approach can have unintended side effects. Therefore, we've chosen to stick to setting `hspeed` to 0 when there's something in the way.

4. **Sound Effects.** We have swapped these for more appropriate ones.

5. **View.** The size of the main view into the room has been expanded from 512x300 pixels up to 1024x600. The size of the port on the screen remains at 1024x600, so this means our view is no longer being scaled up as it is drawn to the screen. We scaled up the view in *Zool* because the sprites were so small, but we don't need to scale up *Shadows on Deck* because the sprites and view are much larger to begin with.

6. **Grid.** As a result of scaling up the view, we're also going to scale up the grid size. So all the basic collision objects (platforms, slopes, and so forth) that were 16x16 pixels are now 32x32 pixels. Our Room Editor is now also set up to use a 32x32 grid, accordingly.

So how does the game play after these quick modifications? Well, the level design is clearly no longer appropriate for a character Flynn's size, but it does actually help us identify (and fix) some initial problems. If you try and make your way toward the right side of the room (the long way around), then you should find that you can jump and climb your way across most of the landscape fairly well. Clearly, there are some adjustments we need to make for climbing walls, and the sliding animation doesn't work particularly well for Flynn, either. Nonetheless, it's certainly a good basis for developing Flynn's movement mechanic. Unfortunately, once you eventually make it to the collection of ledges on the far right of the room, you are likely to encounter a serious problem (see Figure 11–7).

Figure 11–7. *Flynn can't move into contact with the ground because of ledges going through his body*

It's not difficult to get completely stuck amongst either set of ledges, as there is a fundamental problem with using such a relative giant under our existing "engine". The problem is that many of our collision events use the `move_to_contact_with` script to place the character on the surface of the landscape. This script works by moving the object one pixel at a time until it collides with something solid, but it doesn't account for the possibility that the object is already in contact with something solid, because it has a ledge through the middle of it! (See Figure 11–7). In these situations, the `move_to_contact_with` script does absolutely nothing, and so the character ends up being stuck, unable to make contact with the ground.

This is a similar problem to the "The Ninja Elbow Walk" issue from earlier: it's just that our new character is so much bigger. We solved that problem by inventing a new script called `check_standing_on` that performed collision checks in a small area beneath the character's bounding box. We can partly solve this problem by expanding upon that with a new version of `move_to_contact_with` that only checks for collisions beneath the character's bounding box in exactly the same way.

Move On Top

Load `shadows1.gmk` and open the new script resource called `move_on_top_of`. This version of the script only has two arguments, as it is always assumed that the direction of movement is 270 degrees. Other than that, it is practically identical to `move_to_contact_with`, except that it uses the script `check_standing_on` instead of the built-in function `place_meeting`.

This is the important line:

```
if( check_standing_on( contact_obj, 1, 0 ) == true ) then return true;
```

So in practice, this script moves the instance pixel by pixel until it finds the required object within the 1-pixel high rectangle beneath the bounding box. This contrasts with the approach of `move_to_contact_with` that checks whether the entire bounding box overlaps with the object and then returns the previous position. As a result, we have a script that isn't affected by ledge objects that are already inside the character's bounding box when the script is called.

We can now use this new script in place of `move_to_contact_with` in all the places where Flynn is moved directly downward following a collision (so any kind of ramp or slope collision as well as conditional statements that move Flynn down to keep him walking on top of platforms). This prevents situations where Flynn gets stuck between two ledges such as that shown on the left of Figure 11–7, but doesn't improve the situation shown on the right. This is because the airborne collision event with platforms has to use the more general `move_to_contact_with` script, to cope with collisions in all directions that can happen in mid-air. We'll need to give that some more thought.

Ignoring Ledges in the Air

You might think that the **Collision** event between `obj_flynn_air` and `obj_ledge` is all you need to worry about when considering collisions with ledges in the air. Unfortunately it's not as simple as that because ledges are also *a kind of* `obj_solid`, and as such are also included in collision checks wherever the `move_to_contact_with` script is used. So even if the original collision event was not with a ledge, ledges still get included in the way that collision is resolved.

Open up the `obj_solid` **Collision** event of `obj_flynn_air` and remind yourself of how it works. It is a general-purpose collision event that uses the `move_to_contact_with` script to cope with collisions in all directions, and thus is vulnerable to the ledge problem. Unfortunately, we can't replace it with `move_on_top_of`, as this wouldn't work for horizontal collisions with solid objects, such as when Flynn jumps into the side of a platform (it would actually transport him down onto the floor when he did so). However, there is another way to make sure ledges are ignored in such a collision and that is simply to deactivate them. Game Maker provides a range of functions that allow you to deactivate certain instances, so that they simply behave as if they don't exist anymore, yet can be brought back into existence at a later point. The following listing shows how we've used the `instance_deactivate_object` function to deactivate all instances of a `obj_ledge` (which includes lifts) at the start of the collision code and `instance_activate_object` to reactivate them again afterward.

```
 1:  {
 2:      instance_deactivate_object( obj_ledge );
 3:
 4:      x = xprevious;
 5:      y = yprevious;
 6:
 7:      move_to_contact_with( direction, -1, obj_solid );
 8:
 9:      if( place_meeting( x, yprevious+vspeed, obj_solid ) == true )
10:          vspeed = 0;
11:      else
12:          y = yprevious+vspeed;
13:
14:      if( place_meeting( xprevious+hspeed, y, obj_solid ) == true )
15:          hspeed = 0;
16:      else
17:          x = xprevious+hspeed;
18:
19:      if( check_standing_on( obj_platform, 1, 0 ) == true )
20:          instance_change( obj_flynn_land, true );
21:
22:      instance_activate_object( obj_ledge );
23:  }
```

This approach doesn't stop ledges from working, as there is an entirely separate collision event with obj_ledge that gets called independently when the character lands on a ledge. Even if it causes Flynn to pass through a ledge in some obscure situations, this is a price worth paying in order to solve our problem with Flynn getting stuck so easily.

Empty Collisions

One final thing we need to do to fix the ledge problem is to make sure that all our other character state objects have empty collision events with obj_ledge. We already have one of these in place for obj_flynn_land to make sure that sideways collisions with obj_ledge are ignored when Flynn is walking. It is simply an **Execute Code** action containing the exit command, meaning "do nothing"—and significantly *don't* call the general collision event with obj_solid that would otherwise bring Flynn to a halt. The same events therefore need to be added to obj_flynn_ice and obj_flynn_wall to cope with the extra potential for Flynn to have his body within a ledge while doing something else.

All these tweaks work together to fix the original problem we had with Flynn getting stuck between ledges. Play shadows1.gmk from the Chapter11/Games directory on the CD and see for yourself.

Congratulations

Okay, so we've reached the end of the chapter and there's not been so much as a whiff of sea air, or a pirate ship. Don't worry, the ninjas haven't finally wiped out all the pirates, it's just far easier for you to understand GML within the familiar context of a game you've already worked on. We have already taken the first steps toward including our new protagonist in the game and seen the problems that a larger character can create.

Nonetheless, it's time to start practicing your best pirate voice, as you'll truly earn your sea-legs in the next chapter by creating a vertical slice of the finished game. A vertical slice might sound like some kind of strange pirate punishment, but it is actually a reference to a slice of a cake rather than anything gruesome. Of course, this particular slice of cake contains sinister skeletons, deadly spear-traps, merciless pirates, and relentless skull-bats, but that's really beside the point....

■ ■ ■

CHAPTER 12

Rogues' Rendezvous: Vertically Sliced

We're aiming to produce one complete level for *Shadows on Deck*, or what is often called a "vertical slice" of gameplay. In a professional game development studio, it is quite common to create a small section of a game like this in order to prove the concept's worth to a publisher. Console games often cost many millions of dollars to develop, and these days it is usually only the big-name publishers who can afford to pick up this kind of bill. Nonetheless, they don't just hand over that kind of money based on a design document, however good it may be. Publishers are always looking for AAA titles,[1] but the truth is that it is actually impossible to design such a game on paper! The art of game design is an interactive, step-by-step process and quality games evolve into being; they are not simply implemented according to a meticulous plan.

Consequently, publishers often fund an initial, short period of development called *preproduction* in order to try and find the fun in the concept. In that phase, the designers compile the game design, the artists create concept art for the characters and environments, and the programmers create game play and technology prototypes. A vertical slice is often seen as a single complete level that has the feel of the finished game, but exists in isolation. The success of this initial prototype will determine whether the publisher decides to continue to fund the development of the project, and whether the team's hard work and enthusiasm for their concept will ever see the light of day....

Animated Driving

Large, well-defined sprites may look great, but they bring with them a whole range of additional problems. We've already seen some of the issues it can create with collisions, but there are animation problems, too. Sliding feet in walk cycles, sudden transitions between different animations, and the synchronization of sound effects are all issues that are much harder to ignore with larger character sprites. The hierarchical animation systems used in 3D games typically have the ability to dynamically access or modify animation data on the fly, so they do not suffer from

---

[1] Pronounced, *triple-A*. Refers to the very best games that have been both critically acclaimed and commercially successful.

the same issues. This ability to change animations means that the game-logic can drive the animations. Unfortunately, this isn't an option for games like ours that use pre-rendered sprites, so one alternative is to make the animations drive the game logic instead.

In this section, we're going to revert to a step-by-step approach, so make sure you have an unaltered version of shadows1.gmk from the Chapter12/Games directory open and ready to go. We're going to change the way that Flynn moves and animates, replacing the friction and acceleration approach used for *Zool* with a constant movement speed that is driven by the animations (a little like *Fishpod*). We'll also provide a less ninja-like way of climbing up onto the top of platforms, and introduce the double-jump feature, so be prepared for a bit of typing.

Best Foot Forward

The most significant way that the animations will be made to drive the game logic is in the walking mechanic. We're going to replace the friction and acceleration approach used for *Zool* with a constant movement speed. To prevent Flynn's feet from sliding, his movement speed needs to accurately match the frames in his animation. Changing his movement speed over time would make that even harder. We'll also only stop his speed in an **Animation End** event, which is what makes his movement dependant on the animation. We've made sure the animation is fairly short (so it only includes a single step), but it still means Flynn can only move fixed distances at a time. Nonetheless, bear in mind that the final levels that Flynn will navigate will be far more open and spacious than the one we're using at the moment, and there won't be pixel-perfect jumps to make, so it shouldn't impact the game play too severely.

Adjusting Flynn's Walking Mechanic

1. Reopen obj_flynn_land and edit the code of the **Create** event. Set the friction to 0 rather than 1 and include a line that sets hspeed to 0 as well. Unlike for *Zool* (where we didn't want jumping to break his stride), we want *Shadows on Deck* to be a more thoughtfully paced platform game, so coming to a halt between states is actually desirable this time.

2. Select the **Begin Step** event and have a quick peek at its code. All it did was to default the state to the standing state. We no longer need to do this, as Flynn should remain in the walking state until the end of an animation cycle. Therefore, you can delete the **Begin Step** event entirely from the obj_flynn_land object.

Figure 12–1. *Looking at Flynn's walking animation in the Sprite Editor, we can see that his foot touches the ground in subimage 7*

3. Select the **End Step** event and change the line dealing with footsteps that says:

    ```
    if( global.step_count mod 8 == 0 )
    to:
    if( image_index == 5 )
    ```

    In *Zool*, we just wanted footsteps to be played at regular intervals (once every 8 steps). His legs were too small and moved too fast to worry too much about exactly when they were touching the ground. Flynn is much larger and it's clearer to see that his foot touches the ground on about subimage 7 (see Figure 12–1). Therefore, we will play a sound effect a couple of steps before this happens (subimage 5) as it generally takes a little time for the sound effect to reach the critical part of the sound. Achieving the desired result can take a little experimentation.

4. Now, add the following two lines within the same block of code that depends on the `if( state == FSTATE_WALK )` condition:

    ```
    if( x == xprevious )
        state = FSTATE_STAND;
    ```

    This will reset the walking state back to the standing state if Flynn doesn't actually manage to move horizontally during a step. In other words, we won't keep playing the walking animation if Flynn has been blocked by an obstruction.

5. Edit the code for the **Keyboard, Left** event and change the line that subtracts 2.5 from hspeed (using minus equals "-=") to one that sets hspeed to -10 (using just "="). Now include the following lines directly below that one to reset the walking animation back to its starting frame when Flynn enters the walking state:

    ```
    if( state != FSTATE_WALK )
        image_index = 0;
    ```

6. Do the same for the **Keyboard, Right** event, setting hspeed to 10 and including the same two lines shown in step 5 immediately after it.

7. Add an **Other, Animation End** event and include an **Execute Code** action (**control** tab) containing the following code:

    ```
    {
        state = FSTATE_STAND;
        hspeed = 0;
    }
    ```

    This will put Flynn back into the standing state and stop his horizontal movement at the end of each animation cycle.

8. Select the **Collision** event with obj_solid. There is a tweak we will make to the way that collisions are handled with solid objects, as essentially there are two types of collisions: those with Flynn's feet and those with the rest of his body. Previously, we have assumed all collisions are with his whole body and should bring Flynn to a halt, but there are rare situations (when ascending ramps) where he can collide with the corner of a platform with his feet and come to a halt (see Figure 12–2). We can fix this problem by adjusting the collision event to check if Flynn is standing on the object he has collided with and handling the collision like we would do for a ramp instead. We still need the other collision code (when he is not standing on the object), as Flynn should still come to a halt if his head or upper body collides with a platform too. Change the code to read as follows:

```
 1:  {
 2:      if( check_standing_on( other.id, 1, 0 ) == true )
 3:      {
 4:          y -= speed;
 5:          move_on_top_of( -1, obj_solid );
 6:      }
 7:      else
 8:      {
 9:          x = xprevious;
10:          y = yprevious;
11:
12:          move_to_contact_with( direction, -1, obj_solid );
13:
14:          hspeed = 0;
15:      }
16:  }
```

Figure 12–2. *Flynn cannot move right from this position, as his bounding box (blue) keeps colliding with the corner pixel of the platform object (green) and putting him back into his previous position (red)*

9. We'll make another small tweak that affects the walking mechanic when switching to the ice state and back again. It is easy for the larger Flynn character to end up standing on both ice and land at the same time, you can get "fighting" (rapidly switching back and forth) between the two states on the borders between ice and land. Open obj_flynn_ice and select the **Collision** event with obj_solid. Edit the **Execute Code** action to include an extra line above the last two:

```
if( check_standing_on( obj_slope, 1, 0, 0 ) != true )
    if( check_standing_on( obj_platform, 1, 0, 0 ) == true )
        instance_change( obj_flynn_land, true );
```

This now helps to prevent fighting between the two states by essentially making ice take priority over land, as it will only switch back to the land state when there is a platform below Flynn, and there is no ice.

So try walking Flynn around the test level now. Hopefully, you can see what we mean about a constant movement rate and fixed movement distance. Nonetheless, the animated effect of the character is much more believable and visually consistent as a result. We can't make all our transitions between animations as smooth as this, but as walking is the most common one, it has the most effect on the overall impression of the game.

Over the Top

Next, we're going to address climbing animations including an animation for when Flynn climbs to the top of a wall and pulls himself onto the surface above. Not only is this a particularly hard movement to animate, but it can also be difficult to integrate it within the game in a way that makes it look like the character is physically interacting with the landscape. Fortunately, the simple solutions are often the best, so we'll just use an animation that has all the movement as part of the animation (see Figure 12–3). This kind of animation is set up to make it look as if Flynn is moving in the game world when he actually isn't (his coordinates and bounding box will remain on the side of the wall). As a result, we will need to quickly move the Flynn instance into the new position at the end of the animation so that it appears as if his climb is one continuous sequence.

Adjusting Flynn's Climbing Mechanic

1. Create a new constant called `FSTATE_CLIMB_TOP` set to a value of 7.

2. Create two new sprite resources called `spr_flynn_climb_top_right` and `spr_flynn_climb_top_left` using the appropriate files from the `Chapter12/Resources/Sprites/Flynn` directory on the CD.

3. Modify the mask of `spr_flynn_climb_top_right` to use a **Rectangle Shape** and **Manual Bounding Box** set to **Left**=48, **Right**=80, **Top**=144, and **Bottom**=298, with an **Origin** of X=64, Y=208.

4. Modify the mask of `spr_flynn_climb_top_left` to also use a **Rectangle Shape** and **Manual Bounding Box**, but set to **Left**=128, **Right**=160, **Top**=144, **Bottom**=298, and with an **Origin** of X=144, Y=208.

There are two things worth observing here, so take a careful look at the sprites and animations. As already discussed, the sprites include Flynn's movement on top of the wall as part of the animation, and that makes them larger than all the other sprites. Flynn's first subimage is offset to one side of the sprite to make room for the animation and the sprite's **Origin** has been offset to match (set just above his knee in the first subimage). Secondly, Flynn's bounding box remains in the same position throughout the animation, which is something we'll need to consider later.

5. Now, edit the **Draw** event of `obj_flynn` and add a new case for drawing the climb top sprite within the block for `FACE_RIGHT`:

    ```
    case FSTATE_CLIMB_TOP: sprite_index = spr_flynn_climb_top_right; break;
    ```

    and then `FACE_LEFT`:

    ```
    case FSTATE_CLIMB_TOP: sprite_index = spr_flynn_climb_top_left; break;
    ```

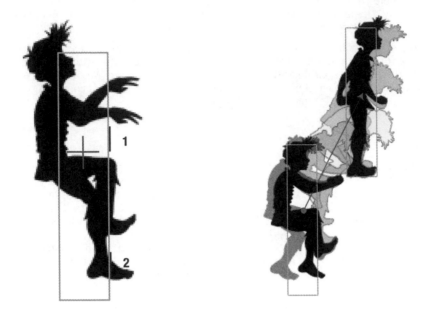

Figure 12–3. *(Left): The new script will check for walls in two different positions (marked in red). (Right): Unlike most of Flynn's animations, the climbing animation will not take place "on the spot" but will show Flynn moving in space and then his position will be moved at the end of the animation (blue arrow)*

6. Next, we're going to write a new script resource that provides a consistent way of detecting walls that Flynn can climb. At the moment, the game contains a number of subtly different checks for walls in various situations and none of them cope well with larger characters. We will replace all of these with calls to a single script that will make sure there are sections of wall adjacent to Flynn at both hand and foot heights at the same time (see Figure 12–3, left). Only when both are present will we allow Flynn to hold onto a wall; otherwise, his climbing animation looks a little odd. Create a new script resource called `is_climbable` and carefully type the following code into it:

```
 1:  {
 2:      var yoff, xdirn, x1, y1, x2, y2;
 3:
 4:      xdirn = argument0;
 5:      yoff = argument1;
 6:
 7:      if( xdirn > 0 )
 8:      {
 9:          x1 = bbox_right;
10:          x2 = bbox_right+1;
11:      }
12:      else
13:      {
14:          x1 = bbox_left-1;
15:          x2 = bbox_left;
16:      }
17:
18:      y1 = y+yoff-32;
19:      y2 = y1+32;
20:
21:      if( collision_rectangle(x1, y1, x2, y2, obj_wall, true, true) > 0 &&
22:          collision_rectangle(x1, y1+80, x2, y2+80, obj_wall, true, true) > 0)
23:          return true;
24:      else
25:          return false;
26:  }
```

This script takes two arguments: the first indicates the direction to look for walls (a negative value for left and a positive for right), and the second provides an optional vertical offset (for when you want to "look-ahead" above or below the character).

Lines 7–16 set up the left and right boundaries of a very thin rectangle that starts at the edge of the bounding box and extends just one pixel beyond (see Figure 12–3, left).

Lines 18 and 19 then set the top and bottom boundaries of this rectangle to correspond to the area just below Flynn's hands, and then lines 21 and 22 check for instances of obj_wall within both this rectangle and one 80 pixels beneath it. The use of the && (and) operator means that the script will only return true if both tests succeed; otherwise, it returns false.

7. So there are now a number of places where we will use this script instead of the existing code that checks for walls. Open obj_flynn_air and obj_flynn_land in turn and edit their **End Step** events. In each one, change the line that reads:

    ```
    if( place_meeting( x+facing, y, obj_wall ) == true )
    ```

    to:

    ```
    if( is_climbable( facing, 0 ) == true )
    ```

8. Open obj_flynn_wall and edit the **End Step** event. Change the line at the start of the action that reads:

```
if( place_meeting( x+facing, y, obj_wall ) != true )
```

to:

```
if( is_climbable( facing, 0 ) != true )
```

9. Still in the **End Step** event of obj_flynn_wall, remove the middle two lines (plus the comment) that cope with Flynn extending too high above the top of the wall (by making him slip down). Happily, this situation can't happen anymore as there has to be a wall at Flynn's hand position in order for is_climbable to return true.

10. Next, change the last line that sets image_index to 0 so that it sets image_speed to 0 instead. This will stop Flynn from snapping back to the first frame of the animation each time he stops climbing. Stopping the speed will bring the animation to a halt on its current frame instead, which looks more natural.

11. Edit the **Begin Step** event for obj_flynn_wall and add the following line directly above the line that defaults the state to FSTATE_CLING.

```
if( state != FSTATE_CLIMB_TOP )
```

This prevents the state from being changed back to clinging when the climbing up animation has started. It's also worth indenting the line after it to keep things tidy.

12. Now, edit the **Keyboard, Up** event of obj_flynn_wall. There are a number of changes to make here, so we'll just provide you with the result so that you can adjust it accordingly:

```
1:  {
2:      if( state == FSTATE_CLIMB_TOP )
3:          exit;
4:
5:      if( is_climbable( facing, -3 ) == true )
6:      {
7:          vspeed = -3;
8:          image_speed = 1;
9:          state = FSTATE_CLIMB;
10:     }
11:     else
12:     {
13:         if( place_meeting( x+(facing*60), y-130, obj_solid ) == false )
14:         {
15:             state = FSTATE_CLIMB_TOP;
16:             image_index = 0;
17:             image_speed = 1;
18:         }
19:     }
20: }
```

Notice that this event exits without doing anything if Flynn is already in the climbing-on-top state. He clearly can't climb any higher if he is already in this state.

Line 5 checks to see if it is possible to move 3 pixels up from Flynn's current position and then lines 7–9 start him moving up at a speed of 3 pixels per step if he can. This speed looks about right for the climbing animation, and we need to make sure the animation is playing forward by setting image_speed to 1 (we'll need to play it backward when he moves down the wall).

If it's not possible to move any further up the wall, then line 13 checks to see if Flynn would collide with anything solid if he was moved 60 pixels in the direction he is facing and 130 pixels up. Why these values? Well, that's the relative distance between Flynn in the first frame of the climbing up animation and the last frame (the blue arrow in Figure 12–3, right). We only want him to start climbing up if the end position is free of obstructions. If it is free, then lines 15-17 put Flynn into the climbing on top state and set his animation playing at a normal forward speed starting from the first frame.

13. Now, edit the **Keyboard, Down** event of `obj_flynn_wall`. Again, we will just provide the result of the changes required:

```
 1: {
 2:     if( state == FSTATE_CLIMB_TOP )
 3:         exit;
 4:
 5:     if( is_climbable( facing, 3 ) == true )
 6:     {
 7:         vspeed = 3;
 8:         image_speed = -1;
 9:         state = FSTATE_CLIMB;
10:     }
11:     else
12:     {
13:         instance_change( obj_flynn_air, true );
14:     }
15: }
```

This event also exits without doing anything if Flynn is already in the climbing-on-top state because aborting the animation half-way to climb down again would look odd.

Lines 5-10 cope with checking and moving downward from Flynn's current position. However, note that `image_speed` is set to -1 to make the animation play backward when Flynn is climbing down, as this looks much more realistic.

Finally, line 13 makes Flynn fall down if he has reached the bottom of a wall and there is nothing more to hold on to.

14. Now, add an **Other, Animation End** event to `obj_flynn_wall` and include an **Execute Code** action that contains the following code:

```
 1: {
 2:     if( state == FSTATE_CLIMB_TOP )
 3:     {
 4:         x += facing*60;
 5:         y -= 130;
 6:         move_on_top_of( 10, obj_solid );
 7:         instance_change( obj_flynn_land, true );
 8:     }
 9: }
```

Remember that despite appearances, Flynn's x and y position is actually still on the side of the wall. So this event will trigger on the final subimage of the animation, teleporting Flynn into a new position that matches the final frame of the animation. It actually moves up a few more pixels than should be necessary in line 5 and then places Flynn back on the surface of the new platform on line 6. This is because Flynn's y position relative to the top of the wall can vary a little according to where he started climbing from and the speed at which he is moving up it.

15. Finally, edit the **Create** events of obj_flynn_land and obj_flynn_dead and include an extra line in each that sets image_speed to 1. We've been setting this to -1 in obj_flynn_wall to make animations play backward, but we wouldn't want this to affect any other states, so this will make sure it is back to normal for other objects. The obj_flynn_land and obj_flynn_ice objects already handle this for themselves so there's no need to add anything for them.

And that's it for climbing. If you try out the game now, then you should find that Flynn navigates around the test level quite convincingly now—despite it being a less-than-appropriate level design for a larger character like this. If you have any problems with your version, then compare it to the file shadows2.gmk in the Chapter12/Games directory on the CD.

One thing you will notice is that the screen position jumps at the end of the climbing on top animation when Flynn is moved on top of the platform. Don't worry about that for the moment, as we'll be fixing that later by adding our own code to control the view position.

Jump High, Fall Hard

The double jump is a key part of the design for *Shadows on Deck*. It will give Flynn the ability to nimbly avoid his enemies as well as help him to navigate the more precarious heights of the level. It will be especially useful to be able to make a second leap in mid-air, as the result of Flynn falling too far to the ground will be instant death (followed by a convenient restart, of course). We will therefore consider both the double jump and death by falling next.

Adjusting Flynn's Jumping Mechanic

1. We'll begin by creating four new constants. We need two new states: FSTATE_BEND set to a value of 8 and FSTATE_RECOVER set to 9, as well as two constants for controlling how far Flynn can fall before he dies: FALL_DIST_RECOVER set to 300 and FALL_DIST_FATAL set to 600. Also, rename the constant SKID_SPEED to JUMP_SPEED with a new value of -33 and create a new constant called DRIFT_ACCEL (acceleration) with a value of 3.

2. Create a new sprite resource called spr_flynn_bend_right using the appropriate file from the Chapter12/Resources/Sprites/Flynn directory on the CD. Modify its mask to use a **Rectangle Shape** and **Manual Bounding Box** set to **Left**=48, **Right**=80, **Top**=32, and **Bottom**=186 and **Center** its **Origin**.

3. Duplicate spr_flynn_bend_right to create a new sprite called spr_flynn_bend_left. Click on **Edit Sprite** and use the **Transform** menu to **Mirror/Flip** the sprite horizontally with the **Apply to all images in sprite** option checked (see Figure 12–4). This saves you having to load and set up the collision mask of the opposite facing sprite.

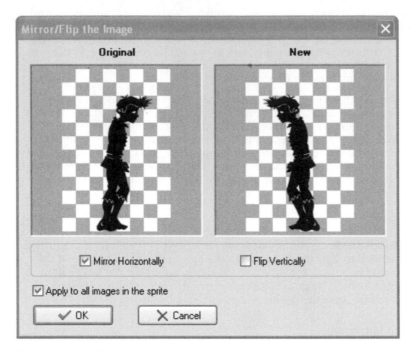

Figure 12–4. The fastest way to create the left flipping sprite is to flip the right-facing one

4. Create another new sprite resource called `spr_flynn_recover_right` using the appropriate file. Modify its mask to use a **Rectangle Shape** and **Manual Bounding Box** set to **Left**=64, **Right**=96, **Top**=32, and **Bottom**=186 and **Center** its **Origin**.

5. Duplicate `spr_flynn_recover_right` to create a new `spr_flynn_recover_left` sprite in the same way as before.

6. Reopen `spr_flynn_fall_left` and click on **Edit Sprite**. Notice that this sprite currently only has one subimage. Now go to **File**, **Create From File** and select the `spr_flynn_fall_left` sprite. It now has two subimages: one for "normal" falling and one for when Flynn has fallen too far. If you close the Sprite Editor and look at the mask, you'll see that loading the new sprite in this way hasn't changed the mask as it would do if you just used **Load Sprite**.

7. Repeat the process for `spr_flynn_fall_right`.

8. Open `obj_flynn` and edit the **Create** event. Add a new line of code *before* `instance_change` is called that sets the variable `peak_height` to `y`. We will use this value to calculate how far Flynn has fallen.

9. Now, edit the **Step** event of `obj_flynn` and include these two new lines at the end:

```
if( object_index != obj_flynn_air || y < peak_height )
    peak_height = y;
```

The first part of this condition will ensure that Flynn's `peak_height` variable is updated to match his y position, when he is not in the air state object (so not jumping or falling). The second part adds an exception to this condition using the *or* (||) operator so that `peak_height` *is* updated while jumping or falling if Flynn's current y position is higher than the previous peak height. So as a result, the `peak_height` variable will always contain Flynn's highest y position since he last stood or held onto solid ground.

10. Finally, for `obj_flynn`, edit the **Draw** event and add new cases for setting the bend and recover sprites in the usual way. It doesn't matter what order the new states come in the list of cases, but don't forget to do both left- and right-facing sprites.

11. Open `obj_flynn_land` and edit the **Key Press, Space** event. Change the line that sets `vspeed` to `-22` so that it sets `vspeed` to `JUMP_SPEED` instead (the constant already includes the minus, so there is no need to include it here).

12. Do the same for the **Key Press, Space** event of `obj_flynn_ice`. We now have one constant that can be changed to globally alter the jump speed, which is a bit neater.

13. Open `obj_flynn_air` and edit the **Create** event. Change the existing code to set `gravity` to `3.5` and then add three new lines that set `image_speed`, `image_index`, and then `jump_count` all to the value 0. Now that we have two frames for our falling sprite, we need to control the index and speed of the animation manually.

14. Edit the **End Step** event of `obj_flynn_air`. Most of this code is included in a condition that only occurs when Flynn is falling (`vspeed > 0`). Remove the line that sets `gravity` to 2 (we're not bothering with the extended jump for Flynn, as the double jump replaces it). Insert the following lines of code in its place:

```
1:      var fall_dist;
2:      fall_dist = y - peak_height;
3:
4:      if( fall_dist > FALL_DIST_FATAL )
5:          image_index = 1;
6:      else
7:          image_index = 0;
```

So when Flynn is falling, this calculates how far Flynn has fallen so far and selects the appropriate subimage according to whether the fall is "safe" or "fatal." We'll use a similar approach to decide what to do at the end of a fall later.

15. In the same code, remove the last two lines that check to see if Flynn is jumping and always set the `image_index` to 0 if he is. We're going to use different subimages for jumping and double jumping, and we've already made sure the subimage won't change on its own by setting `image_speed` to 0 in the **Create** event.

16. Edit both the **Keyboard, Left** and **Keyboard, Right** events of `obj_flynn_air` and change the amount added or subtracted from `hspeed` to `DRIFT_ACCEL` (which we set to 3). This will make the drifting mechanic appropriately stronger for the larger Flynn.

At this point, you might think that all we need to do now to support a double jump is add a **Key Press, Space** event to `obj_flynn_air` that launches Flynn into the air based on the value of `jump_count`. Unfortunately, it's not as simple as that, because of the slightly unpredictable way that the **Key Press** events work while changing between instances.

We know the **Key Press, Space** event must have already been triggered in another object (perhaps obj_zool_land) in order to reach the obj_zool_air state. So you wouldn't expect it to be triggered again until the Space key was released and then pressed again. However, when you change the instance in a **Key Press** event, Game Maker can actually end up triggering the **Key Press** event again—in the same step—for the object that you are changing into.

If this was always the case, then it wouldn't be unpredictable, but unfortunately it depends on the order in which objects are stored internally in Game Maker. So changing into obj_flynn_air in the **Key Press** event of obj_flynn_land calls the **Key Press, Space** event in both objects. Yet, changing into obj_flynn_land in the **Key Press** event of obj_flynn_air only triggers it once for the original object (presumably because the other object has already been processed for **Key Press** events by that point).

This means we need a solution that explicitly controls whether the **Key Press** event is counted for the double jump, as we can't rely on Game Maker to do this for us.

17. Edit the **Key Release, Space** event of obj_flynn_air. Delete the line that sets gravity (and the comment) and include the following two lines instead:

    if(jump_count == 0)
        jump_count = 1;

18. Now, add a new **Key Press, Space** event for obj_flynn_air and include an **Execute Code** action that contains the following lines of code:

```
1:  if( jump_count == 1 )
2:  {
3:      sound_play( snd_jump );
4:      vspeed = JUMP_SPEED;
5:      image_index = 1;
6:      state = FSTATE_JUMP;
7:      jump_count = 2;
8:  }
```

So now the sequence of events for a double jump works like this:

- The player triggers the **Key Press, Space** event in one of the other state objects that changes it into obj_flynn_air and calls the **Create** event.

- The variable jump_count is set to 0 in the **Create** event of obj_flynn_air, which means the **Key Press, Space** event we've just created won't do anything if it gets automatically called again by Game Maker.

- The player eventually triggers the **Key Release, Space** event by releasing the Space key and jump_count gets set to 1.

- The player can then press the Space key again and this time the **Key Press, Space** event will succeed and allow Flynn to do a double jump. The jump_count variable is also set to 2 so Flynn can't jump again until he leaves this state object and returns back to it (that is, he lands on something and jumps again).

It's quite an involved solution, but it doesn't rely on the order in which objects are created, so it should work in all different situations. Next up, we need to cope with what happens when Flynn lands from a height, making him recover or die depending on the total distance he has fallen.

19. Open `obj_flynn_land` and edit the **Create** event. Remove the line that sets the state to `FSTATE_STAND` and put this code in its place:

```
1:      var fall_dist;
2:
3:      fall_dist = y - peak_height;
4:
5:      if( fall_dist == 0 )
6:          state = FSTATE_STAND;
7:      else if ( fall_dist < FALL_DIST_RECOVER )
8:          state = FSTATE_BEND;
9:      else if( fall_dist < FALL_DIST_FATAL )
10:         state = FSTATE_RECOVER;
11:     else
12:         instance_change( obj_flynn_dead, true );
```

This calculates the distance Flynn has fallen and then sets the state accordingly. If the distance is zero (line 5), then Flynn has probably just moved horizontally from the wall or ice states, but most of the time, Flynn will enter the bend state (line 8) that just displays a couple of frames of him bending his knees. If Flynn has fallen some way, then he will enter the recover state that shows him getting up from his knees (line 10), but if he has fallen too far, then Flynn switches to the dying state object (line 12).

20. Finally, we will prevent the player from interrupting the recover animation by walking or jumping out of that state. For this, you'll need to edit the **Keyboard, Left**, **Keyboard, Right**, and **Key Press, Space** events in turn and put *all* the existing code within a block that depends on the following condition:

```
if( state != FSTATE_RECOVER )
{
    // Existing code goes here and should be indented accordingly
}
```

Have a play around with the game at this stage, as it's the last time we'll be using the old *Zool* level. See if you can jump and fall far enough to make Flynn enter the recover state—it's actually harder than it sounds. If you have any problems with your version, then compare it to the file `shadows3.gmk` in the `Chapter12/Games` directory on the CD.

Half a Pixel

You might have noticed that Flynn stands on his toes at the very start of the level (if you haven't, then take another look and see for yourself). He's not stuck in this position, but it is a little odd-looking and in fact it can happen to Flynn at various points in the level. This happens because there is a slight inconsistency between the way that the `collision_rectangle` and `place_meeting` functions round (or don't round) values internally in Game Maker. It means that one function might consider him to be colliding when he is half-way between one pixel and the next, when the other does not. That sometimes creates a problem in the `obj_solid` **Collision** event of `obj_flynn_air`, as both of these functions are used (directly and indirectly through scripts). So although `move_to_contact_with` resolves the collision, `check_standing_on` can't find a platform beneath Flynn's feet at the end of it.

The easiest way to fix this is simply to add 1 to the value of the y2 variable in the check_standing_on script so that it checks a little bit further down despite any rounding. However, this also breaks the sliding mechanic of obj_flynn_ice, so you'll need to swap all the place_meeting functions in the **Begin Step** event over to use check_standing_on instead. You'll find we've done both of these things for you in the next version of the game.

Lights, Camera, Action!

It's time to take another jump in the implementation of the game. Open up shadows4.gmk from the Chapter12/Games directory of the CD and run it. You should find yourself transported to the beach at the foot of the pirate town: Rogues' Rendezvous (see Figure 12–5). If you explore this level (or look in the Room Editor), then you'll see this is a very tall, thin room with platforms winding their way up between the faces of two cliffs. Apart from changing the room, we've not altered a massive amount since last time, but we've created a host of new resources (which we'll explain as we go along) and made a few tweaks and additions, listed next.

Additions to shadows4.gmk

1. Flynn has a couple of new states that we've implemented for you: FSTATE_BARGE and FSTATE_DEAD. The former will allow Flynn to destroy skeletons by knocking them off platforms or into hazards. The latter is an alternative dying animation for when Flynn loses all of his health. Both come with their own animations and behaviors within the Flynn state objects, but none of it is particularly new or taxing, so you should be able to take a look at the code and figure out how it works for yourself.

2. We've made some changes to how the lifts look. No surprise there, but it's worth peeking at how we've done this. When you place a lift instance in the Room Editor, it looks pretty much as it always did, complete with direction arrows. However, they look quite different in the game and have magic chains that appear at either end. You'll find the interesting code in obj_lift, which is used as a parent by all the other lifts. It uses a new script called cord_attach_height to calculate the end point of the chain and another called draw_cord to draw it. The cord_attach_height script can slow down the game because of the number of collision tests it makes, so it is initially called in the **Room Start** event and not called again unless the lift moves horizontally. Drawing all the chains in the whole level could also slow down the game, so the draw_cord script only draws the chains that are visible within the current view. Without optimizing the chains in this way, the game would start to slow down on less powerful machines.

3. We've also created empty state objects for the skeleton pirates and Archie the parrot. This includes a set of constants for their different states and **Draw** events to display the appropriate sprites in each state. They might look like they're part of the game, but they are doing nothing more than animating at the moment.

Figure 12–5. *Flynn begins his ascent of Rogues' Rendezvous starting from the beach*

Pretty Useful Polly

Archie is not just your average sidekick that simply follows you around offering advice; he is a central part of the core game mechanic for *Shadows on Deck*. That's because Flynn is actually pretty defenseless when it comes to dealing with angry skeletons—or any other kind of foe, for that matter. Enemies will be encountered relatively infrequently compared to an average platform game, but each will require quite a bit of thought and maneuvering in order to get past them. That's the style of game play we're after to compliment the storyline aspects we'll add later. Archie is Flynn's secret weapon, as he is completely invulnerable to enemy attacks, but can lure them into precarious situations where Flynn can dispatch them. We will also allow Archie to perform useful tasks for the player without the risk of ever getting hurt—in fact, it's almost like the enemies aren't trying to harm him at all. . . .

Follow the Leader

Archie's default behavior will be to follow Flynn around the level, hovering just behind his shoulder. We've already created a constant for this state called `ASTATE_FOLLOW`, which along with `ASTATE_COMMAND` and `ASTATE_DISTRACT` are the three states we'll be implementing for Archie. Archie's behaviors aren't complicated enough to justify multiple state objects, so we'll create just one object and use a `switch` statement to handle his state machine within its **Step** event.

Implementing the Follow Behavior for the Parrot Object

1. Open the **Create** event of obj_parrot (in the Flynn group) and edit the **Execute Code** action. Include additional lines of code that create three new instance variables: target_id set to noone and both targetx and targety set to 0. We will use these variables to keep track of what instance Archie is following (if anything) and the point he is moving toward.

2. Add a **Step, Step** event and include an **Execute Code** action containing the following:

```
1:  {
2:      switch( state )
3:      {
4:          case ASTATE_FOLLOW:
5:              break;
6:          case ASTATE_COMMAND:
7:              break;
8:          case ASTATE_DISTRACT:
9:              break;
10:     }
11: }
```

This is the basic framework for constructing a state machine using a switch statement, and we will use it as the basis for creating Archie's different behaviors. Each state has its own case statement that handles behaviors specific to that state (usually including state transitions). Anything common to all states can appear outside of the switch statement, either before or after it, depending on the situation.

3. Now, expand the case statement for ASTATE_FOLLOW to include the following code (note you do not need to include lines 1 and 11 again, as they should already be there):

```
1:      case ASTATE_FOLLOW:
2:
3:          targetx = obj_flynn.x - (obj_flynn.facing*64);
4:          targety = obj_flynn.bbox_top;
5:
6:          if( x > obj_flynn.x )
7:              facing = FACE_LEFT;
8:          else
9:              facing = FACE_RIGHT;
10:
11:         break;
```

Lines 3 and 4 set the target position for Archie to be just above and behind Flynn's shoulder depending on the direction in which he is facing. Lines 6-9 make sure that Archie always looks at Flynn as he is following him around.

4. Now include the following three lines at the end of the code, before the last curly bracket but after the end of the block of code for the switch statement:

```
1:    instance_deactivate_object( obj_ledge );
2:    mp_potential_step_object( targetx, targety, 8, obj_solid );
3:    instance_activate_object( obj_ledge );
```

The second line uses Game Maker's path finding to find its way to the target position at a speed of 8 pixels per step while avoiding solid objects. The lines before and after it effectively make the path finding ignore ledges, as we want Archie to fly straight through them. Ledges are used for rope bridges in *Shadows on Deck*, which can sometimes block the whole path and would otherwise prevent Archie from following Flynn.

Run the game now and you should have Archie following you around the level as you move around. He can't go quite as fast as you, but he's relentless in his pursuit—try as hard as you might, it's (nearly) impossible to shake him off.

Aye Aye, Captain

All of Flynn's behaviors are controlled with the keyboard, but Archie will be controlled with the mouse. Clicking anywhere on the screen will send Archie to that point, where he will stay until he falls out of view. If you click on a pirate, then Archie will follow that pirate around (and eventually distract him) until he disappears from view.

Implementing the Command Behavior for the Parrot Object

1. Add a **Mouse, Global Mouse, Global Left Pressed** event to obj_parrot. This event is executed whenever the player clicks with the left mouse button anywhere in the room. Include an **Execute Code** action containing the following code:

```
1:  {
2:      targetx = mouse_x;
3:      targety = mouse_y;
4:
5:      state = ASTATE_COMMAND;
6:
7:      target_id = collision_point( mouse_x, mouse_y, obj_enemy, true, true );
8:
9:      if( target_id != noone )
10:         sound_play( snd_archie_command );
11: }
```

Lines 2 and 3 set Archie's target position to be wherever the mouse was clicked in the room. This is not actually as straightforward as these two lines of code make it look because we are using a view that only shows a small section of the room. However, Game Maker automatically handles all that for us so we don't need to worry about it.

Line 7 uses the collision_point function to see if there are any instances of obj_enemy at the position the player just clicked. This returns either the id of one object found at that point, or noone if it finds nothing.

Lines 9 and 10 play a sound effect for Archie if the player has clicked on an enemy to confirm that he has identified the enemy instance as a target.

2. Return to the **Step** event of obj_parrot and edit the code again. This time, expand the second case statement to include the following code:

```
1:      case ASTATE_COMMAND:
2:
3:          if( target_id != noone )
4:          {
5:              targetx = target_id.x;
6:              targety = target_id.bbox_top;
7:          }
8:
9:          if( x > targetx )
10:             facing = FACE_LEFT;
11:         else if( x < targetx )
12:             facing = FACE_RIGHT;
13:
14:         break;
```

Although the **Mouse** event will already have set targetx and targety values for Archie to move toward, an enemy would probably have moved by the time he gets there. Therefore, lines 3-7 look to see if there is a target and update the target coordinates accordingly.

3. Add a new **Other, Views, Outside View 0** event and include an **Execute Code** action containing the following code. Basically, this just plays a sound effect (saying "wait for Archie") and then reverts back to the follow state.

```
1: {
2:     if( state == ASTATE_COMMAND )
3:         sound_play( snd_archie_wait );
4:     state = ASTATE_FOLLOW;
5: }
```

Now run the game again and try out Archie's new skill. It's a bit difficult to tell if he is following pirates as they don't move yet, but he should go wherever you click and return to your side when he goes out of view.

Flapping Distraction

Archie's final (and most useful) skill is to be able to distract and lure enemies away from Flynn and into vulnerable situations. To make the animation look a bit more realistic, we have created a path resource called path_distract, which defines a pretty wild path for Archie to take (see Figure 12–6). When you assign a path to an instance in Game Maker, you can either use *absolute* or *relative* coordinates. Absolute coordinates treat points on the path as exact positions in the room, and relative coordinates will map the start position of the path (green square) to the instance's current position and move it relative to the path from there.

Unfortunately, neither of these works for us, as we actually want Archie to follow a path **and** an enemy at the same time. In other words, we want it to be relative, but relative to the moving position of the pirate. The easiest way to do this is simply to create another object that follows the path starting at **X**=0, **Y**=0 (the top left corner of the room) and then add its x and y position onto the moving position of the pirate. We'll even feed this back into the path finding target position so that Archie doesn't move through the landscape too much during his dance.

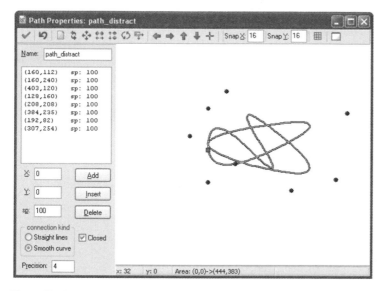

Figure 12–6. *The Path Properties form showing path_distract*

Implementing the Distract Behavior for the Parrot Object

1. Create a new object called `obj_path_offset` in the `Misc` group. Add a **Create** event and include an **Execute Code** action containing the following lines. This sets the object to follow the distract path at a speed of 5 pixels per step, looping back to the beginning when it reaches the end and using relative coordinates.

```
1: {
2:     path_start( path_distract, 5, 1, false );
3: }
```

2. Return to `obj_parrot` and open its **Create** event. Add this additional line that creates an instance of `obj_path_offset` at **X**=0, **Y**=0 when the parrot is created. The `obj_path_offset` object has no sprite so no one will ever see it.

```
instance_create( 0, 0, obj_path_offset );
```

3. Still in the parrot object, add a **Collision** event with `obj_enemy` and include an **Execute Code** action containing the following code:

```
1:   {
2:       if( other.id == target_id && state != ASTATE_DISTRACT )
3:       {
4:           state = ASTATE_DISTRACT;
5:           alarm[0] = 300;
6:       }
7:   }
```

Line 2 checks if Archie has collided with the enemy instance that he's supposed to be targeting and that he's not already in the distract state. If this is true, then lines 4 and 5 put Archie's into the distract state and set an alarm to 10 seconds.

4. Add an **Alarm, Alarm0** event for obj_parrot and include an **Execute Code** action containing the following code. This returns Archie to the follow state once the 10 seconds are up and resets the target.

```
1: {
2:     state = ASTATE_FOLLOW;
3:     target_id = noone;
4: }
```

5. Now, return to the **Step** event of obj_parrot and expand the third case statement to include the following code:

```
1:     case ASTATE_DISTRACT:
2:
3:         targetx = target_id.x - (facing*16);
4:         targety = target_id.bbox_top;
5:
6:         if( facing = FACE_LEFT )
7:             targetx += obj_path_offset.x;
8:         else
9:             targetx -= obj_path_offset.x;
10:
11:         targety += obj_path_offset.y;
12:
13:         break;
```

Lines 3 and 4 set the initial target position to be just in front and above the target's bounding box. Lines 6-11 then add or subtract the position of obj_path_offset from the target position. Note that the horizontal position is added if Archie is facing left and subtracted if he is facing right, flipping the path so that he always remains on the near side of his enemy. This makes it possible to control which direction to lure enemies by using Archie to attack them from the side you want them to move in.

Now, go to the Room Editor and place a couple of instances of obj_skeleton in front of Flynn's start position in order to try out the new moves (don't worry if they float off the ground for the time being). Try distracting them from different directions and make sure the path mirrors correctly. If you have any problems with your version, then you can check it against the file shadows5.gmk in the Chapter12/Games directory on the CD.

Numb Skulls

Pirates are not known for their intelligence, and ours certainly aren't going to break the tradition. Nonetheless, we don't want them to seem completely oblivious to Flynn and Archie, so we will give them the ability to spot and pursue both the player and the sidekick. To make this feel more realistic, we'll do it using a basic line-of-sight test, which will make it possible to sneak up on pirates through clever use of the landscape.

We've already created a hierarchy of skeleton objects, including a parent object `obj_skeleton`, which is itself a child of `obj_enemy`. We've chosen to use two separate state objects to implement the pirate's different behaviors: `obj_skeleton_land` and `obj_skeleton_air`. These follow a similar pattern to the Flynn object, inheriting their **Draw** event from `obj_skeleton` to draw the appropriate sprite in different states. The `obj_skeleton_air` object has already been implemented for you, as it does little more than fall under gravity and recover or die depending on how far it has fallen. This is all behavior you have seen already, but `obj_skeleton_land` will have some more interesting behaviors that are worth implementing for yourself.

Before we begin, also take a look at the new `is_passible_for_enemy` Script resource. It's a simple script that basically just tests for all the different kinds of things that can get in the way of a skeleton's path (including a lack of ground to stand on!) and returns `false` if any of these situations exist—otherwise, it returns `true`. It is easier to have a single way of checking for all these obstructions at the same time because we will need to use it more than once in the code.

Footsteps on Deck

Patrolling up and down is pretty much what you expect as a default behavior for baddies, so this is what we'll implement first. Initially, you should be able to spot some similarities with the Beastie enemy object in *Zool*, but it will soon take on a new direction. We're only intending skeletons to patrol flat areas of the level, and not ramps, but it would be reasonably simple for you to support them too by copying code from `obj_flynn_land`.

Implementing the Moving Behavior for the Skeleton Object

1. Open the **Create** event of `obj_skeleton_land` and change the line that sets the `state` to `ESTATE_WAIT` and set it to `ESTATE_MOVE` instead.

2. Add a **Step, Step** event to `obj_skeleton_land` and include an **Execute Code** action with the following code:

```
 1:  {
 2:      switch( state )
 3:      {
 4:          case ESTATE_MOVE:
 5:
 6:              if( check_standing_on( obj_platform, 1, 0 ) != true )
 7:                  move_on_top_of( -1, obj_platform );
 8:
 9:              hspeed = facing*8;
10:
11:              if( is_passable_for_enemy( facing*32 ) != true ||
12:                  irandom_range( 0, 300 ) == 0 )
13:              {
14:                  state = ESTATE_WAIT;
15:                  alarm[0] = irandom_range( 10, 100 );
16:                  hspeed = 0;
17:              }
18:
19:              if( image_index == 6 || image_index == 18 )
20:                  sound_play( snd_bootstep );
21:
22:              break;
23:
24:          case ESTATE_ATTACK:
25:              break;
26:
27:          case ESTATE_WAIT:
28:              hspeed = 0;
29:              break;
30:      }
31:  }
```

You can see that we are using a switch statement to create a simple state machine again. Lines 6-7 are a brute-force method of bringing the skeleton's feet in contact with a platform and line 9 sets him moving in the direction he is currently facing.

Line 11 checks to see if there are any obstructions 32 pixels ahead that should trigger the next block of code, and line 12 makes it happen just randomly sometimes anyway to make the skeleton slightly less predictable.

Lines 14-16 put the skeleton into the waiting state and randomly set the timer to wake him up again. Then lines 19 and 20 play footstep sound effects on the appropriate frames of the walking animation (as we did for Flynn).

The attacking state case on lines 24-25 is empty for the moment, but we'll come back to it later. Line 28 makes sure that the skeleton stays put in the wait state.

3. Now add an **Alarm, Alarm0** event to obj_skeleton_land and include an **Execute Code**
    action containing the following code:

```
1:  {
2:      if( is_passable_for_enemy( facing*32 ) != true )
3:          facing = -facing;
4:
5:      state = ESTATE_MOVE;
6:  }
```

This uses the same is_passable_for_enemy function to see if the skeleton's path is clear
at the end of a wait, and reverses his direction before entering the move state again if it
is blocked.

Try out the game now and observe the moving skeletons. If you placed some directly in
front of your start point before then you'll need to remove them again now as they won't cope
well with ramps (make sure you don't accidently delete the ramps in the process). You can now
also give Archie a proper test on moving targets. However, the skeletons still don't respond to
the parrot or Flynn, so we'll start to address that next.

A Deathly Stare

So now we'll make the skeleton's behavior a bit more interesting by including the concepts of
pursuit and line of sight. Flynn will need to be fairly close to a skeleton and within its line of
sight in order to trigger a pursuit in the first place. However, you might have noticed that there
isn't actually a state for pursuing. This is because the movement state already does everything
we need; we just have to be more discerning about when to change direction during a pursuit.

In order to make this work, we will force the skeleton into the wait state when he is in
pursuit of a target, but not facing it. At the end of the wait, we will change his direction so that it
is facing his target before moving again. Using this method, skeletons will both pursue the
player and patrol up and down beneath Flynn when he is on a higher platform.

Implementing the Pursuing Behavior for the Skeleton Object

1. Open the **Create** event of obj_skeleton_land and add all of the following variable
    initializations:

```
 1:      target_obj = obj_flynn;
 2:      target_hidden = false;
 3:      target_dist = 0;
 4:      pursuing = false;
 5:      gravity = 0;
 6:      speed = 0;
 7:
 8:      x1 = 0;
 9:      x2 = 0;
10:      y1 = 0;
11:      y2 = 0;
```

As skeletons will be able to pursue both Flynn and Archie, we are using a variable called target_obj to store which of the two is currently being chased. The variables target_hidden and target_dist will be used as part of the line-of-sight tests, and pursuing is self-explanatory. Both gravity and speed are initialized here in case the skeleton comes back into this state after a fall, and the final four variables are the start and end positions of the line-of-sight test. These last four could easily be temporary variables elsewhere, but putting them here will allow us to draw the lines on screen, too. You'll see that in operation a bit later.

2. Reopen the **Step** event of obj_skeleton_land and insert these lines at the start of the code (after the first curly bracket):

```
 1:  x1 = x+(facing*20);
 2:  y1 = y-48;
 3:  x2 = target_obj.x;
 4:  y2 = target_obj.y;
 5:
 6:  target_dist = point_distance(x1, y1, x2, y2);
 7:  target_hidden = collision_line(x1, y1, x2, y2, obj_solid, true, true) ||
 8:                  collision_line(x1, y1, x2, y2, obj_enemy, true, false);
 9:
10:  if( target_obj.x > x )
11:      target_dirn = FACE_RIGHT;
12:  else
13:      target_dirn = FACE_LEFT;
```

Lines 1-4 set up the start and end positions of the line-of-sight test. This begins just in front of the skeletons eyes and ends at the origin of the target object (the center of the sprite for both Flynn and Archie). Line 6 then calculates the distance between these two points, as the skeletons will have a limited viewing distance.

Line 7 performs a collision test by checking if there are any collisions with obj_solid between the start and end points. The last parameter (set to true) determines whether the calling object (the skeleton instance) should be disregarded from collisions in the test. It makes no difference in this case, as obj_skeleton_land is not a kind of obj_solid so such a collision would not be included anyway.

Line 8 performs a second collision test on the same line, but this time for obj_enemy and with the final parameter set to false. As obj_skeleton_land is a kind of obj_enemy, it will be included in the collision test this time. This means that it will detect a collision with itself if the target is behind the skeleton, as the line will pass through the skeletons head. If either this collision test *or* the previous one returns true, then target_hidden will also be true, as the results are combined with a logical *or* operator ("||").

Finally, lines 10-13 determine the direction of the target based on its x position relative to the skeleton.

3. Also within the **Step** event of `obj_skeleton_land`, insert these lines at the start of the `case` statement for `ESTATE_MOVE`, in front of what is there already:

```
 1:     if( target_dist < EPURSUE_DIST && target_hidden == false )
 2:     {
 3:         if( pursuing == false )
 4:         {
 5:             pursuing = true;
 6:             sound_play( snd_alerted );
 7:             state = ESTATE_WAIT;
 8:             alarm[0] = 30;
 9:         }
10:         alarm[1] = 300;
11:     }
```

The first line ensures that this block of code is only executed if the target is close enough (as defined by the constant `EPURSUE_DIST`) and it is not hidden according to the line-of-sight tests.

Lines 3 and 5 make sure that the initial response to sighting the target is only repeated once for each pursuit. This response is to play an alerted sound effect and cause the skeleton to pause for a second, as if they are challenging the target to identify themselves (lines 5–8).

Nonetheless, line 10 will continue to set alarm1 (used for the pursuit timeout) to 10 seconds for as long as the target is in sight. So Flynn will have to stay out of sight for 10 seconds before a skeleton will stop following him.

4. Still within the **Step** event of `obj_skeleton_land`, alter the check that uses the `is_pasable_for_enemy` script, so that it has an additional line at the end as shown.

```
if( is_passable_for_enemy( facing*32 ) != true ||

    irandom_range( 0, 300 ) == 0 ||

    (pursuing == true && facing != target_dirn && target_dist < EPURSUE_DIST) )
```

This has the effect of forcing the skeleton to go into the wait state if it is pursuing something within range, but not facing toward it. At the end of the wait state (in the **Alarm0** event), we will change the skeleton's direction to face its target, and thereby create the pursuit behavior we're after.

All three lines of the check are combined with the logical *or* operator, so this check succeeds if the space in front of the skeleton isn't passable *or* a random number between 0 and 300 returns 0, or the final line is true. However, the final line is actually three separate conditions that are combined with the logical *and* operator ("&&"), so it only succeeds if the skeleton is pursuing *and* it is not facing its target *and* its target is not too far away. Notice that the final line has a set of brackets around the three conditions that are combined with the *and* operators to indicate that they are grouped together into one.

5. Again in the **Step** event of obj_skeleton_land, alter the check before playing the bootstep sound effect to include an additional line at the start, as follows:

```
1:      if( target_dist < EPURSUE_DIST*2 )
2:          if( image_index == 6 || image_index == 18 )
3:              sound_play( snd_bootstep );
```

This stops you from being able to hear footsteps from all skeletons on the whole level at once—just the ones within a reasonable earshot distance. Note that putting two if statements directly after each other in this way is the same as combining the separate expressions with a logical *and* operator, so you could use a single if statement and it would do the same thing:

```
1:      if( target_dist < EPURSUE_DIST*2 &&
2:          (image_index == 6 || image_index == 18) )
3:              sound_play( snd_bootstep );
```

6. Finally, for the **Step** event of obj_skeleton_land, change the case statement for ESTATE_ATTACK to include the following code. This will then play sword sound effects at appropriate points in the animation when we trigger it later on.

```
1:          case ESTATE_ATTACK:
2:              if( image_index = 8 || image_index == 18 )
3:                  sound_play( snd_sword );
4:              hspeed = 0;
5:              break;
```

7. Now you can finally close the **Step** event and add an **Alarm, Alarm1** event to obj_skeleton_land. Include an **Execute Code** action containing the following code to reset the pursuing state. It also resets the target object back to Flynn, as it will sometimes change when skeletons start to pursue Archie as well.

```
1: {
2:     target_obj = obj_flynn;
3:     pursuing = false;
4: }
```

8. Finally, edit the **Alarm, Alarm0** event and include the following code after the first two lines that switch the direction of facing. This code simply changes the skeleton's facing direction to look at its target when it is in pursuit. This is ultimately what creates the pursuit behavior for the skeleton.

```
1: if( pursuing == true )
2: {
3:     if( target_obj.x > x )
4:         facing = FACE_RIGHT;
5:     else
6:         facing = FACE_LEFT;
7: }
```

Before you try this out, you might like to edit the **Draw** event of `obj_skeleton` and remove the commented lines at the end of the event. Just delete the backslash (//) characters at the start of each line (apart from the first one, which really is a comment). Now, try out the level again and see the difference this makes. You can now see exactly what the skeletons can see: a green line means the skeleton's view is obstructed and a red line means he can see you! (see Figure 12–7).

Figure 12–7. *The red line indicates that the skeleton has seen Flynn. This is only displayed during development to check that everything is working correctly and will not appear in the final game*

It can be a bit hard to get very far now as an alerted skeleton makes himself very unhelpful to your progress. Nonetheless, we still have to make the skeleton respond to our secret weapon—the parrot.

Pesky Parrot

The parrot distraction mechanic needs a few loose ends tied up to make it all come together. We'll trigger the pursuit of Archie through a collision event between `obj_parrot` and a skeleton, which will put the skeleton into the attacking state, too. Skeletons will only remain in an attacking state until the end of the animation cycle, but can be sent back into an attacking state by another collision with Archie. As the parrot's distraction path is quite erratic, this can happen randomly during an encounter. This gives the whole interaction an improvised feel, rather than a scripted sequence of events that keeps repeating itself.

Implementing the Distraction Behavior for the Skeleton Object

1. Reopen obj_skeleton_land and add a new **Collision** event with obj_parrot. Include an **Execute Code** action and enter the following code:

```
1:  {
2:      if( state != ESTATE_ATTACK )
3:      {
4:          with( obj_skeleton )
5:          {
6:              target_obj = obj_flynn;
7:              pursuing = false;
8:          }
9:
10:         target_obj = obj_parrot;
11:         state = ESTATE_ATTACK;
12:         pursuing = true;
13:         alarm[1] = 300;
14:         alarm[0] = -1;
15:         sound_play( snd_wings );
16:     }
17: }
```

Line 2 makes sure that this skeleton is not already in the attacking state and lines 4–8 stop any other skeletons from pursing Archie. We only want Archie to be able to distract one skeleton at a time. Lines 10–13 make Archie the target of the skeleton's pursuit for a period of 10 seconds until **Alarm1** calls off the pursuit. Line 14 turns off **Alarm 0** so that it doesn't trigger mid-way through an attack, and cause the skeleton to wander off.

2. Now, add an **Other, Animation End** event to obj_skeleton_land and include an **Execute Code** action containing the following code:

```
1:  {
2:      if( state == ESTATE_ATTACK )
3:      {
4:          state = ESTATE_WAIT;
5:          alarm[0] = 30;
6:      }
7:  }
```

This stops the attacking animation at the end of the cycle, putting the skeleton back into the wait state and resetting the **Alarm 0** timer to awaken him again after 1 second.

And that's it for Archie and the skeletons. The demise of skeletons is already handled for you in the `obj_skeleton_air` object. You should now be able to defeat the skeletons in the test level by using Archie as a distraction. Goad them into standing on the edge of a platform and then barge them from behind using the Control key.

Camera Focus

Finally in this chapter, we're going to implement a better form of "camera" for our game. You might not think of the view as being a camera, but that's effectively what it is—a camera that follows the action around so that the player can see it. Unfortunately, it's not a very flexible camera, because it only follows Flynn and it always keeps him directly in the middle of the screen. It would be preferable if the camera showed more of what was in front of Flynn than behind him and it would also help if it followed Archie a bit when he was out "on a mission." We can achieve all of this fairly easily using a focus object.

Making a Better Camera Using a Focus Object

1. Create a new object called `obj_focus` within the Misc group. Add an **Other, Room Start** event that includes an **Execute Code** action with the following code. This just makes sure that the focus point starts pointing at Flynn.

```
1: {
2:     x = obj_flynn.x;
3:     y = obj_flynn.y;
4: }
```

2. Now, edit `obj_controller` and add this line at the end of the code for the **Create** event in order to automatically create an instance of `obj_focus` in the level:

```
instance_create( 0, 0, obj_focus );
```

3. Now, edit `room_rogue` and select the **views** tab. Change **Object following** to `obj_focus`. The view will now try to keep `obj_focus` in the center of the view area.

4. Add a **Step, Step** event to `obj_focus` and include an **Execute Code** action. This event needs to position the focus object so that it provides a better view of the level. It will do this by placing the focus object some way in front of Flynn's position, depending on which way he is facing. The view will then center on this instead of Flynn and provide a longer view of the level in front of him. Add the following code to do this:

```
 1:  {
 2:      var targetx, targety, dx, dy;
 3:
 4:      targetx = obj_flynn.x;
 5:      targety = obj_flynn.y;
 6:
 7:      targetx += obj_flynn.facing*256;
 8:
 9:      if( point_distance( x, y, targetx, targety ) < 1.0 )
10:      {
11:          x = targetx;
12:          y = targety;
13:      }
14:      else
15:      {
16:          dx = targetx - x;
17:          dy = targety - y;
18:
19:          x += dx/16;
20:          y += dy/8;
21:      }
22:  }
```

Line 2 sets up a number of temporary variables, including a target position for the focus point. This is initially set to Flynn's position in lines 4 and 5, and then offset by 256 pixels in the direction Flynn is facing in line 7. Note that this position is a target position, not the actual position. A target position is used to make the actual position of the view slide gracefully toward a new focus point.

Line 9 then checks to see if the current position of the focus object is less than 1 pixel away from its target position. If it is, then it's close enough to snap straight into the actual target position, so that's what lines 11 and 12 do.

If it's further than 1 pixel away, then lines 16 and 17 work out exactly how far away the target position is in the x and y axes. Lines 19 and 20 then add fractions of these differences onto the current focus position. This means that the further the focus is from its target, the faster it will move, and it will slow down as it comes closer to its target (and would actually never get there were it not for the check in line 9).

Now give the new camera a try. You should notice that using the focus object provides a better view of the level in front of Flynn. It also slides into position as you change direction and removes that nasty jump in the view's movement when Flynn reaches the top of a platform. However, it could still do with taking Archie's movement into account too, so we'll add that too.

Including Archie's Movement as Part of the Camera Focus

1. Edit the **Step** event of obj_focus and replace the two lines that initially set targetx and targety with the following lines of code:

```
 1: if( obj_parrot.state == ASTATE_FOLLOW )
 2: {
 3:     targetx = obj_flynn.x;
 4:     targety = obj_flynn.y;
 5: }
 6: else
 7: {
 8:     targetx = (obj_flynn.x*0.75) + (obj_parrot.x*0.25) ;
 9:     targety = (obj_flynn.y*0.75) + (obj_parrot.y*0.25);
10: }
```

Line 1 checks to see if Archie is in the follow state, as there's no point taking his position into account if he's not doing something interesting. If he is just following, then lines 3 and 4 set the target position in the usual way, but otherwise lines 8 and 9 set the target position based on 75% of Flynn's position and 25% of Archie's. This gives a nice compromise that makes it impossible for Flynn to disappear out of view, but allows the camera to follow Archie on his travels.

Try out the final camera again and see what difference it makes to moving Archie around the level. You should now be able to move Archie an entire screen width away from Flynn, before he disappears out of view (see Figure 12–8). A custom camera can add a lot to your game and this is one way to quickly achieve it. You could of course adjust the position of the view directly using the view_xview[0] and view_yview[0] variables without relying on Game Maker to follow a particular object if you want to take direct control of everything.

If you have any problems with your version, then you can check it against the file shadows6.gmk in the Chapter12/Games directory on the CD.

Figure 12–8. *Making the camera take Archie's position into account as well as Flynn's helps the player to use Archie to explore the level and (eventually) collect items too*

Congratulations!

So you've made it to the end of another chapter and there really isn't much further for us to go. We're close to having completed our vertical slice of the game and you can already get a sense for the kind of game play that the "distract and barge" mechanic will produce. Just one more outing will take us back to the Rouges' Rendezvous to include traps and puzzles in the game as well as adding some depth to the story in the form of conversations with NPCs. Once these are in place as well, we will be able to see whether the *Shadows on Deck* game has some sea legs in it or whether it is doomed to remain a land lubber....

CHAPTER 13

■ ■ ■

The Story Begins

Shadows on Deck may belong to the platform game genre, but it is the story and puzzle elements of the game that are the driving force behind the concept. It already looks pretty cool, and has a pretty solid movement mechanic, but this kind of game needs the puzzles, traps, and character interactions set out in the game design to keep the player engaged along the way. These are the elements that will appeal to the game's target audience, moving it away from a hard-core platform game like *Zool* and toward the platform-adventure genre.

In this chapter, we will be putting all these missing elements in place in order to create our finished vertical slice of the game. This is the point at which the roles of designer and programmer meet, and programmers often build custom level editors that allow the designers to place scenery, script interactions, and edit dialogue for themselves. Of course, Game Maker provides programming and design tools in a single package and so this chapter will seamlessly move between the programming and design tasks required to finish the game. Nonetheless, whether you consider yourself a programmer or a designer, we hope this process will give you an insight into the incremental nature of the game design process.

Emotivation

Games are all about motivation. If you're not motivated to play a game, then you simply stop doing it. One advantage of games that include storylines is that it provides the opportunity to get the player to "emote" (express emotions) with respect to the characters and storyline. Emotions are perhaps the most powerful motivators of all and you can truly guarantee the commitment of a player who is emotionally engaged in your game.

Of course getting a player emotionally engaged in your game is very hard. Flynn's story is certainly emotional for him, but even with the greatest storyline, transferring that emotion to the player can take a lot more time than we have in our vertical slice. Fortunately, it is possible to play on a range of more immediate emotions, such as awe, wonder, anxiety, or even fear. These are all emotions that the player will more readily submit to while we work on the long-term aim of getting them to buy into Flynn's plight on a deeper emotional level.

Exhausted from his fight, Flynn is hiding out in the crow's nest aboard the pirate ship. The skeleton crew is down below and he has no idea where the ship is taking him or whether he will be discovered and imprisoned or killed when he gets there. His companion, Archie, is already showing signs of being a little bit sinister and Flynn must be starting to question whether he made the right decision setting out on this journey. If there is one emotion that comes to mind from his predicament, then it is *anxiety*.

Cutting the Scene

Cut scenes are an opportunity to get the player to get emotionally involved in the game. Chapter 9 described the cut scene leading to the Rouges' Rendezvous level as follows:

The pirate ship sails with all speed now. Flynn wonders why nobody notices that the lookout is missing (shh, Flynn is being lured towards the Pirate King, remember?), but is relieved to be left alone.

After days at sea, the ship reaches a hostile-looking island. Huge cliffs loom out of the ocean and the captain seems to be steering the ship right into the rocks. But then at the last minute, a small inlet is revealed and the ship slowly negotiates the narrow channel into an inner pool, completely hidden from the sea (see Figure 9-10). Flynn looks up in awe. A sprawling town inhabits the cliffs. Makeshift houses and huts made from what looks like driftwood fill the gap above the ship. Rope walkways connect the different buildings and pirate flags are flying proudly everywhere.

"Welcome to Rogues' Rendezvous," whispers Archie. "This is where all the pirates meet and barter their newly stolen goods. I don't know if the Pirate King is here, but there must be someone here who can tell us more." Flynn spots a dangling cage hanging high above. A skeleton foot pokes out from the bars. "What's that?" he asks with dread. "Oh that," Archie says with a chuckle, "is a captive held ransom for money. I guess his family didn't raise the money in time."

Flynn looks sideways at the parrot. He seems very much to be on the pirates' side; laughing at a poor prisoner. And this is his mother's pet? Does that mean that Mary is as ruthless when it comes to making money? He hopes not. The skeletons tie up the ship and, except for a grumpy-looking crew member left as guard, the ship is quickly deserted. Flynn sneaks past with ease. Archie says: "Let's go find out if Mary has been here and whether the King is here himself. We better avoid the skeleton crews, but some of the other bandits must know something."

To set about turning this description into a cut scene, we began by turning it into a storyboard (Figures 13–1 and 13–2). It's fairly easy to create a low-effort animation sequence by panning a camera over a set of panels like this. With the addition of music and text to tell the story, you can quickly create an effective cut scene entirely from 2D artwork.

Music is probably the fastest way to provoke an emotional response in a player and it's more likely to happen with higher-quality music. Fortunately, there are many web sites that provide access to professional-quality music that you can license for use in games within a limited budget. Using the word "anxious" as a search term, we quickly found a track that really seemed to fit the bill. As an orchestral piece, it fitted the period of the game and the horns rising and falling really seemed to conjure up the image of cliffs rising out of the ocean.

As we didn't have editorial control over the music, we were forced to fit the images to the music. This meant that only part of the story could be told, using some of the images, but this is probably not a bad thing, as cut scenes shouldn't outstay their welcome.

Figure 13–1. *The first page of the cut scene storyboard.*

Figure 13–2. *The second page of the cut scene storyboard.*

There are a wide range of video editing packages you could use to create a cut scene like this, but we used Pinnacle Studio Plus, which is both affordable and doesn't overwhelm the novice user with features. No actual video is involved in creating the movie, it simply uses the pan and zoom facility to focus on different points of the static storyboard images (see Figure 13–3).

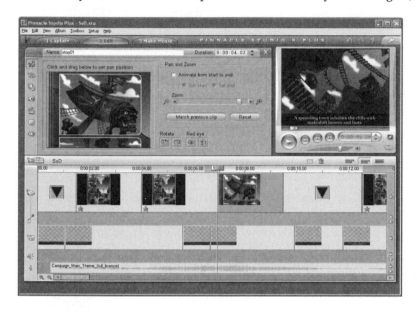

Figure 13–3. *Pinnacle Studio Plus version 9.*

Fetch the Popcorn

At a complete length of 1 minute 17 seconds, you'd be lucky to finish more than a mouthful of popcorn during this movie, but take a moment to view the final result nonetheless. You'll find the file shadows.wmv in the Chapter13/Games directory on the CD, and it should play in Windows Media Player (or any other default player) by double-clicking on it. Make sure that you watch it full-screen (Alt-Enter in Windows Media Player) and with the sound turned up (or headphones on) to get the full emotional effect.

If we've done our job, then you should come out of the other side excited and anxious about playing the level ahead—as well you might, because it's a dangerous place to be....

Level Design

Good level design can turn an average concept into a great game, but poor level design can turn a great concept into a terrible game! Our aim in this vertical slice is to give a taste of the kind of game play the game will offer, which means bringing together all of the designer's skills for storytelling and level design.

Theory in Practice

We've talked a lot about the theory of game design and storytelling in this book. The problem with theory is that great-sounding ideas and principles can be quite hard to convert into practice, so we'll review how some of the theory from previous chapters can help us to plan out the level design for our vertical slice. Let's reiterate some of the important points about game design from both this and the previous book:

- **Challenges**: Above all, players need **achievable** challenges, with **clear goals** and **accurate feedback** in terms of **rewards** or **fair punishments** for their actions.

- **Progression:** Plan the **difficulty curve** of the game to maintain achievable challenges. Slowly introduce your features one at a time, allowing the player time to gain skill in each. Having a **balanced progression** will keep the game challenging and fun.

- **Interactivity: Empower** the player by giving them control over **powerful situations** where their **actions** and **choices** have a **meaningful effect** on the game.

- **Mentoring:** Remember that the player is your apprentice. Your goal is not to beat the player, but to **teach** the player how to beat your game.

- **Storytelling**: Engage the player in the narrative context of your gaming world with **believable characters** and **intriguing storylines**.

We will use a walkthrough of our level to illustrate how these relate in a practical way to the design of our game. This will mainly focus on the first four of these, as storytelling will be covered in its own section later on in the chapter.

Progression

The level we're using as our vertical slice is Rogues' Rendezvous, the pirate town hidden in the cliffs. We've already planned out the difficulty ramping for the whole game, including what new features we want to introduce for every level in the game. We've tried to select features carefully to create a game that is well-balanced and interesting without getting chaotic. Too many elements will result in a mishmash of ideas, and too few makes the game boring.

Although we will start with our planned progression, we should remain willing to make changes. What looked like a fun design on paper might need tweaking if it turns out to not work well. We'll also keep our eye out for happy accidents; while creating the game, we might stumble on unexpected features or unexpected uses of planned features that are worth keeping. At this point in the game:

- Flynn will already have his jump, double jump, and climb abilities and should be fairly confident at using them after the action in the rigging from the previous level.

- Flynn will have already seen a range of hazards and monsters, but always had to avoid them up to this point in the game.

- Flynn will be used to receiving advice from Archie and using him to collect items and solve puzzles.

And in this level, we want to introduce two new features:

- Flynn will be given the charge ability that allows him to kill certain monsters by pushing them into danger when they are looking the other way.

- Archie will be given the distract ability, which allows him to lure certain monsters into dangerous situations so that Flynn can dispatch them.

We also included booby traps in this level, even though the planned progression for the game doesn't include them by this stage. Sometimes, a vertical slice may include (or exclude) features, to make sure that a single level can give a good account of the game. It also gives us the chance to show you how they work. So for the purposes of the example level, we will not only include traps, but act as if they are already familiar to the player.

Micro Curves

Difficulty curves apply on a micro level, too, so we now have to carefully design up this level with our new features in mind. It will make sense to start off with a single pirate that needs to be dispatched using the new charge ability. Archie will explain to Flynn and the player how the new charge move works:

Archie: Send me out to distract the brute, and when he's not looking, charge him from behind using the Control key. Push him over the edge, but watch out for that saber.

The charge is the last move Flynn gets and is more advanced than any of the earlier ones. The player has to charge an enemy from behind or he'll be hurt by the monster's weapon, so we nearly always need to use Archie to set this up. Enemies don't automatically die once they have been charged either—they have to be pushed into danger. The simplest form of danger is falling off a platform, so this is a good way to set up the player's first conflict.

Our job will be to teach the player the different ways that they can use the charge, such as pushing enemies onto spikes instead of from platforms and dealing with two baddies at the same time, and so on. To make confrontations even harder, we can also start to mix the charge ability with challenges the player is already familiar with, such as hazards and moving platforms.

We'll make sure that many of the enemies on this level need to be dealt with using the charge, so that we know the player has practiced this move a lot before he meets the boss.

There is some variety to the enemies Flynn meets in this level. Some of them you actually have to talk to in order to progress. The two types are visually different to help distinguish them. The kill-on-sight enemies are skeletons, and the ones the player can circumvent look human. They are also audibly different, in that the skeletons have strange guttural sounds, while the human ones can speak (albeit using text).

Walkthrough

At this stage of the design process, a designer would often create plans of the layout of the level, along with a description of how to complete it. This is often called a *walkthrough*, and you're probably familiar with the concept from web sites that do the same thing after a game is released to show players how to complete them. We're going to provide a walkthrough of how to complete the level, which is illustrated by the actual graphical plan of the level (Figures 13–4 and 13–5), but it could just as easily have been a rougher set of sketches produced by the designer before the level was created.

Walkthrough of Part One of the Rouge's Rendezvous Level

1. **Briefing**. At the very start of the level, Archie will brief Flynn on his level objective to reach the main entrance to the pirate town, and allude toward a sub-goal of finding a way past the guards. This ensures the player has **clear goals** to begin with.

2. **Skeleton #1**. Flynn won't get very far off the ship before his ascent will be blocked by a mean-looking skeleton guard. This is the player's first encounter with a monster that he can destroy, so we will need to ensure that the player is **mentored** through the experience. Archie will alert him to the baddie and explain exactly how to dispatch him by using Archie as a distraction (setting a **clear goal**). The overhead platform will provide temporary refuge for Flynn while Archie lures the skeleton back the other way to the edge of the platform (with his back to Flynn). This creates the simplest situation in which Flynn can drop down and barge him off the edge. This first skeleton encounter is with a single skeleton and the environment is relatively free of hazards to ensure that the goal is **achievable** and the progression is **balanced**. The player is **rewarded** by seeing the skeleton dissolve into a strange vortex with accompanying audio **feedback**. The skeletons are powerful-looking, so this makes the player feel **empowered**.

3. **Barrel Trap**. This suspended platform will be booby-trapped. It will move slightly as Flynn touches it, releasing a barrel down the slope toward him. He'll need to pull off a move that Mario would be proud of in order to avoid being hit. There is only the one barrel, and the slope provides a convenient way up to the next platform.

4. **Skeleton #2**. The second skeleton will be patrolling the rope bridge as Flynn climbs up to it, so he'll need to time his climb to reach the safety of the top of the hillock. From this vantage point, he will be able to use Archie to tempt the skeleton away toward the left and follow behind to reach the hanging platform. From here, Archie can lure the skeleton in front of the big set of spikes, for Flynn to dispatch. The challenge is a little more complicated here, as the spikes can also harm Flynn. Nonetheless, there is still only a single skeleton (**balanced progression**).

5. **Key**. The player will need to click on the key for Archie to grab it. Flynn will then head back on to the hillock and down the slope toward the prisoner.

6. **Prisoner #1**. The young prisoner will tell the player that they need a key to rescue him, setting another **clear goal**. Archie needs to fly up with the key to unlock the ship's wheel above the prisoner's head. If Archie touches the wheel without the key, then he will reassert that they need a key (**accurate feedback**). Once it is unlocked, it will send the cage tumbling to the ground (**reward**) while also bringing up a handy platform in the form of the counterweight. The pit is too deep for Flynn to fall down and survive, so Archie will suggest that they find another way down (avoiding **unfair punishment**). Once he has found and talked to the released prisoner, they can use the counterweight to get up to the next level of platforms.

7. **Poster #1**. To reach the prisoner, Flynn will need to retrace his steps back down the cliff and use the alternative route into the bottom of the cave. Once there, they will find that the prisoner is not actually much help, but the nearby poster provides a clue to prevent the player from falling for the guards' trick later on (a **reward** for thorough play).

Figure 13–4. *The first half of the level contains two skeletons and one prisoner.*

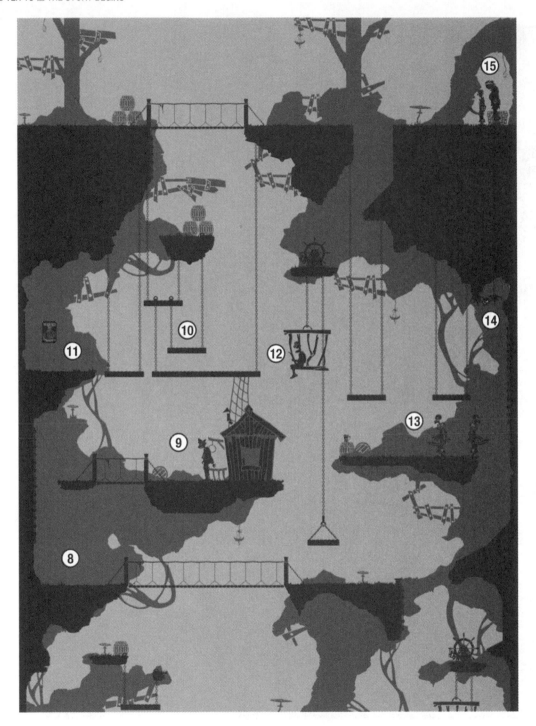

Figure 13–5. *The second half of the level contains two skeletons, three pirates and one prisoner.*

8. **Spear Trap.** Crossing an almost invisible tripwire will trigger a spear trap that sends spears thrusting out of the ground. The tripwire is placed beyond the spears, as this is the first time Flynn has encountered this particular trap, so we'll make it hard to get hurt by it. Nonetheless, it should surprise the player and we'll get Archie to point out the tripwire, just in case the player doesn't realize what caused it (avoiding **unfair punishment**).

9. **Thirsty Pirate.** Initially, the platforms above this point are all out of reach, but there is a lever on the cliff wall opposite the pirate that activates a lift. The pirate explains that he will help Flynn if he finds his tankard for him (which is over near the two skeletons). The player doesn't *need* to do this to continue, and can find the lever for themselves, but fetching the tankard will spring an arrow trap on Archie (who is invincible), preventing it from harming Flynn later on. This provides a level of **meaningful effect** from the **choice** of helping out the thirsty pirate. A sort of good/bad Karma effect, if you like.

10. **Barrel Trap.** Another one—this time coming from above.

11. **Poster #2.** A wanted poster for Mary. This has no effect on the game play, but helps to build the story. There is also another spear trap beneath it.

12. **Prisoner #2.** The second prisoner can be released in the same way as the first, and he will offer Flynn the temptation of helping him to fulfill his main **goal** of getting past the guards to the pirate town (15). However, getting the key is much trickier this time because of the skull bat (14) and two skeletons (13).

13. **Skeletons #3&4.** These skeletons will be more difficult to take out as a pair, but the player should be in a better position to cope by now (**balanced progression**). Archie only distracts skeletons one at a time, so it is possible to split them up and push them over the edges of the platform. However, if Archie hasn't already triggered the arrow trap, then touching the tankard will add to Flynn's difficulties in this situation.

14. **Skull Bat.** The bat will guard the key and stop Archie from getting to it. Archie will suggest that Flynn distracts it, and hint towards skewering it on something (**clear goal**). The skull bat will chase Flynn if he gets close enough and pursue him relentlessly from then on. Luring the bat into any hazard will destroy it, but the most convenient one is the lower of the two spear traps (8).

15. **Pirate Guards.** Two pirate guards will guard the main sailor's entrance to the sheriff's mansion (and the next level), but they need proof that Flynn is a member of a ship's crew to continue. This is provided by the second prisoner, after rescuing him. Even so, the guards will engage in a conversation to try and catch the player out. If the player has paid attention to the first poster (7), then they should be able to give the right answers; otherwise, they may end up losing health as the guards rough Flynn up a bit.

General Principles

As well as the specific layout and mechanisms of the level design, there are some general principles that we have applied to the level design in line with the game design theory.

- Although Flynn can die from falling, we have been very careful to make sure that this only happens when the player makes a true mistake. Most of the heights of platforms have been adjusted to make sure that Flynn won't die by dropping off the end of a rope ladder, for example. We have even put in little slopes that push the player toward the safety of a platform in such cases. This helps to avoid **unfair punishment**.

- This level has a lot of talking in it. When we pull the player into a conversation where he can't move, it's important to make sure that he is in a safe spot. It would be **unfair punishment** if the player can get killed while unable to move, so we will make sure that whenever Flynn has to choose between dialogue paths, he is out of danger from patrolling baddies.

- We'll try to make a clear distinction between aggressive skeleton pirates that need to be dispatched using the charge and more friendly human pirates that Flynn can reason with. Establishing unwritten rules like this in your game helps to provide **clear goals**.

- As Archie is the only one who can collect items, we have tried to make sure that they are always somewhere high out of Flynn's reach so that the player doesn't assume he can collect things too.

Saving

How often should we allow the player to save? As you probably know, Game Maker allows you to save and load at any point using F5 and F6. This is a very handy feature, especially when you're testing, but it could make the game too easy. We think that part of the challenge of our levels is to successfully do a succession of the challenges before you are allowed to save, so we have disabled the save feature and instead added invisible save points that activate the first time the player collides with them.

Game Play Tweaking

One thing you'll no doubt find when you build your own levels is that no matter how carefully you've planned beforehand, once you've actually got the level in front of you, some things will work and some will not. The walkthrough may give the impression that we know exactly how the player will react to our level—but we really don't. We may think that this should provide a good progression, but it may not. Not even the world's greatest game designers can plan something like this on paper and have it work first time, so there's nothing wrong with tweaking your design and deviating from your plan as you go along.

In fact, if you're not changing things, then something's wrong because game design is an iterative (step-by-step) process. However, beware of changing something after two weeks of playing the same level, just because it seems far too easy for you and you're getting a bit bored with the layout. Unfortunately, this is the game designer's lot. You won't enjoy your own games as much as you do others, because you will have tested them so many times that it all strikes you as far too easy. You will have heard the jokes you wrote in the dialogue until you're sick of them. Remember, the player comes into this for the very first time. Get your friends to test your levels for you, and notice where they get stuck and where they laugh. They're a much better indicator of how your players will react to the game.

Traps and Puzzles

So now that we know more about the plan for the level, it's time we started implementing some of the features. The puzzle elements of the game are all simple interactive behaviors of the kind that you should be very familiar with by now. You can summarize nearly all of these behaviors as a collision event between two instances that changes the state of an instance. One of the colliding instances is nearly always Flynn or Archie and the instance that changes state could be either of the colliding objects, or a third object that is not involved in the collision. The best way to see this is to see some examples, so we have created a version of the game that contains all the puzzles for this level in the file shadows7.gmk in the Chapter13/Games directory on the CD. In this section, we'll discuss some of the less familiar concepts that we've used to make the traps and puzzles work, but first take a look at the game.

Play it now. You should be able to complete it fairly easily with the information from the walkthrough, but it's pretty hard without restart points. We'll address that later, but now that you've seen what the level has to offer, we can take a closer look at how some of these traps and puzzles have been implemented so that you could add more if you wanted to.

Traps

We've chosen to include a few simple traps in this level because we wanted to show you how to implement them for yourself. Take a look at the barrel trap as an example (obj_barrel in the Hazards group). All of the traps use a single object called obj_trap as their parent and have a variable called activated to determine when they should trigger. This is initially set to false in their **Create** events, but can be set by any object in an appropriate event (often a **Collision** event) by using the following code.

```
var trap;
trap = instance_nearest( x, y, obj_trap );
trap.activated = true;
```

We've created a new kind of lift object called obj_lift_trigger to trigger the barrel traps. You'll find this code in the **Step** event of obj_lift_trigger to activate nearby traps. Using the instance_nearest function in this way means that we don't need to hard-code exactly which object triggers which trap and any object can do the job for any trap, provided they are positioned near to one another on the level.

The barrel trap is triggered by the lift trigger platform when Flynn is above but not overlapping the platform. The barrel is initially created with gravity turned off, but setting the activated variable turns gravity on and lets it fall down the slope toward the player. The trigger lift turns into a falling lift (obj_lift_fall) until it hits something and then back into a "normal" static lift again (obj_lift). All this means that the lift trigger is only a single use trigger, but the barrel actually resets itself after a couple of bounces so that it could be triggered again.

Another example of this on the level is the spear trap. This uses an identical mechanism to trigger the nearest trap, but both the trigger (obj_tripwire) and trap (obj_spears) reset themselves after a period of time so that they can be used again. Using this system, you could just as easily set up a lift trigger to set off some spears of a tripwire to set off the barrel.

The file traps.psd in the Chapter10/Traps directory contains a range of artwork for different traps that you could include in the game. Using this system, you can make sure that they are all interchangeable to keep the player (quite literally) on their toes.

Puzzles

The design of the level itself provides a puzzle in terms of physically reaching each new area, and there are three distinct puzzle-episodes within this. These take the form of the two prisoner cages and the thirsty pirate, so there are really only two different types of puzzle. In this section, we'll look at these in turn and highlight the main points of their implementation.

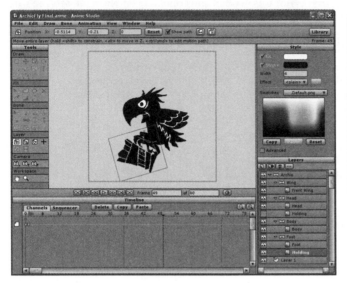

Figure 13–6. *You can create new object animations in Anime studio (left). The final animation just contains the object and not the entire parrot image (right).*

Carrying Objects

Both of the puzzle types require the player to retrieve and use objects within the game. We thought it would be more interesting to allow Archie to carry items and rather than worry about an inventory system, we're only allowing him to carry one at a time. We've introduced a new variable called `holding` for `obj_parrot` along with a new set of constants for defining which objects Archie is carrying (`HOLD_NOTHING`, `HOLD_KEY`, and `HOLD_TANKARD`). Archie's **Draw** event then draws this object on top of his character sprite when the `holding` variable is set.

You should find it easy enough to add a new object to the code, but creating an animation is a bit trickier. You'll need to render a new version of Archie's flying animation using your object image in place of one of the "Holding" layers in the animation hierarchy (see Figure 13–6). You then need to hide all the other layers and render the animation out again so that just the object appears in the animation. See Chapter 10 for more information on the whole process of rendering out animations from Anime Studio and getting them into your game.

Prisoner Cages

The main puzzles in this level revolve around the prisoner cages that need to be unlocked by using Archie to retrieve a key and take it to the lock. We've implemented the behavior of the prisoner cages using three component objects that you'll find the Misc and NPCs groups: a ship's wheel (obj_wheel), a cage (obj_cage), and a counterweight (obj_counterweight). The ship's wheel acts much like a trap trigger, finding the nearest cage and activating it after a collision with an instance of obj_parrot. However, the wheel is supposed to be locked so this **Collision** event makes sure that Archie is holding a key before activating the cage.

Like the traps, the cage object has an activated variable that makes it fall to the ground and release the prisoner. The level is designed to make sure this happens off-screen, so that we don't need additional collision animations for the prisoner or cage. In fact, the prisoner is part of the cage object and is drawn within its **Draw** event. The prisoner sprite drawn depends on the value of the prisoner variable, with a value of 1 drawing the young prisoner and a value of 2 drawing the older one. However, you won't see this variable set in the cage's **Create** event, as this would result in the same prisoner for every cage. Instead, it is set within **Creation Code**, which is specific to each instance.

You can set **Creation Code** within the Room Editor by right-clicking on an instance with the Control key held down and selecting **Creation Code** from the menu. This opens up the code editor so that you can add code that just needs to be executed for that instance (see Figure 13–7). We've simply put the line prisoner = 1 (or 2) into this **Creation Code** depending on the prisoner required in each position in the room.

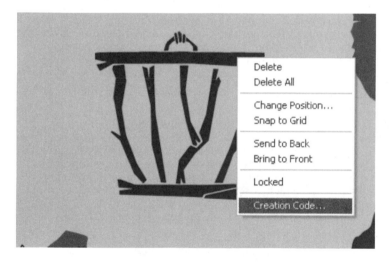

Figure 13–7. *Using the Creation Code option in the Room Editor.*

The counterweight object is the final object that makes up the cage behavior. It is basically just a lift platform that looks for the nearest cage and moves in the opposite direction to it. This makes the counterweight move up when the cage moves down and vice versa. Both the cage and the counterweight use the same chain drawing routines as the lift platforms, so that the length of the chains is handled automatically. Together, these create a convincing-looking pulley system for making the cages work.

Thirsty Pirate

There are two parts to the thirsty pirate puzzle. The first is simply collecting the tankard and giving it to him. This is handled in a **Collision** event for the `obj_pirate_thirsty` object, and simply checks that Archie is holding the tankard before proceeding. The other part is a switch that starts a lift moving. Ideally, this would be done in the same way as the traps, but because any number of instances can make up lifts, it is not so easy to use the `instance_nearest` function. Instead, we have created one large `obj_lift_long_vlimit` object that uses the usual `obj_lift_vlimit` object as its parent. When Archie collides with the button object (`obj_button`), it finds this object using `instance_nearest`, and then deletes it. This then allows the lift to start moving and provides Flynn with a way up.

Storytelling

This level was designed to have more dialogue than earlier levels, so it's perfect for showing you some of the ideas that help tell the story. In each level, we want to set the mood of the location, populate it with believable characters, and advance the overall story.

Mood

The mood of the scene is very much conveyed by the atmospheric artwork. The location is the pirate town of Rogues' Rendezvous. It's full of ramshackle buildings and sharp, inhospitable cliff faces. Already it shows us that Flynn has moved completely away from what he is used to. He comes from soft beaches and a friendly, sleepy little village. This one is harsh and unforgiving and he needs to watch his step. Hopefully, that tells players to be wary, not believe every word they hear, and to watch out for danger. The people they will meet help set the mood as well.

Characters

The characters Flynn meet are very important in setting the mood and giving flavor to a level. It can be a somewhat daunting task to populate a whole level with interesting characters, but if we approach it systematically, we'll get there in no time. We start by checking which roles the game play requires us to fill. The previous walkthrough already tells us what we need to support the game play. There are a number of rather unimportant NPCs in this level, whose characters don't have to be particularly deep. Nevertheless, it will be useful for us to flesh them out in a bit more depth just to illustrate how it's done.

   We talked about assigning characters a role in terms of an archetype. Let's do this as we make the list.

1. **Skeleton pirates.** These are obviously **shadows**, and they don't need much personality other than wanting to kill Flynn on sight.

2. **First Prisoner.** This guy is pretty useless. He turns out to not help Flynn at all in his search, so he is a **trickster**, lying for his own gain. Plenty of scope for depth here.

3. **Thirsty Pirate.** A drunken pirate like this is in danger of becoming a stereotype, so we need to give him a twist. He actually serves as an **ally**, for although he demands something in return, he does help Flynn on his way.

4. **Second Prisoner.** His role in the game play is to help Flynn along, so he is an **ally**. But we can set him up as a **shapeshifter**, so that Flynn isn't certain whether to trust him or not—particularly after the previous prisoner. That should make it more interesting.

5.   **Pirate Guards**. While these two are **shadows**, they are also **threshold guardians**. They are here to check whether Flynn is ready to proceed. They are less eager to kill than the skeletons, but are willing to rough Flynn up a bit if he doesn't answer their questions.

There. That was easy. So with the help of these guidelines, we can now make up little stories for each of our characters. Giving them a few traits will help us think of lines they might say in the game, and give them some personality.

First Prisoner

Out trickster is the first character Flynn talks to in this level. He will have several dialogues, so there is opportunity to make his personality shine through. He used to be a happy ship's boy, but unfortunately he got locked up by the skeleton pirates. It has recently dawned on him that neither his ship-mates nor his family is particularly eager to come rescue him or pay his ransom. This makes him disappointed and angry. He is now only interested in helping himself and will lie through the teeth to get out of his cage. You can't really blame him.

Thirsty Pirate

This fellow has some comedy value. He is addicted to lemonade and down on his luck. The only thing he looks forward to in life is the next swig of the sweet bubbly. Even though he is a pirate, he has grown a bit soft in his old age, and considers himself an honorable man. He knows Archie for what he is and doesn't particularly like him, so he drops hints to Flynn about what is going on. Archie actually ends up being put into danger by retrieving the booby-trapped tankard. Perhaps this is just a coincidence, but he keeps his word to Flynn and tells him the truth about the secret lever.

Second Prisoner

Next we have another prisoner. As mentioned, we'll try to make him a bit of a shapeshifter. He looks like a pirate and was serving on a pirate ship. But he fell out with his captain and was sold along with the prisoners he had helped capture on other ships. He is not happy about that—at all! He doesn't care about Flynn or his quest (being starved to near death does that to most people), but he'll do anything he can to get out and to get even with these pirates who don't even have the honor of common thieves. So he tells Flynn how to get close to the sheriff, hoping to stir up trouble.

Pirate Guards

Threshold guardians are usually very single-minded. That's how they got the job in the first place. So they won't be eager to join into conversation at all, but they still need to make it clear what the player needs to do to get past.

They are brothers and one very much dumber than the other. The "smart" one thinks highly of himself, and is eager to show how clever he is. He is telling anecdotes about the sheriff when Flynn gets close enough to listen.

Once all the characters have their traits, we can plan out a quick outline of who will be talking and who won't and start writing their dialogue. If you have a big level with lots of characters, it might be useful to first give them all placeholder dialogue. Then, when you have everything in place, you can embellish their speech at leisure.

For instance, the first prisoner had a placeholder dialogue that simply said, "Boohoo, I need help, and you will agree to help me, but I will not give you anything useful in return." Later, the larger script was planned out in detail.

Bigger Story

The characters so far have been mainly serving the immediate needs of game play, rather than developing the bigger story. We have an opportunity to elaborate a bit on the main characters as well since Archie and Flynn are always around. This is the trial and tribulation part of the story, and at this stage, Flynn is still learning who he is and what he can do (represented nicely in a practical sense, as he is still learning new moves). He has almost solved the riddle of finding his mother, so he must be starting to worry about what he is going to find.

Mary

Flynn will be nervous about meeting his mother for the first time. We can bring this to the player's attention by letting Flynn bump into reminders of Mary—reminders that show us that she is indeed a pirate, and a pretty fierce one. We could have a 'wanted' poster of Mary, to affirm her status as a part of this underworld (pasted up before the Pirate King captured her). Flynn already knows that she is a pirate, but would probably be happy to forget it. Pirates might be awesome in theory, but would you want one as your mother?

Wanted Poster

Wanted!

Dead or alive,

Preferably dead:

Mary Jones.

Distinctive features:

Deadly temper and annoying parrot.

Archie comments: Bah! Annoying temper and deadly parrot more like.

Archibald

We should also be giving the player some clues here as to the trickster, Archie. We will foreshadow that he might not be all that nice. Archie drops comments about how great it was to roam the seas with Mary, instilling fear in everyone. Flynn's responses will always be less than enthusiastic, as he has not made up his mind about his Mom yet. Archie can also show a bit of his true nature while we are interacting with the less-important NPCs. He is inclined to not believe anyone is telling the truth and happy to let the prisoners rot in their cages.

Setting a Prisoner Free

Archie: You know, your mother would have just knocked the guy on the head and grabbed his badge while he slept.

Flynn: Maybe so… But I'm not my mother.

Keeping Track of What the Player Knows

If you think about the design so far, there is actually quite a lot of the story the player can actually miss.

- We don't force the player to go back to talk to the first prisoner once he's down, so the player might miss hearing Raffi's name the first time.

- Clicking on the posters is optional and the player might miss these altogether.

- The player might miss the speech that gets triggered while he is jumping around–the two guards talking to each other, for instance.

This is completely by choice. We have added extra story and information for players who like to investigate. But they are perfectly free to race ahead.

If you leave information in your game that is optional, such as the wanted poster, then be careful if you refer back to it at a later point. It can be hard to keep track of these things, but will be very rewarding for the player. If a player has actually read this poster, then they could later use that information to gain access to the sheriff. We can give Flynn the option to say that he has come about the reward. Feeding back to the player in this manner is a nice touch, as it rewards them for being observant earlier on.

Make sure that all the information that is vital to game play and vital to understanding the story isn't placed where the player can by-pass it. For instance, while we do have to save the first prisoner in order to progress (the extra platform doesn't appear until we have unlocked the wheel), the player can choose to not go down and talk to him again. So we need to place any vital information in the first conversation and not the second. If you want the player to hear the second bit as well, then you need to make sure that they can't progress without hearing it. Keep your eye on these things. It's perfectly fine to let the player miss some of the dialogue (in fact it's nice to let them choose how much they'd care to listen to), as long as they never get stuck because they didn't get a certain piece of information.

Implementing Dialogue

Most of methods we used to implement the traps and puzzles should be fairly familiar to you and by now we hope you would be able to expand upon these without too much difficulty. However, creating conversation trees is something completely new, so we will go into this in more detail. We'll begin by looking at how the dialogue script is created, and then look at the finer details of displaying text on the screen one word at a time.

Scripting Dialogues

The way the dialogue system works is completely independent from the rest of the game, so we can actually work in a completely different .gmk file to illustrate how it operates. In addition to branching dialogue, we want a neat-looking text system that displays the lines spoken by the characters one word at a time—as you expect in this kind of game.

Open up dialogue1.gmk from the Chapter13/Games directory on the CD and run the example. Not much happens yet, but you should see a picture of the first prisoner's face and a blue rectangle. This is where the spoken text will eventually appear, but first we'll take a quick overview of what is already in place.

Exploring dialogue1.gmk

1. There is a range of different sprite resources for the faces of different characters and a mouse icon. There is nothing particularly special about these.

2. There is a font set up for you (font_speak) that includes all of the letters, numbers, and special characters of the font you have selected. This will usually default back to Arial unless you happen to have the same font installed as us. Feel free to choose something more appropriate for the pirate theme, but make sure it is clear and readable.

3. There are four objects already created for you that form the basis of the dialogue system. The obj_text object handles drawing a single sequence of text one word at a time and selecting that text with the mouse. The obj_dialog object is the parent object for all dialogues. Dialogue objects such as obj_dialogue_test store information about all the different sequences of text in a complete dialogue, including the way in which they branch. Finally, obj_controller simply exists to create two instances of the obj_text object in its **Create** event at the start of the game. These are assigned to global variables so that you can use the same instances to handle all the dialogue text in the game. The positions of these instances arc hard-coded so that the text will appear within the blue rectangle at the bottom of the screen. Note that the coordinates are specified relative to the top left corner of the view, rather than a position within the room.

    ```
    global.text1 = instance_create( 135, 500, obj_text );
    global.text2 = instance_create( 135, 540, obj_text );
    ```

4. The dialogue object (obj_dialog) includes a number of different events that are inherited by all dialogues, including the **Create** event, the **Global Left Pressed** mouse event, the **User Defined 0** event, and the **Draw** event. We'll explore these in turn next.

5. The **Create** event sets up a number of key variables that include the current sequence of text being displayed (sequence), the next primary sequence of text (next_sequence1), and the next secondary sequence of text (next_sequence2). These primary and secondary sequences are used to create the branches in the dialogue. If there is only one path for the dialogue, or the player has chosen the first option, then next_sequence1 is used, but when the player chooses the second option, then next_sequence2 is used. Finally, there is a variable that stores who is talking (talking), which is simply used to decide which face is displayed adjacent to the text.

6. The **User Defined 0** event is an event that is called when the dialogue needs to advance to the next sequence, either as a result of a mouse click, or because of a timeout.

```
 1:  {
 2:      if( talking == TALK_NOONE || global.text1.finished == false )
 3:          exit;
 4:
 5:      if( global.text1.selected == true )
 6:      {
 7:          sequence = next_sequence1;
 8:          global.text1.text = "";
 9:          global.text2.text = "";
10:      }
11:
12:      if( global.text2.selected == true )
13:      {
14:          sequence = next_sequence2;
15:          global.text1.text = "";
16:          global.text2.text = "";
17:      }
18:  }
```

It begins on lines 2–3 by checking if no one is talking or if the current sequence of text hasn't finished displaying (one word at a time) yet. If either of these situations is true, then it exits the script.

Lines 5–17 simply check which of the two global text objects are selected and advances the current sequence accordingly. In both cases, the actual text strings of the text objects are reset back to the empty string ("") as well. Note that where there is no choice to be made (such as when another character is talking), the first text object will always have its selected variable set to true.

7. The **Global Left Pressed** event simply calls the **User Defined 0** event using the event_perform function.

event_perform(ev_other, ev_user0);

As already discussed, we use the **User Defined 0** event to handle advancing to the next sequence, so it needs to be called when the mouse is clicked. Of course, we could have put that code in this **Global Left Clicked** event, but we will need to call the same code from more than one place, so this allows us to do that. It's another way of achieving a similar effect to using a script resource, if you like. You can get Game Maker to call any event in this way—see the help file for details on the parameters for different events.

8. Finally, the **Draw** event draws the character faces and the background rectangle for all the dialogue objects.

```
 1:     vx = view_xview[0];
 2:     vy = view_yview[0];
 3:
 4:     switch( talking )
 5:     {
 6:         case TALK_NPC: face_index = sprite_index; break;
 7:         case TALK_ARCHIE: face_index = spr_parrot_face; break;
 8:         case TALK_FLYNN: face_index = spr_flynn_face; break;
 9:     }
10:
11:     if( talking != TALK_NOONE && sequence != 999 )
12:     {
13:         draw_sprite( face_index, 0, vx + 60, vy + 540 );
14:
15:         draw_set_color( make_color_rgb( 0, 0, 64 ) );
16:         draw_set_alpha( 0.5 );
17:         draw_rectangle( vx+122, vy+490, vx+1014, vy+590, false );
18:         draw_set_alpha( 1.0 );
19:     }
```

Like a number of the other objects, we use vx and vy variables to store the position of the view at the start of the **Draw** event (lines 1-2). This then provides a shorthand way of adding the view position onto coordinates in lines 13 and 17 so that the face sprite and blue rectangle follow the player's view around the room. The values **X1**=122, **Y1**=490 and **X2**=1014, **Y2**=590 represent the top left and bottom right coordinates of the blue rectangle within the view. Adding vx and vy then makes these relative to the view position in the room. Notice that we set (and reset) the alpha value of the drawing operations so that the level can be seen through the rectangle.

Lines 6-8 determine which face sprite is displayed alongside the text. Rather than have constants defined for every character, we use TALK_NPC for all characters other than Flynn and Archie and display the default sprite for this object (sprite_index). Each of the dialogue objects in the final game use the appropriate face sprite as its default sprite, which makes it easier to identify it when it's placed within the room.

9. The actual content of the dialogue is controlled within obj_dialogue_test. This is the initial conversation that takes place between Flynn and the first prisoner in the game, as set out in Table 13–1. Open the **Step** event of obj_dialogue_test and observe how the entire conversation is mapped out within a state machine. Each case statement within the switch corresponds to the ID column of the table and the speaker column corresponds to the talking variable.

Table 13–1. *The Conversation Tree for the First Prisoner Flynn Encounters*

ID	Speaker	Speech	Next
1	NPC	Oh, please set me free. Help a poor boy down on his luck.	2
2	Archie	Ha. I bet you got yerself into this mess. We haven't got time to release you.	3
3	NPC	Oh, but I can help you. I see everything that goes on from up here.	4
4	Flynn	Will you help me with some information? We're looking for someone. Who are you and how did you end up in that cage?	5 6
5	NPC	Of course. You save my hide and I'll tell you what you need to know.	7
6	NPC	I was the ship's boy on the Spice Queen. They're holding me for ransom, but my family hasn't got any money.	7
7	Flynn	Have you seen a woman called Mary Jones? She's... a pirate. We're looking for the Pirate King. Is he here in the town?	8 9
8	NPC	Mary Jones? I know her. Set me free and I'll tell you exactly where to go.	10
9	NPC	Sounds like you're looking for trouble. I can tell you where to find him, but first you gotta help me out.	10
10	Archie	He's a liar. The boy knows nothing.	11
11	Flynn	You're probably right Archie, perhaps we should leave him. Maybe so, but we can't leave him here.	12 13
12	NPC	I promise I can help you. I will die in this cage if you don't free me. Find the key to release that wheel up there.	End
13	NPC	You won't regret it mate. Find the key to release that wheel up there.	End

Linear spoken sequences of text set the speak variable of the first global text instance (global.text1.speak) to the string that should be spoken, and set the next_sequence1 variable to the next sequence in the dialogue.

Branching sequences of text set the select variables of both global text objects (global.text1.select and global.text2.select) to the appropriate strings and set both the next_sequence1 and next_sequence2 variables depending on the outcome of each choice of dialogue.

Note that each sequence starts with a value of 0 and ends with a value of 999.

10. It's also worth considering the following lines that appear at the beginning of the code for the **Step** event:

```
if( global.text1.timeout == true )
    event_perform( ev_other, ev_user0 );
```

The text object will use a timeout variable to record when the text has been displayed in full for a reasonable amount of time. Therefore, this code automatically calls the **User Defined 0** event when this variable gets set.

Punctuating Text

So the objects we've given you already handle the big picture as far as the dialogue is concerned, and these will change for each new character and conversation. However, we still need to implement the functionality that displays the text on the screen. The convention for spoken text in games is for it to appear one word at a time, but this is not straightforward to achieve. Nonetheless, if you understand how it works, then you should be able to incorporate a similar system into your own games, so it's worth going through step by step.

The Word Script

There is one main script that lies at the heart of making the text appear one word at a time. This script will take a string and a number of words as arguments, and return the length (in characters) of that number of words from the start of the sentence. We'll call our new script string_length_words, as it's similar to the Game Maker string_length function that returns the length of a complete string (in characters).

Once we know how many characters to display for a given number of words, we can then use Game Maker's string_copy function to create a new version of our original string that just contains the number of words required. Keep performing this process with an increasing value for the number of words and you can create spoken text that appears one word at a time.

Creating the string_length_words Script

1. Working from dialogue1.gmk, create a new script called string_length_words and type the following code:

```
 1: {
 2:     var str, words, count, index, length;
 3:
 4:     str = argument0;
 5:     words = argument1;
 6:
 7:     index = 0;
 8:     count = 0;
 9:
10:     length = string_length( str );
11:
12:     while( count < words && index < length )
13:     {
14:         index +=1;
15:
16:         if( string_char_at( str, index ) == " " )
17:             count += 1;
18:     }
19:
20:     return index;
21: }
```

The script works by moving through the string one character at a time looking for spaces (because spaces mark the end of words). The index variable is used to keep track of the current character position within the string, and the count variable is used to keep track of how many words have been counted so far. Both of these are initialized to 0 in lines 7 and 8 and the complete length of the string is also calculated in line 10.

A while loop is set up in line 12 that will repeat the subsequent block of code as long as the number of words counted is less than the target number, and index is less than the total length of the string. This means it will stop when it has counted the required number of words, or it has reached the end of the string. Line 14 increases the index variable one character at a time and line 16 uses the string_char_at function to check if this character is a space. If it is, then the word count is increased as well.

By the time the function reaches line 20, count will either be equal to words (we've found the end of the required number of words) or index will be equal to length (we've reached the end of the string). Either way, index is returned to provide the number of characters at the point the script reached within the string.

The Speaking Object

Our next task is to implement the obj_text object, which will need to keep track of such things as the text string and the number of words that are currently being displayed from that string. It will also need to draw the text and maintain finished, timeout, and selected variables so that other objects can tell when it has finished displaying the current string of text, or when the mouse pointer is over the text.

Implementing the obj_text_speak Object

1. Edit the **Create** event of obj_text and replace it with the following code:

```
 1: {
 2:     text_width = 760;
 3:     word_delay = 3;
 4:     mouse_icon = true;
 5:
 6:     text = "";
 7:     speak = "";
 8:     select = "";
 9:     text_previous = "";
10:     displayed_words = 0;
11:     displayed_index = 0;
12:     displayed_text = "";
13:
14:     finished = false;
15:     timeout = false;
16:     selected = false;
17:     selectable = false;
18:
19:     alarm[0] = word_delay;
20: }
```

The text, speak, and select variables will all be used to hold the current complete string of text, and other objects will change these variables directly to alter what is being spoken. The text_previous variable will be used to keep a record of the previous string of text so we can tell when another object has altered one of these variables (as it will no longer be the same as text_previous).

The displayed_words variable will be used to keep track of the number of words currently being displayed. Similarly, the displayed_index variable will record the number of characters that make up those words. Based on these values, the displayed_text string will hold the actual string that needs to be displayed at any point in time.

The finished variable will be used to signal when the entire speech text is being displayed, and the timeout variable will signal that it has been displayed for a reasonable amount of time. The selected variable will be set when the mouse pointer is positioned on top of the text, and the selectable variable determines whether the words should be highlighted when they do. The final line of the **Create** event sets **Alarm 0** to go off after the number of steps defined by word_delay.

2. Now add the **Alarm, Alarm0** event and include an **Execute Code** action containing the following code. This simply adds one to the number of words being displayed and then sets the alarm to go off again in another three steps. It provides the timing mechanism for displaying text word by word.

```
{
    displayed_words += 1;
    alarm[0] = word_delay;
}
```

3. Next add a **Step, End Step** event and include an **Execute Code** action containing the following code:

```
 1: {
 2:     displayed_index = string_length_words( text, displayed_words );
 3:     displayed_text = string_copy( text, 0, displayed_index );
 4:
 5:     if( displayed_index == string_length( text ) && finished == false )
 6:     {
 7:         finished = true;
 8:         alarm[1] = 300;
 9:     }
10: }
```

This code begins by using our string_length_words script to get the number of characters that make up displayed_words within the text string. It then copies this string to the displayed_text variable in line 3 ready to be drawn in the **Draw** event.

Line 5 checks to see if we're displaying the entire string, but haven't already set the finished variable to true. If this is the case, then the finished variable is set to true and **Alarm1** is set to 10 seconds.

4. Now add that **Alarm, Alarm1** event and include an **Execute Code** action containing the following code to set the timeout variable after the 10 seconds have expired.

```
{
    timeout = true;
}
```

5. We will also allow the player to skip quickly through the text by jumping to the end of the sentence after a single mouse click and automatically setting the timeout variable after a second click. Add a **Mouse, Global Mouse, Global Left Pressed** event and include an **Execute Code** action containing the following code:

```
{
    if( displayed_words < 999 )
        displayed_words = 999;
    else
        finished = true;
}
```

6. Now add a **Draw** event that draws the text. and include an **Execute Code** action containing the following code:

```
 1: {
 2:     vx = view_xview[0];
 3:     vy = view_yview[0];
 4:
 5:     if( text == "" )
 6:         exit;
 7:
 8:     draw_set_font( font_speak );
 9:
10:     if( selected )
11:         draw_set_color( c_white );
12:     else
13:         draw_set_color( c_gray );
14:
15:     draw_text_ext( vx+x, vy+y, displayed_text, 25, text_width );
16:
17:     if( finished == true && mouse_icon == true )
18:         draw_sprite( spr_mouse, global.step_count/30, vx+x+text_width+30, vy+y );
19: }
```

Most of this is fairly straightforward, but observe the use of the draw_text_ext function on line 15 to draw multiple lines of text. This function automatically breaks down the string into lines of text that are text_width long and separated by 25 pixels:

Also notice that the final two lines draw the mouse icon once the whole line of text has finished appearing. This uses the global.step_count variable to change between the mouse icon's two subimages once every 30 steps (1 second) while the game is waiting for the player to click the mouse button.

7. Now return to the **End Step** event and add the following above the existing code:

```
 1:      if( speak != text_previous )
 2:      {
 3:          text = speak;
 4:          select = speak;
 5:
 6:          displayed_words = 0;
 7:          displayed_index = 0;
 8:          selected = true;
 9:          selectable = false;
10:          timeout = false;
11:          finished = false;
12:          mouse_icon = true;
13:          alarm[1] = -1;
14:
15:          text_previous = text;
16:      }
```

This code checks if the speak variable has been changed by another object and sets up the internal variables to display a string of text that is displayed one word at a time. Notice that it also sets `alarm[1]` to `-1` just in case the timeout alarm had already been set for the previous string of text. We wouldn't want it to time out before the entire string has even been displayed!

8. Now we need to add support for selectable text as well. This doesn't appear word by word, but will need to detect when the mouse cursor is placed over the text. Add this code in front of the existing code in the **End Step** event again.

```
 1:      if( select != text_previous )
 2:      {
 3:          text = select;
 4:          speak = select;
 5:
 6:          displayed_words = 999;
 7:          selected = false;
 8:          selectable = true;
 9:          timeout = false;
10:          finished = true;
11:          mouse_icon = false;
12:          alarm[1] = -1;
13:
14:          text_previous = text;
15:      }
```

As you can see, other objects will trigger selectable text by setting the select variable rather than the speak variable, but it operates in a similar way, other than setting the internal variables to different values.

9. Now add the following to the *end* of the **End Step** event code to add support for the selectable text.

```
1:    text_height = string_height_ext( text, 25, text_width );
2:
3:    if( selectable = true )
4:    {
5:        if( mouse_x > vx+x && mouse_x < vx+x+text_width &&
6:            mouse_y > vy+y && mouse_y < vy+y+text_height )
7:            selected = true;
8:        else
9:            selected = false;
10:   }
```

Notice how the `string_height_ext` function is used to find out how high the string of text is, as the `draw_text_ext` function may have broken the text into many lines. The rest of the code then just tests the mouse position against the "bounding box" of the text in order to see whether the `selected` variable should be set or not.

Now run the game and check that it behaves as you would expect. If you have any problems, then compare your version to the file `dialogue2.gmk` in the `Chapter13/Games` directory on the CD. You should now see the spoken text displayed on the screen one word at a time, unless you deliberately click through it. You should also be able to make selections at various points in the dialogue that change the path of the conversation.

Hopefully, this provides a system that you will feel comfortable modifying for yourself. The best way to create a new dialogue is to duplicate an existing one and change the states and text to represent the conversation that is required. Remember that you can include all sorts of additional code within the states to activate objects, or change other states in the game depending on the outcome of different conversations. In this way, you can make sure that the dialogue really affects the way that the game plays.

Congratulations

If you've managed to hold out this far, then it's definitely time to play the finished version of *Shadows on Deck*, containing a vertical slice of game play with traps, puzzles, and dialogues. Load `shadows8.gmk` from the `Chapter13/Games` directory on the CD and take some time to enjoy the fruits of your labor by playing it all the way through (alternatively, you can run the `shadows.exe` executable from the `finished` directory on the root of the CD). If you have any problem completing the level, then refer back to the walkthrough provided earlier.

We hope that you find the finished level enjoyable, but we also expect that you can see plenty of flaws and improvements that could be made, too. The point of producing a vertical slice is to prove a concept has potential, but it is also the first opportunity for a designer to experience their concept for real and see what is and isn't working about their design. At this stage in a game's development, it is still possible to take quite drastic changes in direction: perhaps even changing the core mechanics, or basic emphasis of the game.

There are certainly ways of improving the way the game is programmed, too. For example, a better solution to the dialogue system would be to take a "data-driven" approach in which all the text and flow of dialogues is stored in external data files rather than scripted in the code (see the file `dialog_alternative.gmk` in the `Chapter13/Games` directory for a starting point on how you might achieve this using arrays).

It is now up to you whether this concept will become a finished game, and what the form of that game will look like. You are free to use the resources from *Shadows on Deck* in your own Game Maker games, or even create new levels for the game based around our design. We only ask that you share your games on the YoYoGames web site at `http://www.yoyogames.com` so that we can enjoy what you have produced.

Final Words

Learning is a journey and not a destination. This book and its predecessor were never intended to be a collection of pre-digested facts about game development, but active journeys that allow you to form your own understanding through engaging projects. We hope that accompanying us on our latest journey has achieved just that; perhaps challenging some of your existing ideas about game development and hopefully introducing some new ones, too.

One of the exciting things about this field is that it is continually evolving and advancing, which means that the journey never ends. There is certainly plenty left to discover in Game Maker, too. We would love to tell you more about data-driven approaches, hierarchical animation, particle effects, external DLLs, blend modes, drawing surfaces, and many others, but these will have to wait. Nonetheless, we hope that your own journey will not end here and that you are brimming with ideas for changing, adding to, and improving the example games in this book. We would encourage you to do just that and we would love to see the results on the YoYoGames web site. *The Game Maker's Companion* may have led you through this particular journey, but the path ahead is now entirely up to you.

Jacob, Nana, Martin and Kevin, 2010

PART 4

Reference

When it finally comes down to the nitty-gritty job of game development, you'll soon discover there are all sorts of challenges you will have to find solutions for. To help you out, this reference covers a number of very popular game features. Just explore the pages of this library and steal away its small treasures to your heart's content....

■ ■ ■

CHAPTER 14

Feature Reference

This is a good time to congratulate yourself.

You've hopped your way through a game that couldn't have been set in earlier times, you gave Zool his extravaganza of super moves, and you've battled to shape Flynn's epic quest to find his mother and a fabled treasure. Along the way, you've learned about platform game mechanics, the tricks of the art trade, and the principles behind the power of storytelling.

Fuelled by the sugar rush you got from recreating *Zool*'s Sweet World, you've probably already started a project of your own. You've drafted the storyline, penned down character descriptions and dialogues, and drawn the first sketches of your artwork. You are now spending most of your time developing in Game Maker, where you are mixing everything together in a tightly knit game.

But as you add features to your game, you'll sometimes find yourself stuck for solutions. How, for example, can you link several rooms together in your epic Role-Playing Game? How do you create a mini-map? How do you make scrolling credits, cheat codes, smoke trails, and patrolling enemies, how do you move and shoot in a particular direction?

These and a selection of other questions are answered by this reference section through an alphabetically ordered list of features. Step by step, we'll explain how to add a certain feature to your game. Each feature starts with a simple example file with the resources set up for you so that you can try out the steps for yourself. This way, you can test a feature before implementing it into your own game.

To keep things simple, we've used drag-and-drop actions where we can, but where things get a little bit more complicated, we've had to use the *Game Maker Language* (GML) as well. If your GML knowledge is a bit rusty, then you can refer to the final chapters of *The Game Maker's Apprentice* to refresh your memory—but rest assured we've added explanations where required.

■**Tip** Don't limit yourself to our instructions—sometimes, you'll find that the best solution depends on how you've made your game. Our suggestions are just a few out of many solutions. Trying things out for yourself is one of the best ways to master Game Maker!

We hope that you have purchased the Pro edition of Game Maker by now, as it is essential to some of the features in this reference. However, in case you don't have it, then we've marked features that require the Pro version with the symbol shown in Figure 14–1, so that you can skip them.

Figure 14-1. *Features with this image require the Game Maker Pro edition.*

Browse around to see what's here, and add those finishing touches to your game—or just try them out to learn, to tinker, and to have fun.

360-Degree Movement

If you've read *The Game Maker's Apprentice*, you are probably familiar with one form of 360-degree movement, where you used a sprite with rotated subimages to move in any direction. If you have Game Maker Pro, however, there is another, simpler way to rotate the sprite. We'll create an Asteroids-like space ship to show you how.

Start with: Reference/Framework/spaceship1.gmk

Creating 360-Degree Movement

1. Open spr_spaceship and note that the sprite contains two subimages that we will use to show and hide the jet flames. Click the **Center** button—this is important because a sprite rotates around its origin!

2. Create a new object, call it obj_spaceship, and set the **Sprite** to spr_spaceship.

 3. Add a **Create** event and insert the **Set Variable** action with **Variable** image_speed and **Value** 0. This stops the sprite from animating.

 4. Add a **Keyboard, <Left>** event and include a **Set Variable** action with **Variable** image_angle and **Value** 5, **Relative**. This action rotates the sprite counter-clockwise.

 5. Add a **Keyboard, <Right>** event and include a **Set Variable** action with **Variable** image_angle and **Value** -5, **Relative**. This action rotates the image clockwise.

 6. Add a **Keyboard, <Up>** event and include a **Move Free** action. Set **Direction** to image_angle and **Speed** to 0.2. Check the **Relative** box.

 7. In the same event, include a **Set Variable** action with **Variable** speed and **Value** min(speed,6). This keeps the speed limited to 6.

 8. Add a **Key Press, <Up>** event and include a **Set Variable** action with **Variable** image_index and **Value** 1. This will show the subimage with a fired engine.

 9. In the same event, include a **Play Sound** action for snd_engine. Set **Loop** to **true**.

 10. Add a **Key Release, <Up>** event and include a **Set Variable** action with **Variable** image_index and **Value** 0. This returns to the subimage with the inactive engine.

 11. In the same event, include a **Stop Sound** action for snd_engine.

12. Add an **Other, Outside Room** event and include the **Wrap Screen** action and set it to wrap **in both directions**.

13. Finally, include an instance of obj_spaceship in the test room.

Result: Reference/Result/360_degree_movement.gmk

360-Degree Shooting

If you can move in every direction, chances are you want to shoot in every direction, too. We'll use the spaceship we created in the previous feature and give it some firepower.

Start with: Reference/Framework/spaceship2.gmk

Creating 360-Degree Shooting

1. Create a new object and call it obj_bullet. Set **Sprite** to spr_bullet and the **Depth** to 10 to make bullets appear under the spaceship.

2. Add an **Other, Outside Room** event and include the **Destroy Instance** action.

3. Now open obj_spaceship and add a **Key Press**, **<Space>** event. Include a **Create Moving** action. Set **Object** to obj_bullet, **X** to lengthdir_x(12,image_angle), and **Y** to lengthdir_y(12,image_angle). Set the **Speed** to 10, the **Direction** to image_angle and check the **Relative** box. This action takes care of placing the bullet in front of the spaceship in the direction it is facing (explained after these steps). We're using image_angle rather than direction because we want to shoot in the direction we are facing, not in the direction we are moving!

4. In the same event, include a **Play Sound** event and set the **Sound** to snd_shoot and **Loop** to **false**.

Result: Reference/Result/360_degree_shooting1.gmk

In the 360-degree shooting example, the lengthdir_x and lengthdir_y functions are used to create the bullet directly in front of the spaceship, which is 12 pixels away from the spaceship's origin. This works fine if the gun is mounted on the front of the ship facing forward, but you'll need to do a little more arithmetic if the guns are mounted in a different place (for example, if you wish to shoot from the wings of the spaceship). We'll change the example to show you how.

Creating 360-Degree Shooting from Custom Gun Mounts

1. The most important step is finding out where the bullets should be placed when coming out of the gun mounts. Double-click spr_spaceship and click **Edit Sprite**, then double-click on the first image.

2. Zoom in on the picture using the magnifier button. It helps to toggle the grid so you can see gridlines around the pixels.

3. Hover the mouse in front of the top engine, which we will imagine to be the left gun. Check the coordinates in the status bar at the bottom of the window. You'll see that at position (33,9), the mouse cursor is in front of the engine. The bullet sprite is 7x7, with its origin in the middle, so this coordinate would be the place to create the bullet.

4. Do the same for the bottom engine. The coordinates you find should be mirrored from the top engine, at (33,38).

5. For each of these coordinates, we now need to find out how far they are from the origin, both horizontally and vertically. We can do this using the function `point_distance`. Double-click `obj_spaceship`, select the **Create** event, and include a **Set Variable** action with **Variable** `distgun1` and **Value** `point_distance(24,24,33,9)`. This calculates the distance from the origin at (24,24) to the position where the bullet should be created.

6. Include another **Set Variable** action with **Variable** `distgun2` and **Value** `point_distance(24,24,33,38)`. This does exactly the same for the other bullet position.

7. Again, include a **Set Variable** action, with **Variable** `anglegun1` and **Value** `point_direction(24,24,33,9)`. This calculates the difference between the angle of the front of the spaceship, and the top gun.

8. Include a **Set Variable** action with variable `anglegun2` and **Value** `point_direction(24,24,33,38)` to do the same for the bottom gun.

9. Open the **Press Space** event and double-click the **Create Moving** action. Change **X** to `lengthdir_x(distgun1,anglegun1+image_angle)` and **Y** to `lengthdir_y(distgun1,anglegun1+image_angle)`. This creates the bullet at the distance we've calculated in the **Create** event for the top engine. The angle of the gun is added to the image angle to place it at the appropriate angle.

10. Copy the **Create Moving** action and paste it in the same event so that you now have a duplicate.

11. Double-click the duplicate **Create Moving** action. Change **X** to `lengthdir_x(distgun2,anglegun2+image_angle)` and **Y** to `lengthdir_y(distgun2,anglegun2+image_angle)`. This does the same as the previous action, for the bottom engine.

Result: Reference/Result/360_degree_shooting2.gmk

■**Note** In the real world, bullets would move at a speed relative to the speed you're moving at. In other words, the speed and direction of the gunner is added to the speed and direction of the bullet. We're not doing that here, because in a game, where bullets travel slow enough to see and dodge them, it doesn't feel right to have bullets travelling at different speeds. We often happily ignore real-world physics anyway—imagine playing a space game without sound....

Cheat Codes

Cheat codes are like candy to game players. Type in the magic words and all of a sudden you've skipped a level, gained invincibility, or received a load of weapons with unlimited ammo. Sometimes though, the game developer tricks you and you find yourself surrounded by an evil horde of enemies. For developers, cheat codes have always been a method to test particular features of the game. You may not strictly need them, as you have the source for your game under your fingertips, but the players will love them.

Here is how you can create cheat codes. In our bouncing cog example, we'll use the cheat code *gimmemore* to burst 100 extra cogs from the center of the screen.

Start with: Reference/Framework/bouncing2.gmk

Creating a Cheat Code

1. Create a new object and call it obj_cheatcode. Don't give it a sprite.

2. Add a **Key Release** event for **<Any key>**. Include an **Execute Code** action and insert the following lines:

```
1:  {
2:      if ( string_pos('gimmemore',string_lower(keyboard_string)) )
3:      {
4:          repeat ( 100 ) instance_create(320,240,obj_cog);
5:          keyboard_string = '';
6:          sound_play(snd_activate_cheat);
7:      }
8:  }
```

This script uses Game Maker's system variable keyboard_string, which returns a string of, at most, the last 1024 characters that have been entered on the keyboard. The function string_pos returns the position where the text 'gimmemore' was found. If it's larger than 0, the condition is automatically true and the lines between the brackets are executed. So it doesn't matter if any other keys are typed during the game, we're specifically looking for one sequence of characters between them. The function string_lower makes all keyboard input lowercase, so that we don't have to worry about the state of the Caps-Lock key.

Line 4 does what our cheat was all about, which is creating 100 cogs from the center of the room. Line 5 clears all previous keyboard input, to make sure the cheat isn't triggered again. Finally, line 6 plays a sound to indicate the cheat has been activated.

3. Place one instance of obj_cheatcode in the game's room.

Result: Reference/Result/cheat_code.gmk

■**Note** Cheat codes must be typed in lowercase within the script code, but it doesn't matter whether you type it in uppercase or lowercase during the game!

Countdown Clock

One simple way to increase the intensity of a game is to force the player to finish a task in a given amount of time. In our click-the-ball game, we'll display a digital clock, set the timer, and make it count down to zero. Once time runs out, a message appears and the game ends.

Start with: Reference/Framework/bouncing1.gmk

Creating the Countdown Clock

1. Create a font for the digital clock and give it the name fnt_countdown. Set the **Font** to Courier New, the **Size** to 16, and make it **Bold**. Set the **Character Range** to 48 Till 58. As you may know, computers represent characters using numbers internally. The numbers tell Game Maker which characters from the font we wish to use. The numbers come from the *American Standard Code for Information Exchange* (ASCII for short). You can look up the characters by value in a so-called ASCII table. For now, it is enough to know that characters 48 to 58 represent the characters for the numbers 0-9 and the colon, which we'll use in the time presentation.

2. Create an object and give it the name obj_countdown. Set the **Depth** to -1000. We want the clock to always appear in front of everything else.

3. Add a **Create** event and include the **Set Alarm** action. For **Alarm 0**, set the **Number of steps** to 90*room_speed. The room speed decides the amount of steps in a second, so this sets the alarm to 90 seconds.

4. Add an **Alarm 0** event and add the **Display Message** action. Set the **Message** text to Time is up!

5. In the same event, include an **End Game** action.

6. Add a **Draw** event and include the **Execute Code** action. Insert the following lines:

```
 1: {
 2:     var time, min, sec;
 3:     time = round(alarm[0]/room_speed);
 4:     min = string(time div 60);
 5:     sec = string(time mod 60);
 6:     if ( string_length(sec) < 2 ) sec = '0'+sec;
 7:     draw_set_font(fnt_countdown);
 8:     draw_set_color(c_black);
 9:     draw_set_halign(fa_center);
10:     draw_text(320,32,min+':'+sec);
11: }
```

We're using the alarm to keep track of the time, but we need to convert the steps into a readable time format and that's what this script is all about.

Line 2 first defines three variables we will be using to calculate the time. Line 3 converts the steps to the amount of seconds by dividing by the room_speed (remember that the room speed sets the number of steps in a second). Line 4 does an integer division of the time by 60, so we get the number of minutes without decimals. Line 5 does a modulo division by 60, so we get the remainder in seconds. Both are converted to numbers using the string function.

Because we want seconds to always consist of two digits, line 6 checks the length of the min variable and if it is less than 2, it inserts an extra zero. Lines 7-8 set the color and font, while line 9 tells Game Maker to center-align when drawing texts. Line 10 finally draws the time with a colon between the minutes and the seconds.

7. Add an instance of obj_countdown to room_first.

Result: Reference/Result/countdown_clock.gmk

Fancy Buttons

So far, the buttons in our games have been little more than clickable images. We'll spice them up by making them behave more like real buttons that can actually appear highlighted and pressed. This example shows you how.

Start with: Reference/Framework/space2.gmk

Creating Fancy Buttons

1. Take a quick look at the sprites we've added to the framework file. Note that each sprite contains three subimages for the button states, one for the regular state, one for the mouse-over state, and one for the pressed state. We will be creating the interaction with the player in the next steps.

2. Create a new object and call it obj_button. This will be the parent object for all buttons that defines how buttons behave. Add a **Create** event and include a **Set Variable** action with **Variable** image_speed and **Value** 0. This makes sure Game Maker doesn't actually animate the sprites.

3. Add a **Mouse, Mouse Enter** event and include a **Set Variable** action with **Variable** image_index and **Value** 1. This switches to the highlighted button sprite once the user moves the mouse over the instance.

4. Now add a **Mouse, Mouse Leave** event and include a **Set Variable** action with **Variable** image_index and **Value** 0. This switches back to the regular state once the user moves the mouse away from the instance.

5. Add a **Mouse, Left Pressed** event and include another **Set Variable** action with **Variable** image_index and **Value** 2. This switches the image to the pressed state.

6. Include a **Play Sound** event for snd_click.

7. Add a **Mouse, Left Released** event and include an **Execute Code** action. Insert the following script:

```
1: {
2:     if ( image_index == 2 ) event_user(0);
3:     image_index = 1;
4: }
```

User events are a special kind of event which are only executed when we (the user) explicitly tell Game Maker to do so. The name is a little confusing as in this case "user" means "the programmer" of the game, and is nothing to do with the player.

This script executes user event 0 only if the button was already pressed for this instance (as indicated by the value of image_index). This excludes the situation where the mouse button is released over the button, but was initially pressed somewhere else on the screen. Line 3 sets the button back to its highlighted state.

8. Create four objects obj_button_help, obj_button_options, obj_button_quit, and obj_button_start, and set the sprites to spr_button_help, spr_button_options, spr_button_quit, and spr_button_start respectively. For each object, set the **Parent** to obj_button.

9. For each object, add an **Other**, **User Defined**, **User 0** event. This event describes what the button does once it is pressed. For our example, we have made obj_button_help open the game information and obj_button_quit end the game. Note that by using the parent object, we define the button behavior once for all our buttons, but we made each button have its own sprite and its own specific action using the user event.

10. Finally, place instances of obj_button_help, obj_button_options, obj_button_quit, and obj_button_start somewhere in the test room.

Result: Reference/Result/fancy_buttons.gmk

Four- and Eight-Way Movement

Having reached this far in the book, controls for moving the player around in four directions should hardly be difficult for you. You would just create an event for each key and set sprite and speed accordingly. However, sometimes (see for example Grid Movement), it can be more convenient to script everything related to player movement in a single event. We'll show you how to do this for a simple top-down game, where our explorer's movement is limited by a maze of walls.

Start with: Reference/Framework/explorer2.gmk

Creating Four-Way Movement

1. Create a new object obj_wall and set the **Sprite** to spr_wall. Note that the framework file already contains the sprites for this feature.

2. Create a new object called obj_explorer. You may give the object any of the explorer sprites if you want, but we'll let the object change sprites on its own.

 3. Add a **Create** event and include a **Set Variable** action with **Variable** image_speed and **Value** 0.

4. Add a **Step**, **Step** event and include an **Execute Code** action. Insert the following lines:

```
1:  {
2:      var dx, dy;
3:      hspeed = keyboard_check(vk_right)-keyboard_check(vk_left);
4:      vspeed = keyboard_check(vk_down)-keyboard_check(vk_up);
5:      if ( hspeed != 0 ) vspeed = 0;
6:      speed *= 4;
7:      if ( speed != 0 )
8:      {
9:          switch ( direction )
10:         {
11:             case 0: sprite_index = spr_explorer_right; break;
12:             case 90: sprite_index = spr_explorer_up; break;
13:             case 180: sprite_index = spr_explorer_left; break;
14:             case 270: sprite_index = spr_explorer_down; break;
15:         }
16:         image_speed = 0.5;
17:     } else image_speed = 0;
18:     dx = lengthdir_x(speed,direction);
19:     dy = lengthdir_y(speed,direction);
20:     if ( place_meeting(x+dx,y+dy,obj_wall) ) speed = 0;
21: }
```

This script requires some explanation. Line 2 first defines two variables that we wish to use only in this script. Lines 3–4 set the vertical and horizontal speed, dependent on the state of the arrow keys. We've taken advantage of the result of keyboard_check, which either returns 1 (**true**) if the key is pressed or 0 (**false**) otherwise. These values are used to calculate a vertical and horizontal speed. For example, if vk_right (the right arrow key) is being pressed while vk_left (the left arrow key) is not, then the outcome is 1-0 = 1. The other way around, if vk_left is being pressed but vk_right isn't, then the outcome is 0-1 = -1. If neither are being pressed, then the outcome is 0-0 = 0 and if both are being pressed, then the result is 1-1 = 0. This is correct as it shouldn't go left or right on either occasion.

Line 5 limits the speed we have computed to only horizontal or vertical movement, just in case the player is pressing both a left/right key and an up/down key. Line 6 multiplies whatever speed we ended up with by four so the explorer actually moves faster than one pixel per step.

Lines 7–17 change the sprite and animation speed, depending on the current speed. One cool thing about Game Maker is that when we change hspeed and vspeed, then the variables speed and direction are automatically adjusted. So, Line 7 first makes sure that speed doesn't animate it, because we only want to change the sprite if a key was pressed. Lines 9–15 then check the direction and change the sprite accordingly (0 for right, 90 for upward, 180 for left, and 270 for downward).

Line 16 sets image_speed to 0.5 to animate the sprite, while the else statement doesn't animate it if the speed was 0 to begin with.

Lines 18–20 deal with running into walls. The lengthdir_x and lengthdir_y functions help us calculate how much the instance would travel horizontally and vertically with the current speed and direction. We then check if there is a wall in that direction. If there is, we set the speed to 0 to prevent the explorer from going that way.

5. Open `room_test` and create a a number of long walls and corners using `obj_wall`. Finally, place a single instance of `obj_explorer` somewhere in the maze.

Result: Reference/Result/4_way_movement.gmk

For eight-way movement, you only need to make a few small adjustments to the script:

Changing Four-Way Movement to Eight-Way Movement

1. Open the **Step**, **Step** event and double-click the **Execute Code** action. Remove the fifth line of code that says `if ( hspeed != 0 ) vspeed = 0`. This will allow the player to move both horizontally and vertically when they press more than one key.

2. In the same event, add four extra `case` statements in the `switch` statement block for the directions 45 (right + up), 135 (left + up), 225 (left + down), and 315 (right + down). You can either use new sprites for these directions or choose any of the available sprites; we've done the latter in our example.

Result: Reference/Result/8_way_movement.gmk

Grid Movement

Grid movement limits the freedom of the player's movement (and his enemies) to a grid of (invisible) squares. There can be several reasons to do this—for example, to make sure all instances are lined up nicely when opening doors, pushing objects, or forming combinations. It's easier to deal with grid movement if you realize that it conforms to the following rules:

-   Changing direction is only allowed when a moving object is aligned with a grid square.

-   A moving object should not stop moving until it has reached its target square.

-   The moving objects themselves are not bigger than the size of the grid squares.

We'll take our explorer example and give it grid movement. We'll also deal with an example of enemy movement. Before you continue, make sure to read the Four-Way and Eight-Way Movement section, as we will pick it up from there.

Start with: Reference/Framework/explorer3.gmk

Creating Grid Movement

1. The first step is to check the requirements for grid movement. Our example contains block and explorer sprites that are 32x32 pixels, so each square in the grid will be 32x32. In a room of 640x480 pixels, this means that the room consists of 20x15 squares. It also means that the explorer will have to move 32 pixels horizontally or vertically to go to the next square. The dimensions are important to know when setting or adjusting the speed of the instances, because we need to make sure objects are always set to move at a speed that allows them to line up exactly with the next square!

2. For `obj_explorer`, open the **Step, Step** event and double-click on the **Execute Code** event. The good thing about this object is that all the logic relating to movement is contained in a single script—we don't have to check four arrow key events to see if we can allow the player to change direction! Insert the following line of code at line 2:

    ```
    if ( !place_snapped(32,32) ) exit;
    ```

    This single line checks if the instance is not snapped to a horizontal and vertical position in a grid using squares of 32x32 (notice the exclamation mark just before the function—it means the same as checking the **NOT** option for an action). So, if it's not snapped into position, it immediately exits the script. The result of this is that the player can't adjust the direction until the condition becomes true. The speed of the explorer is 4 when it moves, which means it will end up on the next square in 8 steps (because 8x4=32). A speed of 3 wouldn't work correctly because 32 doesn't divide into steps of exactly 3!

Result: Reference/Result/grid_movement1.gmk

Now let's add an enemy to the room that starts to follow the explorer around. It lives by the same rules as our explorer: its sprite should be 32x32, it can only change direction at the grid positions, and it should keep on moving until it hits the next square. Just like the explorer, it should not be able to walk through walls.

But there are a few more problems when you start to introduce several enemies with the same behavior. For example, we don't want two enemies to occupy the same grid spot, otherwise the player can't see how many enemies there are. In other words, one grid spot should contain exactly one instance. So, we need to make sure enemies won't go where other objects are already standing, and we should also avoid two enemies walking toward the same grid square because both "see" it as empty at the same time. We need to find a way to keep a position reserved when one instance has decided to start moving there. Be prepared for a little bit of advanced scripting!

Obviously, our next example is just one out of many possible enemy behavior patterns, but it should give you a good idea of what is involved in creating grid movement intelligence.

Creating Enemy Grid Movement

1. Take a brief look at the resources—there are four sprites there for a scorpion moving in four directions, as well as a sprite called spr_reserved. This sprite will be used in an object that keeps a grid position reserved once an enemy has decided to move there.

2. Create an object obj_impassable. This is going to be the parent object for all objects that our scorpion enemies are not allowed to pass through. This is much easier than creating conditions for every single object.

3. Create an object obj_reserved and set its **Sprite** to spr_reserved. We're going to let our scorpions place this where they plan to walk, so that no other enemy can go there. Set the **Parent** to obj_impassable and uncheck the **Visible** option.

4. In the same object, add a **Create** event and include a **Set Alarm** timer for just 5 **Steps** in Alarm 0.

5. Add an **Alarm**, **Alarm 0** event and include a **Destroy Instance** action. This makes obj_reserved kill itself after a few steps, which is more than enough to allow the instance that placed it there to start moving in that direction and occupy the spot.

6. Double-click obj_wall and set the **Parent** to obj_impassable.

7. Now create an object obj_scorpion and assign it any of the scorpion sprites. Set the **Parent** to obj_impassable.

8. Let's give each scorpion a random start position in the grid. Add a **Create** event and include an **Execute Code** action. Insert the following lines:

```
1:  {
2:      do move_random(32,32)
3:      until ( place_empty(x,y) && distance_to_object(obj_explorer) > 128 );
4:  }
```

The move_random function does the simple task for us of putting the instance in a position that aligns to our grid of 32x32. However, we need to make sure it is an empty place and reasonably far away from the explorer, which is why we do repeat the placement until the instance placed there meets no other instance and is more than 128 pixels away (5 grid moves). You may guess you shouldn't fill up the game with too many instances, as it may take Game Maker long before it finds a free spot.

9. Add a **Step, Step** event, include an **Execute Code** action, and insert the following lines:

```
1:  {
2:      if ( place_snapped(32,32) )
3:      {
4:          speed = 0;
5:          image_speed = 0;
6:          if ( !instance_exists(obj_explorer) ) exit;
7:          var dx, dy;
8:          dx = obj_explorer.x-x;
9:          dy = obj_explorer.y-y;
10:         hspeed = sign(dx);
11:         vspeed = sign(dy);
12:         if ( place_meeting(x+hspeed*32,y,obj_impassable) ) hspeed = 0;
13:         if ( place_meeting(x,y+vspeed*32,obj_impassable) ) vspeed = 0;
14:         if ( vspeed != 0 && hspeed != 0 )
15:             if ( abs(dx) > abs(dy) )
16:                 vspeed = 0
17:             else
18:                 hspeed = 0;
19:         if ( speed != 0 )
20:         {
21:             instance_create(x+hspeed*32,y+vspeed*32,obj_reserved);
22:             speed *= 2;
23:             image_speed = 0.5;
24:             switch ( direction )
25:             {
26:                 case 0: sprite_index = spr_scorpion_right; break;
27:                 case 90: sprite_index = spr_scorpion_up; break;
28:                 case 180: sprite_index = spr_scorpion_left; break;
29:                 case 270: sprite_index = spr_scorpion_down; break;
30:             }
31:         }
32:     }
33: }
```

It's a long script, so let's break it down. Line 2 should be familiar to you—it ensures that all code in the following block (which relates to moving the instance) is only executed if the scorpion is aligned with the grid. When it is aligned, lines 4-5 first stop it moving and stop the sprite's animation. We do this because we can't be sure the instance should still be moving after this event.

Line 6 checks if obj_explorer still exists. If it doesn't, we simply exit this script. This is necessary because the rest of this script tries to locate obj_explorer and then move toward it!

Lines 8–9 figure out where obj_explorer is relative to the scorpion. The line dx = obj_explorer.x-x calculates the horizontal difference between the scorpion and the explorer, while dy = obj_explorer.y-y calculates the vertical difference. Because the scorpion may be further to the right or further down than the explorer, these values may be negative.

In lines 10–11, we can now use the sign of dx and dy to adjust the speed toward the explorer. This is what the function sign does in the line hspeed = sign(dx): it makes hspeed equal to -1 if obj_explorer is to the left of obj_scorpion, 0 if it is on the same horizontal position, and 1 if obj_explorer is to the right of obj_scorpion. The same is done for vspeed with regard to the vertical distance, so obj_scorpion would now start to move toward obj_explorer.

But we can't allow it to move through any impassable objects, and that's where lines 12–13 come in. The function place_meeting checks if there would be any collision with obj_impassable (which includes obj_wall, obj_reserved, and obj_scorpion—this is where inheritance saves us work) if the current instance is placed at (x+hspeed*32,y). So, it checks 32 pixels to the left of obj_scorpion if hspeed is -1, or 32 pixels to the right if it is 1 (if hspeed is 0, it checks the current position, but nothing happens since that is where the instance is). If there would be a collision, then hspeed is set to 0, as we cannot allow it to move that way. The same is done for the vertical speed, so we eliminate horizontal and/or vertical movement if necessary.

After all these checks, we may still have both a horizontal and vertical speed, which means the scorpion would move diagonally, which is something we won't allow in our grid game. Line 14 checks for diagonal movement, and if it finds some, we decide whether we're going to allow vertical movement or horizontal movement in lines 15-18: if the horizontal distance is greater than the vertical distance, we're going to stop vertical movement; otherwise, we stop horizontal movement (the function abs returns an absolute number, making it easier to compare the difference). This will make the scorpions zigzag their way toward the explorer.

Before we continue to setting up movement, line 19 first checks if there is any speed left, as there is no point in continuing if there isn't. Line 21 reserves the position so no other enemy instance will start moving there. The variables hspeed and vspeed are used to figure out where to place obj_reserved.

Line 22 multiplies speed by 2. We've waited until here to increase the speed because all of our previous calculations wouldn't work had it gone any faster. We also set a speed for animating the sprite, and line 23 starts its animation. The last few lines deal with assigning the correct facing sprite dependent on the direction, which is derived from its speed.

10. Finally, open room_test and place five instances of obj_scorpion in the room. It doesn't matter where, as they will move to random positions. Take a test run and see if you can keep out of the scorpion's reaches!

Result: Reference/Result/grid_movement2.gmk

It's time to deal with death... You might be tempted to simply use a **Collision** event and make the explorer die upon contact with a scorpion, but in grid-based games, player characters typically die when there is considerable overlap between the player sprite and his enemies, sometimes only when they both fully occupy the same square. We could do this by changing the collision masks, but it's just as easy to build a check in the collision event.

Dealing with Collisions

1. Create an object obj_hat and set the **Sprite** to spr_hat. We'll drop this hat where the explorer dies.

2. Add a **Create** event and include an **Align to Grid** action with **Snap hor** and **Snap vert** both set to 32. This makes sure that wherever we drop the hat once the explorer dies, it always aligns to the grid.

3. Double-click obj_explorer and add a **Collision** event for obj_scorpion. Include an **Execute Code** action and insert the following lines:

```
1:  {
2:      if ( abs(x-other.x) <= 16 && abs(y-other.y) <= 16 )
3:      {
4:          instance_create(x,y,obj_hat);
5:          with ( other ) instance_destroy();
6:          instance_destroy();
7:      }
8:  }
```

Line 2 checks the horizontal and vertical distance between obj_explorer and its colliding enemy. Only if they are both smaller than 16 (half of both sprites) do we register the kill. The lower the values you use, the closer the instances must be together, and If you set them at 0 then they must be lined up exactly. Lines 4–6 drop the hat and kill both instances in the collision. It doesn't matter if the explorer was halfway two squares as the hat drops itself neatly in the nearest square.

Result: Reference/Result/grid_movement3.gmk

Homing Missiles Pro

Practically not to be missed in any shoot-'em-up are the good old fire-and-forget homing missiles. Rather than taking a clear aim at your target, let the missile do its own targeting using a little bit of Game Maker logic. In this example, we'll use it to clear an asteroid field.

Start with: Reference/Framework/spaceship3.gmk

Creating Homing Missiles

1. First, open the sprites spr_missile and spr_asteroid and set the **Origin** to the **Center** for both. Note that the origin is what we'll use to move instances and what the missiles will be aimed at, so always make sure your targets have their origin set to the center—you don't want missiles to aim for the top-left corner of a sprite.

2. Next, create an object called obj_missile and set the **Sprite** to spr_missile.

3. We will make the spaceship shoot a missile in the direction it's facing exactly like we did in the 360-Degree Shooting example. Open obj_spaceship and add a **Key Press**, **Space** event. Include a **Create Moving** action. For **Object**, select obj_missile. Set **X** to lengthdir_x(20,image_angle), **Y** to lengthdir_y(20,image_angle), **Speed** to 6, and **Direction** to image_angle. Check the **Relative** check box.

4. In the same event, insert a **Play Sound** action and set the sound to snd_fire_missile.

5. We're now able to fire a missile, but we still need it to find a target and properly track it. Reopen obj_missile and add a **Create** event. Include a **Set Variable** action with **Variable** target and **Value** instance_nearest(x,y,obj_asteroid). This finds the instance ID of the asteroid nearest to the missile and put its ID in the variable target. We're going to use this ID to track it!

6. Next add a **Step**, **Step** event and include an **Execute Code** action. Insert the following lines:

```
1:  {
2:      if ( instance_exists(target) )
3:      {
4:          delta = point_direction(x,y,target.x,target.y)-direction;
5:          if ( abs(delta) > 180 ) delta =- delta;
6:          if ( abs(delta) > 4 ) direction += 4*sign(delta);
7:      }
8:      image_angle = direction;
9:  }
```

It looks complicated, but all this script does is check where the target is and then decide whether the shortest turn toward the target is clockwise or counter-clockwise, turning at a speed of 4 degrees per step.

Line 4 sets up a variable `delta` that contains the difference in angle between the direction the missile is currently going in and the direction it needs to turn into to face the target, and we use `point_direction` to get this angle. If it's positive, it means the missile must turn counter-clockwise (increase its angle of direction); if it's negative, the missile must turn clockwise (decrease its angle of direction).

Line 5 checks if the difference is bigger than a 180-degree turn (the function `abs` always returns a positive value, which helps us in our `if` statement). If it is, we invert `delta` because it will be quicker to turn the other way!

Line 6 changes the direction with 4 degrees multiplied by the sign of `delta`: if `delta` is negative, `direction` is lowered by 4; otherwise, it is increased by 4. We only do this, however, if the difference is greater than 4, otherwise our missile will wiggle toward the targeted direction. The final line adjusts the image's angle to the direction.

7. That's all we need to track it. Now for some destructive power, add a **Collision** event with `obj_asteroid` and include a **Create Effect** action (**draw** tab) with **Type** `firework`, **Size** `small`, and **Where** set to `above objects`, and check the **Relative** box.

8. Include a **Play Sound** action and set **Sound** to `snd_explosion`.

9. In the same event, include two **Destroy Instance** actions, one that **Applies to Self** and one to the **Other**.

10. Finally, include an **Other**, **Outside Room** event and include a **Wrap Screen** action, **in both directions.**

Result: Reference/Result/homing_missiles1.gmk

Try out a few shots, and notice how our missile never fails to meet its target—unless another asteroid gets in the way! It even turns around if the asteroid wraps to the other side of the screen, and if its target was destroyed by another missile, it just keeps flying straight until it hits something. You'll notice that its effectiveness is dependent on the speed with which we allow it to make turns—the slower we let it turn, the longer it takes before it is back on track toward its target. Now it's up to you to invent all kinds of variations on the theme—do you want it to set a different target if its target is destroyed? Or should it self-destruct immediately or after a given amount of time? One cool variation is to make the missile heat-seeking, targeting anything that is within a certain range.

Changing the Missile to Heat-Seeking the Nearest Object

1. Open `obj_missile` and delete the **Create** event.

2. Select the **Step** event and open the **Execute Code** action. At line 2, insert the following two lines:

```
target = instance_nearest(x,y,obj_asteroid);
if ( distance_to_object(target) > 100 ) target = noone;
```

Instead of setting a target only once in the **Create** event, this changes target to the nearest instance every step. But if the target is more than 100 pixels away, we set it to `noone`—which means that the missile will just fly straight without changing direction.

Result: Reference/Result/homing_missiles2.gmk

Mini-Map

Do you have a large room with a small view? Then you may want to give the player a bit of help in navigating around by creating a *mini-map* somewhere on the screen. With the power of views, we'll describe several variations on the theme using a small unfinished space shooter in which you track down and obliterate asteroids.

Start with: Reference/Framework/spaceship4.gmk

Creating a Simple Mini-Map Showing the Entire Room

1. Let's first check the current configuration. In room_test, select the **settings** tab. The room's dimensions are currently at 1600x1200 pixels, so we'll use these values to create the mini-map. Now, select the **views** tab. As you can see, there is only one view configured. It's set at 640x480 and will follow obj_spaceship around. The borders are half the view's size, which makes Game Maker center the view around the spaceship anywhere unless it nears the borders of the room.

2. Click on **View 1** and check the **Visible when room starts** check box. Views are drawn on top of each other, with view 0 being the bottom view, view 1 on top of that, view 2 on top of that, and so forth. We could actually stack up to eight views if we wanted to!

3. The **View in room** settings specify what part of the room will be visible in our mini-map. Leave **X** and **Y** set to 0, but change the width and height (**W** and **H**) to 1600 and 1200, respectively.

4. The **Port on screen** settings specify where on the screen our view will be drawn. You would probably want to put this in an area that is not used by any of the other views, but for the moment, we'll just place it in the top-left corner. For both **X** and **Y**, enter 20. The width and height (**W** and **H**) allow us to change how much of the room is to be resized. You should keep the proportions in line with the room, otherwise you'll squeeze or stretch the projection. We'll just make the mini-map 10 times smaller than the room itself, so specify 160 for the width and 120 for the height.

5. The mini-map is ready, but if you would do a test-run at this point, you'd notice an issue with it: it also draws the score. And it looks really strange, as the score is set to follow the view around. To fix this, double-click obj_display, select the **Draw** event, and double-click the **Execute Code** action. This action takes care of drawing the score in the right place in the view, but it should not be drawn in the first view. Change it to read the following:

```
 1:  {
 2:      if ( view_current == 0 )
 3:      {
 4:          draw_set_font(fnt_score);
 5:          draw_set_color(c_white);
 6:          draw_text(view_xview[0]+480,
 7:              view_yview[0]+20,'Score: '+string(score));
 8:          dx1 = view_xview[0]+view_xport[1];
 9:          dy1 = view_yview[0]+view_yport[1];
10:          dx2 = dx1+view_wport[1];
11:          dy2 = dy1+view_hport[1];
12:          draw_rectangle(dx1-1,dy1-1,dx2+1,dy2+1,true);
13:      }
14:  }
```

This script takes some explaining. The entire room is redrawn once for each view, which actually means that all draw events are executed twice: once for view 0 and once for view 1. The variable view_current keeps track of which view is currently being drawn. We check it in line 2 so we can draw the score only in view 0 (lines 4–7).

Lines 8–12 draw a rectangle around view 1, which must also be done in view 0. In fact, just like the score, the rectangle must follow view 0 around (which, in turn, follows the spaceship) to keep it on the screen. The variables dx1, dy1, dx2, and dy2 are used to calculate the positions in the room between which the rectangle must be drawn so that it always appears in the top-left corner of view 0, which is our main view. Line 12 finally draws it, making it a pixel larger than view 1 on each side.

Result: Reference/Result/mini_map1.gmk

You'll have noticed that making the room ten times smaller in the mini-map view doesn't make it any easier to see what's going on in the mini-map. It sometimes makes sense to map only a portion of the room that is only somewhat larger than what is actually shown in the main view.

Changing the Mini-Map to View Only Part of the Room

1. Open test_room again, select the **views** tab, and click **View 1**. Because we're only going to show part of the room, we'll have to make it follow the spaceship around. Set **Object following** to obj_spaceship.

2. First, let's decide how large the viewed area is. Once again, it is a good idea to set this in proportion to the port of the view. To size things up, halve the values in **View in room** to 800 for width and 600 for height. It shouldn't be any smaller than this, because the main view is 640x480.

3. Let's try to center the spaceship in the mini-map view as well. Set **Hbor** to 400 and **Vbor** to 300—this sets the horizontal and vertical borders around the spaceship to exactly half the size of the view in the room set previously, which centers the spaceship in the mini-map.

Result: Reference/Result/mini_map2.gmk

There is another issue with the mini-map: it blocks our view of what is happening in that corner in the screen. It would be better if view 1, the mini-map, was transparent-showing only the objects but not the background. We can make it transparent by simply disabling the background before view 1 is being drawn.

Making the View Transparent

1. First, open `test_room` and select the **backgrounds** tab. Background colors are part of the background and would be visible even if we remove the background, so remove the flag at **Draw background color**, if there is one.

2. Double-click `obj_display` and select the **Draw** event, then open the **Execute Code** action. Change it to read the following:

```
 1: {
 2:     if ( view_current == 0 )
 3:     {
 4:         draw_set_font(fnt_score);
 5:         draw_set_color(c_white);
 6:         draw_text(view_xview[0]+480,
 7:             view_yview[0]+20,'Score: '+string(score));
 8:         dx1 = view_xview[0]+view_xport[1];
 9:         dy1 = view_yview[0]+view_yport[1];
10:         dx2 = dx1+view_wport[1];
11:         dy2 = dy1+view_hport[1];
12:         draw_rectangle(dx1-1,dy1-1,dx2+1,dy2+1,true);
13:         draw_set_color(c_blue);
14:         draw_set_alpha(0.2);
15:         draw_rectangle(dx1,dy1,dx2,dy2,false);
16:         draw_set_alpha(1);
17:         background_visible[0] = false;
18:     }
19:     else background_visible[0] = true;
20: }
```

The changes start at lines 13–16. Because our mini-map is going to be fully transparent, we will add a nice transparent blue backdrop. This is by no means a requirement, but it certainly looks prettier than just making it entirely transparent. Line 14 sets the alpha (transparency) value to `0.2` (20% opaque) before drawing. Line 15 draws the rectangle in the appropriate position in the room.

Line 16 sets the alpha value back to 1 (100% opaque)—if we don't reset it, subsequent draw events would also draw with an alpha value of `0.2`, making everything partially transparent! Line 17 hides the background image. This won't take effect until Game Maker starts to draw view 1. The `else` statement in line 18 is executed when the current view is *not* view 0 (meaning, view 1), switching the background back on again. Remember that all draw events are executed once for every view, so this script is executed twice every step.

Result: Reference/Result/mini_map3.gmk

Mouse Aim-and-Fire

A must-have feature in any shooter: aim your mouse at your hapless target and fire away, while your other hand is controlling your movement on the keyboard. Almost all 3D first-person shooters have this feature, and some 2D games have it too. In our spaceship example, we'll mount a cannon on top of the ship and make it aim and fire at the mouse position.

Start with: Reference/Framework/spaceship5.gmk

To Create Mouse Aim-and-Fire

1. First, open `spr_cannon` and set the **Origin** to (10,15). The cannon will be rotated around this point.

2. Create a new object called `obj_bullet` and set `spr_bullet` as its **Sprite**.

 3. Add an **Other**, **Outside Room** event and include a **Destroy Instance** action.

4. Now create an object called `obj_cannon` and set `spr_cannon` as its **Sprite**.

 5. Add a **Step**, **Step** event and include a **Set Variable** action with **Variable** `image_angle` and **Value** `point_direction(x,y,mouse_x,mouse_y)`. This function gives us the angle between the cannon's current position and the position of the mouse, and turns the sprite's image accordingly.

 6. Add a **Mouse**, **Global Left Pressed** event. It is important to use a global mouse event because the player will not be clicking on his own ship when firing. Include a **Create Moving** action and set **Object** to `obj_bullet`. Set **X** to `lengthdir_x(18,image_angle)` and **Y** to `lengthdir_y(18,image_angle)`. Set **Speed** to 10, **Direction** to `image_angle`, and check the **Relative** box. This creates a moving bullet instance in the direction the cannon sprite is facing, 18 pixels from the cannon's center.

 7. Include a **Play Sound** action and set the sound to `snd_shoot`. The cannon is almost done but we still need to keep it fixed on the spaceship.

 8. Because the cannon should only exist if there is a spaceship, we make the spaceship responsible for creating the cannon. Open `obj_spaceship` and click on the **Create** event. Include a **Create Instance** action and select `obj_cannon` as the **Object**. You can ignore the other parameters.

 9. The cannon should also disappear when the spaceship is destroyed. Add a **Destroy** event and include a **Destroy Instance** action. Select **Object** and set it to `obj_cannon`.

 10. Now we need to make sure the cannon follows the spaceship around. Open `obj_cannon` again and add a **Step**, **End Step** event. It's important to use the **End Step** event because we need to make sure the ship's position has been updated before we move the cannon there! Include a **Jump to Position** event and set **X** to `obj_spaceship.x` and **Y** to `obj_spaceship.y`. Note that the cannon's origin is set to the ship's origin, which means it will automatically be placed on the right spot.

Result: Reference/Result/mouse_aim_and_fire1.gmk

If you need more than one ship to have a cannon (for example, when enemies have gun mounts as well), you'll notice a problem with the current setup: only one of them would carry all cannons! This happens because Game Maker's actions address all instances of obj_cannon at once, rather than the one we've created specifically for that ship. To fix this, we need to keep track of the cannon instance each ship creates for itself.

To Make Each Spaceship Keep Its Own Cannon

1. First, open obj_cannon, select the **End Step** event, and click **Delete**.

2. Now, open obj_spaceship, select the **Create** event, and delete the **Create Instance** action. Include an **Execute Code** action and insert the following lines:

```
1:  {
2:      cannon = instance_create(0,0,obj_cannon);
3:  }
```

This script snippet stores the ID of the instance in a local variable called cannon. We can now use this variable to reference only the cannon we've created for this ship.

3. Because only the spaceship knows which cannon is its own, we'll make it responsible for keeping it in the correct place. Add a **Step**, **End Step** event and include an **Execute Code** action. Insert the following lines:

```
1:  {
2:      cannon.x = x;
3:      cannon.y = y;
4:  }
```

4. Now, open the **Destroy** event and remove the **Destroy Instance** action. Include an **Execute Code** action and insert the following lines:

```
1:  {
2:      with ( cannon ) instance_destroy();
3:  }
```

5. If you wish to test this, place a few more instances of obj_spaceship in the room. Keep in mind they're all controlled by the same mouse and keys! Maybe you could make a game of that...

Result: Reference/Result/mouse_aim_and_fire2.gmk

Mouse Cursor

Do you think the Windows mouse cursor is rather dull? Or do you need a game where the mouse cursor consists of crosshairs to shoot with? Here is how you can replace the default mouse cursor with a sprite of your own.

Start with: Reference/Framework/bouncing3.gmk

Creating a Custom Mouse Cursor

1. A mouse pointer uses a single pixel within its image as the tip with which you click things. The tip can be set using the origin. We've used a tiny sword as our mouse pointer: open spr_mouse and set the sprite's **Origin**'s **X** to 15 and **Y** to 1 (the sharp tip of the sword).

2. Add an object and give it the name obj_mouse. Set the **Sprite** to spr_mouse and the **Depth** to -1000 to make sure it is drawn in front of everything else.

 3. In the same object, add a **Step**, **Step** event and include the **Jump to Position** action. Enter mouse_x for the **X** value and mouse_y for the **Y** value.

4. Double-click on the **Global Game Settings** in the resource tree, select the **graphics** tab, and switch off **Display the cursor** to hide the real mouse cursor.

5. Place an instance of obj_mouse anywhere in room_first. If you think the mouse moves somewhat sluggish, try increasing the room's **Speed** to 60.

Result: Reference/Result/mouse_cursor.gmk

■**Caution** It's not easy for game players to get accustomed to a mouse cursor that looks different from what they are used to, so they may easily be annoyed by your choice. Only change the mouse cursor if it makes sense within your game and make sure the player can easily guess where the tip would be.

Moving Through Rooms

No dungeon crawler or RPG can do without an extensive world. In Game Maker, we could make one large room for this, but if the world becomes too big it may become too slow or too difficult to organize. Instead, we will make a large area out of several rooms, and introduce a technique for moving between the rooms where exiting one room will make you enter the next.

Start with: Reference/Framework/explorer4.gmk

Before you do anything else, *make a map of how you want the game world to be.* It is going to be vital once we get to the point of linking the rooms. It doesn't matter how you make your initial map; you could draw it on a sheet of paper, draw it in your favorite drawing program, or by stitching together the room screenshots. For our example game, in which the player must collect amulets while avoiding enemies, we've done the latter.

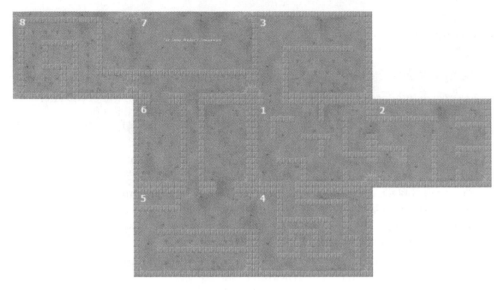

Figure 14–2. *Our game map.*

In our example game, there are eight rooms numbered room_1 through to room_8, which we want to form the world above. As you can see, most rooms consist of a border of blocks, in which we've left gaps. The gaps can be any size, but there are two important rules:

- For two adjacent rooms, the gaps *must* be of equal size.

- The gaps *must* fit together exactly; in other words, vertical gaps must be at the same vertical position, while horizontal gaps must be at the same horizontal position.

If you do not take these rules into account, you will at some point get the player stuck in a wall when trying to move from one room to another.

Creating Room Movement

1. In this game, we want the player to collect amulets. If they return to a room they have previously visited, then the amulets that were already collected should no longer be there. Normally, all the instances are reset every time you jump to a room in Game Maker, but you can let the room preserve the state it was left in by making the room **Persistent**. Open room_1, select the **settings** tab, and mark the **Persistent** check box.

2. Repeat the first step for room_2, room_3, room_4, room_5, room_6, room_7, and room_8. Note that persistent rooms are reset by restarting the game, which is what we will do when the player is killed.

3. Now open obj_explorer and check the **Persistent** option for this object. Persistence for objects does something different: as long as the instance is not destroyed, it makes obj_explorer move to any room we jump to. It doesn't execute the **Create** event when it is moved to the new room, and it keeps all its variables in the same state, placing it exactly where we last left it. That's why we will have only one instance of obj_explorer in the game. We've put it in room_1.

4. Create an object `obj_compass` and set the **Sprite** to `spr_compass`. For each room, this object will store what the rooms are when going in northern, southern, eastern, and western directions. We don't want it to actually be visible, so unmark the **Visible** check box.

5. Now open `obj_explorer` again and add an **Other**, **Intersect Boundary** event. This event occurs when the instances cross the boundary (limits) of the room. We use this event rather than the **Outside Room** event simply because we wish to keep the explorer on the screen at all times. Include the **Execute code** action and insert the following lines:

```
 1: {
 2:     transition_steps = 30;
 3:     if ( x <= 0 )
 4:     {
 5:         x += room_width-sprite_width;
 6:         transition_kind = 14;
 7:         room_goto(obj_compass.west);
 8:     }
 9:     if ( x >= room_width-sprite_width )
10:     {
11:         x -= room_width-sprite_width;
12:         transition_kind = 15;
13:         room_goto(obj_compass.east);
14:     }
15:     if ( y <= 0 )
16:     {
17:         y += room_height-sprite_height;
18:         transition_kind = 16;
19:         room_goto(obj_compass.north);
20:     }
21:     if ( y >= room_height-sprite_height )
22:     {
23:         y -= room_height-sprite_height;
24:         transition_kind = 17;
25:         room_goto(obj_compass.south);
26:     }
27: }
```

Don't worry—room movement doesn't get more complex than this script. To understand it, imagine that the explorer is standing near a western exit. If the explorer continues to move left, we want the screen to quickly pan to the next room and have the explorer appear on the right-hand side of the new room at the same height he left the previous room. This is essentially what this script does for all directions, and it's using a room transition to create the panning movement.

Line 2 first sets up the speed for the room transition, which we want to be the same for all directions. We make it equal to the room speed (30), which means the transition we select will take exactly one second. Line 3 checks if the explorer is leaving from the left end of the screen. If so, line 5 resets the x position by adding the room width minus the sprite's width—this places the obj_explorer at the entrance in the new room. Remember, obj_explorer is persistent, so it will be going to the new room while preserving its x and y position and that's why we need to change them.

Line 6 sets the transition_kind. This is a Game Maker system variable with which you can set what transition to use when changing rooms. A value of 14 means *Push from left*, making the room we go to push the current room away from the left. Line 7 tells Game Maker to jump to the room stored by obj_compass.west. The variable west is a local variable of obj_compass that we'll set up later.

Lines 9–14 do the same thing, but now we check if obj_explorer is leaving on the right-hand side of the room. Note that because the sprite's origin is in the top-left corner of the sprite, the sprite may already be overlapping the eastern boundary— that's why we subtract its width in the comparison in line 9. Line 11 is simply the opposite of line 5, making sure the x position of the explorer is reset to the left-hand side of the room. Line 12 sets the transition to 15 (*Push from right)* and line 13 jumps to the room stored in the variable obj_compass.east.

In the same way, lines 15–19 deal with movement in upward (northward) direction using a *Push from top* transition and lines 21–26 deal with movement in a downward (southward) direction using a *Push from bottom* transition.

We're done with the logic! The next step is to place a compass object in each room and tell it where the exits lead. This is where our map a few pages back comes in handy, because it will help us to quickly look up which exit leads where.

Setting Up the Map

1. Open room_1 and place an instance of obj_compass in the room. This object will be invisible during the game so it doesn't matter where you put it—just put it somewhere where it won't bother you when adding other instances. Make sure you put only one instance of obj_compass in the room.

2. If you take a look at the map, you'll see that for room 1, north leads to room 3, east to room 2, and south to room 4. There is no westward exit. Hold the Control key, right-click the obj_compass instance, and select **Creation Code…** from the context menu. By setting a creation code for an instance, you give it a custom script that is only executed for that instance in that particular room. We use this feature to set the directions in each room. Insert the following lines:

```
1: {
2:     north = room_3;
3:     east = room_2;
4:     south = room_4;
5: }
```

These variables will be used by obj_explorer once the **Intersect Boundary** event is executed to know which room to go to.

3. There is always the chance that we're going to add or remove instances in a room, so we might as well lock this instance to save it from accidentally being deleted. Hold the Control key, right-click the instance again and select **Locked**.

4. The compass works as an exit only, so nothing will bring the explorer back unless we don't add compass instances to other rooms. Open room_2 and add an instance of obj_compass again. This room has only one exit, so set its creation code to read:

```
1: {
2:     west = room_1;
3: }
```

Don't forget to lock the instance. Notice that if you wanted to, it is actually quite easy to make the explorer return to a completely different room. Some games apply this "magic" trick to confuse the player.

5. Now, use the map as a guide and complete the process for room_3, room_4, room_5, room_6, room_7, and room_8.

6. Test your game to make sure that all exits lead to the correct room. Check all exits in both directions! But don't touch the baddies on the way, or you can start your walk all over....

Result: Reference/Result/room_movement.gmk

■**Tip** The player is always immediately placed at the entrance of the room. Make sure to keep this area free of dangers—it isn't fair on the player to enter a room and immediately end up in trouble.

Orbiting Objects

Whether it's for planets, for activated power-ups such as shields, or just for show, sometimes you'll need one or more objects to orbit another object and follow it around wherever it goes. In the next example, we'll make some stars circle our spaceship.

Start with: Reference/Framework/spaceship6.gmk

Creating Orbiting Objects

1. Create an object and call it obj_star. Set spr_star as its **Sprite**.

2. In the same object, add a **Step**, **End Step** event. Because this event will be responsible for adjusting the star's position to the spaceship, we use the **End Step** event to make sure that the ship's position has been updated first. Include an **Execute Code** action and insert the following lines:

```
1: {
2:     x = obj_spaceship.x+lengthdir_x(100,angle);
3:     y = obj_spaceship.y+lengthdir_y(100,angle);
4:     angle += 5;
5: }
```

The `lengthdir_x` and `lengthdir_y` functions are used to set the instance to a relative distance of 100 from the spaceship's position. The variable `angle` is set up further below and decides the current angle of position with regard to the spaceship. Line 4 sets a rotation speed; use negative values for clockwise rotation.

3. Open the `obj_spaceship` object. We use the **Create** event to create the orbiting stars, but obviously you may add it in a more appropriate place. Include an **Execute Code** action and insert the following lines:

```
1:  {
2:      var i;
3:      for ( i = 0; i < 360; i += 36)
4:          with ( instance_create(0,0,obj_star) ) angle = i;
5:  }
```

This script creates ten evenly distributed stars that each start at a different angle. Line 2 first defines a variable we will use for a `for` loop. Line 3 sets up the loop from 0 to 360 in steps of 36, which amounts to 10 steps (10 stars). Line 4 creates an instance of `obj_star`. Note that we do not specify any position here, as this is taken care of in the star's **End Step** event using the instance's angle. Using the `with` statement, we set the `angle` variable of the created instance to the value of `i` (0, 36, 72, 108, and so forth).

4. Because the stars are dependent on the existence of the spaceship, we should destroy them when the spaceship is destroyed. Add a **Destroy** event and include a **Destroy Instance** action. Select **Object**, and choose `obj_star`.

Result: Reference/Result/orbiting_objects.gmk

Patrolling Enemies

Enemies do not always chase the player—often, they're just harmlessly patrolling an area, and the player's only danger is in touching them. Having enemies walk around a maze with lots of turns and corners would be a difficult job if it weren't for Game Maker's awesome path mechanisms.

Start with: Reference/Framework/explorer5.gmk

Creating Patrolling Enemies

1. Create a new object `obj_mummy` and assign any of the mummy sprites to it. Also create an object `obj_scorpion` and assign it any of the scorpion sprites.

2. Now add a path resource and call it `path_mummy1`. To the top right of the path window, click the **Indicate the room to show as background** button (it's on the far right at the top of the window), and select `room_test` from the drop-down box. Resize the window if necessary to show the entire room.

3. Uncheck the **Closed** check box. Make sure that **Connection kind** is set to **Straight lines**.

4. Clicking on the grid will now create a path! But before you start clicking away, keep in mind that the path line we're going to create describes the path of the origin of the sprite. Since this will be a mummy path, and the mummy's sprite origin is at (0,0), this means that the line describes the path of the top left corner of the sprite. It's important to know this because we don't want our mummy to move through any walls! Let's add the following points: (224,368), (48,368), (48,48), (304,48), and (304,144). Note that you can drag points if you have placed them in the wrong spot.

5. Create a path called path_scorpion1 and again set room_test as the background. This time, keep the path closed and add the points (192,144), (432,144), (432,336), (304,336), (304,240), and (192,240). Put both paths in a group called room_test. It's best to keep them grouped, as they only apply to this room.

6. Now place an instance of obj_mummy and obj_scorpion in the room. It actually doesn't matter where you place them, as we'll let the path take care of placement, but it's a good idea to place them somewhere near their paths.

7. We now need to tell these instances which path to use. There are actions for these, but because your game is probably going to be littered with enemies of the same type, it makes little sense to create lots of copies of them with a different path stored in each. So we'll use the instance's **Creation Code**. Still in the room editor, **objects** tab, hold the Control key and right-click on the mummy instance. Select **Creation Code...** from the context menu. Insert the following lines:

```
1: {
2:     path_start(path_mummy1,2,3,true);
3: }
```

This line tells the instance to start the path path_mummy1 with speed 2. The third parameter is the **End action** and determines what should happen if the end of the path is reached. A value of 3 means the path should be reversed, making the instance turn back on the same path. The last parameter tells the instance that the points in the path are **Absolute**, which means they are room coordinates rather than coordinates relative to the instance's position.

8. Now hold the Control key and right-click the scorpion instance, and select **Creation Code...** again. Insert the following lines:

```
1: {
2:     path_start(path_scorpion1,2,1,true);
3: }
```

The only changes in this script are the path and the **End action**, which now equals 1 (continue from start). This will make the scorpion loop its path.

9. We still need to make obj_mummy and obj_scorpion face in the direction they're walking, and walk at a decent speed. We can make use of the fact that Game Maker automatically adjusts the direction variable depending on the path! Open obj_mummy and add a **Step**, **Step** event. Include an **Execute Code** action and insert the following lines:

```
 1: {
 2:     switch ( direction )
 3:     {
 4:         case 0: sprite_index = spr_mummy_right; break;
 5:         case 90: sprite_index = spr_mummy_up; break;
 6:         case 180: sprite_index = spr_mummy_left; break;
 7:         case 270: sprite_index = spr_mummy_down; break;
 8:     }
 9:     image_speed = path_speed/8;
10: }
```

Using a switch statement, we check the direction and change the sprite accordingly: a value of 0 means we're going to the right, 90 is upward, 180 is left, and 270 is downward. Finally, we set the sprite's animation to be relative to the path speed. This means that if you ever change the path speed, the animation pace changes as well.

10. Right-click this **Execute a piece of code (Execute Code)** action and select **Copy** from the context menu. Now open obj_scorpion, add a **Step**, **Step** event, right-click in the **Actions** list, and select **Paste**. Next, open the event and replace every occurrence of mummy with scorpion, and set image_speed to path_speed/4.

Result: Reference/Result/patrolling_enemies1.gmk

It's easy to make more than one enemy share a path, so that a particular area is patrolled more heavily.

Putting Multiple Enemies on a Single Path

1. Open room_test and place three other instances of obj_scorpion in the room.

2. Hold the Control key and right-click the first of the new instances of obj_scorpion. Select **Creation Code...** from the menu and insert the following lines:

```
1: {
2:     path_start(path_scorpion1,2,1,true);
3:     path_position = 0.25;
4: }
```

The path position indicates where on the path this instance should be placed, a number between 0 and 1 inclusive. If not specified, it defaults to 0 (the start of the path). We set it at 0.25, which means it is a quarter of the way along the path.

3. Set similar creation codes for the third and the fourth instance, with path positions at 0.5 and 0.75, respectively.

Result: Reference/Result/patrolling_enemies2.gmk

If you've been watching the different enemies long enough, you may have noticed that they sometimes walk into each other. The easy solution to this, of course, is to make sure the paths never cross. If that's not always an option, we can make sure that enemies check ahead for a possible collision, and turn around if necessary.

Avoiding Enemy Collisions by Turning Around

1. First, create a new object called obj_enemy. We'll use this object as a parent to help us check for collisions with all enemies, as well as define the required turn-around behavior for all of them.

2. Add a **Collision** event and include a **Set Variable** action with **Variable** path_speed and value -path_speed (note the minus sign).

3. Now, open obj_mummy and set the parent to obj_enemy. Do the same for obj_scorpion.

4. To test this, add another obj_mummy to the room and set its **Creation Code** to read as follows:

```
 1: {
 2:     path_start(path_mummy1,2,3,true);
 3:     path_position = 0.5;
 4: }
```

Result: Reference/Result/patrolling_enemies3.gmk

Of course, you may want the enemies to try and complete their path regardless of what crosses the road. So let's make the enemy wait for other enemies passing through.

Avoiding enemy collisions by waiting

1. Open obj_enemy and remove the collision event with obj_enemy.

2. Add a **Step**, **End Step** event and include an **Execute Code** action. Insert the following lines:

```
 1: {
 2:     dx = x+lengthdir_x(2,direction);
 3:     dy = y+lengthdir_y(2,direction);
 4:     if ( collision_rectangle(dx,dy,dx+sprite_width,
 5:         dy+sprite_height,obj_enemy,false,true) )
 6:     {
 7:         path_position = path_positionprevious;
 8:         image_speed = 0;
 9:     }
10: }
```

Lines 2–3 calculate the x and y position just in front of the object if it would continue in its current direction. The first parameter in each lengthdir function specifies the distance—the larger it is, the further away it waits.

The collision_rectangle function in lines 4–5 checks if there would be a collision with obj_enemy at that position with a rectangle the size of this instance's sprite. We use collision_rectangle rather than instance_place because instance_place would use precise collision detection as set in our sprites and this can cause instances to detect collisions too late and get stuck. The last two parameters indicate that precise collision detection should not be used at all and that the current instance should not be checked in the detection.

In case of a collision, lines 7–8 set the path's position back to its previous position and stop the sprite from animating (remember that sprite animation is changed in the step event, so it will automatically kick back in action if this condition is no longer true).

3.   The mummies make head-on collisions and that would make them wait forever upon their meeting, so remove the second instance of obj_mummy in room_test (the mummy with a **Creation code** assigned).

4.   The mummy's path is a bit long to see the effect, so let's shorten it. Open path_mummy1, select the first point in the point list, and click **Delete** three times.

Result: Reference/Result/patrolling_enemies4.gmk

Pausing the Game

No fast-paced game can do without a pause button. Your game players will be grateful for the opportunity to temporarily stop the game, take a breath, and fuel up on the caffeine that keeps them awake at night while they battle through your levels.

The easiest way to force Game Maker to pause is to set an infinite loop and wait for the player to press a key. This will stop everything in its tracks, but we need to make sure the game isn't taking up the computer's processing power running the loop. Fortunately, there is a command to make the computer take a break too, or at least to tell it to prioritise other applications. In the following example, we'll use the space bar as the game's pause key.

Start with: Reference/Framework/bouncing4.gmk

Creating a Pause Feature

1.   Create an object and call it obj_pausegame.

2.   Add a **Key Press**, <**Space**> event. Include an **Execute Code** action and insert the following lines:

```
1: {
2:     io_clear();
3:     draw_sprite(spr_gamepaused,0,80,200);
4:     screen_refresh();
5:     while ( !keyboard_check_pressed(vk_anykey) ) sleep(100);
6: }
```

Line 2 first clears all input from mouse and keyboard. This is necessary to avoid entering and immediately exiting this event when the user presses the space bar. Line 3 then draws the "game paused" sprite centered on the screen, and line 4 refreshes the screen so the message will immediately be visible (normally Game Maker doesn't show anything until all instances are drawn). Finally, the last line creates a loop that keeps running until the user presses a key. The `sleep(100)` tells Game Maker to pause everything and temporarily give other processes on the computer some time to run before checking back on the loop 100 milliseconds later.

3. For all rooms in the game where you want to allow pausing, add an instance of `obj_pausegame`.

Result: Reference/Result/pausing_the_game.gmk

■**Tip** Don't forget to tell the player which key allows them to pause the game!

Pushing Boxes

If you know the game Sokoban, you need no introduction to this feature. If you don't, just imagine a game where the player object can push boxes around to cover holes, to push them into enemies, or to clear exits. For as simple and logical as it looks on a screen, it's not always a trivial thing to build into your game. Here are some things to keep in mind:

- The player object should be lined up correctly next to the box to be able to push it (the player object should not be able to push it with only a fraction of its sprite).

- The box needs to be moved into the direction the player object is walking into.

- It should not be possible to push the box if there is something behind it.

We're going to use our Grid Movement example and extend it to push boxes, so read that section first, earlier in this chapter, to understand this one. We're using grid movement because grid alignment always takes care of putting the instances straight next to each other. Once the player starts moving in the direction of the box, we simply make it move 32 pixels in that direction all by itself using an alarm to stop its movement.

Start with: Reference/Framework/explorer6.gmk

Creating Boxes That Can Be Pushed

1. Create an object `obj_impassable`. This object will do nothing more than serve as a parent to group all objects that a box cannot be pushed through. This way, we only have to check moving the boxes against one object!

2. Double-click to open `obj_wall` and set its **Parent** to `obj_impassable`.

3. Add an object called `obj_box` and set its **Sprite** to `spr_box`. Set its **Parent** to `obj_impassable` too (we should not be able to push boxes through other boxes).

4. Open obj_explorer, select the **Step** event, and double-click the **Execute Code** action. Change it to read the following:

```
1:  {
2:      if ( !place_snapped(32,32) ) exit;
3:      var dx, dy;
4:      dx = keyboard_check(vk_right)-keyboard_check(vk_left);
5:      dy = keyboard_check(vk_down)-keyboard_check(vk_up);
6:      if ( dx != 0 ) dy = 0;
7:      if ( place_meeting(x+dx*32,y+dy*32,obj_wall) )
8:          speed=0
9:      else
10:     {
11:         hspeed = 4*dx;
12:         vspeed = 4*dy;
13:     }
14:     box = instance_place(x+dx*32,y+dy*32,obj_box);
15:     with ( box )
16:     {
17:         if ( instance_place(x+dx*32,y+dy*32,obj_impassable) )
18:             other.speed = 0
19:         else
20:         {
21:             hspeed = other.hspeed;
22:             vspeed = other.vspeed;
23:             alarm[0] = 32/speed;
24:         }
25:     }
26:     if ( speed!=0 )
27:     {
28:         switch ( direction )
29:         {
30:             case 0: sprite_index = spr_explorer_right; break;
31:             case 90: sprite_index = spr_explorer_up; break;
32:             case 180: sprite_index = spr_explorer_left; break;
33:             case 270: sprite_index = spr_explorer_down; break;
34:         }
35:         image_speed = 0.5;
36:     } else image_speed = 0;
37: }
```

It's a long script, but if you have been reading Grid Movement, then most of it should already make sense. Lines 2–13 deal with obj_explorer's regular grid movement: check if it is aligned with the grid, calculate the direction to move into based on the keyboard input, make sure that it moves either horizontally or vertically, but not both, and that it isn't trying to run into walls. At the end, lines 26–36 set the sprite and animation speed dependent on the speed and direction.

Lines 14–25 are new. Line 14 looks for an instance of obj_box in the direction of the grid square where obj_player would walk into if it started to move. The instance ID of this box is placed in the variable box. The with statement in line 15 then executes the code in lines 16–25 within the context of the found box. In other words, what happens in that script happens inside the found instance of obj_box and not in obj_explorer. Note that if no instance of obj_box was found in that direction, this code is not executed at all!

The code executed for the found box first checks, in turn, if there is an impassable object (wall or box) in the direction where we're trying to move it (line 17). If this is the case, it sets the speed of obj_explorer to 0. It's important to realize here that within a with statement, the keyword other refers to the instance calling the with statement.

If there is no box or wall in the way, lines 21–22 give the box the same horizontal or vertical speed as the explorer. So rather than pushing the box, we let it move on its own accord. That's why we also set alarm 0 in line 23 relative to the speed and the size of the grid. We'll make it deal with stopping the box next.

5. Double-click obj_box again and add an **Alarm, Alarm 0** event. Insert the **Set Variable** action with **Variable** speed and **Value** 0. This makes sure the speed is set to zero again once the alarm reaches zero.

6. Finally, place a few instances of obj_box in the test room and start pushing them around to see if it works.

Result: Reference/Result/pushing_boxes.gmk

Scrolling Text (Horizontal)

We call it scrolling text, but news channels call it a *ticker tape*: a line of text that scrolls slowly from right to left, usually at the bottom of the screen. In a game, it's great for showing credits.

Start with: Reference/Framework/space1.gmk

Creating the Horizontally Scrolling Text

1. Create a new font for the ticker tape and give it the name fnt_tickertape. Select Verdana for the **Font** and set the **Size** to 24.

2. Create an object and give it the name obj_tickertape. Set the **Depth** to -1000.

3. Add a **Create** event and include an **Execute Code** action. Insert the following lines:

```
1: {
2:     ticker = "The Game Maker's Companion was written by Jacob ";
3:     ticker += "Habgood, Nana Nielsen and Martin Rijks, with ";
4:     ticker += "artwork by Kevin Crossley. This is an example ";
5:     ticker += "text for a ticker tape. It will wrap once it has ";
6:     ticker += "disappeared from the screen..."
7:     x = room_width;
8:     hspeed = -4;
9: }
```

This script sets a string variable called ticker containing the text to scroll. Strings are like variables in the sense that you can add information to them using the + operator—we're using this to break the text in several lines. Line 7 places the instance at the right border of the room, and line 8 sets the horizontal speed for the ticker tape.

4. Add a **Draw** event and include an **Execute Code** action. Insert the following lines:

```
1:  {
2:      draw_set_color(c_white);
3:      draw_set_font(fnt_tickertape);
4:      if ( x < -string_width(ticker) ) x = room_width;
5:      draw_text(x,y,ticker);
6:  }
```

Lines 2-3 first set the appropriate color and font. Line 4 makes sure the text wraps once it has completely disappeared from the screen. We do this by checking if x is smaller than the negative value of the width (in pixels) of the ticker string—this is equal to checking if the text is entirely left of the room. If so, the x value is reset to room_width to place it at the right of the room again. Line 5 finally draws the text at the current position of the instance.

5. Open room_test and place an instance of obj_tickertape somewhere in the lower half of the room. Only the vertical position matters as the x value is taken care of by the code.

Result: Reference/Result/scrolling_text_horizontal.gmk

■**Note** Your text can only be read at the speed at which it scrolls. Test if your text is not too slow, too fast, or too long! And if the scrolling text doesn't look smooth to you, see the Smooth Motion feature.

Scrolling Text (Vertical)

You've seen it at the end of a movie, where they call it the *end credits*: several rows of text listing the people involved in making the flick. We can do this in much the same way as horizontally scrolling text (see the previous feature).

Start with: Reference/Framework/space1.gmk

Creating the Vertically Scrolling Text

1. Create a new font for the end credits and give it the name fnt_endcredits. Select Times New Roman as the **Font** and set it to **Bold** with **Size** 16.

2. Create an object and give it the name obj_endcredits. Set the **Depth** to -1000.

3. Add a **Create** event, include an **Execute Code** action, and insert the following lines:

```
 1: {
 2:     credits = "The#Game Maker's#Companion###written by##Jacob ";
 3:     credits += "Habgood#Nana Nielsen#&#Martin Rijks##with ";
 4:     credits += "artwork by##Kevin Crossley####";
 5:     credits += "This is example text for scrolling end credits.#";
 6:     credits += "Feel free to add as many lines as you want.#";
 7:     credits += "The end credits will wrap once#";
 8:     credits += "the last line of the text has disappeared#";
 9:     credits += "from the screen...";
10:     y = room_height;
11:     vspeed = -1;
12: }
```

This script sets a string variable called credits containing the text to scroll. Just like in the horizontally scrolling feature, the text is broken up over several lines using the + operator. Note that it is a single line of text, but you can use the hash character (#)to indicate where you want a new line when you draw the text on the screen. Line 10 places the instance at the bottom border of the room and line 11 sets the vertical speed for the credits.

4. Add a **Draw** event and include an **Execute Code** action. Insert the following lines:

```
 1: {
 2:     draw_set_color(c_white);
 3:     draw_set_font(fnt_endcredits);
 4:     draw_set_halign(fa_center);
 5:     if ( y <- string_height(credits) ) y = room_height;
 6:     draw_text(320,y,credits);
 7: }
```

Lines 2–3 first set the desired color and font. Line 4 makes sure the lines of text are centered to the draw position rather than using the draw position as the top left corner. You can compare this to setting the x origin of the text to the center of the text, much like you can do with sprites.

Line 5 makes sure the text wraps once it has completely disappeared from the screen. We do this by checking if y is smaller than the negative value of the height (in pixels) of the `credits` string—this is equal to checking if the text is positioned entirely above the room. Note that the function `string_height` returns the total height regardless of the number of lines used in the string when using the hash character. If the text is out of the screen, the value of y is reset to `room_height` to make it start at the bottom again. Line 6 finally draws the text at (320,y). A value of 320 is the middle of our room and the text lines are centered around this.

5. Open `room_test` and place an instance of `obj_endcredits` anywhere in the room.

Result: Reference/Result/scrolling_text_vertical.gmk

■**Tip** Put your end credits in a special room and always give the player the possibility to go back to the title screen.

Smoke Trail

If it flies or drives, it burns fuel. And whether it's rockets, aircrafts, or cars, it just has to smoke! After all, it's only a game, so we can temporarily forget about clean emission and the Kyoto Protocol. Game Maker Pro users can use *particle effects* to create smoke trails. The challenge is in making sure that these trails appear at the right place at the right time. We'll use our spaceship example and make it blow smoke every time the engines are burning. It just takes a single step using one of Game Maker's built-in default particle effects.

Start with: Reference/Framework/spaceship2.gmk

Creating a Smoke Trail

1. In our example, the engines are burning as long as the Up arrow key is being pressed. Open the object `obj_spaceship` and select the **Keyboard**, **Up** event. At the end of the action list, include a **Create Effect** action. Note that although this action draws effects on the screen, you don't need to use it in the **Draw** event. Rather, you use it to start the effect and Game Maker takes care of drawing it.

   In the action, select **smoke** as the **Type**. For **X**, use `lengthdir_x(-36,image_angle)`, for **Y** use `lengthdir_y(-36,image_angle)`. We use `image_angle` rather than `direction` because we always need to create smoke relative to where the spaceship is facing. Note that we use negative values as the first parameter because we want to put the smoke behind the ship rather than in front of it. Set **Size** to **small** and set the **Color** to white or gray. Set **Where** to **above objects** and check the **Relative** box.

Result: Reference/Result/smoke_trail.gmk

■**Note** For all visual effects, there is a simple rule—don't overdo it. Too much smoke will only annoy the player! You may even want to create the effect only once every few steps using timelines or alarms.

Smooth Motion

Ever wondered why your game's movement doesn't always look as smooth as in the commercial games you've played? There are two reasons for this:

- The default room speed is set at 30, which means Game Maker only redraws the screen 30 times per second. Most CRT screens "refresh" the screen at twice that rate.

- The updates by Game Maker and those by the screen are not synchronized. While the screen is half-way displaying the old image, Game Maker switches to the next. The result is a mixed image between two steps, an effect commonly known as "tearing."

As you might guess, it's not difficult to get your game to look much smoother, but there is a golden rule to save you a lot of work: *apply these changes before you create anything else in your game.* This is important because we'll increase the room speed, and this influences the speed of almost everything else: sprite animations, path following, instance movements, alarm time, particles, background scrolling, and so forth. You don't want to go back to adjust everything!

Start with: Reference/Framework/bouncing1.gmk

Creating Smooth Motion

1. Double-click the **Global Game Settings** in the resource tree and go to the **resolution** tab. Enable **Use synchronization to avoid tearing**.

2. For all rooms in the game, open the room editor, go to the **settings** tab, and set the room speed to 60.

3. If necessary, adjust all game speeds. In the case of our example, the original room speed was 30 and has now been doubled, which means that the speed of all movement needs to be halved. Fortunately, for this game there is only one place where we need to do this. Open obj_cog, select the **Create** event, and double-click the **Set direction and speed of motion** (**Move Free**)action. Set the speed to 2.5 + random(4).

Result: Reference/Result/smooth_motion.gmk

■**Note** Not all screens refresh at a speed of 60 updates per second, but it is the best common value for most computer users. Monitors don't go below 60 and anyone playing at a higher refresh rate will still get good results.

Snap To Grid

If your game is made up of a fixed grid in which instances need to be placed, you may require the mouse to snap to these positions—either to help the player place game elements in the right places, or to facilitate a level editor. In the following example, we'll make the mouse snap to a 32x32 grid to place wall objects in the room.

Start with: Reference/Framework/explorer1.gmk

Creating Grid Snapping

1. Create a new object `obj_wall` and give it the sprite `spr_wall`. This is the instance we'll be placing around the room.

2. Create a new object `obj_gridcursor` and and set the **Sprite** to `spr_gridcursor`. Set the **Depth** to `-10` to make sure it appears in front of everything else.

3. Add a **Step** event and include a **Jump to Position** action. For **X** specify `mouse_x`, for **Y** specify `mouse_y`. The system variables `mouse_x` and `mouse_y` keep track of where the Windows mouse cursor is within the room.

4. In the same event, include an **Align to Grid** action. Our grid has squares measuring 32x32, so set **Snap hor** to `32` and **Snap vert** also to `32`.

5. Open the **Global Game Settings**, **Graphics** tab and remove the check for **Display the cursor**. We have our custom cursor now, so we should hide Windows' mouse cursor. All this is enough to snap the instance to the grid—the next steps are only required to for instance placement and removal.

6. Open `obj_gridcursor` again and add a **Mouse, Global Left Button** event. We're using the global rather than the regular left button event, because the latter looks for a collision of the Windows mouse pointer with `obj_gridcursor`, which is neither necessary nor always the case. We're also not using a press or release event because we wish to be able to drag the mouse, painting the room with wall instances. Insert a **Check Object** action and select `obj_wall` for the **Object**. Check the **Relative** and **NOT** boxes—this checks if there is a collision with `obj_wall` in the current (snapped) position, because we only want to place a wall instance if there wasn't one already.

7. Just below it, insert a **Create Instance** action for `obj_wall`. Check the **Relative** box and don't change the values. It will use the snapped coordinates of `obj_gridcursor` to place the wall instance.

8. Now add a **Collision** event for `obj_wall` and include a **Check Mouse** action. Set the **Button** to **right**.

9. In the same event, add a **Destroy Instance** action and set **Applies to** to **Other**. You can now right-click on a wall object to have it removed again.

10. Because deletion is based on collision detection, it's a good idea to make sure the sprite cursor is as large as a grid square; otherwise, it may not be able to delete smaller objects. Open `spr_gridcursor` and uncheck the **Precise collision checking** box.

11. Finally, open `room_test` and place an instance of `obj_gridcursor` in the room.

Result: Reference/Result/snap_to_grid.gmk

Toggle Music and Sound Effects

No game can do without sound effects and some cool music to set the mood. But for all your efforts in sound design, the player may not be as happy with your choices are you are. We should give them the opportunity to switch either of them off. We can't simply set the global volume to 0, as that will influence both at the same time, so there is a little more work involved. Most games have configuration screens to do this, but flexible as we are, we allow users to toggle music and sound effects at any time in the game, by either clicking on an icon or pressing a key.

Start with: Reference/Framework/spaceship7.gmk

Creating Toggles for Music and Sound

1. Add an object called `obj_music_toggle` and set its **Sprite** to `spr_music_toggle`. This will be our music switch, which needs to always appear in front of other objects, so set the **Depth** to -1000.

2. Add a **Create** event and include an **Execute Code** action. Insert the following lines:

```
1: {
2:     if ( !variable_global_exists('playmusic') ) global.playmusic = true;
3:     image_index = global.playmusic;
4:     image_speed = 0;
5: }
```

This code requires some explanation. We're going to keep track of whether music should be played or not by using a global variable called `global.playmusic`. We use a global variable so we can check this value in any room in the game. After all, if music was switched off in one room, we shouldn't start playing again in the next!

We will let our music toggle create this variable and set it to `true` (play music) by default, but we only do this if the variable does not yet have any value. This check is required because it may have been set in another room, and we don't want to reset it, and we can't check a variable that doesn't exist. In short, using the function `variable_global_exists()` in line 2 makes sure the variable is properly initialized without being reinitialized (remember that the Boolean operator ! means **not**).

Line 3 sets the subimage to the value of `global.playmusic`. The variable will be either 0 for `false` or 1 for `true`, so this nicely switches to the appropriate subimage. The last line stops the sprite from animating.

3. Add a Script resource and call the script `music_play`. We will be using this script anywhere in the game where we want to play music, rather than using Game Maker's action for playing sound. It will check for us whether or not the music should be played at all. Insert the following lines:

```
1: {
2:     global.music = argument0;
3:     if ( global.playmusic ) sound_play(global.music);
4: }
```

This Script takes the music we want to play as its argument. The value of `argument0` is stored in a global variable `global.music` so we can keep track of which music was selected last in case we toggled it. Line 3 plays the music only if `global.playmusic` is `true`. In other words, if the music was switched off, nothing is played.

4. Add another Script resource called `music_toggle` and insert the following lines:

```
1:  {
2:      global.playmusic = !global.playmusic;
3:      if ( global.playmusic ) sound_play(global.music)
4:      else sound_stop(global.music);
5:      image_index = global.playmusic;
6:  }
```

The value of `global.playmusic` should either be 1 (true) or 0 (false). Rather than using an `if` statement to check and change, we're using the Boolean operator ! (**NOT**), because it flips the value around for us. Line 3 checks if we should either play or stop playing the music (line 4) and line 5 changes the subimage.

5. Open `obj_music_toggle` again and add a **Mouse**, **Left pressed** event. Insert an **Execute Script** action and set **Script** to `music_toggle`.

6. Add a **Key Press** event for the letter **M** and include another **Execute Script** action. Again, set **Script** to `music_toggle`. We can now either click the object or press the M key to toggle the music.

7. Place an instance of `obj_music_toggle` in the top-right of the test room.

8. It can't work without any music, so we need to make sure we play some music in the same room. Open `obj_spaceship` and add an **Other**, **Room Start** event. We use this event because it is executed after all **Create** events have been handled, so the `global.playmusic` variable will already have a value. Here comes the most important part—we're no longer going to use the **Play Sound** action to play sounds or music. Include an **Execute Script** event and set **Script** to `music_play`. Set **Argument0** to `snd_music`. Notice there is no longer a drop-down menu, so we'll have to enter the correct values ourselves.

9. Now, add an object called `obj_sfx_toggle`, set the **Sprite** to `spr_sfx_toggle`, and the **Depth** to -1000. The toggle for sound effects works in much the same way as `obj_music_toggle`, as you'll see shortly.

10. Add a **Create** event, include an **Execute Code** action, and insert the following lines:

```
1:  {
2:      if ( !variable_global_exists('playsfx') ) global.playsfx = true;
3:      image_index = global.playsfx;
4:      image_speed = 0;
5:  }
```

11. Add another Script resource and call it `sfx_toggle`. Insert the following lines:

```
1:  {
2:      global.playsfx = !global.playsfx;
3:      image_index = global.playsfx;
4:  }
```

You'll notice that unlike `music_toggle`, we're not trying to stop the sound. This is because we don't actually know which sounds are currently playing, and we can't stop them all because it will stop any music that was playing as well. Most sound effects, fortunately, will end by themselves at some point.

12. We'll now need replacements for Game Maker's `sound_play` and `sound_loop` commands, just like we needed them for the `music_play` command. Add a new script resource and call it `sfx_play`. Insert the following lines:

```
1:  {
2:      if ( global.playsfx ) sound_play(argument0);
3:  }
```

13. Add another script resource and call it `sfx_loop`. Insert the following lines:

```
1:  {
2:      if ( global.playsfx ) sound_loop(argument0);
3:  }
```

14. Open `obj_sfx_toggle` again and add a **Mouse**, **Left pressed** event. Insert an **Execute Script** action and set **Script** to `sfx_toggle`.

15. Now add a **Key Press** event for the **S** key. Insert another **Execute Script** action and set the **Script** to `sfx_toggle` again. The S key now toggles sound effects.

16. Our example file already had a few sound actions in it, but they're still being played by the ordinary **Play Sound** action. We need to change those to use the script. Open `obj_spaceship` and select the **Press <Space>** event. Remove the **Play Sound** event for `snd_laser` and include the **Execute Script** event. Select `sfx_play` as the **Script** and enter `snd_laser` for **Argument0**.

17. Now, select the **Press <Up>** event and again replace the **Play Sound** action with an **Execute Script** event, this time with **Script** `sfx_loop` and **Argument0** `snd_engine`. As you may have guessed, if you're going to include this feature in the game, it helps to do this early on to prevent you from having to replace countless sound actions!

18. Finally, put an instance of `obj_sfx_toggle` into the room, next to `obj_music_toggle`.

Result: Reference/Result/toggle_music_and_sfx.gmk

Rogues' Rendezvous: Dialogue

Object	obj_dialog_archie_start		
Position	At the very start of the level.		
Case	**Who**	**Speech**	**Next**
1	Archie	Right. The main entrance to the pirate town is further up. We'll need to figure out a way through, as it'll be guarded.	End

Object	obj_dialog_archie_skeleton		
Position	Just before meeting the first skeleton.		
Case	**Who**	**Speech**	**Next**
1	Archie	I can smell sea legs... maybe I should go first?	2
2	Archie	Send me out to distract the brute, and then when he's not looking, charge him from behind using the Ctrl Key.	3
3	Archie	Push him over the edge of the platform, but watch out for that saber.	End

Object	obj_dialog_prisoner1_attract	
Position	On the approach to the first prisoner.	
Case	Who	Speech	Next
1	NPC	Help.	End

Object	obj_dialog_prisoner1_help	
Position	In front of the first prisoner.	
Case	Who	Speech	Next
1	NPC	Oh, please set me free. Help a poor boy down on his luck.	2
2	Archie	Ha. I bet you got yerself into this mess. We haven't got time to release you.	3
3	NPC	Oh, but I can help you. I see everything that goes on from up here.	4
4	Flynn	Will you help me with some information? We're looking for someone. Who are you and how did you end up in that cage?	5 6
5	NPC	Of course. You save my hide and I'll tell you what you need to know.	7
6	NPC	I was the ship's boy on the Spice Queen. They're holding me for ransom, but my family hasn't got any money.	7
7	Flynn	Have you seen a woman called Mary Jones? She's... a pirate. We're looking for the Pirate King. Is he here in the town?	8 9
8	NPC	Mary Jones? I know her. Set me free and I'll tell you exactly where to go.	10
9	NPC	Sounds like you're looking for trouble. I can tell you where to find him, but first you gotta help me out.	10
10	Archie	He's a liar. The boy knows nothing.	11
11	Flynn	You're probably right, Archie, perhaps we should leave him. Maybe so, but we can't leave him here.	12 13

| 12 | NPC | I promise I can help you. I will die in this cage if you don't free me. Find the key to release that wheel up there. | End |
| 13 | NPC | You won't regret it, mate. Find the key to release that wheel up there. | End |

Object		obj_dialog_archie_wheel	
Position		Next to the first wheel lock.	
Case	**Who**	**Speech**	**Next**
1	Archie	Yup, it's locked alright. We're going to need a key.	End

Object		obj_dialog_archie_key	
Position		Next to the first key.	
Case	**Who**	**Speech**	**Next**
1	Archie	Ouch—that's gotta hurt. If only you had a pair of wings.	End

Object		obj_dialog_archie_prisoner1	
Position		Triggered by the first prisoner cage falling.	
Case	**Who**	**Speech**	**Next**
1	NPC	Ouch.	2
2	Archie	I suppose we'd better find another way down and see if he's alright.	End

Object	obj_dialog_prisoner1_rescued		
Position	Next to the first rescued prisoner.		

Case	Who	Speech	Next
1	NPC	Thank you so very much. I won't forget this.	2
2	Archie	So spill the beans already, what do you know?	3
3	NPC	Only that the guy in charge around here is Raffi the Sheriff. He knows everyone and everything.	4
4	Flynn	But you said you knew about...	5
5	NPC	Well no, but Raffi does. That is, if he doesn't lock you up first.	6
6	Archie	Knew we couldn't trust him.	End

Object	obj_dialog_archie_poster1		
Position	On top of the missing poster down the cage pit.		

Case	Who	Speech	Next
1	Archie	MISSING. Ship's cat from the Black Penny. Reward for information leading to painful death of those responsible. Answers to the name of Robinson.	End

Object	obj_dialog_archie_tripwire		
Position	On top of the first tripwire.		

Case	Who	Speech	Next
1	Archie	Aark! Mind the tripwires, Flynn!	End

Object		obj_dialog_thirsty_attract	
Position		On the approach to the thirsty pirate.	
Case	Who	Speech	Next
1	NPC	Yo-ho-ho and a bottle of... Where's me lemonade?	End

Object		obj_dialog_thirsty_help	
Position		Next to the thirsty pirate.	
Case	Who	Speech	Next
1	Flynn	Excuse me. I wonder if you could help us out, sir?	2
2	NPC	Ah there you are. I'll have a refill please, lad. Put it on my bill. Yo-ho-ho and all that.	3
3	Flynn	Have you seen a woman called Mary Jones? Do you know where I can find the Pirate King?	4 5
4	NPC	Women... *hic*. Never trust 'em lad. Take my advice and stick to lemonade. It never lets you down.	6
5	NPC	The King? Where? Don't get me into trouble boy. I only want to enjoy my lemonade.	6
6	Archie	Forget it, Flynn. This guy is useless. Leave him for the guards to deal with.	7
7	NPC	Listen lad, you shouldn't take advice from devious parrots. This one is no good, take it from me.	8
8	Flynn	He's more useful than you are! And why should I trust anything you say?	9 9
9	NPC	I might look like an old fool to you, lad, but pirates still had honor in my day. Fetch me my tankard and I'll show you the way forward.	10

Object	obj_dialog_thirsty_tankard		
Position	Next to the thirsty pirate.		
Case	**Who**	**Speech**	**Next**
1	NPC	You're a good lad. There's a lift above your head that will take you further up. The switch to operate it is above that mushroom over there.	2
2	Archie	We could have found that ourselves, old man.	3
3	NPC	Watch your tongue, Archie, or I might tell this lad what you're up to.	4
4	Archie	Forget it Flynn. He's rambling again, the old fool.	5
5	Flynn	Is he? How did he know your name?	6
6	Archie	Mary and I used to come here all the time. I told you that before. Let's go.	End

Object	obj_dialog_archie_poster2		
Position	On top of the wanted poster above the second spear trap.		
Case	**Who**	**Speech**	**Next**
1	Archie	WANTED. Preferably dead. Mary Jones. Noticeable features: Deadly temper and annoying parrot.	2
2	Archie	Bah! Annoying temper and deadly parrot, more like!	End

Object	obj_dialog_prisoner2_attract

Object		obj_dialog_prisoner2_help	
Position		Next to the second prisoner.	
Case	Who	Speech	Next
1	NPC	Listen, boy. You have to get me out of here. I'll make it worth your while.	2
2	Archie	Hah! That's what the other one said.	3
3	NPC	My crew sold me out. All because of a little gambling debt. I want revenge on the Pirate King.	4
4	Flynn	How are you going to get that? I'm not looking for trouble.	5 6
5	NPC	By helping you get past his guards. I've been watching you, but you'll need some help getting further up.	7
6	NPC	You wouldn't be sneaking in here if you weren't. I can see everything you've been doing from up here.	7
7	NPC	Get me down from here and I'll give you my ship's badge. You'll need it to get past Raffi's goons up there.	End

Object		obj_dialog_prisoner2_rescued	
Position		Next to the second rescued prisoner.	
Case	Who	Speech	Next
1	NPC	Thanks, lad. I'm very grateful to ya.	2
2	NPC	Here's the badge I promised you. Show it to the guards and they'll let you through.	3
3	Flynn	Why are they looking for badges? Won't you come with us?	4 5
4	NPC	If you have a badge, then it means you work for one of the pirate ships. Show's you're not a spy.	End
5	NPC	The badge will only let one person through. Besides, I need to get myself a weapon. Good luck, kid.	End

Object	obj_dialog_archie_prisoner2		
Position	Just after leaving the second prisoner.		
Case	**Who**	**Speech**	**Next**
1	Archie	You know your mother would have just knocked the guy on the head and grabbed his badge while he slept.	2
2	Flynn	Maybe so... but I'm not my mother.	3

Object	obj_dialog_guards_attract		
Position	On the approach to the guards.		
Case	**Who**	**Speech**	**Next**
1	NPC	So Tony sets his hat on fire... Hur hur!	2
2	NPC	Hahahaha!	3
3	NPC	Raffi is dead scared of him now.	4
4	NPC	Hahah! I'd have paid good money to see that.	5
5	NPC	Better not let the boss hear you say so.	End

Object	obj_dialog_guards_challenge		
Position	Next to the guards.		
Case	**Who**	**Speech**	**Next**
1	NPC	Go away, boy. Only pirates who can prove they belong to a ship are allowed further up.	2
2	Flynn	Let me through or you'll be sorry! But I have a badge.	3 4
3	NPC	Hur Hur. Very likely.	End

4	NPC	Ah the Black Penny. Is Robinson still the First Mate?	5
5	Flynn	Erh, Yessir, he is. I don't know any Robinson.	6 7
6	NPC	Oh really? Robinson is the ship's cat. You're not from the Penny.	8
7	NPC	Just testing. You can pass.	End
8	Archie	Aark. He's only joking mate. Everyone knows Jenkins is the mate.	9
9	NPC	Did you see that Bob? A talking parrot...	End

Object		obj_dialog_archie_bat	
Position		Next to the skull bat.	
Case	Who	Speech	Next
1	Archie	Aark. I'm not messing with that! You distract it, Flynn. If only we could skewer him on something...	End

Object		obj_dialog_archie_quay	
Position		On the wrong side of the main path up to the town entrance.	
Case	Who	Speech	Next
1	Archie	That's the main route back down to the quay, Flynn. We need to go the other way.	End

Object		obj_dialog_archie_finish	
Position		Beyond the guards.	
Case	Who	Speech	Next
1	Flynn	Well we're in, Archie. I hope you know where you're taking me.	End

Index

■ ■ ■

■ G

Important License Information

The software on the CD provided in this book is the copyright of YoYo Games Ltd and is included on the CD as a service to the reader. You must not sell or redistribute this software in any form and you must agree to the license agreement provided with the software in order to use it.

ZOOL and the ZOOL logo are registered trademarks of Urbanscan Ltd. All rights reserved. The Zool game resources are provided solely for use with *The Game Maker's Companion* and should not be redistributed without written permission from the copyright holder.

The background music track ("Campaign") used in the *Shadows on Deck* cut scene is the copyright of Jonathan Geer and licensed for use in this product through www.Royalty-Free.tv. This music is synchronized with the video media, and may not be used separately without purchasing an additional license.

The remaining resources on the CD are the copyright of the authors. By purchasing this book, the authors grant you permission to use the remaining electronic resources (sprites, backgrounds, sounds and scripts) from the *Fishpod*, *Shadows on Deck* and *Reference* chapter examples in your own Game Maker games, including for commercial use. However, redistribution of these resources in their own right is prohibited, as is their use for games not made with Game Maker. The copyright of the original concepts behind these games (including names and characters) remains with the book's authors.

The contents of the CD are provided "as is". Apress and the authors ("we") disclaim all warrantees, conditions or representations (whether expressed or implied, oral or written) with respect to the software and the accompanying files. We do not warrant that the software or files will function without interruption or be error free. We do not warrant that they will correct all deficiencies, errors, defects or nonconformities or that the software and files will meet your specific requirements.

We shall in no event be liable for any direct, indirect, incidental, consequential, or exemplary damages resulting from use of the software or files. This limitation shall apply whether or not we have been advised of or should have been aware of the possibility of such damages. In jurisdictions where the exclusion or limitation of liability for consequential or incidental damages is not allowed our liability of is limited to the greatest extent permitted by law.

Apress is providing this CD as a service to the reader through permission from YoYo Games Ltd and the authors. Apress has no rights to or interest in the contents of the CD.